BOOK LOAN

Please RETURN or RENEW it no later
than the last date

Kingdoms and Communities in Western Europe, 900–1300

Second Edition

SUSAN REYNOLDS

CLARENDON PRESS · OXFORD
1997

Oxford University Press, Great Clarendon Street, Oxford OX2 6DP

Oxford New York

Athens Auckland Bangkok Bogota Bombay
Buenos Aires Calcutta Cape Town Dar es Salaam
Delhi Florence Hong Kong Istanbul Karachi
Kuala Lumpur Madras Madrid Melbourne
Mexico City Nairobi Paris Singapore
Taipei Tokyo Toronto Warsaw

and associated companies in
Berlin Ibadan

Oxford is a trade mark of Oxford University Press

Published in the United States
by Oxford University Press Inc., New York

Second edition published 1997

British Library Cataloguing in Publication Data
Reynolds, Susan
Kingdoms and communities in Western Europe,
900–1300.
1. Europe—History—476-1492
I. Title
940.1   D117
ISBN 0-19-873148-5
ISBN 0-19-873147-7 (Pbk)

Printed in Great Britain
on acid-free paper by
St Edmundsbury Press
Bury St Edmunds, Suffolk

Acknowledgements

Preparatory versions of parts of this book have been presented to seminars or other groups at Columbia, Edinburgh, Iowa, Leicester, Michigan, and Toronto Universities, at Dartmouth and Haverford Colleges, at a conference of the British Legal History Society at Bristol, and at a colloquium on 'Legitimation by Descent' at the Maison des Sciences de l'Homme, Paris. I am very grateful to my hosts for giving me the chance to try out my ideas and to all those who listened and criticized and discussed them with me. Bits of the book have also been published already, namely the greater part of chapter 1 and a little of chapter 2 in the *American Journal of Legal History*, xxv (1981), 205-24, and parts of chapter 8 in *History*, lviii (1983), 375-90. Parts of chapters 1 and 2 are also being published in *Law and Social Change in British History*, which is being edited by John Guy. I am grateful to the respective editors for allowing me to use these papers or parts of papers again.

I probably owe thanks to many people from whom I have picked up ideas without realizing where they came from. I also owe apologies to those who may think that my citation of their works misrepresents them: I have sometimes cited books or articles because the information they give seemed to me susceptible of being interpreted so as to support my argument even if this was not how it was interpreted by the authors. This may be rather irritating for the authors but it seemed preferable to going into detailed controversy, often on small points, in the footnotes.

Over the past five years I have built up an even bigger debt than I already owed to the staffs of the Institute of Historical Research and the British Library: between them the two places provide near perfect conditions for the sort of work this book has required. Many friends have endured my obsession with medieval collective activity, have listened with patience and even sympathy, and have made criticisms and suggestions. I am particularly grateful to Geoffrey Barrow,

John Blair, David Carpenter, Bill Kellaway, Tim Reuter, Pauline Stafford, Romila Thapar, and Paola Zambelli. The greatest help and encouragement has come from Peggy Brown, Michael Clanchy, Tom Green, and Barbara Harvey, who all either read large chunks or gave detailed advice or both. Peggy Brown has corrected so many mistakes on French history that I am the more aware of the number which must remain on areas where I did not have her expert and pains· taking guidance. My sister Vickie Macnair has read the whole thing and done her best to clarify my arguments. Lastly, Richard Jeffery, of Oxford University Press, removed a mass of small errors and infelicities from my typescript. I am grateful to all of them.

Contents

Note on References

The figures in square brackets [ ] after the titles of the works cited in the footnotes to the main text refer to the numbered entries in the List of Works Cited, pp. 340–75, where further details and a list of abbreviations are given. Works cited in the Introduction to the Second Edition that are in that List are cited in the same way. The rest are given separately, in a single alphabetical series, on pp. lxvii–lxxv.

Introduction to the Second edition, 1997[1]

A dozen years later I have not changed my mind about the arguments I put forward in the first edition of this book. That is not to say that I think there is nothing wrong with it. Apart from such small mistakes as I have noticed and corrected—and no doubt many more that I have not—what I have read since 1984 makes my reading before then look even thinner than it seemed at the time. I should have read more and cited more primary sources. On the other hand, if I had tried to cover the subject fully I would not yet have published the book. I like to think that it was useful in raising questions that were worth discussion, whether or not the answers I suggest turn out to be wrong.

One element of the book that I partly regret was its title. I was seduced by alliteration into using a word—communities—which has virtually lost all meaning.[1] Combined with 'kingdoms' it may suggest that the book was a general account of medieval Europe in which 'kingdoms' represent traditional political narrative and 'communities' cover popular movements, particularly in towns. For those acquainted with German historiography it probably suggests a contrast between *Herrschaft* and *Genossenschaft* which, as I explain

For works cited, see Note on References.

[1] My brief discussions of the meaning of community (pp. 2–3, 332–9) were supplemented by Smith, '"Modernization" and the Corporate Village Community', which appeared at almost the same moment. Oexle, 'Die mittelalterliche Zunft' and 'Gruppenbindung', has called for more study of medieval groups, their forms and structures. Althoff, *Verwandte, Freunde und Getreue*, discusses individuals in relation to each other and to groups more than groups themselves, which he suggests (p. 4) have not been studied in their general form and content. On late medieval England: Rubin, 'Small Groups', and Carpenter, 'Gentry and Community'. More generally: Calhoun, 'Community'; Cohen, *Symbolic Construction*, though the historical background seems weak; Wellman and Berkowitz, *Social Structures: A Network Approach*, 1–13, 123–9; Scott, *Social Network Analysis*, 8–38, 56–117. On communitarian use of historical evidence: Phillips, *Looking Backward*. In 1984 I inexplicably failed to cite Cheyette, *Lordship and Community*, whose introduction anticipated several points I made in 1984 about medieval community and in 1994 (in *Fiefs and Vassals*) about feudalism.

below, was not at all what I meant. 'Lay Collective Activity in Western Europe, 900–1300' would have been a more accurate, if less catchy, title. Not that I thought the book was only about activity. I meant it also to be about ideas: that is, the ideas of lay people about the rights and activities of groups, but I thought that these could best be explored through the evidence of their activities. At the time I thought that starting with chapters on custom and law, inserting a section about academic writing in the chapter on the community of the realm, and saying something in other chapters about the attitudes that I thought lay behind the activities I discussed would together make the book's relevance to the history of political theory clear. For some readers it did, but I now think that I should have been more explicit and more expansive about ideas. This introduction includes an attempt to remedy that.

I have not made any attempt to remedy the gaps in the book that I mentioned in the original introduction (pp. 3–4, 8–9). Nor have I added anything about the centuries before 900, although, having since read more about them, I now suspect that it would have made good historical sense to have started earlier. Separate essays by, for instance, P. Fouracre, H. W. Goetz, P. D. King, J. L. Nelson, and C. Wickham, as well as those collected in *The Settlement of Disputes in Early Medieval Europe*, suggest that some of the assumptions and attitudes about collectivities that I found in sources after 900 were much older.[2] That is not to say that I think that nothing changed. My view is that real changes in the form and nature of collective activities took place before, during, and after my period. What I argued then, and will repeat later in this introduction, is that few of the changes were initially provoked by new ideas, whether theories that trickled down from academics to the laity, or revolutionary demands for new kinds of popular government that seeped out from the towns. So far as I can see, now as in 1984, new ideas were only

[2] Fouracre, 'Carolingian Justice' and 'Cultural Conformity'; Goetz, 'Regnum'; King, 'Barbarian Kingdoms'; Nelson, 'Kingship and Empire', and [606–7] in List of Works Cited; Wickham, *Land and Power*, esp. 121–99, and 'Rural Society'; Davies and Fouracre, *Settlement of Disputes*. For a 5th-cent. suggestion of collective judgement in rural Gaul: Van Dam, *Leadership and Community*, 46–7.

slowly worked out to justify or resist new practices of government and law which were themselves made possible by
economic and social changes—among which I include the
spread of literacy, account-keeping, and higher education.

My work since 1984 has convinced me more firmly than
ever that our understanding of all of this has been impeded
by a very old custom of teleological historiography, firmly set
within the separate academic traditions that have developed
within the boundaries of modern states.[3] It is not that no historians study other countries than their own, or that no comparisons are made, but we are all so accustomed to the
interpretations we have inherited that we hardly notice them
as interpretations.[4] Medieval historians today do not always
seem to realize how many of their assumptions derive from
arguments put forward by lawyers, historians, and political
writers of the eighteenth and nineteenth centuries whose preoccupations were totally different from those of anyone in the
middle ages. The more I have tried to compare medieval evidence with what has been done with it since the seventeenth
century, the more convinced I have become of the need to
examine our own assumptions and ideas, and where they
come from, if we are to separate them from the assumptions
and ideas of medieval people enough to be able to see the
medieval ideas clearly. I am not so naïve as to suppose that
self-consciousness will enable us to eliminate all distortions
and get our history right. But we can at least think about the
problem and try to avoid starting from premises of eigh-
teenth- and nineteenth-century ideas about society and history that no longer look adequate. We shall never be able to
get our history right, but we have to try to get it less wrong.

My attempt to clarify and amplify the arguments I put forward in 1984 starts therefore with a discussion of the way
that ideas about medieval groups and collective activities
have developed since the sixteenth century. I follow this with
a sketch of what I suggest medieval people between the tenth
and the early twelfth century thought or assumed about
groups and collective activities, how far I think their ideas

[3] I have discussed different aspects of this in *Fiefs and Vassals*, 'Idea of
Incorporation' and 'Historiography of the Medieval State'.
[4] Wickham, 'Problems of Comparing Societies', 222–5.

had changed by 1300, and how far I think that their ideas may in general have affected their practice.

A few small corrections were made in the 1991 reprint. I have made a few more now, where what I said in 1984 seems absolutely wrong, especially about feudo-vassalic matters (pp. 45, 237, 241). Otherwise, to avoid an impractical amount of alteration, I have drawn attention to points that I think badly need correction, either in the text of this introduction (at the reference to notes 156, 158), or in the notes to it (e.g. notes 21, 92–3, 120). The notes here also include references to some works published since 1984 that relate to what I have discussed in the introduction. I have not attempted to bring the 1984 bibliography up to date beyond that. If I started on a systematic revision I would probably end by having to rewrite the whole thing, and I have no intention of doing that. This is a book published in 1984, with a few mistakes corrected, and a new introduction added.

The historiography of medieval community

One common way of looking at the middle ages since the early nineteenth century has been to see it as feudal. A feudal society, in the non-Marxist sense of the word, has come to be seen as one in which there was little or no sense of the common good, so that the main bond of free and noble society was the relation between individual lords and their individual vassals.[5] Another view, focused on the history of villages, towns, and what are generally called 'craft-guilds', can make medieval society into a golden age of communal brotherliness. Discounting the exaggerations of disapproval or nostalgia, there is no necessary contradiction between these two pictures, for the first, though relying, as I argued in *Fiefs and Vassals*, on later evidence, purports to depict the earlier middle ages while the second depicts the later. Consideration of the way that both were first sketched and then elaborated, however, raises the question whether the apparent paradox is really to be explained by changes in

---

[5] e.g. Maitland, *Constitutional History*, 143; Bloch, *Feudal Society* [252], 148–9, 156, 231–2; cf. Reynolds, *Fiefs and Vassals*, 17–22. For the acceptance of this idea of 'feudal society', e.g. Blok, 'Variations in Patronage', 367.

medieval society. I suggest that it is just as much, or more, the result of combining together traditions of historiography produced by the varying interests of different historians and the political preoccupations of their times.

The following sketch of the traditions that seem to me relevant to ideas of medieval collective activity starts in the seventeenth century and works, more or less chronologically, through to the twentieth. In the hope that this will make it easier for readers to find their way, I have divided the ideas I discuss into three themes, which I call the feudal, the communal, and the religious/intellectual. The names are the roughest approximations and the three themes are simply conveniences for setting out my argument. I do not claim that they are the major themes of all writing on medieval history. Even in the context of the paradox I have mentioned, they are merely themes rather than separate traditions. Many of the works I mention in connection with only one theme (as well as many that I do not) could be used to illustrate one or two of the others. The third—the religious/intellectual—is perhaps the most pervasive and fundamental: historians of the middle ages have quite often said or implied that a sense of community, common welfare, and public spirit is something difficult that medieval people acquired gradually with the help of Christianity and intellectual sophistication. Because the implications of this point of view began to be explored relatively recently, however, I shall start not with the religious/intellectual but with the feudal theme, then the communal, and then the way that these two came to be combined, ending with the religious/intellectual. Although I refer in passing to other historians from the seventeenth century on, I have chosen four from the nineteenth—Hallam, Guizot, Gierke, and Ernest Semichon—for rather fuller discussion. The first three were major scholars of wide influence. The fourth was much less distinguished and important, but his book seemed to me an interesting example of the religious/intellectual theme. Wider reading would probably reveal other historians who were equally or more significant. My four nevertheless seem to me to illustrate both the way that my three themes came to be combined in the nineteenth century, and the way that they and their combinations have affected views of medieval collective activity, and of medieval ideas about it, ever since.

Before 1789

From the sixteenth century on many scholars interested in the centuries that lay between them and the ancient world approached them through the academic feudal law of the later middle ages.[6] Until well on in the eighteenth century few if any of them seem to have been interested in vassalage as an affective interpersonal relation that bound society together. Despite their different interests and the different preoccupations that they absorbed from their different polit- ical and social circumstances, historians seem to have seen the academic law of fiefs or feudal law as what indeed it was—a system of property law.[7] When theories of social evo- lution began to be worked out the feudal or agricultural stage formed an important stage, but one that was still envisaged primarily in terms of property relations. Opinions varied about how feudal law had worked: Kames, concentrating on England and Scotland, thought that it had bound a people to their sovereign by giving him a hold over their persons and property. Adam Smith, like French historians, considered that it left kings too weak to control violence, rapine, and disorder—what Mably called 'la monstrueuse anarchie du gouvernement féodal'.[8] Either way, the political and social

---

[6] Reynolds, *Fiefs and Vassals*, 3–10.

[7] Dumoulin, *Opera*, i: *De feudis*. Church, *Constitutional Thought*, 184–7, seems to have read into Dumoulin a sense of 'personal' ('a man's personal relation- ships with those above and below him') that Church derived from modern ideas of the interpersonal relations of lords and vassals. Dumoulin's contrasts between *personale* and *haereditarium* or *temporale* (*Opera* 24 (§§ 116, 117), and cf. 22 (§ 104), like those of late medieval jurists, are concerned with property rights, not political or social relations in general. Also primarily concerned with prop- erty relations: Hotman, *De feudis* ; Sigonio, *Opera Omnia*, ii, cols. 33–4, 442–3; Craig, *Jus Feudale*; Spelman, *Reliquiae Spelmanniae*, 1–46, 172–86; Brady, *Complete History*; Boulainvilliers, *Histoire*, i. 118, 291–320, and *Essais*, 102–24; Muratori, *Antiquitates*, i, diss. XI; Dubos, *Histoire critique*, i. 545–9; Kames, *Essays*, 3–25, 123–92; Montesquieu, *L'Esprit des lois*, bks. 28–30; Bouquet, *Droit public*, 30–6, 94–101; Dalrymple, *Essay*, 1–75, 159–226; Smith, *Lectures in Jurisprudence*, 52, 187–8, 244–61, and *Wealth of Nations*, ii. 365–6; Hume, *History of England*, i. 159, 397–424; Bréquigny, introd. to *Ordonnances des roys de France* [144], xii, pp. iv-v, ix; Millar, *Origin of Ranks*, 189–213.

[8] Kames, *Essays*, 25; Smith, *Wealth of Nations*, ii. 366; Mably, *Observations*, i. 221.

implications of feudal law and feudal government were not seen as having very much to do with the loyalties or affective relations of individuals.[9] They had even less to do with anything of the sort in the French legal works about *les droits des fiefs*, which dealt with the contemporary rights of nobles over their non-noble tenants, rather than with the relations of lords and more or less noble vassals that had been the subject of older works of feudal law.[10]

It seems to have been an interest in chivalry rather than in vassalage that brought personal motives and interpersonal relations to the fore. Historians had been interested in chivalry long before the eighteenth century and some had noted its importance as a force for order. Its invention and use to preserve the peace and protect the weak were generally attributed to the clergy, but sometimes to French kings, who were said to have started or used it, just as they used the clergy, in their struggle against disorderly and rebellious feudatories.[11] The eighteenth-century discovery of medieval vernacular literature and the beauties of the Gothic cast a richer glow over chivalry and over medieval society in general. Knights errant who protected the weak and confronted dangers as individuals also fitted well with political theories that focused on individuals with their own natural rights, apart from either society or the state and prior to both. La Curne de Saint-Palaye, as one of the first students of medieval romances, may not have been affected, at least consciously, by ideas of this sort, but he was clearly affected by current ideas about feudal anarchy. Chivalry had helped French government come out of the chaos that followed the end of the Carolingian monarchy. It may have enabled barons to strengthen the bonds of *la féodalité* by adding the grant of arms to the ceremony of homage.[12] For La Curne,

[9] Vico, *La Scienza nuova*, ii. §§ 1046–85; Robertson, *History of Scotland*, 12–18, 37n, 65–7; Ferguson, *Essay*, 124, 200–1; Justi, *Staatswirthschaft*, i. 374, ii. 132–3, 400–12, and *Historischen und juristischen Schriften*, 212–33; Smith, *Lectures on Jurisprudence*, 52, 128, 187–8, 244–61, and *Wealth of Nations*, ii. 364–6.

[10] Robin, 'Fief et seigneurie'. Mackrell, *Attack on Feudalism*, seems to read 'feudalism' rather readily into his sources.

[11] Pasquier, *Recherches*, 81v; Boulainvilliers, *Essais*, 131–8; Saint-Palaye, *Mémoires*, i. 69–80.

[12] Saint-Palaye, *Mémoires*, 68–9.

as for his followers, knights were vassals, while vassalage came to mean dying for one's lord as much as holding land from him.[13] In 1817 the *Encyclopaedia Britannica* depicted 'the intercourse betwixt' lord and vassal before 'the romantic ideas of chivalry ceased' as 'of the most tender and affectionate kind'.[14] As yet, however, vassals and their lords existed, in true romantic fashion, in a social void. Writers on chivalry were not thinking about social bonds. By 1817, however, historians were beginning to make a further combination of feudal anarchy and chivalry with elements deriving from my second or communal theme.

In the form of the medieval assumption that kingdoms and lesser units of government were communities of descent and custom, what I have called the communal theme is genuinely medieval, and can be traced back a long way.[15] In the fifteenth century it was given new vigour, and a new twist, by the discovery of Tacitus' *Germania*.[16] As scholars elaborated Tacitus' picture of the noble simplicity of the second-century Germans, two points came to be stressed. First, the ancient Germans (that is, the adult male householders and property-owners among them) were free. Even if some of them were noble, they were equal in their upstanding independence, subject only to the authority of the local or tribal assemblies in which they all met. Second, they gave unstinting loyalty to the war-leaders they elected in these assemblies. The same

---

[13] The connection between chivalry and feudal laws, knights and vassals, is made very clear in Saint-Palaye, *Mémoires*, i. 300–14, ii. 5–6, 112, 128–30, Hurd, *Letters on Chivalry and Romance*, 83–4, 157, and Percy, *Reliques*, iii, pp. iii–iv. Hume, *Hist. of England*, i. 404, 423 may also count as an early suggestion of the newer synthesis, though in general he seems to have envisaged feudal law more in terms of property (above n. 7) and his early 'Historical Essay on Chivalry' does not suggest a link with it. Herder, *Ideen zur Philosophie der Geschichte*, XIX. 3. 5–6, XX. 2 is also suggestive, though the English translation by F. E. Manuel (Chicago, 1968) adds extra feudo-vassalic terminology that is not in the original. The use of the word 'vassal' in medieval French may have helped to make the connection between chivalry and vassalage: T. Venckeleer, 'Faut-il traduire vassal par vassal?'. In general: Gossman, *Medievalism*, 273–84; Smith, *Gothic Bequest*.

[14] *Encyclopaedia Britannica* (5th edn. London, 1817), viii. 597, 598. Scott's *Essays on Chivalry, Romance and the Drama* were also written for the *Encyclopaedia*: see esp. p. 45.

[15] Below, at n. 158 and pp. 251–61.

[16] See, *Deutsche Germanen-Ideologie*, 9–33; Ridé, *L'Image du Germain*, 129–40, 1057–94, 1193–1209; Kelley, 'Tacitus noster'.

kind of loyalty or fidelity was transferred to the kings whom the Franks acquired during and after their settlement in Gaul. When and how the reward of warriors with booty was changed to their reward with alods or fiefs, or first with alods and then with fiefs, was a matter of controversy.[17] A related problem was that of explaining the apparent loss of liberty and equality that was entailed in the change, and either justifying it or showing how liberty at least had been preserved or might be recovered. Claims to long-lost national freedom could be revolutionary, as they were in seventeenth-century England.[18] By the eighteenth century, however, Germanic liberties were generally—though not invariably—seen in more noble, and therefore less dangerous, terms.

The most obvious example of non-nobles who had recovered liberties lost under feudal oppression were the inhabitants of privileged towns, but in the eighteenth century they were often seen as having been given their liberties rather than having seized them. French kings had favoured the 'rise of the communes' as a counterpoise to *la puissance féodale*. Hume thought that the Anglo-Saxons had preserved their ancient liberties: even after the Normans made England into a feudal kingdom freedom was still kept alive in the county courts. After the Conquest kings of England followed 'other European princes' in encouraging and protecting the lower and more industrious orders for two centuries before Edward I added 'the house of burgesses, who were the true commons' to parliament.[19] Eighteenth-century histories of individual towns might derive their liberties from either ancient Romans or ancient Germans. In Germany there were many towns that, like the smaller states in which they lived, evoked a strong local patriotism, but, whatever their claims to ancient liberties, they presented a picture of cosy corporate life rather than seeming like bastions of liberty in the present.[20] To the

[17] e.g. Mably, *Observations*, i. 356–63; Montlosier, *De la monarchie française*, 345–61; Hallam, *View of the State of Europe*, 113–22, esp. 114n.

[18] Hill, *Puritanism and Revolution*, 50–122, does not stress the Tacitean influence, but cf. MacDougall, *Racial Myth*, 42–9, 59.

[19] Boulainvilliers, *Histoire*, i. 309–13; Bréquigny, *Ordonnances* [144], xii, introd.; Hume, *History*, i. 141–60, 401–2, 411, ii. 89–95.

[20] Walker, *German Home Towns*, 148–50, 174–82 *et passim*, and 'Rights and Functions'.

citizens or burgesses of towns there and elsewhere their trade
and craft associations represented happy harmony and togetherness, but to enlightened outsiders they looked more and
more like bastions of privilege and restrictions on trade.[21]
Liberty and community were increasingly seen as the rightful
property, not of small local groups but of nations. Once
expressed as *liberté, égalité, et fraternité*, they seemed to a good
many people to have become incompatible, or barely compatible, with monarchy.

The nineteenth century

The French Revolution affected every European historian
who lived through it or after it. Those who studied medieval
history came to see feudal government in a new light. Even
in the aftermath of revolution and war, however, Henry
Hallam was in a position to view the state of continental
Europe in the middle ages with a comparatively complaisant
detachment. He is important in my argument because,
though there may be earlier works that put the warm interpersonal relation of lord and vassal into a real social context,
his is the first I have found. Like many historians of medieval
Europe after him, Hallam concentrated his attention on
France. In his judgement the ancient Germanic liberties
described by Tacitus were lost soon after the Franks settled
in Gaul, as warriors were dispersed, became landowners, and
stopped going to assemblies of the nation.[22] The 'state of
anarchy, which we usually term feudal, was the natural result
of a vast and barbarous empire feebly administered, and the
cause, rather than effect of the general establishment of feudal tenures.'[23] In the breakdown of all law after the death of
Charlemagne, 'the powerful leaders, constantly engaged in

---

[21] Associations of trades and craftsmen were by now generally called guilds
or companies in England and *arti* in Italy. In French the word *corporations* (which
I wrongly noted below, p. 72, as medieval) came into use only in the eighteenth
century: Coornaert, *Les Corporations* [337], 23–5. In Germany various words
were by then in use, of which Walker, *German Home Towns*, 78n. says the most
common were *Zünfte* and *Ämter*. Cf. Schmidt-Wiegand, 'Gilde und Zunft',
360–1. The word *Korporation* was also then applied to them and to many other
collectivities, including many that would fall barely, if at all, within later definitions of legal personality: its varying uses are briefly but clearly disentangled
by Oexle, 'Gilden als sozial Gruppen', 287–8.

[22] Hallam, *View*, i. 101–9.   [23] Ibid. i. 226.

domestic warfare, placed their chief dependence upon men whom they attached by gratitude, and bound by strong conditions.'[24] As a result, 'the relations of a vassal came in place of those of a subject or citizen' and 'the connexion of lord and vassal grew close and cordial.'[25] Although the bulk of the people were degraded by servitude, that had no connection with feudal tenures as such. While chivalry 'inspired virtues of independence, as opposed to those founded on social relations', the feudal system might—at least as it developed in England—involve the principles of representation and consultation.[26] The feudal relation fostered 'the peculiar sentiment of personal reverence and attachment towards a sovereign, which we denominate loyalty; alike distinguishable from the stupid devotion of eastern slaves, and from the abstract respect with which free citizens regard their chief magistrate.' Later on, fealty to a lord was transferred to a monarch. 'In ages when the rights of community were unfelt, this sentiment [of fealty] was one great preservative of society.'[27]

The feudal system was destroyed by the rise of commerce and even more by the institution of free cities and boroughs, which Hallam suggests was due as much to the townspeople's spirit of resistance to oppression as to royal protection.[28] Later, following Thierry (who himself followed the German, Wilda) he suggested the private, personal, and voluntary association of the guild as the origin of the urban commune.[29] Hallam did not make much of communes, however, probably because the English liberties he cherished did not seem to owe much to them, while the liberties acquired by the common people of France in the middle ages did not look very impressive, and he must have disapproved of the way the modern French had enlarged them.[30] By the end of the middle ages royal hostility to the Estates General ensured

---

[24] Ibid. i. 117.   [25] Ibid. i. 218, 219–20.
[26] Ibid. i. 226–9, ii. 541, and cf. ii. 168–75, 216, 220.   [27] Ibid. i. 228.
[28] Ibid. i. 209–18.
[29] *View* (10th edn., London, 1853), 350, incorporating *Supplemental Notes* first published separately in 1848. Cf. Thierry, *Récits*, 1. 267–303; on Wilda, *Gildenwesen*, see below, at n. 54.
[30] Though 'a sound Whig' he disapproved of the Reform Bill of 1832: *Dictionary of National Biography*, 24. 96–8.

that the opportunity 'for establishing a just and free constitution in France was entirely lost.'[31] England, however, had
preserved both effective government and ancient Germanic
liberty, not least—as Hume had thought—through the
county courts. English towns acquired less independence
than those of Italy or Germany, but they were protected by
the same vigour that Norman kings used against the feudal
aristocracy. It was, naturally, parliament as a whole, including the borough members, that in Hallam's account came to
embody 'the ancient constitution of the Northern nations
. . . [that is] the participation of legislative power with the
crown'.[32]

Hallam was a scholar. The *View of the State of Europe* was
based on critical and perceptive reading of medieval sources
and of French and Italian (though not apparently German)
scholarship of the previous hundred years. Its interpretataion
of changes in social and political relations was nevertheless
based, as it was bound to be, less on the often gnomic sources
than on ideas about society and politics that were current in
Hallam's day and surroundings. 'No unbiassed observer', as
he said at the beginning of his chapter on the English constitution, 'who derives pleasure from the welfare of his
species, can fail to consider the long and uninterruptedly
increasing prosperity of England as the most beautiful
phænomenon in the history of mankind'.[33]

Only a few years later F. P. G. Guizot produced more
completely worked out, as well as more rhetorically elaborated, accounts that may well have been influenced by
Hallam's, as well as by German scholarship that Hallam did
not use.[34] Despite his admiration of the English constitution,
however, Guizot's point of view was bound to be different.
He was more unambiguously hostile to the feudal regime,

---

[31] *View*, i. 185. [32] Ibid. i. 182, ii. 207–41. [33] Ibid. i. 127.
[34] *Essais sur l'histoire de France*; *Cours d'histoire moderne: histoire de la civilisation en
France depuis la chute de l'empire romain jusqu'en 1789* (Paris, 1829–32). I cite the
Essais and the five-volume *Cours* on France (both in effect ending in the 14th
cent.) as more revealing than his much briefer general history of Europe (1828).
The *Essais* have more footnotes than the *Cours*. Guizot cited secondary works
less often than Hallam but he cited Hallam with relative approval, e.g. *Essais*,
128, 167. He used Savigny (*Cours*, i. 390–1) and also K. D. Hüllmann (*Essais*,
89, 123, 153; *Cours*, iv. 307), on whom see Koller, 'Zur Entwicklung', 5–7.

which had never, he said, received habitual acceptance and obedience.[35] Talk of mutual rights and obligations going right through the feudal hierarchy was, he thought, unreal, while he seems to attribute only slight influence to chivalry, the poetic daughter of the feudal regime.[36] Feudal society began to develop from the sixth century, as a necessary stop-gap (*une sorte de pis aller nécessaire*) in the complete breakdown of both barbarian and Roman society.[37] Charlemagne's government failed because, in the infancy of civilization, in the midst of ignorance and barbarism, and without communications and contacts to unite men by the community of ideas and the reciprocity of interests, great states were impossible. The Franks had no sense of the public and could handle only direct relations between man and man.[38]

Guizot is clearer than Hallam on the importance of ideas, though his distinction between public and personal is not always unambiguous: his idea of the public seems to be closely connected to the Roman-law distinction between public and private, while he uses 'personal' sometimes to contrast with 'public', sometimes for what one might call interpersonal relations, though in some places they are personal as opposed to real (i.e. based on property). This last distinction is important: the purely personal relation of the barbarian chief with his followers was changed when he granted them land and they secured hereditary rights in it.[39] Guizot, however, made less of this change than later historians would when they talked of the union of vassal and fief.[40] When he said that the personal relation remained the basis of feudal society, it is fairly clear that he meant that relations—such as they were—did not go beyond the interpersonal. In any case he did not think that they amounted to much: the essence of the feudal regime was the independence and isolation of individuals—that is, in effect, of seigniorial families in their

---

[35] *Cours*, iv. 18; *Essais*, 352–3, which suggest a deliberate response to Hallam, *View*, i. 218.

[36] *Cours*, iv. 10, 108–9, 181–99; though cf. *Essais*, 351–64.

[37] *Essais*, 351–70 (quotation on p. 362); *Cours*, i. 299–317, iv. 77–103.

[38] *Essais*, 81, 98, 122–3; *Cours*, iv. 94, 137, 298.

[39] e.g. *Essais*, 98–104, 122–3, 154–5, 344; *Cours*, iv. 286–92, 363–9.

[40] Brunner, *Deutsche Rechtsgeschichte*, ii. 274; Reynolds, *Fiefs and Vassals*, index *sub* union.

castles.[41] The only principle of association was the bond
between suzerain and vassal. Where that was lacking there
was no society with laws and obligations.[42] 'L'infériorité de
l'élément social à l'élément individuel, c'est là le caractère
propre et dominant de la féodalité.'[43] The result for France
was five centuries of chaos or anarchy, with lords exercising
arbitrary and despotic power in their domains.[44]

Guizot thought that the feudal regime was ended by the
rise of the monarchy and the communes. Liberty is conta-
gious. Townspeople and peasants saw the liberty of the lords
and strove ceaselessly to win it for themselves. Guizot did
not, however, make much of their feelings of collective solidarity. Despite his remark about peasants striving for liberty,
non-nobles who lived outside towns in the middle ages
appear in his pages—as in those of many of his contemporaries—simply as peasants and objects of feudal oppression.
As for townspeople, Guizot did not apparently take up
Thierry's suggestion about guilds. He made the internal government of those French towns that secured a measure of
autonomy sound almost as oppressive and conflict-ridden as
the earlier feudal anarchy. Only in modern times would liberty and security be combined.[45] In the middle ages what
would become the third estate had, like the nobility, no collective unity and merely helped to create the absolute monarchy.[46] It only won through in the long run by creating both
the French Revolution and the constitutional monarchy, thus
absorbing all the other estates.[47] In Italy towns had for a
while become glorious republics, but where, as in the
Netherlands, liberties had been preserved into modern times,
towns had become petty oligarchies, favouring the predominance of partial and local interests. Centralization had
brought France more prosperity and glory than she would
have gained if local independence and local ideas had

---

[41] *Cours*, iv. 164–71. Hallam, though he considered Guizot's work epoch-
making, thought he exaggerated this: *View* (10th edn., 1853), pp. x–xi, 321.
[42] Ibid. iv. 317.   [43] Ibid. iv. 364.   [44] *Essais*, 354–8.
[45] Ibid. 363–70; *Cours*, v. 128–35, 209–17, 222–6.
[46] *Essais*, 364–70, 516: he was more negative about the unity of the third
estate, and equally so about urban government, in his *Histoire de France*
(1872–6), ii. 31, which presumably reflects his final thoughts on the topic.
[47] *Cours*, v. 122–3, 129, 516–17.

remained preponderant. The contrast with the parliamentary government of England and its embodiment of national unity might have been a cause for sorrow before the Revolution. After it, despite all the evils along the way, it was not. French liberties were all the better for being achieved after social equality and enlightened civilization.[48]

The proud—not to say smug—confidence of Hallam and Guizot was impossible for Germans, but the predicament in which they found themselves in the early nineteenth century was productive of great historiographical results. This is said subject to the caveat that my knowledge of nineteenth-century Germany is more sketchy even than my knowledge of nineteenth-century Britain and France. Nevertheless, unless my reading is yet more inadequate than I think, and unless I have misunderstood a great deal of it, it seems not too rash to deduce that a great deal of what has been written since about medieval collective activity reflects ideas that were worked out in response to conditions in nineteenth-century Germany.[49] Any German who was concerned about current politics, and wanted to understand how they had got to where they were, knew that Germany, however divided at present, was a nation with a glorious imperial past and an even older heritage of law and liberty.[50] Current ideas of nations and national liberty made it difficult to reconcile the past with the present. Not that all educated and thoughtful people wanted the kind of centralized state in which Guizot and Hallam took pride. The pull of loyalty to existing states was strong, and not only for outright conservatives. The result was a conflict of loyalties which in turn produced a ferment of ideas about nations, states, liberty, and law. Law mattered partly because of the prominence in government and society of

---

[48] *Cours*, v. 122–30, 212–43; *Essais*, 371–517, esp. 371, 381, 442–3, 493, 509–17.

[49] I have found particularly helpful Koller, 'Zur Entwicklung der Stadt-geschichtsforschung'; Nipperdey, 'Verein als soziale Struktur'; Oexle, 'Mittelalterliche Zunft' (especially useful about the connection of of 19th-cent. terminology and ideas with medieval historiography); Schmidt, 'Landes-geschichte'; Schröder, 'Zur älteren Genossenschaftstheorie'; Böckenförde, *Verfassungsgeschichtliche Forschung*; and, in English, Walker, *German Home Towns*; Whitman, *Legacy of Roman Law*; Reulecke and Huck, 'Urban History Research'.

[50] Hegel, *Verfassung*, 461–8, 550–1, 575–6; *Philosophie der Geschichte*, 419–26.

lawyers trained in the universities. It also mattered because
of the conflicts posed by the rival claims both of rationaliz-
ing codification and supposedly organic development, and of
Roman and German law—all highly debatable categories in
themselves. What made all this so important for medieval historiography was that the prevailing climate of political and
legal ideas made problems of law into problems of legal history.

The more free the ancient Germans had been the more
necessary it was to explain how they had lost their national
liberty and unity. It seems to have been fairly widely
accepted that the original Germanic states had been formed
from below, when the rights of free Germans over their
households and property were combined in the local communities (*Gemeinden*) of the marks, and then in *Gauen* and
Länder, and finally in the kingdom or empire. According to
Ficker, higher levels of government therefore had no right to
interfere in matters with which lower levels could deal.[51] The
transition from the free communities of early Germans to the
feudal society of medieval kingdoms was explained by showing—in varying ways and with varying emphasis—how the
personal *Treue* owed by the Germanic warrior to his war-
leader was replaced by the fidelity owed by a vassal to the
lord who granted him a fief. The strength of the German
legal tradition shows here: personal relations were contrasted
with 'real' (*dinglich*) relations, that is, with those concerned
with property, while private relations were contrasted with
public in the sense of those concerned with the state.[52] The
sense of interpersonal and affective seems less clear than it
was in Guizot or Hallam, though something of the sort seems
sometimes to be implied.[53] Feudal law also helped to explain

---

[51] Hüllmann, *Deutsche Finanz-Geschichte*, 3; Wilda, *Gildewesen*, 56–7; Roth,
Feudalität, 19–23; Ficker, *Deutsche Kaiserreich*, 54–5.

[52] Hüllmann, *Geschichte des Ursprungs der Stände*, 16–17, 27–9; Eichhorn,
Deutsche Staats- und Rechtsgeschichte, i § 158, ii. § 364; Roth, *Beneficialwesen*, pp. iii–
vii, 106–7, 203, 379, and *Feudalität*, 23–31, 280–1, 312–16; Waitz, *Deutsche
Verfassungsgeschichte*, ii. 606–7; v. 309; Hegel, *Philosophie der Geschichte*, 425–6, 434,
445.

[53] Waitz, 'Lehnswesen', 359, and *Deutsche Verfassungsgeschichte*, 606; iv. 538;
and an additional remark in ii. 673 (2nd edn., Kiel, 1870); Giesebrecht,
Geschichte der deutschen Kaiserzeit, i. 176–7, 282.

the loss of royal power which had left the German nation divided among a mass of states, most of which, by the early nineteenth century, were hard to envisage as the sort of natural communities to which their subjects owed natural and rightful obedience.

When German legal historians looked at the middle ages, they could, however, find that kind of community, not only in the tribes of Germany and the empire that united them, but in towns and villages and the collective liberties that they enjoyed. By the nineteenth century peasant communities no longer existed in law, except in the vestigial form of common property, but they could, with faith, be traced back to the mark-communities that had begun to clear the forests of ancient Germany. Towns, except in Roman areas, were more recent, while their records were for the most part later still. In 1831, however, W. E. Wilda bridged the gap by connecting medieval merchant and craft guilds to the *convivia* described by Tacitus through Scandinavian, Anglo-Saxon, and Carolingian guilds and through the *convivia* that Henry I ordered to be held in tenth-century Saxon fortifications. The love of sociable togetherness was, he thought, deep-rooted in the Germanic character. Guilds created by the Germanic urge to participate in community formed artificial families for those who left their homes to settle in towns.[54] This emphasis on the close affective community as well as the freedom and loyalty of the ancient Germans came at a time when voluntary societies of all kinds were burgeoning in Germany and when lawyers in universities and in government service were struggling with the problem of which groups ought to have legal rights or not, and why.[55] Until the 1830s the prevailing legal doctrine maintained that groups could own property and act at law as individuals only if they were authorized by the state. From then on it came under fire from Germanist lawyers who pointed out how little sense it made both of Germanic freedom and of past and present practice.[56] As the

[54] Wilda, *Das Gildenwesen*, 4, 24, 40–1. See Oexle, 'Gilde als soziale Gruppen', 293–6.

[55] Nipperdey, 'Verein als soziale Struktur'; cf. e.g. Riehl, *Land und Leute*, 79–82 *et passim*, and works cite above n. 49.

[56] Schröder, 'Zur älteren Genossenschaftstheorie'; Hallis, *Corporate personality*, pp. xxxix, 1–28.

nineteenth century wore on, problems of industrialization
and worry about trade unions gave a new edge to all these
questions, making the past, with its small towns and brotherly guildsmen, look increasingly attractive. Nostalgia for
medieval towns, villages, and guilds was not restricted to
Germany, or to conservatives, as the example of William
Morris suggests. What made Germany's contribution to ideas
about medieval communities so important and long-lasting
was the intellectual quality, the sheer richness of ideas link-
ing past and present, that were evoked by the political, social,
legal, and economic circumstances in which lawyers and
scholars there found themselves in the nineteenth century.

All this came together in the work of Otto Gierke.[57] In the
first volume of *Das deutsche Genossenschaftsrecht*, published in
1868 as *Rechtsgeschichte der deutschen Genossenschaft*, Gierke combined interpersonal feudal relations and the Germanic roots
of community in a fully worked out dialectical relationship.[58]
The dialectic was complex. Alongside the contrasting principles of the vertical relations of lordship or government from
above (*Herrschaft*) and the horizontal relations of community
or fellowship (*Genossenschaft*), were the corresponding principles of unity and freedom, and also those of property (patrimonial) relations and personal relations. One could add a
further dialectic, implied but pervasive, of German with
Roman or foreign. Gierke saw the dialectic working itself out
in five stages.[59]

The first stage, which ran to AD 800, was that of the free
community which was originally based on kinship and patri-
archal relations. From the start, however, the contrary principle of lordship was present, at first in the form of personal
service, but later gradually transformed by property relations
and the development of the state. The second period
(800–1200) was dominated by feudal and property (patrimo-

---

[57] I have not used Gierke's 'von' since he acquired it only in 1911, after
three volumes of *Das deutsche Genossenschaftsrecht* had been published: *Neue deutsche
Biog.* vi. 373–4.

[58] On Gierke and dialectic: Dilcher, 'Genossenschaftstheorie', 331–2; 'Boldt,
'Otto von Gierke', 9. Extracts from vol. i, including the introductory outline of
the stages of history, together with smaller parts of vols. ii and iii, are translated as Gierke, *Community in Historical Perspective*.

[59] *Das deutsche Genossenschaftsrecht*, i. 8–11.

nial) relations. All peace, law, and power came from above, all law became private law, contract was all, and the only legal relations were those between individuals.[60] But the German corporative spirit was so strong that it formed first the group based on common subjection (*die abhängige oder herrschaftliche Genossenschaft*) and then a new and mightier form of community. This was the community based on voluntary, free union (*Einung*[61]) which, in contrast to feudal government from above, grew up spontaneously from below. In towns it produced the oldest local community (*Gemeinde*) and the oldest state on German soil. The principle of free union dominated the third period, which lasted until the end of the middle ages. This was the heyday of free urban communities and of free guilds of merchants and craftsmen within them; of leagues of towns and nobles; of unions of clergy; of universities of scholars; of communities of estates within the different provinces or lordships; and even of communities of peasants, though these last were not really free unions.[62] Although German law, as Gierke explained in a later volume, did not have any theory of corporations as such, the free communities of this third period were envisaged as having a collective personality so that they owned property and were able to act at law as if they were individual people.[63] With time, however, they became ever more rigidly confined by differences of status, by the application of academic theories of corporations developed out of Roman and canon law, and by the transformation of lordship over land into the sovereign state. The fourth period, from 1525 to 1806, was that of sovereign states, fortified by Roman law, and of privileged corporations that were dependent on the state and ruled by private law. The keynotes of this period were the absolute

---

[60] Ibid. 154, 189. Despite the much more legal cast Gierke gives this it is tempting to relate it to Guizot. Being concerned only with German history, Gierke cites few non-German works. Guizot's essays and lectures on French history were apparently not translated into German before 1910, though the lectures on European history were translated in 1844. Hallam's *View* was translated in 1820–1.

[61] For the difference for Gierke between *Einung* (voluntary in formation) and *Genossenschaft* (lasting longer and comprehensive in purpose): *Deutsche Genossenschaftsrecht*, i. 297n.

[62] *Das deutsche Genossenschaftsrecht*, i. 588–9, 609.   [63] Ibid. iii. 1–4.

state and the absolute individual. In 1868 Germany stood at the beginning of a fifth period in which the spirit of the old German community had reawoken and was finding new forms of free association. These were different from the old because they lived under a powerful state and, rather than embracing the whole of their members' lives, were formed for a mass of various and particular purposes.[64] Nevertheless, Gierke said in his introduction to volume i, they were transforming public and private life and would go on to achieve even greater things in the future.

Gierke was 27 when this first volume was published—1,111 pages of it, with many references to medieval sources—and a second volume (on the history of German ideas of community) appeared only five years later. It was an astonishing achievement and, as has been said, it put the whole idea of different forms of community and association at the very centre of social history.[65] According to O. G. Oexle, Gierke's arguments ran too much against the dominant trend of the time to have much influence on German historians until after the First World War and have now rather fallen into neglect once more.[66] The contrast between *Herrschaft* and *Genossenschaft*, however, is only one striking example of something that seems to have been first clearly formulated by Gierke and has been discussed, or simply taken for granted, by later German historians.[67] Something like it was introduced to Anglophones, though hardly quite naturalized, in Walter Ullmann's formulation of descending and ascending themes of government.[68] In any case, Gierke's influence on both sociology and legal history was rapid and undeniable.

[64] *Das deutsche Genossenschaftsrecht*, i. 882; Oexle, 'Die mittelalterliche Zunft', 25–6, is particularly clear on Gierke's distinctions.

[65] Boldt, 'Otto von Gierke'. Brentano's essay in Smith, *English Gilds* [188], though reflecting a similar background of German concerns, was written independently of Gierke: Oexle, 'Die mittelalterliche Zunft', 26.

[66] Oexle, 'Otto von Gierkes "Rechtsgeschichte"'.

[67] *Geschichtliche Grundbegriffe*, ii. 854, iii. 86–8 do not trace the contrast back before Gierke, but Hüllmann, *Geschichte des Ursprungs der Stände*, 509, and Roth, *Feudalität*, 15–16, are suggestive.

[68] Ullmann, *Principles*, 20–9, 216, *et passim*; cf. his review in *R. H. D.* 26 (1958), 360–6, where he alludes to Gierke just before postulating ascending and descending theories but does not make the connection. For Ullmann, however, descending theories were hierocratic rather than feudal: see the comments of Black in Gierke, *Community in Historical Perspective*, p. xxix.

Ferdinand Tönnies's *Gemeinschaft und Gesellschaft* (1887), which has had far-reaching effects within sociology and beyond it, has often been interpreted in a way that simplifies Gierke's connection between types of community and periods of history so far as to be almost a caricature. Tönnies postulated two ideal types of community, the natural, organic, affective *Gemeinschaft*, and the artificial, purposive, instrumental *Gesellschaft*. These easily became identified respectively with the rural and small-town society of the premodern, pre-industrial ages and the urban, industrialized conditions of modern society.[69] Max Weber also spread some of Gierke's ideas more widely. Part of what both Tönnies and Weber took from Gierke has been recycled rather uncritically back into medieval history, which makes it important to note that they both tended to generalize what he said about medieval Germany (often from rather late medieval sources) more or less explicitly to cover the European middle ages in general.[70]

In legal history Gierke's biggest impact may have been made by his third volume (1881), where he discussed the history of the idea of legal personality or incorporation. The way that nineteenth-century German scholarship envisaged the connections between the nature, political rights, and legal position of groups or communities made this an essential part of Gierke's argument. He had to explain how what he saw as foreign, Romanist ideas of legal personality had been used by early modern states to crush free German communities. It was part of this volume that F. W. Maitland translated into English. What attracted Maitland to Gierke's work is obvious: it embodied a wealth of historical imagination and ideas that he could never have found in what had been written about English common law before he himself started on it. For many British medievalists Maitland's enthusiasm for Gierke's ideas—more, perhaps, than his rather mid-North Sea translation—ensured that Gierke would be referred to with respect, though generally from a safely unread distance. That seems to be how he is regarded elsewhere too. As a result,

---

[69] See Phillips, *Looking Backward*, 81–8; Oexle, 'Die mittelalterliche Zunft', 32–8; and below, pp. 333–7.

[70] Weber's use of Gierke is suggested e.g. in *Wirtschaft und Gesellschaft*, 431–2, 433 (Eng. trans. 716–17, 720).

although it has been suggested—surely rightly—that his historical work was driven by preoccupations with his own
time,[71] his interpretation of medieval history seems to be seldom questioned.[72] This matters because, so long as Gierke's
arguments and their relation to the evidence are not examined, they cannot be assessed as seriously as both their intrinsic interest and their indirect and sometimes garbled
influence on later historians demand. *Das deutsche Genossenschaftsrecht* is a monument of fertile ideas and of wide and
deep scholarship, but, like the works of Hallam and Guizot—
and everyone else—it is a work of its time. Looking more
closely at the context in which Gierke grappled with the
problems of group personality makes it harder to accept that
nineteenth-century legal ideas about corporate groups can be
traced back as far as he traced them in volume iii. Much of
the vast quarry of material he presented in volume i supports
details of argument that individually still seem to stand up
well. But if one looks at it, not in the long perspective of
German uniqueness that Gierke surveyed from 1868, but in
the light of the range of evidence we now have about
medieval Germany, about the rest of medieval Europe, and
about other societies outside Europe, the larger argument
into which it is fitted looks highly questionable. As a result
the details need to be questioned too. Gierke's selection and
interpretation of all his evidence is clearly determined by the
extraordinarily consistent vision that informs volume i. The
very coherence of his argument makes it hard to detach the
details from the dialectic into which he fitted them without
questioning their interpretation and the context into which
they now need to be fitted.

My third theme, which I have called the religious/
intellectual, can be dealt with more briefly. The idea of the

---

[71] Janssen, *Otto von Gierkes Methode*, 38–9, 55.

[72] It seems to be implicitly accepted or is not discussed e.g. by Janssen, *Otto
von Gierkes Methode*; Boldt, 'Otto von Gierke'; Hallis, *Corporate Personality*, 139.
Dilcher, 'Genossenschaftstheorie', 360–1, points out that Gierke's dialectic of
Herrschaft and *Genossenschaft* is too simple. Oexle, 'Otto von Gierkes "Rechstgeschichte"', 209, argues against the Germanic origins of the guild and suggests that many other details could be criticized. Black, introd. to Gierke,
Community in Historical Perspective, and *Guilds and Civil Society*, 28, 210–17, makes
interesting criticisms.

middle ages as the age of faith did not originate in the nineteenth century: Herder, for instance, envisaged medieval
society as floating on the sea of the church, with feudal lordship as one side of the ship and episcopal power the other.[73]
The religious climate of the nineteenth century favoured a
greater emphasis on the church as the source of all or most
medieval morality except for the barbarian values of courage
and loyalty; on its transmission to the middle ages of such
relics of Roman civilization as ideas of *res publica* and public
spirit; and on monasteries not only as peaceful communities
in themselves but as fostering ideas of brotherly peace and
harmony for others to copy.[74] The book on the peace of God
which Ernest Semichon published in 1857 is not a much
remembered or particularly distinguished example of the
scholarship of the Catholic revival but it illustrates well some
of the ideas that were around.[75] Semichon's was the first serious study of the peace movement. Although not an academic
but, in his own words, *appartenant au monde et aux affaires* (he
was a lawyer), he used a considerable number of the available sources.[76]

Semichon repudiated both the customary belief that Louis
VI created the communes and any desire to look for origins
of medieval associations in Germanic, Gaulish, or Roman
survivals.[77] The first development of the third estate started
in the eleventh century and was the work of the church and,
more specifically, of the clergy. France had fallen into a sad
condition of feudal anarchy under the later Carolingians
(there is a reference to Guizot here) and only the church
cared.[78] The church taught the weak their rights and put in
their hands the powerful weapon of association, in the form
of brotherhood (*la confrérie*), which had been born in the first

---

[73] Herder, *Ideen zur Philosophie der Geschichte*, XIX. 3. 1.
[74] See the interesting survey of Van Engen, 'The Christian Middle Ages'.
[75] Semichon, *La Paix*: the 2nd edn. (1869), which I cite, incorporates a chapter on Germany that profited from Kluckhohn's *Geschichte des Gottesfriedens*,
which is much slighter, alludes only in passing (p. 122) to the contribution of
the ecclesiastical movement to urban communes, and is in general more academic, more legal, and apparently less religious in inspiration. On both: Paxton,
'History, Historians'.
[76] Semichon, *La Paix*, i, p. xii; Lorenz, *Catalogue*, v. 386.
[77] Semichon, *La Paix*, i. 196–7; ii. 113–19, 213–14.
[78] Ibid. i. pp. v, 7, 14, 18, ii. 193–7.

centuries of Christianity but now took on a new form and
new importance.[79] Diocesan associations led to parish mili-
tias and so to the sworn communes of towns and villages.[80]
The church thus saved political society in the eleventh century, and, by a bold application of the principle of association, gave birth to the modern world.[81] Chivalry, the revival
of philosophy, and the growth of the schools were all the
work of the church: like other works of the eleventh century,
the revival of learning was both profoundly national and profoundly Christian.[82] Of course, not all historians of the time
agreed that the church was responsible for so much: as
Semichon said, his contemporaries were too disposed to
attribute the progess of the modern world to a vague, philo-
sophic form of Christianity, independent of the church and
the clergy.[83] Nevertheless the quantity and quality of nineteenth-century scholarship that was imbued by Catholic piety
carried its influence to many medieval historians who were
neither Catholic nor even avowedly Christian.[84] While some
historians stressed the hostility of the clergy to communal liberties, that did not necessarily involve questioning how many
of the basic values of community came originally either from
Christianity—perhaps in the vague form Semichon
deplored—or from Roman ideas that the church had
absorbed.

This summary of Semichon's views suggests why I put
together my third theme as both religious and intellectual.
Important and influential approaches to the social and political ideas of the middle ages had earlier been made through
law, through German interest in the conflicts of popes and
emperors, and, of course, through feudalism. But the connection between religious and intellectual history that
Semichon illustrates was reinforced after a papal encyclical of
1879 encouraged the study of medieval theology.[85] As the
study of theology and canon law led on to the study of
medieval academic thought in general, medieval political

[79] Semichon, *La Paix*, ii. 201–11.   [80] Ibid. i. 208–13, ii. 113–19.
[81] Ibid. ii. 210–11.   [82] Ibid. i. 153, 179–90.
[83] Ibid. ii. 193–4.
[84] Among Protestants, compare Hallam, *View*, ii. 1–125, 417–22, 435–42,
569–82, with the less negative tone of Adams, *Civilization*, chs. 3 and 6.
[85] Van Engen, 'Christian Middle Ages', 520.

thought came to be studied almost exclusively through academic and polemical treatises, with problems of church and state, papacy and empire to the fore.

The twentieth century

Much has been written in the past hundred years that touches in various ways on medieval collective activity and on medieval ideas about it. So far as I can see, however, the subject has not generally been looked at as a whole. Specialization has enabled most historians to avoid the problem of reconciling the initial paradox that I noted and that Gierke resolved by his dialectic of *Herrschaft* and *Genossenschaft*, feudal rule from above and Germanic community. Perhaps the generally fragmented approach explains why so much that has been done seems to accept the categories devised by the historians I have discussed so far and to reflect their preoccupations: no historian now, confronted with so much more evidence and so much more secondary literature, can afford their wide sweep and bold generalizations.

Noble society—what is often called feudal society—is generally studied rather apart from that of humbler lay communities. The main group-consciousness which nobles are thought to have had tends to be that of the family or kin, while their collective activity outside it is thought of primarily in terms of vassalage, conspiracy, or rebellion.[86] Beyond the kin and the conspiracy the primary bond of noble society is still often seen as starting from the interpersonal relation described by Hallam and Guizot. When noble property—generally described as fiefs—became secure and hereditary (which is often thought to have happened around the eleventh century) the personal relation became territorial or 'real' (i.e. mediated through real property). In so far as this made the relation less affective, the change made for less solidarity rather than more.[87] German historians have found signs of the development of 'transpersonal' kingship or a 'transpersonal' state from the eleventh century, while the English follow Hallam in seeing England as a nation and a state from even earlier. In either case, what is being

[86] See e.g. the essays in Reuter, *Medieval Nobility;* Althoff, *Verwandte.*
[87] I have questioned all this at length in *Fiefs and Vassals,* chs. 2–5.

described is a type of government, which affected the relation between the king and his subjects, but did not reflect or necessarily even promote what I have called regnal solidarity.[88] Feelings of regnal solidarity, together with collective activity on a regnal scale, are generally postponed to the age of estates, dawning national consciousness, and 'state formation' in the later middle ages.[89] Before then the 'community of the realm' is only envisageable in England, and even there it is generally thought of in exclusively baronial terms.

Most twentieth-century medieval historians have associated collective activity primarily with what Guizot and Semichon called the Third Estate, and above all with towns. Although increased use of archaeological evidence has helped pushed the rise of towns further back, twentieth-century urban historians have tended to follow earlier traditions connecting the formation of urban communities with the use of the word 'commune' and the formal grant of liberties in the twelfth century. The investigation of the Latin words that are taken to indicate the achievement of legal personality is another obvious inheritance from Gierke.[90] Other nineteenth-century preoccupations include almost anything to do with 'craft guilds', as they are still called. It also sometimes seems to be assumed that medieval townspeople were concerned with the right of association and the relative merits of free trade that preoccupied people in the nineteenth century. Attention has therefore focused on the economic purposes of guilds or craft guilds (often taken as synonymous) and on economic reasons for official disapproval of them.[91] In reaction against the more sentimental views of 'craft guilds' held by those who were worried by nineteenth century industrialization, twentieth-century historians have tended to stress the selfishness of 'guildsmen', urban 'patriciates', and the conflicts their oppressions provoked. Those who argue about medieval patriciates and urban oligarchies have not been

---

[88] On 'transpersonal': below, p. 293; on 'regnal', p. 254.

[89] Below, ch. 8, and index *sub* estates. I have discussed 'state formation' and ideas of states more fully in 'The Historiography of the Medieval State'.

[90] Michaud-Quantin, *Universitas* [586]; below, pp. 59–64, 168–83; Reynolds, 'History of the Idea of Incorporation'.

[91] Most recently: Epstein, *Wage Labor*.

much bothered by the absence of the terms from their sources.[92] The attention paid recently to what are sometimes called social and religious guilds or fraternities, though concentrated more on the later middle ages, suggests a welcome rethinking of some of the old categories.[93]

Rural communities have received much more attention in the past century and much new material has been produced, along with new ideas about it.[94] But once again it is possible to wonder whether some of it has not slipped rather too easily into old paradigms. One of these is the belief that there were no real local communities in the countryside before the eleventh or twelfth century.[95] One reason adduced for this is that peasant communities, according to Marxist reasoning, would have been formed when heavier seigniorial pressure created a new class solidarity. Another is that archaeological evidence suggests that concentrated settlement, at least in some areas, is not much older than the twelfth century, while documentary evidence suggests that co-operative open-field agriculture started only at about the same time or later.[96] Both these explanations rest on good evidence of the explanatory phenomena but rather insubstantial links between them and the existence of solidarity or community. In so far as community is to be found in co-operative and collective activity, then the suggestion that either seigniorial pressure or concentrated settlement were necessary to it is as

[92] 'Oligarchy' is not quite so foreign as I suggested on p. 198: see below, at n. 145.

[93] e.g. Black, *Guilds and Civil Society*, though keeping the old terminology of 'guilds' and 'craft-guilds', and accepting the significance of 'legal personality', is an interesting exploration of the historiography and of medieval ideas. Oexle, 'Gilden als soziale Gruppen' and 'Conjuratio und Gilde', casts serious doubt on the pagan origin of guilds that I was inclined to accept (below, p. 67). On late medieval fraternities, e.g. *Le Mouvement confraternel*; Rosser, 'Going to the Fraternal Feast'.

[94] Wickham, *Comunità e clientele*, 199–254 surveys the literature on Italy, Spain, France, and England.

[95] Wickham, *Comunità e clientele*, 14–15, and Rösener, *Peasants*, 149–54, are exceptional in making clear the distinction between community (as a matter of collective activities and social relations) and formal, institutional autonomy.

[96] Since 1984: e.g. Blair, *Anglo-Saxon Oxfordshire*; Bourin-Derruau, *Villages médiévaux*; Fossier, 'Les Communautés villageoises'; Harvey, 'Initiative and Authority'; Hooke, 'Early Medieval Estate and Settlement Patterns'; Rösener, *Peasants*; Sivéry, *Terroirs et communautés rurales*; Spiess, 'Bäuerliche Gesellschaft'; Wickham, *Mountains and the City*, and 'Rural Society'.

questionable as the assumption that it started with charters of liberties.[97]

Once some kind of rural community was formed, medieval historians have generally come to stress economic divisions between richer and poorer among the peasants, just as they have stressed divisions and conflicts within towns. Some, however, like the early sociologists and recent communitarians, have made medieval villages seem more happy and harmonious.[98] In the case of those sometimes called the 'Toronto school', this may reflect the ideas of the Catholic social movements of the nineteenth century as much as the work of Gierke or Tönnies.[99] 'Peasant studies' by social anthropologists have formed a more recent influence—though anthropologists too have not always been immune from a rather similar inherited nostalgia. Analogies drawn from peasant societies elsewhere have provoked Alan Macfarlane to argue that, since peasant communities are by definition self-contained and dominated by collective behaviour, English villages, in contrast to those elsewhere, were by the thirteenth century not peasant communities at all. Instead, 'the majority of ordinary people in England from at least the thirteenth century were rampant individualists, highly mobile both geographically and socially, economically "rational", market-oriented and acquisitive, ego-centred in kinship and social life.'[100] Here too the contrast between collectivist and individualist suggests the concerns of nineteenth-century and later thought.

Increased study of medieval political thought has in some ways widened the gap between the study of political and legal practices of the middle ages on the one had and the study of medieval academic writings on the other. As J. L. Nelson put it in 1987: 'The ideology presented by historians of medieval political ideas has sometimes seemed divorced not only from

---

[97] Wickham, 'Rural Society'; Sivéry, *Terroirs et communautés rurales*; cf. (on 19th–20th centuries) Holmsen, 'Old Norwegian Peasant Communities'.

[98] On communitarians: Phillips, *Looking Backward*.

[99] Their work is discussed by Smith, ' "Modernization" and the Corporate Village Community'; the suggestion about the connection with Catholic social thought is just a guess of my own.

[100] Macfarlane, *Origins of English Individualism* [560], 163. See the comments of Smith, ' "Modernization" and the Corporate Village Community'.

the realities described by historians of medieval politics but from the ideas of most of those involved in medieval government.'[101] For the Carolingian period, which she was then discussing, the gap has been bridged by her and others.[102] After 900 the bridges, though they exist, tend to be one-way and rickety. There are almost none before the papal-imperial quarrels of the later eleventh century and the academic explosion of the twelfth. The reason generally given for this is the absence of evidence before then, but that is valid only if one assumes that lay people did not think and that academic treatises are the only or best source for what anyone thought. It is odd that historians who will not risk deducing attitudes and values about collectivities from charters, chronicles, and laws are happy to take the norms and values of feudo-vassalic relations from modern works that are themselves based on late medieval treatises as interpreted by even later historians.[103] The prevalence of feudo-vassalic values is so taken for granted that direct contemporary evidence is thought to be unnecessary. From the twelfth century, historians of medieval thought often seem to assume that serious thought about politics, having started among the clergy in the eleventh century, was thereafter the prerogative of academics. It has even been suggested that western Europe was saved from a stark alternative of anarchy or absolutism by the ideas of hierarchy, community, and consent that developed in the church, stimulated by its conflicts with the state.[104] Semichon's emphasis on the clerical origins of the Peace of God has been continued and developed by those who see secular lordship in the eleventh century as essentially violent and lawless and the Peace as directed against it, or at least against the lesser lords.[105] Ideas of representation are said to have been embodied in church assemblies well before

[101] Nelson, 'The Lord's Anointed', 105.   [102] See n. 2 above.

[103] Most recently, e.g. Luscombe, 'Formation of Political Thought', 159–62; Black, Individual and Society', 589–90, 593; Althoff, *Verwandte*, 10–11. Cf. Reynolds, *Fiefs and Vassals*, especially chs. 2, 4–6.

[104] Tierney, *Religion, Law*, 5–12, 40–2, and 'Freedom and the Medieval Church', 64–6.

[105] E.g. Bisson, 'Feudal Revolution', 18–21; Van Engen, 'Sacred Sanctions', 219. Martindale, 'Peace and War', 156–7, esp. n. 26, suggests that this interpretation originated with Duby, 'Les Laïcs'. Cf. Goetz, 'Kirchenschutz', 206 (Eng. version, 260).

they percolated through to the laity.[106] Perhaps the most striking development of all lines of thought derived from nineteenth-century Germany is to be found in the attention that historians of medieval political thought have devoted to ideas of legal personality or incorporation.[107]

Some Inherited Problems

The fact—if, as I suggest, it is a fact—that some of the ideas and assumptions that twentieth-century historians have in the back of their minds when they approach the collective activities of the medieval laity are rather old does not necessarily mean that they are wrong. Old ideas are not always any worse than new ones. But it is worth looking hard at our presuppositions to make sure, first, that we really think they are right and, second, that we are not imposing them on the evidence. Looking harder at them, though it will never stop us from seeing things from our own point of view, may help to guard against the more gross distortions.

One inheritance from the nineteenth century which surely needs examination is the assumption that liberty, equality, and community go together.[108] A look at other traditional societies, past and present, suggests that there is no reason why they should do so in a society that had never heard the slogan 'liberty, equality, and fraternity'. Collective self-government gives opportunities for new sorts of collective activity but it also gives rise to new divisions. Solidarity can be created by collective oppression, while groups without formal autonomy can sometimes act collectively whether or not they feel oppressed. Nor is equality always conducive to unity. However distasteful we—or some of us—find it, inequality may actually make cohesion easier. Subordination is more likely to be accepted in societies where people have not been brought up to believe that they are all born as free, equal, and separate individuals whose submission to author-

---

[106] Tierney, 'Freedom and the Medieval Church', 82–4.

[107] See most recently, with reference to earlier literature: Canning, 'The Corporation'.

[108] C. Helliwell, 'A Just Precedency', though modern ideas of individualism can create a contrary tendency to associate collectivity with hierarchy when looking at traditional societies outside Europe: Jolly, 'Epilogue: Hierarchical Horizons'.

ity is voluntary and contractual. Their subjection may seem part of a natural and ordained pattern in which superiors and inferiors each fulfil their functions.[109] Perhaps we do not need to worry about the origin of medieval communities or how they cut across the supposedly interpersonal, vertical relations of feudal society. Perhaps communities as such were always there, in the sense that groups of people acted together over long periods, at least in part voluntarily, and took their mutual responsibilities and solidarities largely for granted. If so, what we need to study are the ways in which communities and their responsibilities and solidarities changed; the ways their autonomy was increased, reduced, or circumscribed by formal, recorded rules; and the ways that the new conditions provoked new conflicts, solidarities, and methods of internal government. The contrast between feudal and communal, *Herrschaft* and *Genossenschaft*, is one that made sense in the nineteenth century but, I shall argue, does not translate very well into medieval terms. We may find the contrasting concepts a useful analytical device but that may be all they are. We need to be careful that we are not just assuming that, if we explained them to intelligent people in the middle ages, they would have seen what we were getting at and have found the categories useful.

It is easy to see why Gierke believed in the peculiar gift of the German people for forming communities, and why people in other countries have tried to claim their share of the Germanic heritage of liberty and community.[110] Such beliefs now look untenable. Relics of the arguments once used to support them, however, may survive in places where no one has examined their relation to the evidence. One obvious example of this is in comparisons between Europe and elsewhere. The way that the European economy developed so as to make modern western society different from any previous societies has encouraged a search for anything in medieval and early modern Europe that may have been

[109] Aristotle, *Politics*, I. ii, v–vii; III. iv–vii; Dumont, *Homo Hierarchicus*, 36–55, 104–19; though see Jolly, 'Epilogue: Hierarchical Horizons', for criticisms and later literature on the subject.

[110] Gierke, *Deutsche Genossenschaftsrecht*, i. 3; Gollwitzer, 'Zum politischen Germanismus'.

unique to it and that might explain later developments. Some claims to uniqueness have been made by Europeans with apparently rather scant knowledge of anywhere else and some seem rather unlikely to explain the change. One supposedly unique feature of medieval society that has attracted attention is the autonomous, sworn craft guild.[111] The only way I can explain this is that 'craft guilds' became so embedded in the minds of historians in the nineteenth century that many of their successors have taken the autonomy and the identity of craft and guild as given, despite problems in the evidence. It may be that the oaths which seem to have generally been imposed on guild members (though whether on all practitioners of crafts is less clear) were unique to Europe.[112] Since people in western Christendom seem to have been much given to taking oaths in all sorts of circumstance, however, that may not in itself be evidence that their sworn associations were any more cohesive—let alone independent—than unsworn associations elsewhere. Another way that Europe can be made to look unique, and uniquely given to forming free communities, is by making the definition of 'full urban communities', fit a definition of medieval European towns devised by nineteenth-century legal and constitutional historians.[113] The definition does not fit many European towns either in the middle ages or since any better than it fits those in many other societies. The reputation of Weber, who used it, has inhibited serious historical comparisons between the rise of towns in Europe and elsewhere ever since. Weber's range of learning was enormous but his evidence and arguments about medieval Europe and about other continents are no longer uncontested.

---

[111] Weber, *Wirtschaft und Gesellschaft*, 433–4, 437–9 (Eng. trans. 720, 725–9); Hintze, *Staat und Verfassung*, i. 163–4, and cf. 175–6; these are both cited by Oexle, 'Gilden als soziale Gruppen', 353. The construct is then accepted by those concerned with non-European towns and their internal organization: e.g. Lapidus, *Muslim Cities*, 92–107; Stern, 'Constitution of the Islamic City', though see also Hourani's introduction to the volume in which Stern's essay appears, esp. pp. 14–15, which has not apparently been sufficiently noticed. Also Venkatarama, 'Medieval Trade, Craft, and Merchant Guilds in S. India'.

[112] Oexle, 'Gilde als soziale Gruppen', 353, and 'Conjuratio und Gilde'; cf. Prodi, *Il Sacramento del potere*.

[113] Weber, *The City*, 80–1.

We need to look at medieval collective activity in a less Eurocentric, less teleological, and more analytical way. Comparisons with non-European societies should start by examining at least some of the evidence about collective activity in them which has been ignored by those who assumed European (or Germanic, or German) uniqueness and looked only for what seemed to prove it. Virtually all traditional societies studied by social anthropologists seem to be full of collective activities and to be generally unbothered about justifying them or setting limits to them.[114] There are plenty of conflicts within groups that might seem to raise questions of principle about the rights of individuals as such against the rights of the community, but they do not often seem to do so. Concern about such matters is not apparently an innate aspect of human nature. There is, of course, no reason to assume that medieval Europe shared assumptions about collective activity and collective responsibilities with, say, traditional African societies. On the other hand, so long as medieval Europe used non-professional, customary law and collective judgement, a comparison with others societies that do the same may be illuminating and suggestive. In such societies it may be difficult to distinguish between what Tönnies called *Gemeinschaften* and *Gesellschaften*. It seems likely that acting collectively and forming associations of all sorts is easier in societies that do not distinguish between what a modern lawyer would call corporate and unincorporated groups.[115]

More comparisons within Europe are also needed. The difference between national historiographical traditions make these difficult, not least because they make it necessary to get behind the secondary literature—and to do so more thoroughly than I did in this book. Use of medieval evidence is essential if we are to get behind such stereotypes as feudalism, craft guilds, and the communal movement, into which the evidence has been forced, and see what is genuinely

---

[114] e.g. Clastres, *La Société contre l'état*; Dumont, *Homo hierarchicus*; Gellner, 'Trust, Cohesion, and the Social Order'; Gluckman, *Politics, Law and Ritual* [789]; Mair, *Primitive Government* [807]; Maquet, *Power and Society in Africa*; Moore, *Law as Process*; Popkin, *Rational Peasant*; Roberts, *Order and Dispute*.

[115] Moore, 'Legal Liability'.

common to Europe and what varied—not necessarily along
the lines of modern political boundaries. It needs to be noted
too that generalizations about Europe in this context usually
relate to something much smaller than the whole continent
or, as it might better be described, subcontinent. This book
covers only a small part of it.

We also, as I suggested at the beginning of this introduction, need to discuss both ideas and practice, distinguishing
them from each other but also relating them to each other.
In doing so, it is, I suggest, essential to try to distinguish
words, concepts, and phenomena. As I have argued in discussing fiefs and vassals—and as others have said before
me—there is no necessary connection between any particular word and the concept or notion that people may have in
their minds when they use the word.[116] When words such as
universitas, collegium, communia, or *communitas* occur in medieval
sources in contexts that seem to suggest something like what
a modern lawyer means by a corporate group (though legal
definitions are less simple than historians of medieval political thought sometimes imply), that does not mean that anyone in the middle ages, even academic lawyers, had anything
like the modern legal concept in their minds.[117] Even if they
had, phenomena are different from both words and concepts.
The way that people thought about groups is important, but
it needs to be related to the ways they acted in groups.
Interesting and thought-provoking as it would be to try to
construct a typology of medieval groups, it surely cannot be
right to think of starting it from the study of Latin nouns that
were used to denote groups. If the nouns chosen for study
omit, for instance, *regnum, gens,* and *natio,* then the study omits
categories of medieval thought that were, I suggest, so fundamental that they seldom needed to be argued about.[118]

If we are concerned with phenomena—that is, whether
there were groups of people who acted together on a fairly
permanent basis, how they did so, and how their activities

---

[116] Reynolds, *Fiefs and Vassals,* 12–14. Schmidt-Wiegand, 'Historische
Onomasiologie' discussed this in a medieval context before I did.

[117] Below, pp. 59–64; Reynolds, 'History of the Idea of Incorporation'.

[118] Michaud-Quantin, *Universitas* [586], suggested by Oexle, 'Die mittelalterliche Zunft', 40, as the starting-point for a typology.

changed—and with the concepts or notions they had about the rights and wrongs of their collective activities, then it may be useful to start by looking hard at the ideas about medieval communities that we have inherited from nineteenth-century historians, the circumstances in which they put them forward, and the evidence they used. Was the period before about 1000 or 1100 deficient in collective activities and solidarities—whether at local, regnal, or intermediate level? Is the idea that it was deficient based on evidence or merely derived from old ideas about feudal anarchy in tenth- and eleventh-century France, fortified by the romantic image of the chivalrous knight dying for his lord in a social void? In other words, does the idea depend—even a little—on an exaggerated idea of the troubles of the time, fortified by a literary topos? Does it also require that we either ignore the majority of the population or assume that there was a complete barrier between their ideas and values and that of the 'feudal classes'? Was the idea of the affective bond between lord and man perhaps fostered by intermittent misunderstandings when the use of 'personal' as opposed to 'real' or territorial by legal historians was translated to political and social history?

If the period before 1100 was not devoid of collective activities and solidarities, how does that affect the 'communal movement' of the twelfth century? How far did new economic and political conditions, new kinds of document, new legal procedures, and new words reflect or create new ideas about group rights and solidarities? Finally, when we examine the economic controls established in medieval towns, and the groups by which and for which they were established, we need to be sure that we are not reading into them either nineteenth-century nostalgia for lost harmonies or nineteenth-century hostility to the selfish oligarchies that seemed to have survived from the middle ages.

Lay ideas about collectivity

The argument that the relation of lord and vassal was the main social bond of earlier medieval society would be weak even if it relied on the lack of evidence of other bonds in a period when evidence is scarce. That is because, as I have argued elsewhere, the idea of vassalage, as generally understood, is a construct of later historians who built on academic treatises of the later middle ages, on which, as I have argued above, affective relationships from vernacular literature were later superimposed. *Vassi* in the earlier middle ages were soldiers and servants rather than fiefholders, while the relation between most free men or nobles and those they considered their lords or rulers was not apparently based either on the lord's grant of land to them or a supposed grant to one of their ancestors in the past. It was more like that of a subject to a ruler.[119]

In any case we do not need to deduce the absence of transpersonal or collective relations from the absence of evidence about them. As I argued below, in Chapter 8, the stories that were told, at least from the sixth and seventh centuries, about the origin and migrations of peoples, suggest that kingdoms and the peoples that inhabited them were envisaged as permanent, continuing entities.[120] So do other references to peoples, such as those in the titles of kings, which described them as kings either of one people or of several peoples—but always of peoples as collectivities, not just haphazard collections of individuals. More substantial evidence comes from the records of law, especially chronicles or documents that recount the settlement of disputes. Legislation is useful too, but in an age of customary law accounts of arguments, however cursory, may give more accurate indications of what people thought right and wrong than do more explicitly normative texts. Where laws or charters were written for kings or other laymen there does not seem to be much reason to doubt that the king or lord had at least a rough idea of what was said in his name or that he approved of it. Quotations from scripture may have been added by clerical scribes, and appeals to God and the saints

---

[119] Reynolds, *Fiefs and Vassals*, ch. 2 *et passim*.

[120] Below, pp. 256–60. Most of what I said on p. 291 about the name of the kingdom of Germany was wrong: see Müller-Mertens, *Regnum Teutonicum*, though I still think that those who served in German armies in Italy must have had some sense of regnal solidarity. On the sense of a kingdom in France before the 13th cent.: Schneidmüller, *Nomen Patriae*. On 12th-cent. England: Gillingham, 'Henry of Huntingdon'.

elaborated, but most if not all kings believed in God and his judgement of their activities, even if their ideas about it all were sometimes sketchy.[121] Even chronicles and cartularies compiled to defend churches against what monks or bishops saw as lay oppression give some idea of lay attitudes and values, if only by deploring their consequences.[122] Before the twelfth century all the evidence is scattered and some of it has to be read between the lines, but there is more to be found than is generally suggested. There is certainly as much or more that implies the existence of collective solidarities as there is about the values associated with noble vassalage and fiefholding. What the evidence that I have found suggests to me is that lay people's ideas and assumptions about politics and society combined the values of lordship and community, *Herrschaft* and *Genossenschaft*, in a way that makes the effort to separate and distinguish them seem anachronistic.[123]

'Lordship' here does not mean the rule of lords as distinct from kings. As I argued in Chapter 8, kings were the archetype of rulers. When historians refer to medieval kings as leaders they are presumably borrowing unconsciously from the modern vocabulary of politics. Medieval kings were not leaders whom their subjects could choose to follow as citizens of a modern democracy choose to follow those who lead parties. Once a king was installed the members of the community he ruled were his subjects who owed him obedience and loyalty. I suggested in 1984 that it is misleading to describe a medieval king as *primus inter pares*.[124] I still have not found the source of that phrase and I continue to suspect that it is post-medieval. The great men or peers of a kingdom were not the peers of their king. Nevertheless, though kings were responsible to God for the justice of their government and the protection and welfare of their people, that does not mean that they were absolute or sovereign in the sense of having total authority. They were responsible to the

---

[121] I have argued this further in 'Social Mentalities'.

[122] On apparently different ecclesiastical and lay ideas about property and inheritance: Reynolds, *Fiefs and Vassals*, 63–4, 171–7.

[123] I shall not give references for most of what I say in this section, as it is based on what I have used in the rest of the book.

[124] Below, p. 259.

community of their people as well as to God, as is shown in the constant reference to consultation and consent.

The ruler's duty to consult implies that his subjects, though not his equals, were like enough to him to be able to advise him. They had rights which, like all rights, came ultimately from God and which their earthly superiors were supposed to respect. Those who had authority under kings, whether by formal delegation or by custom, ought not to be deprived of their offices or property at the king's whim. Government was exercised in layers, with rights and obligations at every layer. This is sometimes represented as meaning that medieval ideas of the structure of government were remote from modern ideas of sovereignty. They were certainly different. Rights and obligations rested on different grounds from those in modern states, but the idea of layers of government with rights against each other is not in itself all that different from what is found under federal constitutions today. At each layer of medieval government the subject was supposed to be obedient but the ruler was supposed to consult and to rule justly and according to custom. Respect for rank and authority was embedded in medieval values, but so was respect for custom and justice. In other words, the norms conflicted, but then norms generally do: there is not much point in having them otherwise. Much of the time the tension between the demands of hierarchy and obedience on the one hand and justice and the customary rights of subjects on the other could be contained. When government became too lawless and oppressive the accepted view seems to have been that free men coul take up arms to defend themselves, though, if they did, it was better that they should do so as a community under the leadership of the community's greater members. Best of all would be for the great men to remonstrate with the ruler on behalf of all, taking up arms only as a last resort.

Respect for custom and justice meant that rulers, from kings down to mere lords over peasants, were supposed to consult with the people under their authority. So far as kings were concerned, that was stated clearly in the tenth century by Abbo of Fleury.[125] Though Abbo was writing the kind of

---

[125] Abbo, *Collectio canonum*, col. 478.

treatise that is not, as I maintain, the best evidence for lay values, the evidence of countless charters and reports of assemblies makes it impossible to believe that he was saying anything different from what laymen took for granted. Those whom a king or lesser lord was supposed to consult were such of his subjects, and as many of his subjects, as seemed to represent the rest. In practice that probably meant in the first place the greatest landowners—even if, in a village, that meant no more than the villagers with the least small holdings. When power was exercised for any length of time custom would turn it into legitimate authority. Legitimate authority over land conferred status. Even bishops and abbots, who in principle had a different basis for their status, owed some of it in practice to their land. But status was not everything. Some descriptions of 'feudal society' that stress the legal barriers between classes or orders may be influenced by the old tradition of interpreting the middle ages in terms of the Ancien Régime.[126] Although the wergelds of early laws give an impression of precisely defined status groups, it is pretty clear that, like everything else in a world of local custom and poor records, the status of individuals was in practice often unclear and disputable, and sometimes changeable. To be noble in the earlier middle ages was not to have fixed privileges at law but to be the sort of person who could swing opinion in assemblies against those who in that setting seemed less noble.[127]

Great men were needed in assemblies because, apart from reasons of practical politics, their wealth and status gave them the right and duty to represent the rest. Nevertheless, attendance at assemblies does not seem to have been restricted to the great. For the declaration of custom and doing justice, the more of the community who were present the better—apart, of course, from women, children, and servants. When custom was at issue—and it often was—age could give someone of relatively mediocre status a hearing.

[126] Weber, *Wirtschaft und Gesellschaft*, 137, 148–9 (Eng. trans. 237, 255–8) was obviously influenced by 19th-cent. German interpretations of late medieval or post-medieval German feudal law.

[127] Bloch, *Feudal Society* [262], 286–8, though I think he put the making of clear distinctions a bit early: Reynolds, *Fiefs and Vassals*, 41–5.

He could even speak up without being asked, as an old knight apparently did in a meeting of an English county in the mid-twelfth century at which bishops and barons were present.[128] They were discussing a question of jurisdiction that arose during what was in effect a trial for treason, which illustrates very well the way that law and politics were often discussed in much the same sort of meetings. Both were matters that needed consultation with those who represented the community and could declare its custom. In tenth-century Germany, according to Widukind, the whole people (*omnis populus*) of the Franks and Saxons chose Otto I as king (*principem*). For Widukind, it seems, the great men—and no doubt some less great—who gathered to acknowledge and acclaim Otto represented two whole, collective peoples.[129] Community and inequality thus went together—so much so that, in so far as hierarchy may imply the arrangement of layers within a whole, it may be better to describe the values of medieval society as hierarchical rather than merely unequal or stratified.[130] In practice the hierarchy was very untidy, but at present my concern is with the values and assumptions that I think I detect in the sources, not with the way they worked in practice.

The combination of lordship and community—or *Herrschaft* and *Genossenschaft*—in all this is, I hope, obvious. It is not just that kings consulted representatives of their communities in a way that, in Gierke's terms, revealed the dialectic of *Genossenschaft* working against *Herrschaft*, or that tempted earlier English historians to see the origins of parliaments in what they called the Witenagemot. Groups like guilds, brotherhoods, or communes, that Gierke saw as embodying the values of *Genossenschaft* and that sometimes explicitly proclaimed the equality of their members in their own documents, do not, on closer examination, look like hotbeds of nascent democracy. Whatever elections they held, such groups tended to be ruled by those of their members who

---

[128] Cam, 'An East Anglian Shire Moot' [103].
[129] Widukind, *Rer. gest. Sax.* [81], 63 (II. 1).
[130] Dumont, *Homo hierarchicus*, 104–5, 131, 329–30. But cf. Bloch, *Feudal Society* [262], 443, who perhaps had some other sense of the word in mind (cf. ibid. 288, 332).

were pre-eminent in wealth and status and who often served for long periods without—apparently—much demand for re-election. That was not necessarily a betrayal of the true or original aim of the group.[131] Equality clearly mattered. It mattered in sociable groups such as guilds just because people were conscious of pervasive inequality. They could be more relaxed and sociable among those who, at least in that setting, were to be reckoned as peers, even if some were more equal than others. It also mattered, for instance, when some-one was accused by a lord or official and felt he could get a fairer judgement from his peers. The feeling was evidently regarded as reasonable. Judgement by peers was officially and explicitly recognized as a form of collective, consultative judgement that was particularly suited to such circum-stances.[132]

When it came to government, or to representing any group to the outside world, however, responsibility normally fell, and was apparently supposed to fall, on the older, the richer, and the more powerful. So far as guilds, towns, and similar groups are concerned, the best evidence of this comes from the thirteenth century and later, but it seems reasonable to guess—providing one acknowledges that that is what one is doing—that the same assumptions were made earlier. Wealth, age, and general standing in the community imposed a duty as well as a right to represent the community and to govern it. The kingdoms and communities of my title were not contrasted forms of society and politics.[133] Kingdoms were assumed to be communities and all communities seem to have tended, if not towards monarchy, then to a respect for the kind of authority that looks to us undemocratic. At moments of stress demands were made for wider representa-tion, and even for elected representatives, but there is very little evidence in the whole of my period of any demand for anything like an equal say and equal responsibility in

---

[131] Cf. Cohen, *Symbolic Construction of Community*, 33–6

[132] E.g. *M. G. H. Dipl.* [156], Conrad II, no. 244; Magna Carta, c. 20–2, 39 (Holt, *Magna Carta* [475], 322, 326); comments in Reynolds, *Fiefs and Vassals*, 199–207, 384. On collective judgement in general, in addition to pp. 23–34, 51–9 below, see esp. Davies and Fouracre, *Settlement of Disputes*.

[133] My title apparently deceived at least one historian to think I meant that they were: Head, 'The Judgment of God', 236.

government for all adult male householders, let alone for all adult males or—obviously—women. Describing popular movements of discontent as democratic or populist is liable to evoke modern movements that are based on quite different political ideas.[134] However great the tension between ascending and descending forms of government was in practice, it was not a tension between ascending and descending *theories* of government. The rival theories are modern, not medieval.

So is the tendency to think of collectivity as an enemy of individual liberty. Individuals in the middle ages frequently came into conflict with their communities, as, for instance, when they committed crimes or when the consensus went against them in disputes with other individuals. This does not, however, seem to have provoked the conscious polarization of the two principles that it has in recent centuries.[135] Grants of collective liberties included clauses that seem to me not unlike bills of rights for individuals.[136] That applies not only, for instance, to Magna Carta, but to the much earlier charter granted to the people of Nonantola in 1058.[137] Such grants were generally made—and are sometimes known to have been made—in response to demands. Even if the recipients did not get all they wanted, what they got suggests some of the things they wanted. These often included something called being free or enjoying liberties.

Freedom was, as it always is, a matter of different degrees and kinds, all of them culturally conditioned. Some twentieth-century historians, reacting against nineteenth-century ideas of the middle ages as the nursery of modern freedom, have suggested that, because the liberties that appear in medieval charters were in effect privileges, whether individual or collective, to be enjoyed by those to whom the char-

---

[134] Ullmann, *Principles* [720], 20, 215–16, may have been unaware of the connotations of 'populist' in English usage: *O.E.D.* [212], xi. 1126. The words corporatism and corporatist seem to me unsuitable for similar reasons. On 'democratic' tendencies in late 12th-cent. learned works: Buc, *L'Ambiguité*, 312–78.

[135] Black, 'Individual and Society'.

[136] *Pace* Harding, 'Political Liberty', 434.

[137] Below, p. 131. Also the even earlier charter to Tenda (Alpes-Maritimes): Daviso, 'Carta di Tenda'.

ters were granted, the idea of liberty as such did not exist. That is surely as culture-bound and anachronistic as the idea it replaces. Even if we now all agreed what we mean by freedom or liberty—which even those in western democracies clearly do not—it would be nonsense to suggest that our idea of freedom or liberty is the only valid one.

The maxim *Stadluft macht frei* (town air makes you free) was a product of Germanist legal history rather than of the middle ages, but the freedom from external demands that many town charters promised was a real freedom as far as it went.[138] Freedom from arbitrary exactions, the right to be judged by one's neighbours on one's own home ground, collective freedom to collect and pay over dues without outside intervention, individual freedom to move around, and make one's choice of work—all these were clearly real freedoms. Whatever the words used for it, and whatever the particular form of it that was at issue, the quality of freedom or liberty, of being free in some general way, was obviously desirable and desired in medieval society.[139] No one was entirely free of obligations, any more than they are in any society, but some sorts of obligations were honourable, and therefore tolerable for free men, even if, as individuals, some of them tried to avoid them. When individuals or groups tried to get out of their obligations to their ruler and the community that he ruled, they might or might not succeed, according to power, influence, and payment. Such occasions do not seem to have given rise to disputes about conflicting principles of individuality and collectivity. The most effective defence that a free man had against injustice was precisely the community of which he formed part: hence the right to judgement by one's peers, or by the men of one's locality and by its custom.

So much was collective activity taken for granted, and indeed required for the working of government, that it is often hard to distinguish purely voluntary groups (such as

---

[138] Some of the vast literature on the maxim is surveyed in Henn, 'Stadtluft macht frei?'; cf., more recently, Diestelkamp, 'Freiheit der Bürger'. For the origin of the proverb: Brunner, *Abhandlungen*, i. 366, 412–13. See below, p. 165.

[139] Fried, 'Über den Universalismus der Freiheit', and 'Einleitung'; Harding, 'Political Liberty'; Constable, 'Liberty'.

guilds or brotherhoods) from those formed compulsorily for governmental purposes (such as armies, rulers' councils, or associations formed to police craftsmen). Each could turn into the other, as can be seen in the obscure and complex relations between crafts and guilds or in the way that lawful petitioners could turn, or be turned, into conspirators or rebels. One liberty, or freedom, that all free men took for granted was the freedom to act collectively, provided that their activities were not subversive. Even the unfree could do so, and were often required to do so, though their activities were more likely to be suspect as subversive. The proviso about subversion was important, but the liberty and its restriction together illustrate again the combination of community and lordship that, I maintain, was so characteristic of medieval values. They also illustrate the danger of trying to understand medieval collective activities and medieval ideas about them if one starts by putting them into the context of modern legal distinctions. At the risk of seeming obsessed by a legal technicality, I think it is important that, as I maintain, any kind of group, with the most undefined membership, could act as what we might call a corporate body, without needing to be incorporated.[140] There is nothing surprising about this absence of distinction, which the European middle ages shared with many other societies, but the way that medieval communities developed, and the way that rulers regarded them, make better sense if it is taken into account. New groups could be formed and could acquire rights, discipline their members, and negotiate with the outside world much more flexibly and easily than they could have done if modern legal ideas of incorporation had prevailed. When rulers forbade collective activity they did so because subversive or rebellious groups were more dangerous than subversive or rebellious individuals would have been. Collective activity was fine, so long as it suited rulers. No one seems to have tried to work out rules about the rights and responsibilities that belonged only to individuals as opposed to groups or what sort of group could or could not acquire them and how.

[140] Below, pp. 35–6, 59–64; Reynolds, 'History of the Idea of Incorporation'.

The same lack of theoretical polarity between individual and community is apparent in economic regulation. It was generally up to the members of a group to co-operate or not and work out how to do it, provided that they did not subvert good order or the supposed needs of the community of which they formed part. Rulers had as much right and duty to regulate economic as any other affairs, provided they did so after consultation, in the interests of justice and the good of the whole community. The chief impediment to harmonizing different interests was not, in the view of contemporaries, an inherent and inevitable conflict of interests, but sin and greed. Given sin, it was difficult to protect the poor and weak against the rich and powerful, but it was not apparently perceived as intrinsically more difficult in economic matters than in others. Prices were supposed to be just, which meant in effect that they should conform to the going market rate. There was constant emphasis on trading publicly in the open market.[141] Long before twelfth-century schoolmen began to argue about the just price the Carolingians had tried to stop both the sale of goods to the poor at unfairly inflated prices and the forced purchase of land from them at unfairly low prices.[142] The influence of Christian teaching is clear in this legislation, as in the accompanying prohibitions of usury, but there is no need to see the underlying idea of fairness in trade as coming only from the clergy. Apart from the fact that bishops and prelates were apparently among the guilty, some non-Christian societies have had much the same sort of ideas about fair prices. The just price was less a matter of either high theology or incipient Christian socialism than an expression of the kind of values that produce modern condemnations of dealers who buy antiques from little old ladies for a song. The regulation of trade and prices which appears in town records as soon as they get going seems to have been following these older traditions, though in conditions that made the job ever more difficult, controversial, and liable to provoke corruption.

[141] Baldwin, 'Medieval Theories of the Just Price', esp. 31–4; Gilchrist, *Church and Economic Activity*, 58–62, 116–18.

[142] *Capitularia*, nos. 44, 46, 88; *Concilia*, ii. 166 (c. 4), 645–6 (c. 52–3). The Anglo-Saxon laws about trading in public markets or before witnesses seem, however, to be concerned about theft rather than fairness.

So far as direct taxes are concerned, their irregularity made complaints about them particularly shrill and noticeable, but that is partly because most of the complaints that we read came from the rich, and especially from rich monasteries. It seems to have been taken for granted that taxes, like military service, ought to be roughly proportional to wealth. In practice, landowners passed the burden of taxation on to their subjects and tenants, who already bore other heavy burdens for them. That particular burden may not have seemed more unfairly distributed than others. What is clear is that the exemption of nobles from direct taxes was not the result of applying old and generally recognized norms but of negotiations in particular political circumstances in the later middle ages. When the rulers of more or less independent towns in the twelfth century and later assessed their poorer neighbours too high and themselves too low, it was considered unjust. The poor were supposed to know their place, respecting and obeying their betters, but the rich and powerful were supposed to treat the poor fairly: not equally in the sense we might expect, but justly and according to custom.

Changes in ideas

I have tried to deduce most of these very general ideas and assumptions from sources that date from before the mid-twelfth century. From that time the evidence becomes both more plentiful and different in character. Great social and economic changes had been taking place during the past couple of centuries. The population was growing, more land was coming into more intensive cultivation, and landowners were becoming richer. Much more trade—local and long-distance, in luxuries and everything else—was carried on between a growing number of towns, among which great centres of trade and industry were beginning to emerge from the mass of small market centres. In the twelfth century literacy became much more widely diffused while universities and other schools grew and multiplied. This last phenomenon produced the men who wrote the works on which historians of medieval thought depend. It is, however, still my contention, as it was in 1984, that what the academics, polemicists, and lawyers wrote articulated and refined the old ideas rather than producing entirely new ones.[143] This is not to say that their achievement was inconsiderable or unimportant for the future. It may be true that the distinctions they drew and the controversies in which they engaged contributed as much or more to the eventual development of fundamentally new political ideas as did the premises that they took for granted.[144] Articulating ideas focuses minds and sharpens controversy. But the premises of arguments, the background of values and assumptions that are taken for granted by a society, matter too, especially if one is interested in what people thought at the time as much as in the teleology of the long run.

The arguments of medieval scholars and polemicists about the relation between custom, law, and right, about representation, about the rights of kings over churches and of emperors or popes over kings, and about the moral responsibilities of members of groups, need to be seen against the background of values implied in charters, disputes, and laws for centuries before the academics got going. It was not just a background of practice or 'social reality',[145] but of ideas and values, however unarticulated and unsystematic, that academics learned from their parents and absorbed from their neighbours, as well as from their more formal instructors, in the same way as people in all societies acquire the ideas and values current and assumed in their particular societies. Intellectuals are not the only people in any society who think. What they think, however innovative and interesting, is affected by what their unintellectual neighbours take for granted. While grateful for the slightly backhanded compliment of a reviewer who thought it odd that such an intellectual book should be written to prove how ineffectual the learned can be, I was surprised by its implications. Intellectuals, even if they write in their society's vernacular and have access to ample technologies of popularization, surely do not have as big an effect on their societies' values and assumptions as their societies' values and assumptions have on them?

---

[143] Below, pp. 319–29.
[144] Southern, *Scholastic Humanism*, 1–2, 12–13, 181, though cf. 134–62.
[145] Tierney, *Religion, Law*, 11–12.

I suggest that the expansion of education in the twelfth century affected politics and society first and foremost, not by bringing in new ideas but by improving communications, making law more professional and government more bureaucratic. More important disputes, especially between more important people, began to be settled less often in general-purpose meetings in which age, social status, and experience of life conferred authority, and more often in courts dominated by legal experts arguing according to their own rules. The difference in our terms between the rules and character of arguments at departmental or college meetings and the rules and character of argument in law-courts may not be too far-fetched an analogy. Whether the new expertise made law more rational is hard to say:[146] it certainly made it more rigid and incomprehensible to outsiders, as it became the custom of the community of lawyers rather than of the community at large. The spread of professionalism was slow and patchy but even where university-trained lawyers did not appear the influence of their sort of law was felt.[147]

One result of more professional law and of more consistent record-keeping was the establishment of boundaries between jurisdictions and of the relation between jurisdictions. Since this also stimulated clearer thinking about jurisdiction and authority, it is a good example of the difficulty of deciding whether new ideas were produced more because changing practice needed them or because academics offered them. As old ideas of the responsibility of kings came to be expressed in hierarchies of jurisdiction, with regular appeals to higher levels, so the holders of subordinate jurisdictions came to be more regularly held to account. The Roman lawyers who told Frederick I that all jurisdiction derived from the emperor were responding to his entirely traditional demand that the cities of Italy should acknowledge their subordination, but their response was all the more effective, presumably,

---

[146] Davies and Fouracre, *Settlement of Disputes* gave much reason for abandoning the idea of 'primitive law' as rigid and ritualistic. Most recently: White, 'Proposing the Ordeal'.

[147] Bonfield, 'Nature of Customary Law'; Ourliac, 'Communautés villageoises', 19. Ourliac and Gazzaniga, *Histoire du droit privé*, concentrates on Roman law when discussing professionalization. Cf. *Fiefs and Vassals*, 65–73 (and index *sub* law).

because of the crispness of the rule and the authority and prestige of its source. The theory of the delegation of authority they set out still seems to me to deserve much more attention than it appears to have had so far. It is clearly related to the way that government was developing and it illustrates well the tension between the sharpness of new ideas and the continuing force of old norms. Even in England, where the theory was pushed farthest, though without apparently being explicitly stated, a powerful king with a team of top lawyers could not in the end override rights established by long custom.[148] Ideas about representation and about the relation of kings to law which had long been implied in royal consultations and in collective judgement and consent were also clarified by being expressed in phrases from Roman law.[149]

More systematic and professional government sharpened conflicts between rulers and their subjects. The contrast between king and community is crystal clear at moments of crisis in thirteenth-century England or Jerusalem and in early fourteenth-century France. But it was not drawn consistently or constantly enough to stimulate those involved to work out the kind of theories of the inherent difference between them that Gierke called *Herrschaft* and *Genossenschaft*. Such theories would have cut across the combination of hierarchy and community that seems to me to have lain at the heart of medieval ideas about society and politics. Solving the problems of deciding when kingship became tyranny and whether tyrannicide was ever justified would, as I argue below, have involved deriving a whole new political theory from a wholly new set of premises.[150] Neither theory nor premises would probably have been what anyone wanted.

In any case, at the same time as internal conflict was sharpening, increasingly bureaucratic governments were beginning to justify the increasingly regular dues and taxes they demanded by propaganda designed to foster regnal loyalties and solidarities. The result, by the end of the thirteenth century, is sometimes seen as a growth in national feeling

---

[148] Below, pp. 47, 172, 327. See *Fiefs and Vassals*, index *sub* delegation.
[149] Below, pp. 327–8.   [150] Below, pp. 328–9.

and, by implication, in political consciousness.[151] This may
be right, in so far as hostility to outsiders promotes solidarity
within, but medieval solidarities had always rested on habits
of collective activity as well as on external hostilities.
Historians may be beguiled by national teleologies into taking solidarities within what look like predestined nation-states
(or early modern 'territorial states') as more significant than
earlier solidarities. There may, however, have been as much
sense of community in the smaller populations of smaller
units early on, which could be maintained without the propaganda and organization that were now being deployed.[152]

Economic and social change, and the changes in government and law which it stimulated and made possible, intensified conflicts between different groups within kingdoms and
other units of government as well as those between rulers and
subjects or between different kingdoms as communities. The
grant of autonomy or privileges to particular groups drew
harder lines between ingroups and outsiders. In what R. I.
Moore has called a persecuting society, foreigners, Jews,
heretics, and the unfree all suffered more, though to different degrees, as their legal disabilities were defined more
exactly and enforced more consistently.[153] Economic growth
was also a great sharpener of conflict. Local lords, sometimes
earlier, sometimes later, profited from the same skills as were
used at higher levels of government to extract more dues and
services from their subjects and tenants. By the thirteenth
century woods and common lands were coming under pressure so that the rights of commoners came more obviously
into conflict with those of lords.[154] The multiplication of specialized trades and the conflicting interests of buyers and sell-
ers caused endless problems for municipal governments that
were supposed to regulate trade in the interests of all.[155]
Italians who wrote about civic politics in the thirteenth cen-

---

[151] E.g. Guenée, *States and Rulers*, 4–6, 45–65, 216–20. Cf. Reynolds,
'Historiography of Medieval State'.

[152] Fouracre, 'Cultural Conformity'.

[153] Moore, *Formation of a Persecuting Society*; cf. Gillingham, 'Beginnings of
English imperialism'; Bartlett, *Making of Europe*, 197–239.

[154] In addition to what I said below, p. 123: Birrell, 'Common Rights'.

[155] In addition to pp. 198–214: Britnell, *Commercialisation of English Society*,
90–7, 173–8, 208, 224–5, 229–30.

tury made more use of Aristotle's categories than I allowed
in 1984, but they made only a rather limited use of the richer
vocabulary he gave them. In so far as they used it they did
so, presumably, because bits of it fitted the problems that
preoccupied them.[156]

The legally defined nobilities that have traditionally been
associated with feudalism were another product of the new
conditions, though the definitions took some time to be
worked out. Formal legal privileges were the natural result of
arguments about taxes and other obligations between the
new record-keeping, tax-demanding governments and the
new professional lawyers employed by their richer subjects.[157] It must have been this widening of political and economic gulfs that provoked the invention of new myths that,
instead of explaining the origin of whole peoples, explained
the separate origins of peasants and nobles within them. In
1984, although I had found one such myth which I thought
dated from about 1200, I considered it more exceptional
than I now know it to have been.[158] Even if governmental
assemblies were only beginning to be divided into estates by
1300, and the divisions had not yet been justified in terms of
ideas of social orders, the new myths suggest that ideas of
hard and fast divisions between economic and social classes
were already around in some parts of Europe well before
1300. The reasons why they appeared in some parts and
not—or only later—in others need investigation.

It may be that contrary ideas of social equality were developing too—or had long been there, underground and
unrecorded. Both peasants and poor townspeople may well
have wanted more equality and freedom than their recorded
demands and rebellions reveal. It is not impossible that some
of them, or even some of their superiors, worked out some
kind of alternative ideology to put in place of the ruling ideas
of hierarchy tempered by custom and justice. If they did, we

---

[156] See the cases cited by Black, *Guilds and Civil Society*, 82–3; Martin,
'Medieval Commentaries'; Mundy, 'In Praise of Italy' (though he sometimes
uses the words democracy and oligarchy when they are not in the extracts he
cites). Also, esp. on electoral systems: Keller, 'Kommune' and 'Wahlformen'.

[157] Reynolds, *Fiefs and Vassals*, index *sub* nobility.

[158] Below, 259; but see Szűcs, *Nation und Geschichte*, 295–304; Freedman,
'Cowardice, Heroism', and *Origins of Peasant Servitude*.

do not know what it was and it would be quite unreal to suppose that anyone was aiming at any of the ideologies that have been worked out since the eighteenth century. By 1300 some of the conflicts embodied in the old norms of hierarchy and custom, authority and justice, had been revealed, but there is, I maintain, little evidence that the norms themselves had been seriously challenged, whether by intellectuals or by anyone else.

Theory and practice

To suggest that medieval ideas about the political and social order were based on ideas of just and harmonious hierarchy does not mean that one has to argue that medieval societies were harmonious and just, even according to their own lights. In reality there were many conflicts, some of which arose from what we may now see as the sort of inherently conflicting interests that the most improbably altruistic rulers would have found difficult to reconcile. Many arose, or became worse, because neither rulers nor subjects were altruistic. They arose from what in medieval terms was sin.

No society lives up to its ideals. Medieval sources suggest that lords were sometimes more oppressive than the accepted inequalities of their society allowed, that ordinary people cheated and bullied each other, and that there was much more casual violence than twentieth-century medieval historians are accustomed to meet in their own lives. So far as the first two centuries of my period are concerned, the old model of French feudal anarchy still seems to cast a shadow, both over France itself and over other kingdoms in which anarchy was far less likely to have prevailed. However much historians declare that 'feudal anarchy' is a misleading expression, and admit that monastic wails about the lack of law and order may be exaggerated, the habit remains strong of taking France as representative of western Europe and of seeing the new lordships of the eleventh century as based on 'the capricious manipulation of powerless people'.[159] In so far as the breakdown of Carolingian government in the western

---

[159] Bisson, 'Feudal Revolution', 18.

kingdom left a vacuum of lawful authority there, the building of new structures to fill it created opportunities for both
violence and manipulation. Violence appeared all the more
deplorable to monks whose churches had relied on royal protection and saw the new powers that loomed over them as
illegal. New rulers were indeed illegitimate until their power
was legitimized by custom and the passage of time. Only
then—though perhaps sooner than aggrieved chroniclers
might admit—would what had been illegal violence be transformed into legitimate coercive force. Something like this
must happen with every political revolution. Barbarian war-
lords were brigands to inhabitants of former Roman
provinces, just as the founding fathers of the American
revolution or the freedom fighters of later British colonies
were violent and illegal rebels to the British authorities.

When custom was largely unwritten, the time taken for
established control to become legitimate was not very long.
Since lords, even in France, seem to have exercised fairly
effective power over peasants fairly consistently, their authority over them was probably recognized as more or less lawful. New dues were a cause of discontent and occasional
revolt but that was not peculiar to this period. Where uncertainty, rivalry for power, and therefore violence and manipulation, were most obvious was at a higher level, between
lords who were trying to protect or extend their patches without any superior authority to protect them against each other
or adjudicate between them. Only in the kingdom of France,
however, was there a real vacuum at the top. The kingdom
of England, once united, was small enough for the king to
keep relatively effective control. Kings of Germany, with a
much bigger kingdom to rule—along, from 962, with the
kingdom of Italy as well—left a good deal of local control to
local nobles, but they intervened when things got seriously
rough or they saw their own authority threatened. In any
case, any suggestion of a moral vacuum even in France is
belied both by the complaints of the clergy and by the evidence of the meetings that were held to settle disputes. The
meetings were not always successful but reports of some of
them suggest that the laymen present had ideas about custom
and rights that were independent of the clergy: sometimes

such ideas led to judgements against the claims of churches.[160] That some lay lords took their responsibility for law and order seriously (no doubt partly because that promoted their authority) is suggested by recent arguments that have directed attention to the leading part played by the duke of Aquitaine in early peace councils.[161]

Whether the more systematic and record-keeping governments of the twelfth and later centuries meant more or less oppression, violence, and injustice is hard to say.[162] Oppression could now be more systematic but growing evidence of it may be the result of better evidence as much as of greater oppression. Rulers could introduce and maintain new customs more easily when the old, being unrecorded, were debatable, while the new would be officially recorded. Wars from now on were bigger, and therefore perhaps more destructive and more burdensome, but taxes had to be negotiated and the rules about them became more explicit. Grants of liberties are recorded as well as grants of taxes. Meanwhile, the new powers exercised by rulers seem to have met with opposition rather on the ground that particular customary rights had been infringed than because wider principles that touched the rights of government in general were questioned. Professional government and law fostered a new kind of violence and manipulation but contemporaries still seem to have complained about government, or justified it, on much the same ground of custom and justice, regnal solidarity, and submission to lawfully constituted authority as they had for centuries.

Underlying many of the norms of medieval society was the assumption that it depended on a great deal of collective activity. In practice, a great deal went on, whether at the command of rulers and for their purposes, or on the initiative of the collaborators for their own ends. Quite often the close relation between government and community meant that the same group seems to have combined both kinds of motives and objectives. The commands of rulers were sup-

---

[160] On conflicting ideas of clergy and laity about property rights: Reynolds, *Fiefs and Vassals*, 63, 77–80, 103–4, 175–7.

[161] Martindale, 'Peace and War'; see above n. 105.

[162] Cf. Bisson, 'Feudal Revolution', esp. 33, 37.

posed to reflect the needs and advice of the community. When there were no commands local communities were expected to look after their own affairs for themselves. Many, if not all, medieval people must have belonged to several overlapping groups or communities. The hierarchical ordering of society meant that people belonged to a hierarchy of communities from their households and families, through villages or towns, up to kingdoms. For people of low status the lowest community was the most real. Only people of high status took much part in the community of the kingdom, but others nevertheless had obligations to it that may have been as hard or harder to get out of than they were for its more active members who had more bargaining power. At every level, moreover, there were overlapping communities, such as the communities of guild, parish, and craft within towns, as well as that of the town itself, and those of manor or lordship, parish, village, and guild in the country. People's relationships do not seem to have been enclosed in the single communities that seem to be implied in descriptions of medieval peasants encased in their separate villages, craftsmen in their guilds, vassals in their lordships, and all in their legally defined and unchangeable orders or social classes. Perhaps their interactions worked more like the networks of modern social analysis, but that analogy, though useful as a corrective, is not entirely suitable either.[163] All medieval communities had more hierarchy and more coercion about them than is implied by either the word 'network' or the word 'community'. Few of them can in practice have been the voluntary, affective communities that sociologists since Tönnies have called *Gemeinschaften*, whatever the ideals of brotherhood and solidarity that they proclaimed. Some people had to be coerced into fulfilling their duties, others did them largely because they were obliged by custom, and some did not do them at all.

The relation between theory and practice, ideas and activities, remains problematical. But the ideas, values, and assumptions about right and wrong that prevailed in lay society still mattered, however badly some of its members

---

[163] On networks, see n. 1 above.

behaved. Rulers are more tempted than their subjects by some sins and get away with them more easily, but that does not mean that they do not know about the norms they ignore. Thought about the rights and wrongs of politics did not start in the twelfth century. Long before 1100, long before 900, kings, lords, and peasants had been thinking about them. Some had high IQs and (if IQs mean anything) thought effectively—although, by the lights of later academics, unsystematically—about the problems that confronted them. Much of the time they probably thought about what it would be prudent or profitable to do rather than what would be right. But even when not thinking directly about right and wrong, they must all, even the more powerful of them, have sometimes had to take into account what their society accepted as right and wrong.[164] Social norms must have modified the behaviour of most. If it seems to us that they did not, then it is worth considering whether we have identified and understood the norms correctly. The norms that I think I detect included more about peoples and the political communities they were assumed to form, about legitimate collective activity, and about every ruler's need and duty to seek counsel and consent, than the old stereotypes about the feudal middle ages have allowed us to see.

June 1996

[164] Cf. Popkin, *The Rational Peasant*, 26–31.

List of Works Cited in the Introduction
to the Second Edition

This list contains only works that are not listed on pp. 340–75. Those that are listed there are cited in the same way as in the original edition, with numbers in square brackets [ ] referring to their place in that list. The full titles of periodicals abbreviated here are listed on p. 340.

Abbo of Fleury, *Collectio canonum*, in *Patrologia Latina*, 139, cols. 473–508.

Adams, G. B., *Civilization during the Middle Ages* (London, 1894).

Althoff, G., *Verwandte, Freunde und Getreue: zum politischen Stellenwert der Gruppenbindungen im früheren Mittelalter* (Darmstadt, 1990).

Baldwin, J. W., *The Medieval Theories of the Just Price* (Trans. Am. Philos. Soc. NS 49 (4), 1959).

Bartlett, R., *The Making of Europe* (London, 1993).

Birrell, J., 'Common Rights in the Medieval Forest', *P&P* 117 (1987), 22–49.

Bisson, T. N., 'The "Feudal Revolution"', *P&P* 142 (1994), 6–42.

Black, A., *Guilds and Civil Society in European Political Thought from the Twelfth Century to the Present* (London, 1984).

—— 'The Individual and Society', in Burns (ed.), *Cambridge History of Medieval Political Thought* (q.v.), 58–606.

Blair, J., *Anglo-Saxon Oxfordshire* (Oxford, 1994).

Blok, A., 'Variations in Patronage', *Sociologische Gids* (Meppel, 1953–76), xvi. 365–78.

Böckenförde, E. W., *Die deutsche verfassungsgeschichtliche Forschung im 19. Jahrhundert* (Berlin, 1961).

Boldt, H., 'Otto von Gierke', in H. U. Wheler (ed.), *Deutsche Historiker*, 8 (1982), 7–23.

Bonfield, L., 'The Nature of Customary Law in the Manor Courts of Medieval England', *Comparative Studies in Society and History*, 31 (1989), 514–34.

Bonnard-Delamare, R., 'Fondement des institutions de paix au xie siècle', in *Mélanges . . . L. Halphen* (Paris, 1951), 19–26.

Boulainvilliers, H. de, *Essais sur la noblesse de France* (Amsterdam, 1732).

—— *Histoire de l'ancien gouvernement de France* (Hague and Amsterdam, 1727).

Bouquet, P., *Le Droit public de France* (Paris, 1756).

Bourin-Derruau, M., *Villages médiévaux en Bas-Languedoc: genèse d'une sociabilité (xe–xive siècle)* (Paris, 1987).

Brady, R., *Complete History of England* (London, 1685).

Britnell, R. H., *The Commercialisation of English Society 1000–1500* (Cambridge, 1993).

Brunner, H., *Deutsche Rechtsgeschichte* (Leipzig, 1887–92).

—— *Abhandlungen zur Rechtsgeschichte*, ed. K. Rauch (Weimar, 1931).

Buc, P., *L'Ambiguité du livre: prince, pouvoir et peuple dans les Commentaires de la Bible au moyen âge* (Paris, 1994).

Burns, J. H. (ed.), *The Cambridge History of Medieval Political Thought* (Cambridge, 1988).

Calhoun, C., 'Community: Towards a Variable Conceptualization for Comparative Research', *Social History*, 5 (1980), 105–29.

Canning, J. P., 'The Corporation in the Political Thought of the Italian Jurists of the Thirteenth and Fourteenth Centuries', *History of Political Thought*, 1 (1980), 9–32.

Capitularia Regum Francorum, ed. A. Boretius (MGH Legum Sect. 2, 1883–1901).

Carpenter, C., 'Gentry and Community in Medieval England', *Journal of British Studies*, 33 (1994), 340–80.

Cawson, A., *Corporatism and Political Theory* (Oxford, 1986).

Cheyette, F. L., *Lordship and Community in Medieval Europe* (New York, 1968).

Church, W. F., *Constitutional Thought in Sixteenth-Century France* (Cambridge, Mass., 1941).

Clastres, P., *La Société contre l'état* (Paris, 1974; trans. R. Hurley as *Society against the State* (New York, 1977)).

Cohen, A. P., *The Symbolic Construction of Community* (Chichester, 1985).

Concilia Aevi Karolini (MGH Concilia ii (1), 1906).

Constable, G., 'Liberty and Free Choice in Monastic Thought and Life', in G. Makdisi *et al.* (eds.), *La Notion de liberté au moyen âge* (Paris, 1985), 99–118.

Craig, T., *Jus Feudale*, ed. J. Baillie (Edinburgh, 1732).

Dalrymple, J., *Essay Towards a General History of Feudal Property in Great Britain* (London, 1758).

Davies, W., and Fouracre, P. (eds.), *The Settlement of Disputes in Early Medieval Europe* (Cambridge, 1986).

Daviso, M. C., 'La Carta di Tenda', *Bollettino storico-bibliographico subalpino*, 47 (1949), 131–43.

Dictionary of National Biography, ed. L. Stephen and S. Lee (London, 1885–1900).

Diestelkamp, B., 'Freiheit der Bürger—Freiheit der Stadt', *V und F* 39 (1991), 485–510.

Dilcher, G., 'Genossenschftstheorie und Sozialrecht: ein "Juristensozialismus" Otto v. Gierkes?', *Quaderni fiorentini per la storia del pensiero moderno*, 3–4 (1974–5), 319–65.

Dubos, J. B., *Histoire critique de l'établissement de la monarchie françoise* (Paris, 1742).

Duby, G., 'Les laïcs et la paix de Dieu', in *Hommes et structures du moyen âge* (Paris, 1973), 227–40; Eng. version in *The Chivalrous Society*, trans. C. Postan (London, 1977), 123–44.

Dumont, L., *Homo Hierarchicus*, trans. M. Sainsbury (London, 1972).

Dumoulin, C., *Opera* (Paris, 1681).

Eichhorn, K. F., *Deutsche Staats- und Rechtsgeschichte* (4th edn., Göttingen, 1834–6).

Epstein, S. A., *Wage Labor and Guilds in Medieval Europe* (Chapel Hill, NC, 1991).

Ferguson, A, *Essay on the History of Civil Society* (Edinburgh, 1767).

Ficker, J., *Das deutsche Kaiserreich in seinen universalen und nationalen Beziehungen* (Innsbruck, 1862).

Fossier, R., 'Les Communautés villageoises en France du nord au moyen âge', *Flaran*, 4 (1984), 29–53.

Fouracre, P., 'Carolingian Justice: The Rhetoric of Improvement and Contexts of Abuse,' *Settimane*, xlii (1995), 771–803.

——— 'Cultural Conformity in Early Medieval Europe', *History Workshop*, 33 (1992), 152–61.

Freedman, P., 'Cowardice, Heroism and the Legendary Origins of Catalonia', *P&P* 121 (1988), 3–28.

——— *The Origins of Peasant Servitude in Medieval Catalonia* (Cambridge, 1991).

Fried, J., 'Über den Universalismus der Freiheit', *Historische Zeitschrift*, 240 (1985), 313–61.

——— 'Einleitung', *V und F* 39 (1991), 7–13.

Gellner, E., 'Trust, Cohesion and the Social Order', in D. Gambetta (ed.), *Trust* (Oxford, 1988), 142–57.

Geschichtliche Grundbegriffe, ed. O. Brunner *et al.* (1972–92).

Gierke, O. von, *Das deutsche Genossenschaftsrecht* (Berlin, 1868–1913); extracts from vols. i–iii, trans. M. Fischer, ed. A. Black, as *Community in Historical Perspective* (Cambridge, 1990), and from vol. iii ed. and trans. F. W. Maitland as *Political Theories of the Middle Age* (Cambridge, 1900).

Giesebrecht, W. von, *Geschichte der Deutschen Kaiserzeit*, i (5th edn., Leipzig, 1881).

Gilchrist, J., *The Church and Economic Activity in the Middle Ages* (London, 1969).

Gillingham, J., 'The Beginnings of English Imperialism', *Journal of Historical Sociology*, 5 (1992), 382–409.

——— 'Henry of Huntingdon and the Twelfth-Century Revival of the English Nation', in S. Forde *et al.* (eds.), *Concepts of National Identity in the Middle Ages* (Leeds, 1995), 75–102.

Goetz, H. W., 'Kirchenschutz, Rechtsbewahrung und Reform', *Francia*, 11 (1983), 193–239; Eng. version in Head and Landes, *The Peace of God* (q.v.), 259–79.

——— 'Regnum: zum politischen Denken der Karolingerzeit', *Z.R.G. Germ. Abt.* 104 (1987), 110–89.

Gollwitzer, H., 'Zum politischen Germanismus des 19. Jahrhunderts', in *Festschrift für H. Heimpel* (Göttingen, 1971), i. 281–356.

Gossman, L., *Medievalism and the Ideologies of the Enlightenment* (Baltimore, 1968).

Guénée, B., *States and Rulers in Later Medieval Europe* (London, 1985), trans. J. Vale from *L'Occident aux xive et xve siècles: les états* (2nd edn., Paris, 1981).

Guizot, F. P. G., *Cours d'histoire moderne: histoire de la civilisation en France depuis la chute de l'empire romain jusqu'en 1789* (Paris, 1829–32).

—— *Essais sur l'histoire de France* (first pub. Paris, 1823, cited here from 2nd edn. 1833).

—— *Histoire de France . . . racontée à mes petits-enfants* (Paris, 1872–6).

Hallam, H., *View of the State of Europe during the Middle Ages* (London, 1818).

Hallis, F., *Corporate Personality* (London, 1930).

Harding, A., 'Political Liberty in the Middle Ages', *Speculum*, 55 (1980), 423–43.

Harvey, P. D. A., 'Initiative and Authority in Settlement Change', in M. Aston *et al.*, *The Rural Settlement of Medieval England* (Oxford, 1989).

Head, T., 'The Judgment of God', in Head and Landes, *The Peace of God* (q.v.), 219–38.

—— and Landes, R. (ed.), *The Peace of God* (Ithaca, NY, 1992).

Hegel, G. W. F., *Werke in zwanzig Bänden*, ed. E. Moldauer and K. M. Michel (Frankfurt, 1970–9): i. 461–581: *Die Verfassung Deutschlands*; xii: *Vorlesungen über die Philosophie der Geschichte*.

Helliwell, C., ' "A Just Precedency": The Nature of Equality in Anthropological Discourse', *History and Anthropology*, 7 (1994), 363–75.

Henn, 'Stadtluft macht frei?', *Soester Zeitschrift*, 92–3 (1980–1), 181–213.

Herder, J. G., *Ideen zur Philosophie der Geschichte der Menschheit* (Darmstadt, 1966).

Hill, C., *Puritanism and Revolution* (London, 1958).

Hintze, O., *Staat und Verfassung* (2nd edn., Göttingen, 1962).

Holmsen, A. *et al.*, 'The Old Norwegian Peasant Communities', *Scandinavian Economic History Review*, 4 (1956), 17–81.

Hooke, D., 'Early Medieval Estate and Settlement Patterns', in M. Aston *et al.*, *The Rural Settlement of Medieval England* (Oxford, 1989).

Hotman, F., *De Feudis* (Lyon, 1573).

Hüllmann, K. D., *Deutsche Finanz-Geschichte des Mittelalters* (Berlin, 1805).

—— *Geschichte des Ursprungs der Stände in Deutschland* (Berlin, 1830).

Hume, D., 'An Historical Essay on Chivalry', ed. E. C. Mossmer, *Modern Philology*, 45 (1947–8), 54–60.

—— *History of England from the Invasion of Julius Caesar to the Accession of Henry VII* (London, 1762).

Hurd, R., *Letters on Chivalry and Romance*, ed. E. J. Morley (London, 1911).

Janssen, A., *Otto von Gierkes Methode der geschichtlichen Rechtswissenschaft* (Göttingen, 1974).

Jolly, M., 'Epilogue: Hierarchical Horizons', *History and Anthropology*, 7 (1994), 377–409.

Justi, J. H. G. von, *Historischen und juristischen Schriften* (Frankfurt and Leipzig, 1760–1).

—— *Staatswirthschaft* (2nd edn. Leipzig, 1758).

Kames, H. Home, Lord, *Essays upon . . . British Antiquities* (Edinburgh, 1747).

Keller, H., ' "Kommune": Städtische Selbstregierung und mittelalterliche "Volksherrschaft" im Spiegel italienischer Wahlverfahren des 12.–14. Jahrhunderts', in G. Althoff *et al.* (eds.), *Person und Gemeinschaft im Mittelalter: Karl Schmid zum fünf- und sechsigsten Geburtstag* (Sigmaringen, 1988).

—— 'Wahlformen und Gemeinschaftsverständnis in den italienischen Stadtkommunen', *V und F* 37 (1990), 345–74.

Kelley, D. R., 'Tacitus noster', in T. J. Luce and A. J. Woodman (eds.), *Tacitus and the Tacitean Tradition* (Princeton, 1993), 152–67.

King, P. D., 'The Barbarian Kingdoms', in Burns (ed.), *Cambridge History of Medieval Political Thought* (q.v.), 123–53.

Kluckhohn, A., *Geschichte des Gottesfriedens* (Leipzig, 1857).

Koller, H. 'Zur Entwicklung der Stadtgeschichtsforschung in deutschsprägigen Raum', in F. Mayrhofer (ed.), *Stadtgeschichtsforschung* (Linz, 1993), 1–18.

Lapidus, I. M., *Muslim Cities in the Later Middle Ages* (Cambridge, 1984).

Lorenz, O. (ed.), *Catalogue général de la librairie française (1840–65)*, v (Paris, 1871).

Luchaire, A., *Les Premiers temps capétiens* (Paris, 1901).

Luscombe, D. E., 'The Formation of Political Thought in the West', in Burns (ed.), *The Cambridge History of Medieval Political Thought* (q.v.), 157–73.

Mably, G. Bonnot de, *Observations sur l'histoire de France* (Paris, 1765).

MacDougall, H. A., *Racial Myth in English History* (Hanover, NH, 1982).

Mackrell, J. Q. C., *The Attack on Feudalism in Eighteenth-Century France* (London, 1973).

Maitland, F. W., *Constitutional History of England* (Cambridge, 1946: 1st edn. 1908).

Maquet, J., *Power and Society in Africa* (London, 1971).

Martin, C., 'Medieval Commentaries on Aristotle's Politics', *History*, 36 (1951), 29–41.

Martindale, J., 'Peace and War in Early Eleventh-Century Aquitaine', in C. Harper-Bill and R. Harvey (eds.), *Ideals and Practice of Medieval Knighthood*, 4 (1992), 147–76.

Millar, J., *Origin of Distinction of Ranks* (4th edn., Edinburgh, 1806).

Montesquieu, C. de Secondat, Baron de, *L'Esprit des lois*: in *Œuvres complètes*, ed. R. Caillois (Paris, 1951), ii.

Montlosier, F. D. de Reynaud, Comte de, *De la monarchie française* (Paris, 1814).

Moore, R. I., *The Formation of a Persecuting Society* (Oxford, 1987).

Moore, S. F., *Law as Process* (London, 1978).

—— 'Legal Liability and Evolutionary Interpretation', in M. Gluckman (ed.), *The Allocation of Responsibility* (Manchester, 1972), 51–108.

Le Mouvement confraternel au moyen âge: France, Italie, Suisse (Collection de l'École française de Rome, 97 (1987)).

Müller-Mertens, E., *Regnum Teutonicum* (Vienna, 1970).
Mundy, J. H., 'In Praise of Italy: The Italian Republics', *Speculum*, 65 (1989), 815–34.
Muratori, L. A., *Antiquitates Italicae*, i (Milan, 1738).
Nelson, J. L., 'Kingship and Empire', in Burns (ed.), *Cambridge History of Medieval Political Thought* (q.v.), 211–51.
—— *The Frankish World* (London, 1996), 99–132: 'The Lord's Anointed and the People's Choice: Carolingian Royal Ritual' (repr. from D. Cannadine and S. Price (eds.), *Rituals of Royalty* (Cambridge, 1987), 137–80.
Neue deutsche Biographie (Hist. Komm. bei der Bayerischen Akad. der Wissenschaften, Berlin, 1953–).
Nipperdey, T., 'Verein als soziale Struktur in Deutschland im späten 18. und frühen 19. Jahrhundert', in H. Boockmann *et al.*, *Geschichtwissenschaft und Vereinswesen im 19. Jahrhundert* (Göttingen, 1972), 1–44.
Oexle, O. G., 'Conjuratio und Gilde im frühen Mittelalter. Ein Beitrag zum Problem der sozialgeschichtlichen Kontinuität zwischen Antike und Mittelalter', *V und F* 29 (1985), 151–214.
—— 'Gilden als sozial Gruppen in der Karolingerzeit', in H. Jankuhn *et al.* (eds.), *Das Handwerk in vor- und frühgeschichtlicher Zeit* (Göttingen, 1981), 284–354.
—— 'Gruppenbindung und Gruppenverhalten bei Menschen und Tieren. Beobachten zur Geschichte der mittelalterlichen Gilden', *Saeculum*, 36 (1985), 28–45.
—— 'Die mittelalterliche Zunft als Forschungsproblem', *Blätter für deutsche Landesgeschichte*, 118 (1982), 1–44.
—— 'Otto von Gierkes "Rechstgeschichte der deutschen Genssenschaft". Ein Versuch wissenschaftlicher Rekapitulation', in N. Hammerstein (ed.), *Deutsche Geschichtswissenschaft um 1900* (Stuttgart, 1988), 193–217.
Ourliac, P., 'Les Communautés villageoises dans le midi de la France au moyen âge', *Flaran*, 4 (1984), 13–17.
—— and Gazzaniga, J. L., *Histoire du droit privé français de l'an mil au code civil* (Paris, 1985).
Pasquier, E., *Les Recherches de la France* (Paris, 1596).
Paxton, F. S., 'History, Historians, and the Peace of God', in Head and Landes, *The Peace of God* (q.v.), 21–44.
Percy, T., *Reliques of Ancient English Poetry* (London, 1765).
Phillips, D. L., *Looking Backward* (Princeton, 1993).
Popkin, S. L., *The Rational Peasant: the Political Economy of Rural Society in Vietnam* (Berkeley, 1979).
Prodi, P., *Il Sacramento del potere: il giuramento politico nella storia costituzionale dell'Occidente* (Bologna, 1992).
Reulecke, J. and Huck, G., 'Urban History Research in Germany', *Urban History Yearbook, 1981*, 39–54.
Reuter, T. (ed. and trans.), *The Medieval Nobility* (Amsterdam, 1979).
Reynolds, S., *Fiefs and Vassals: The Medieval Evidence Reinterpreted* (Oxford, 1994).

—— 'The Historiography of the Medieval State', in M. Bentley (ed.), *Routledge Companion to Historiography* (forthcoming, 1997).

—— *Ideas and Solidarities of the Medieval Laity* (Aldershot, 1995), including 'The History of the Idea of Incorporation or Legal Personality: A Case of Fallacious Teleology'.

—— 'Social Mentalities and the Case of Medieval Scepticism', *T.R.H.S.* Sser. 6, 1 (1991), 21–41; repr. in *Ideas and Solidarities* (q.v.).

—— 'The Writing of Medieval Urban History in England, *Theoretische Geschiedenis*, 19 (1992), 43–57; repr. in *Ideas and Solidarities* (q.v.), and in German in F. Mayrhofer (ed.), *Stadtgeschichtsforschung* (Linz, 1993), 19–36.

Ridé, J., *L'Image du Germain dans la pensée et la litterature allemandes de la redécouverte de Tacite a la fin du xvie siècle* (Lille and Paris, 1977).

Riehl, W. H., *Die Naturgeschichte des Volkes als Grandlage einer deutsche Sozial-Politik*, i, *Land und Leute* (4th edn., Stuttgart, 1857).

Roberts, S., *Order and Dispute: An Introduction to Social Anthropology* (Harmondsworth, 1979).

Robertson, W., *History of Scotland* (London, 1759).

Robin, R., 'Fief et seigneurie dans le droit et l'idéologie juridique à la fin du xviiie siècle', *Annales hist. de la révolution française*, 43 (1971), 554–602.

Rösener, W., *Peasants in the Middle Ages*, trans. A. Stützer (Chicago, 1992).

Rosser, G., 'Going to the Fraternity Feast: Commensality and Social Relations in Late Medieval England', *Journal of British Studies*, 33 (1994), 430 46.

Roth, P., *Feudalität und Untertanverband* (Wiemar, 1863).

—— *Geschichte des Beneficialwesen von den ältesten Zeiten bis ins zehnte Jahrhundert* (Erlangen, 1850).

Rubin, M., 'Small Groups: Identity and Solidarity in the Late Middle Ages', in J. Kermode (ed.) *Enterprise and Individuals in Fifteenth-Century England* (Stroud, 1991), 132–50.

Saint-Palaye, J. B. de la Curne de, *Mémoires sur l'ancienne chevalerie* (Paris, 1759–81).

Schmidt, H., 'Landesgeschichte und Gegenwart bei J. C. B. Strüve', in H. Boockmann and others, *Geschichtwissenschaft und Vereinswesen im 19. Jahrhundert* (Göttingen, 1972), 74–98.

Schmidt-Wiegand, R., 'Gilde und Zunft', in A. Zimmermann (ed.), *Soziale Ordnung* (Berlin, 1979), 355–69.

—— 'Historische Onomasiologie und Mittelalterforschung', *Frühmittelalterliche Studien*, 9 (1982), 49–78.

Schneidmüller, B., *Nomen Patriae: die Entstehung Frankreichs in der politische-geographischen Terminologie* (Sigmaringen, 1987).

Schröder, J., 'Zur älteren Genossenschaftstheorie: Die Begrundung des modernen Körperschaftsbegriffs durch Georg Beseler', *Quaderni fiorentini per la storia del pensiero moderno*, 11–12 (1982-3), 399–459.

Scott, J., *Social Network Analysis* (London, 1991).

Scott, W., *Essays on Chivalry, Romance and the Drama* (London, 1888).

See, Klaus von, *Deutsche Germanen-Ideologie* (Frankfurt, 1970).

Semichon, E., *La Paix et la trève de Dieu* (2nd edn., Paris, 1869).

Sigonio, C., *Opera Omnia*, ii (Milan, 1732).

Sivéry, G., *Terroirs et communautés rurales dans l'Europe occidentale au moyen âge* (Lille, 1990).

Smith, A., *An Inquiry into the Nature and Causes of the Wealth of Nations* (London, 1910).

—— *Lectures on Jurisprudence*, ed. A. Meeks (Oxford, 1978).

Smith, R. J., *The Gothic Bequest* (Cambridge, 1987).

Smith, R. M. ' "Modernization" and the Corporate Village Community', in A. H. R. Baker and D. Gregory (eds.), *Explorations in Historical Geography* (Cambridge, 1984), 140–79.

Southern, R. W., *Scholastic Humanism and the Unification of Europe*, i (Oxford, 1995).

Spelman, H., *Reliquiae Spelmanniae*, ed. E. Gibson (London, 1723).

Spiess, K. H., 'Bäuerliche Gesellschaft und Dorfentwicklung im Hochmittelalter', in W. Rösener (ed.), *Grundherrschaft und bäuerliche Gesellschaft im Hochmittelalter* (Göttingen, 1995), 384–412.

Stern, S. M., 'Constitution of the Islamic City', in A. Hourani and S. M. Stern (eds.), *The Islamic City* (Oxford, 1970), 25–50.

Szücs, J., *Nation und Geschichte* (Budapest, 1974).

Thierry, A., *Récits des temps mérovingiens* (Paris, 1840).

Tierney, B., 'Freedom and the Medieval Church', in R. W. Davis (ed.), *The Origins of Modern Freedom in the West* (Stanford, Calif., 1995), 64–100.

—— *Religion, Law and the Growth of Constitutional Thought, 1150–1650* (Cambridge, 1982).

Ullmann, W., *Principles of Government and Politics in the Middle Ages* (London, 2nd edn., 1966).

Van Dam, R., *Leadership and Community in Late Antique Gaul* (Berkeley, 1985).

Van Engen, J., 'The Christian Middle Ages as an Historiographical Problem', *Am.H.R.* 91 (1986), 519–52.

—— 'Sacred Sanctions for Lordship', in T. Bisson (ed.), *Cultures of Power* (Philadelphia, 1995), 203–30.

Venckeleer, T., 'Faut-il traduire vassal par vassal?', in *Mélanges de linguistique, de litterature et de philologie médiévales, offerts à J. R. Smeets* (photog. typescript, Leiden, 1982), 303–16.

Venkatarama, K. R., 'Medieval Trade, Craft, and Merchant Guilds in S. India', *Journal of Indian History*, 25 (1947), 269–80.

Vico, G. B., *La Scienza nuova*, ed. F. Nicolini (Bari, 1928).

Waitz, G., *Deutsche Verfassungsgeschichte* (Kiel, 1844–78).

Waitz, G., 'Lehnswesen', in J. C. Blunschli and K. Brater (eds.), *Deutsches Staats-Wörterbuch*, 6 (Stuttgart, 1861), 357–67.

Walker, M., *German Home Towns: City, State and General Estate, 1648–1871* (Ithaca, NY, 1971).

—— 'Rights and Functions: The Social Categories of Eighteenth-Century German Jurists and Cameralists', *Jnl. Modern History*, 50 (1978), 234–51.

Weber, M., *The City*, trans. D. Martindale and G. Neuwirth (Glencoe, 1958).

—— *Wirtschaft und Gesellschaft* (5th edn., Tübingen, 1976); Eng. trans. by E. Fischoff *et al.* as *Economy and Society*, ed. G. Roth and C. Wittich (Berkeley, 1978).

Wellman, B., and Berkowitz, S. D., *Social Structures: A Network Approach* (Cambridge, 1988).

White, S. D., 'Proposing the Ordeal and Avoiding It', in T. N. Bisson (ed.), *Cultures of Power* (Philadelphia, 1995).

Whitman, J. Q., *The Legacy of Roman Law in the German Romantic Era* (Princeton, 1990).

Wickham, C., *Comunità e clientele nella Toscana del XII secolo* (Rome, 1995).

—— *Land and Power: Studies in Italian and European Social History, 400–1200* (London, 1994).

—— *The Mountains and the City: the Tuscan Appennines in the Early Middle Ages* (Oxford, 1988).

—— 'Problems of Comparing Societies in Early Medieval Europe', *T.R.H.S.*, ser. 6, 2 (1992), 221–46.

—— 'Rural Society in Carolingian Europe', in R. McKitterick (ed.), *New Cambridge Medieval History*, 2 (1995), 510–37.

Wilda, W. E., *Das Gildenwesen im Mittelalter* (Halle, 1831).

Introduction

This book has three principal arguments. The first and most important is that collective activity was more important and more pervasive in medieval Europe than might be deduced from most recent writing on lay society and politics. Reacting against anachronistic interpretations of medieval communes and parliaments as the product of deliberate strivings towards modern democracy, recent generations of historians have concentrated their attention on kingship and the vertical bonds of society—the links between kings and their subjects, lords and their men. Apart from some rather arid wrangling about the concept of feudalism—a concept foreign to the middle ages themselves[1]—this has been enormously illuminating, but it has been accompanied, as it seems to me, by a tendency to undervalue the horizontal bonds in medieval society. Collective activity, apart from that of families, is too often seen either as a matter for peasants and townsmen or as a vehicle for factious opposition, rather than as a permanent, lawful, and necessary part of all government at every level. The 'communal movement' of the twelfth century is often thought to have introduced new ideas and values of association, so that some—but only some—of the associations then formed achieved a new and more fully corporate character. I shall argue that, on the contrary, all the collectivities which abound in the sources of the twelfth and thirteenth centuries drew their cohesion from ideas and values which were already deep-rooted and that one of their strengths was the continuing absence of any legal distinction between those that were in our terms corporate and those that were not.

Community is a fashionable word nowadays. Almost any class or category of people is sometimes called a community, even if (like the 'ethnic communities' of domestic politics)

---

[1] Brown, 'Tyranny of a construct' [284] argues with what seems to me irrefutable cogency against the use of the term. I shall use the words feudalism and feudal only where I refer to interpretations which make use of them.

they do not act collectively or form anything that most sociologists or anthropologists would call a group. Almost any geographically delimited section of the population can also be described as a local community. The kind of community with which I am concerned, however, is one which defines itself by engaging in collective activities—activities which are characteristically determined and controlled less by formal regulations than by shared values and norms, while the relationships between members of the community are characteristically reciprocal, many-sided, and direct, rather than being mediated through officials or rulers.[2] Few of the groups which I shall discuss were pure communities in the sense that their activities were entirely voluntary, reciprocal, and unmediated. By the tenth century European society was much too complex, rich, and unequal, and much too committed to ideas of hierarchy, to have been able to cope with statelessness.[3] Nevertheless medieval society seems to me to have been full of groups of lay people who acted together, or thought of themselves as acting together, sometimes over long periods, and who appear to have done so—as far as the records show—at least partly on their own initiative and with a relatively small amount of formal regulation and physical coercion.

In some ways the imperfection of their communities by this standard illustrates their acceptance of the ideal of community. Political units which were too large and too full of inequalities for everyone within them to enjoy direct, unmediated, and reciprocal relations with each other were nevertheless perceived as communities at the time. Because everyone accepted the principle of inequality, the underdogs seem to have accepted their passive role but nevertheless felt part of the community, while the active participants in politics remained few enough to be able to work within more community-like relationships with each other. One of the most striking characteristics of the collective activities which I discuss, moreover, seems to me to be that they seldom took

[2] I found Taylor, *Community, Anarchy, and Liberty* [827] very helpful. Cf. the definitions of 'groups' in e.g. Homans, *Human Group* [797], 1, 82–6; Deutsch, *Resolution of Conflict* [778], 48–60.

[3] See e.g. Fried, *Evolution of Political Society* [784]; Mair, *Primitive Government* [807].

place within the small, stable, all-embracing, and mutually exclusive groups which appear to form the ideal type of community. People seem to have been capable of acting collectively in all sorts of different and overlapping groups at once, largely relying in all of them on affective, voluntary co-operation. This did not always work well, but the strength of medieval values of community is demonstrated by their endurance in defiance of experience. It is also demonstrated in the lack of discussion about them. Just as the word *communitas* and its derivatives were used very widely, with a range of meanings which apparently needed little or no definition, so the values they embodied were too fundamental to need much spelling out. They can nevertheless be inferred from a mass of records of collective activity.

This book is intended to explore the collective values and activities of lay society from the tenth century to the thirteenth. It is not intended to be in any sense a general history of the kingdoms and local communities which it discusses. I am concerned only with the way that people acted collectively and the way that they perceived their activities. When I refer to the structure of a community I do not mean the economic and social structure of the population within which it functioned, but simply the structure within which collective activities were organized. How far those activities were, for instance, fundamentally determined by the economic structure of society as a whole is a question with which—thankfully—I am not concerned here. Many important types of collective activity are, moreover, omitted from this exploratory survey. To start with, I am writing only about lay communities, that is, those which consisted primarily of lay people, rather than of either regular or secular clergy. Monasteries, collegiate churches, orders of friars, universities, and so forth, are excluded. So, except for some passing references,[4] are the peace associations of the tenth and eleventh centuries. I have also left out communities of family, household, and kinship, noble households and armies, mercantile companies, nomadic groups of shepherds, pilgrims, ships' companies, expatriate colonies, Jews, and no doubt communities of other sorts which I have not thought of. Craft

[4] See p. 34 and index *sub* peace.

associations are dealt with only briefly, as one aspect of urban communities. Each of these topics is excluded not because I think it is unimportant but because the whole subject is too big and I had to draw lines somewhere. Of all the omissions, that of family and kin may seem most inexcusable. All that we know of medieval society leaves no doubt of the importance of kinship. The medieval imagery of fatherhood, motherhood, and fraternity shows how much ideas of the family permeated other collective groups. Nevertheless, we have in the past tended to stress kinship at the expense of other bonds. Looking at those other bonds apart from it may help to redress the balance. In whatever degree and whatever sense it may be true that other communities were derived from the kin (as the conjectural history of nineteenth-century anthropology maintained), that stage was long past by the tenth century. So far as the metaphors of kinship are concerned, it may be worth noticing that it was the nuclear family that provided images for other communities: fraternity, not cousinhood, was the model. In the end, however, my reason for leaving out families and wider kins is that they would make my subject too vast.

My second argument is that, in order to understand the collective activity of the middle ages, we need to pay more attention than we customarily do to lay political ideas. Medieval political thought is generally studied only, or largely, through the works of systematic and academic writers, and it sometimes seems to be assumed either that lay politics were power-struggles of value-free, rational self-interest or that laymen picked up what political ideas and principles they had from the clergy. Political thought is not, however, the prerogative of political philosophers, jurists, or theologians. Kings, barons, and even commoners, as human beings, thought too, though less systematically. They learned ideas (perhaps just in the form of assumptions) about rights and duties from those who brought them up—as did the intellectuals too, presumably. However much they failed to live up to the principles of their society, we cannot understand their institutions or their conflicts unless we pay attention to the ideas and values that those institutions embodied. I maintain that many of the striking developments in society and politics which took place between 900 and 1300 need to be seen against a background of traditional bonds of community. All the intellectual achievements of the twelfth and thirteenth centuries—the study of Roman and canon law, the rediscovery of Aristotle, and so on—impressive as they were, made very little difference to the fundamental political beliefs of the period, and cannot account for the characteristic forms which so many medieval collectivities shared. The character of communities in the central middle ages was rooted and grounded in older traditions, traditions which simply assumed the existence, rights, and duties of collectivities large and small: responsibilities were owed collectively to collectives, and decisions of every sort were made by groups, though in ways that we would not consider popular or democratic. To understand the ideas which informed lay collective activities we need to look not at treatises written by intellectuals but at the records of law-suits, at charters and chronicles, and at all the other documents in which the activities themselves were recorded. These were written by clerks, and most chronicles, for instance, were written by monks who most emphatically identified themselves with clergy as against laity, but nevertheless they were observers of the lay scene and were much closer to it than were most of the treatise-writers.

In case my concentration on the laity and my belittling of clerical and academic influences may suggest that I regard the church as unimportant, I should make it clear that I start from the premise that lay society was permeated by Christianity, not least in its approach to collective activity. By 900 virtually all of the countries which fall within the scope of this book were firmly Christian. The only exceptions lay in the Scandinavian settlements of the British Isles and Normandy, and they quickly became assimilated to the Christianity around them. To say that western Europe was Christian is not to say that most, or even many, laymen were particularly pious, still less that they were well-informed about the doctrines of their faith. The obstacles to acquiring religious knowledge in the tenth century were great. Nevertheless it is misleading to see medieval Christianity as a clerical invention which filtered downwards from the hierarchy to the more pious and well-informed of the laity. We know so much more about the religion of monks and clerks that it is easy to assume that all religious ideas and movements started with them. Yet one of the great achievements of the tenth and eleventh centuries was the vast proliferation of local churches, the formation of a vast patchwork of parishes which effectively brought the church to the people. Much of this was done on the initiative of the laity: there is little evidence that bishops in general regarded it as a high priority or even did much to encourage it. Some of the monks and hermits who became renowned in this golden age of monasticism seem to have started out very much on their own with little help from official clerical channels or from any very intellectual doctrines. Formal theology often limped along behind popular beliefs. On pilgrimages, crusades, indulgences, the theologians rationalized as best they could doctrines that could not be stopped.

It is beyond the scope of this book to describe or explain how all this came about. The important point here is that lay society was itself Christian. We should not talk of the contributions to the ideas of this period of the Christian ethos and of the military (or 'feudal') ethos of the aristocracy as if the two were separate. The military ethos was a Christian military ethos. This may seem like a contradiction in terms to some anti-militarist twentieth-century Christians, but some aspects of twentieth-century Christianity would have seemed equally odd to a pious eleventh-century knight. Not, of course, that most of the clerical reformers of the tenth and eleventh centuries accepted the validity of Christian knighthood. It only became acceptable later, paradoxically at a time when the reformers seem to have been getting other aspects of their message over rather better. Before 1100 one of the strongest reasons for becoming a monk was the impossibility, as it seemed to many future saints, of living a holy life as a lay noble. But the wickedness of the world was a Christian wickedness: there was no alternative set of religious values.

To talk of military or noble values, therefore, as survivals from pagan times is as unreal as it is to talk of sorcery, popular heresy, or the sociability of guilds in the same way. All these had much in common with beliefs and practices to be found in many other societies, Christian and unchristian, and in western Europe most of them had historically originated in paganism, but so had some Christian beliefs and practices which were—and are—fully integrated into official Christianity. By the tenth century, except perhaps in the Norse and Danish colonies, there is no evidence of any coherent set of pagan beliefs to which lay values could be related. Clerical reformers thought that most of the laity were ignorant and probably damned, but although many people were probably not very religious, and although we know that by the twelfth century some suffered from doubts and some flirted with Judaism or Islam, Christianity offered the only ideology available to most. Nobody could escape its influence.

In looking for the influence of Christianity on lay communities, therefore, we must not think simply of a one-way traffic of ideas from the clergy to the laity, or see the laity as passive recipients of the milk of elementary doctrine. The model of monasticism was probably extremely important in the formation of lay communities but it was not the only model. Monks themselves, moreover, drew metaphors for their life from lay society, notably from the family and the battlefield. The traffic of ideas, in other words, between all sorts of community, including those considered here and those left out, must have been constant. Although I am less entitled to draw even tentative conclusions about the subjects I have not attempted to discuss, it seems to me that all types of medieval collective behaviour were permeated by the assumptions and beliefs which I discuss—and which, of course, others have discussed before me. All clerks and monks started as lay children, if not as laymen.

My third argument is that there was much less difference in social and political organization—not least in its collective manifestations—between different parts of western Europe than seems to be generally thought. Many of the national differences now perceived in medieval institutions seem to me to derive more from different traditions of historical writing than from anything to be found in the sources. The long influence of English common lawyers on the perception and writing of English history, for instance, has ensured that English historians tend to start from the assumption that

England has always been different from continental Europe
—the territory of that amorphous mass of foreigners who
are all fundamentally much more like each other than they
are like Us. 'Continental' historians, discouraged, no doubt,
by the impenetrability of English legal terminology, have
been ready to be convinced by this assumption. England is
sometimes compared with one other country, generally
France, but bilateral comparisons inevitably tend to polarities,
and on the whole it seems to be considered safer to leave
England (and the rest of the British Isles) out of all but the
most general of generalizations. Yet before the twelfth
century, as I shall argue, legal procedures and the ideas they
embody seem to have been very similar in England, France,
Germany, and at least the northern part of Italy. Thereafter
the legal systems which developed within the emerging
political units began to diverge like species on slowly separat-
ing continents. Differences of vocabulary became differences
of concept when they began to be explained by lawyers and
historians brought up within their separate national traditions.
Finally, eighteenth- and nineteenth-century controversies
about the Germanic and Roman origins of European culture
created another retrospective divide across the past, and one
which has still not disappeared.

The documents of the central middle ages seem to me to
come out of a quite different and much more homogeneous
world. The divergencies of law began then but do not seem to
have then been the result of deep-rooted national differences.
Medieval people *thought* of themselves as divided into
distinct and aboriginal peoples (though they did not think of
these as Roman or Germanic in the way that later philological
anthropologists would), but the belief in separate peoples was
itself a shared belief, and not one which seems to have been
induced by any obvious differences between the social and
political arrangements of the various peoples. National differences may thus be seen in one view as a product of medieval
ideas about collective groups.

This book is not, however, concerned with the whole of
western Europe. I have restricted myself to the area which
was represented within my period by the kingdoms of
England, France, Germany, and Italy (or Lombardy). France

and Germany, of course, included the Netherlands and Burgundy between them while Germany included Switzerland and Austria. I have made occasional excursions into Scotland, the papal lands, the kingdom of Sicily, and the kingdom of Jerusalem, but not into Scandinavia, Spain, or the Slav kingdoms. This is not because I think that none of my arguments would apply to them but because my knowledge—including my linguistic knowledge—is already stretched thin enough. In fact it is stretched much too thin, but it seemed important to argue my case from a wide enough selection of areas to avoid easy polarizations and to begin to be able to distinguish differences of vocabulary from differences of institutions. The result may look like a collection of examples found wherever they seem to support my arguments. If so, it is in itself suggestive: if similar forms of collective activity, apparently reflecting similar purposes, can be found here and there in villages, towns, and larger polities in England, France, Germany, and Italy, then it seems fair to argue that they may have been part of a common heritage of ideas about politics and society. That is not to argue for a moment either that local variations were insignificant or that the ideas I detect were universally accepted or were the only important ideas around. It was an essential feature of medieval institutions that they tolerated a high degree of local autonomy and variety. But all this was part of the common culture.

These then were the propositions with which I started work on the book: that lay collective activity was underrated and too often confused with revolutionary or democratic aspirations; that lay ideas could and should be studied through documents or chronicles dealing with lay affairs, rather than through academic treatises, while the academic treatises themselves needed to be seen against the assumptions of lay society; that national differences in social and political organization were overrated and too readily assumed to derive from inherent national differences; that medieval ideas about kingdoms and peoples were very like modern ideas about nations; and also that 'feudalism' and 'feudal' are meaningless terms which are unhelpful in understanding medieval society.

Other ideas emerged as I worked, some of them quite

unexpected but deriving, as it seemed to me, from the primary sources which I read. I was constantly amazed at the way that, after grappling with unfamiliar historical ideas and traditions in the secondary literature, I kept finding the sources to which the modern writers directed me strongly reminiscent of the English sources which I already knew. Among arguments which I found myself propounding against my own original intentions were the similarity of all law as actually practised—whether labelled Roman, Germanic, or feudal; the widespread survival of collective judgements in the thirteenth century, and the absence even then of any concept of legal personality or corporation;[5] the slight evidence of the 'single-tier' parochial system before 1200 in Germany and France;[6] the lack, except in a few areas, of evidence of change from scattered to nucleated settlement; the loose and shifting pattern of rural collective activity, irrespective of the pattern of settlement, and the lack of difference between places with and without charters of liberties;[7] the apparent absence of revolutionary objectives among the lower ranks of urban society even by the late thirteenth century;[8] the cohesion of the German kingdom throughout the period and, apparently, of the Sicilian kingdom in the thirteenth century;[9] the lack of evidence of theories of absolutism, except in England and (though less clearly) Sicily; the lack of evidence of influence from academic ideas on lay politics everywhere, even in the thirteenth century;[10] the similarity in ideas and objectives between those who secured Magna Carta, the French charters of 1315, and even (as I guess) the German *Constitutio in favorem principum*;[11] and the absence of any political theory of estates before 1300.[12] Although all these arguments confirm and extend my original propositions, they were not formulated, at least consciously, for that reason, for I was prepared to argue the original propositions without them. The fact that my conclusions were not prejudged does not mean that they are not wrong. I am well aware that many of

[5] Chapters 1 and 2.   [6] Chapter 4.   [7] Chapter 5.
[8] Chapter 6, pp. 203–14.   [9] Chapter 8, pp. 289–301.
[10] Chapters 2 and 8, pp. 319–29.
[11] Chapter 8, pp. 268–70, 285–8, 296.   [12] Chapter 8, pp. 316–19.

them are based on superficial reading and that I have risked making hypotheses about areas of history about which I know little and others know a great deal. Some of my arguments must be wrong, and some may be based on quite elementary mistakes or failure to look at quite well-known sources. If I had spent ten years rather than a bare five on the book it would have been less vulnerable, but the more I worked on it the more it seemed to me that the subject deserved to be opened up in a book which would cover a fairly wide area and a fair range of types of community, so that others could confirm, refine, or refute my hypotheses. I hope that they will.

1

Collective activity in
traditional law, 900–1140

To start a study of medieval lay communities by considering
the law that lay behind them may imply that law is to be
looked on as an independent, autonomous cause of social
cohesion. That is not what is implied here. Medieval law was
not handed down to medieval society on stone tablets from
Sinai or Rome or on wooden tablets from the forests of Germany. Whatever the ultimate origin of medieval ideas on
custom and justice and the methods used to apply them,
both the content and procedures of medieval law were continually shaped and reshaped—if belatedly—by economic,
social, religious, and political forces. This continual reshaping
was all the easier in the early middle ages, when so much of
the law was unwritten and customary and was not the preserve
of professional lawyers. For that reason, therefore, the records
of law and litigation in the tenth and eleventh centuries,
sparse as they are, provide invaluable evidence of the social
norms that also shaped collective activity. It is the argument
of this chapter that all the forms of communal activity that
become so noticeable in the records of the twelfth and
thirteenth centuries reflected ideas about justice, and the
proper means of achieving it, that took for granted a great
deal of collective responsibility. The legal records of the
preceding centuries, moreover, show that these ideas were
already well established at that stage. Law therefore forms
the starting-point of the enquiry, not because communities
were created by law as an independent variable, but because
the surviving records of traditional law reflect the society in
which the communities originated well enough to explain
quite a lot about the distinctive characteristics which they
shared.

It is, of course, a commonplace of the textbooks that
medieval political thought was based on ideas of law, custom,

and justice, but such ideas are usually illustrated largely from works written after the mid twelfth century.[1] It is easy to see why, for sources of a reflective and reasoned nature are much commoner then, but any argument that the ideas were much older can obviously not rely on them. The evidence used in this chapter will therefore come from before 1140, not because the publication of the *Decretum* was really the beginning of the academic study of law, but because that event forms a convenient landmark. Even though I shall argue that the academic writers of the twelfth century and later reflect traditional lay values much more closely than has often been implied, that cannot be either demonstrated or refuted until the lineaments of the older traditions are perceived without the veils they acquired in the twelfth century. It is, in any case, impossible to understand what made early medieval law such a firm cement in society if one looks at it through legal treatises of the twelfth and thirteenth centuries. It would not have contributed half what it did to medieval politics if it had always distinguished as clearly as did even the more traditional of those works between custom and law, between what is judged and what is right, and between different authorities and jurisdictions. Law between the tenth and early twelfth centuries was the undifferentiated, indeterminate, and flexible law appropriate to a society that was for many practical purposes illiterate (if not strictly preliterate[2]), and it must be understood in those terms, not in the terms of later professional or academic law. In the words of Maine: 'The distinctions of the later jurists are appropriate only to the later jurisprudence.'[3]

Customary law

Until recently the history of early medieval law was dominated by the belief of nineteenth-century evolutionary anthropologists that early law was rigid, formalist, and essentially

---

[1] Carlyle, *Med. Pol. Theory* [309], iii; McIlwain, *Growth of Pol. Thought* [561], 184-94; Kern, *Kingship* [502].

[2] Bäuml, 'Medieval Literacy' [240], 243.

[3] *Ancient Law* [805], 230 (in c. 8). On Maine's analysis in general: Gluckman, *Barotse Jurisprudence* [789], pp. xlii, n. 1, 3, n. 7.

irrational. More recently social anthropologists have discovered that the customary law which is actually used in the surviving small-scale societies that they study is, on the contrary, often very flexible. Despite the occasional use of ordeals and the belief in supernatural sanctions which they imply, it seems to give considerable scope for argument to evaluate degrees of wrong and to fit general principles to particular cases. Formalism is, on the face of it, more likely to characterize professional law than unprofessional customary law. Without written records, forms of words are unlikely to be fixed, and without some form of publication, definitions and decisions cannot become authoritative. Unwritten, customary law therefore cannot be rigid: in individual cases the rules and their application may seem clear, but no permanent agreement about them is possible because there is no permanent record and—sometimes—no one with the authority to enforce it everywhere. Even where there is a regular system of courts and of law enforcement, customary and unprofessional law tends by its nature to blur the boundary between morality and law, while arguments about cases tend not to separate principle from illustration, law from fact.[4] To legal historians accustomed to the highly formalist precisions of the English common law this looks irrational. To non-lawyers it looks like ordinary life—life in which arguments are conducted according to what we tend to call common sense. That sort of argument is more likely to be marred by inconsistency, prejudice, malice, and sloppy thinking than by rigidity or formalism. At its best it may be quite rational, in the sense that it is conducted by people who are applying human intelligence to the solution of problems, arguing about right and wrong, citing precedents, and comparing cases. There is, of course, no reason at all to assume without evidence that what is true of the Barotse or the Moroccan Berbers was true of early medieval Europe, but if one looks at the evidence of tenth- and eleventh-century law in the light of these anthropological analogies more of it seems to make

    [4] Clanchy, 'Remembering the Past' [328]; Gluckman, *Barotse Jurisprudence* [789], 1–26, 268–9; Gellner, *Saints of the Atlas* [786], 45, 105–15; Hamnett, *Social Anthropology and Law* [794], 1–13; on literacy also: Goody, *Domestication of the Savage Mind* [791].

sense than if one starts from the hypothesis that it came out of a highly ritualized and rigid system.

That is not surprising, considering that unwritten custom formed the bedrock of law all over western Europe.[5] Some records were kept, as our knowledge of it shows, but they were too few, and much too little read, for their form to have much effect on procedure in the courts. Few people who followed and declared custom can have read monastic cartularies or law codes. Custom ruled. Even the 'Roman' law in which people in parts of Italy took pride can be seen as not much more than another variety of custom, while the 'Roman' law of southern France was still more diluted. The traditional polarization of 'Roman' and 'Germanic' is misleading:[6] not only had each legal tradition borrowed from the other but both had changed as society had changed. Despite some peculiarities of vocabulary and procedure, the fossilized relics of a past age, the sub-Roman law of the tenth century seems in practice to have enforced much the same sorts of rights and duties, according to a very similar set of values and processes, as did the Lombard law of Tuscany and north Italy. It is true that, thanks to the revival of the notarial profession in tenth- and eleventh-century Italy, law-suits and other transactions were more often and more fully recorded there than they were elsewhere. Since, however, there was no system of publishing decisions and no single authority to decide which precedent was best, that did not significantly promote definition or uniformity in the law at large. By the eleventh century the Italian law schools were beginning to learn more of Justinian's texts and, as they began to understand them better, the practice of law outside the schools began to be affected too. It was not, however, until the twelfth century that a whole new jurisprudence appeared: before then the law actually in use in Italian or south French courts contained

[5] Pollock and Maitland, *Hist. of Eng. Law* [628], i. 106-8; Chénon, *Hist. du droit français* [317], i. 489-92; Krause, 'Gewohnheitsrecht' [511]; Calasso, *Medio evo del diritto* [300], 181-217.

[6] Classen, 'Fortleben' [330]; Checchini, 'I "Consiliarii"' [316]; Leicht, *Scritti vari* [533], ii (2), 5-73; Vaccari, 'Diritto Longobardo' [721]; Didier, 'Le Droit romain' [362]; Poly, *Provence* [629], 43-52. On 'Roman' and 'Germanic' in general: Reynolds, 'Medieval *Origines Gentium*' [653] and below, pp. 251-5.

little that was fundamentally different from traditional custom.[7]

The law that was applied, in both north and south, is to be deduced for the most part rather from grants to individuals and from more or less laconic reports of individual cases, than from general statements. Law codes are rare, except in England, and treatises even rarer. The English codes themselves are short on statements of principle and lack any spirit of codification in the modern sense—which is, of course, just what one would expect in a society dominated by customary law. Their use of the word *riht*, however, is revealing. In some contexts it needs to be translated by 'law', in others by 'justice', but it must often mean what is customary as well as what is lawful or right, since the rights or duties it refers to are so often left unspecified.[8] In Germany too, royal diplomas display customary law as supreme: no boundary was perceived, apparently, between customary law and customs in a more general sense, between right and law, or sin and crime, or between new legislation and the confirmation of existing law. It is true that occasional remarks about the relation of custom to law can be found, while here, as elsewhere, bad customs are occasionally mentioned and suppressed, but it was not until the twelfth century that any real attempt seems to have been made to reconcile contradictions and sort out distinctions.[9] It was not in any case until the twelfth century or later that conditions anywhere in western Christendom began to approximate to those in which any real distinction between law and custom can exist: that distinction must depend not only on the monopoly of law enforcement but on a procedure of legislation, and of recording legislation, that distinguishes law as such from other social rules.[10]

In France the decay of royal authority precluded even the

[7] Calasso, *Medio evo* [300], 229-328; Fried, *Juristenstand* [427], 24-36; Classen, 'Kodifikation' [331]; Stock, *Implications of Literacy* [699], 40-1; Toubert, *Latium médiéval* [715], 1229-36, but cf. 1241-51, 1303-8; Gouron, 'Science juridique' [446]; van Caenegem in *La Preuve* [524], 710-53.

[8] Attenborough, *Laws* [87] and Robertson, *Laws*, [177], indices *sub* riht.

[9] Krause, 'Königtum und Rechtsordnung' [512]; Diestelkamp, 'Reichsweistümer' [363].

[10] Fried, *Evolution of Political Society* [784], 14-26; Gluckman, *Politics, Law and Ritual* [790], 196-202.

repetitive legislation of English kings or such quasi-legislative rulings on custom as were made by kings in Germany and Italy. The word *consuetudines* occurs most often in French sources in the sense of rights and duties owed to a lord.[11] That is to be explained, however, rather by the nature of the sources and the political situation they reflect than by different concepts of law and custom as such. Just as we can live with different senses of the word 'customs' (marmalade for breakfast, import duties), so medieval people who used Latin lived with different senses of the word *consuetudines*. The protean character of the word during this period indeed demonstrates not only the hazy legal categories of the time but the fundamental importance of custom itself. Seigniorial *consuetudines* were presumably so called (in other countries as well as in France) because their validity was assumed to derive from custom as well as from might. Custom, in the sense of customary law, did not come to rule in France or Italy, as is sometimes suggested, merely because of a governmental vacuum. It was the one universal and pre-existing secular authority which survived even in the vacuum.[12] Nor, even in France, was it only the prerogative of lords, for it was what their subjects, even their unfree subjects, looked to for protection, however little it may seem, by our standards, to have given them, even when there was a king to enforce it.[13]

It is only the application of distinctions appropriate to the later jurisprudence that makes it difficult to reconcile the rule of custom with frequent changes in the law. Recent suggestions that the concept of the 'good old law' belongs more to the period after 1100 than before fall into this trap.[14] They start from the hard-edged categories of modern law and only make sense for societies in which law-making is a precisely defined and controlled activity and in which the preservation of exact records makes the moment of change

---

[11] Lemarignier, 'La Dislocation du "pagus" ' [536], 410-10; Duby, *Société mâconnaise* [381], 174-5, 188; Gilissen, 'Loi et coutume' [440], 264-5; Maitland, *Domesday Book* [567], 76-9.

[12] Cf. Fasoli and Bocchi, *Città italiana* [408], 39-40.

[13] Verlinden, *L'Esclavage* [726], 718-47; Violante, *Società milanese* [729], 84-9; Despy, 'Serfs ou libres' [357]; Vollrath, 'Herrschaft und Genossenschaft' [730].

[14] Cheyette, 'Custom, Case-Law' [319]; Kroeschell, 'Recht und Rechtsbegriff' [515] and 'Rechtsfindung' [514]; Köbler, *Recht im frühen Mittelalter* [507].

significant.[15] Records of pleas, charters, and such laws as there are seem to suggest rather that the practice of secular law in the tenth and eleventh centuries was governed by just that immanence of right, authority of custom, and generally hazy categories that analogies from social anthropology would suggest.[16] If these qualities are better discerned after the twelfth century it is because they were then more clearly expressed by more articulate writers, not because they appeared for the first time just when the start of record-keeping and professional jurisprudence began to make them obsolete.

Before that the rule of custom did not mean that the law was in reality old and unchanging.[17] Legislation was always possible. New circumstances arose, bad customs needed to be quashed, and good customs were transferred from one people to another. Just before 900, for instance, Alfred of Wessex and his counsellors chose what seemed most just out of West Saxon, Mercian, and Kentish law, and annulled what they thought wrong.[18] In the tenth century Otto II ruled that women's inheritances should not be taken in claims against their husbands,[19] and in the eleventh Henry III bestowed German law on the Hungarians.[20] As these examples suggest, although customary law all over the west had many similar features, local variation was taken for granted. In some areas where government was particularly weak and local solidarity was therefore weakened too, the principle of what historians call 'personal law' (or even more confusingly, 'the personality of law') obtained: that is, separate groups or individuals within local society, like those who distinguished themselves as 'Romans', 'Burgundians', and 'Franks' in parts of France, followed separate inherited customs of their own. In most areas, however, the general rule by the tenth century was for

[15] Works cited above, nn. 4, 10; Brunner, *Land und Herrschaft* [289], 128-9, 134-8, 150-7, 270-1.

[16] Below, nn. 43-76.

[17] Krause, 'Dauer und Vergänglichkeit' [510].

[18] Attenborough, *Laws* [87], 62-3.

[19] *M.G.H. Dipl.* [156], ii: Otto II, no. 130.

[20] *M.G.H. Scriptores* [54], xx. 800; cf. ibid. v. 125 and Müller-Mertens, 'Zur Rolle' [602], 33. For similar legislation in England in 1284: *Statutes of the Realm* [190], i. 73-4.

variation to be geographical.[21] While kingdoms were increasingly seen as the major units of custom, especially where they became the most effective units of government, discrete customs were also attributed to towns or provinces, to villages or lordships—indeed to almost every sort of social unit.[22] Everywhere immigration kept muddling the general rule, since migrating groups and individuals wanted to take their customs with them. If they were powerful or influential they would be allowed to do so, but the passage of time tended to merge neighbouring sets of customs together.

One corollary of the general acceptance of local variations of custom was the right of members of a local community to be tried within it. Such rights are not widely attested before the twelfth-century grants of customs and liberties, but a few examples can be found earlier.[23] The twelfth-century confirmations or grants of local customs thus reflect rather a change in political circumstances than in legal principles— a point which needs emphasis only because intellectual historians sometimes imply that later academic references to differences of law or custom were part of a new view of the state.[24] Though John of Paris, for instance, like a good academic, cited Aristotle and Augustine as authorities for the legitimate variation of custom, it is highly probable that, like everyone else for centuries past, he took the phenomenon itself pretty well as a matter of course.[25]

Although the details of custom varied from place to place, it was the essence of customary law that at any one time and place it should seem to be the one natural sort of law—an undifferentiated accumulation of rules about what was right and wrong, and about the right procedures for enforcing it. The idea of separate but equally valid systems of law with radically different content and procedures would have been

---

[21] See pp. 258, 276. Pepin II's confirmation in 768 of each man's law, Roman or Salic, already implies a tension between descent and locality: *et si de alia provincia advenerit, secundum legem ipsius patriae vivat*: M.G.H. Capit. [154], i. 43.

[22] See below, pp. 126–9, 164–5.

[23] *Cod. Dipl. Genova* [106], no. 3 (and possibly no. 1); cf. Munoz, *Fueros municipales* [162], pp. 236, 238.

[24] Post, *Studies* [631], 496–8, 502; Mochi-Onory, *Fonti canonistiche* [591], 124–39; Ullmann, *Medieval Foundations* [719], 121–2.

[25] *De Potestate* [45], 180–1 (c. 3).

hard to envisage. There were, of course, matters of morals and ecclesiastical law which particularly concerned the clergy and were sometimes dealt with by them alone, but the procedures they followed do not seem to have been radically different from those followed by laymen.[26] As for other possible categories of law, the contrast between 'folk' or 'popular' law (*Volksrecht*) and royal law (*Königsrecht*) belongs to historians, not to the middle ages. References to feudal law (*ius feodale*) seem to be rare before the later twelfth century, but the words when they do occur, seem to mean something like the right to a fee (*feodum*) or the law about fees (that is, generally, law about property held under a superior lord by a lay person above peasant status), rather than a separate system of law.[27] Cases about fees do not seem to have been normally adjudicated in separate courts according to special procedures.[28] Civil and criminal law do not seem to have been explicitly distinguished either. That does not mean, as has sometimes been suggested, that the system of feud and mutual monetary compensation for injuries excluded any concept of public wrong and any royal concern about it. Penalties for crimes had been paid to kings, as well as to victims, from very early times, while the summary execution of thieves who were caught red-handed shows that the ideas of a public interest in crime and of public punishment were not unknown.[29] Given, however, that the boundary between criminal and civil wrongs is never all that simple to draw, it is not surprising that there is no statement in the surviving records of where it ran. If anyone had needed to make the distinction, he would have drawn it in a way that made sense for one particular place, time, and case. Someone else in different circumstances could have drawn an equally reasonable boundary elsewhere. We cannot make a single consistent set of detailed distinctions out of the customary

[26] Le Bras, *Hist. du droit de l'église* [527], vii. 4-6; Donahue, 'Proof by Witnesses' [371], 128; Morris, 'Judicium Dei' [598]; *Chron. Ramsey* [16], 78-80; Solmi, 'L'Amministrazione' [189], 252-3; Marchegay, 'Duel judiciaire' [150].

[27] References in Niermeyer, *Lexicon* [211], 413; also *M.G.H. Scriptores* [54], xxvi, 44.

[28] See pp. 220-42.

[29] Pollock and Maitland, *Eng. Law* [628], i. 157-8, and below, p. 28, for collective accusations. Cf. Gluckman, *Barotse Jurisprudence* [789], 252-4.

law which was practised, in all its rich variety, all over western Europe for centuries: all we can do is try to deduce such general principles as seem to lie behind it.

Consultative legislation

It is the nature of custom that it presupposes a group or community within which it is practised. Any statement of law will therefore be made in some sense on behalf of the community, and government is likely to involve some kind of consultation with it. That was the case in the earlier middle ages: kings were under an obligation to rule rightly, maintaining right and law even when they changed law and custom, and doing so by and with the advice and consent of their subjects. It seems to me quite wrong to suggest, as is sometimes done, either that the twelfth and thirteenth centuries saw the first attempts to restrict arbitrary royal power or that coronation oaths were the only restraints on it before then.[30] Coronation oaths did not create obligations but attempted to enforce them, and though the twelfth-century development of government increased both the occasions for consultation and the temptation for kings to avoid it, the conflicts that ensued can only be understood in the context of these pre-existing obligations. Kings did not, of course, always fulfil their obligations. Like all rulers, they had good opportunities for breaking them with impunity and strong temptations to do so. In 945 Berengar of Italy replaced a bishop without consulting the other bishops (*nullo concilio habito, nulla episcoporum deliberatione*).[31] In 1040 the emperor Henry III pointed out to the Bohemians, who complained that he was breaking an agreement made by one of his predecessors, that every king adds new laws and that those who make the law are not ruled by it, for the law has a nose of wax while the king has a long and iron hand with which to pull it.[32] It seems unlikely that Henry seriously intended to claim that kings had absolute power by right, in

---

[30] David, *La Souveraineté* [347]; Cheyette, 'Custom, Case-Law' [319]; Radding, 'Medieval Mentalities' [640] and 'Superstition to Science' [641].

[31] Liutprand of Cremona, *Opera* [50], 148.

[32] Cosmas of Prague, *Chronik* [20], 93–4.

the sense that they could or should make law without consulting their great men. He——or the later Bohemian chronicler——was simply emphasizing the hard facts of military domination. The story, like that about Berengar, shows that there were norms to break. Other kings had to pay more attention to them. Ethelred II, Cnut, and Henry I of England each had to make special promises, outside their normal coronation oaths, to rule justly and according to good custom.[33] Whether they then broke them is in this context irrelevant: there were rules, however vague and ineffective, to which kings in difficulty might have to pay lip-service. The lip-service presupposes the rule.

Early medieval government, then, was in its own way both constitutional and representative: constitutional because kings were supposed to be limited by law, custom and consultation; and representative, firstly because the king made and declared law as the supreme representative of his people, and secondly because those with whom he was supposed to consult were themselves representative. The bishops and nobles of a kingdom, like the senior and richer landowners of a province or village, were, in the terms of the time, those who were qualified to speak on behalf of the collectivity of which they were the most solid, respectable, and responsible members.

To judge from the frequent references to consultation in charters and chronicles, as well as in law-codes, kings normally did consult when they made new rulings and often thought it worth while to indicate the weight of support that they had received.[34] In 972 Otto I told Ottobeuren abbey that he could not exempt it from royal service without consulting his magnates (*principes*) and then told the magnates that he left it to them and would abide by their decision.[35] Presumably he did not normally abdicate as far as this: practice no doubt varied according to the needs of the case as well as according to personalities, power, and local circumstances. In

---

[33] Stafford, 'Laws of Cnut' [693].

[34] Krause, 'Königtum und Rechtsordnung' [512]; cf. Bosl, *Frühformen* [268], 135-55; Mor, 'Gouvernés et gouvernants' [594]; Stenton, *Latin Charters* [697], 34-7; for Carolingian ideas and practice: Nelson, 'Legislation and Consensus' [607].

[35] *MGH Dipl.* [156], ii. 881-3.

larger kingdoms or lordships the recognition of local custom must have allowed a good deal of local autonomy. Contemporary clerics noted the peculiar independence of assemblies at Tiel and Birka, but it may have been the unruliness of Tiel and the paganism of Birka that attracted attention and disapproval;[36] there is no reason to suppose that unfettered royal decisions would have seemed preferable.

Collective judgement

Hazy though the boundary between legislation and judgement was, examples of consultative or collective action on the judgement side of it are much more numerous. As a result, it is possible to say that, despite the usual mass of local variations, some kind of collective judgement was normal. It is always dangerous to confuse arguments about the meaning and function of current usage with arguments about its origins, but on this subject it may be useful to start from the general recognition of the Carolingian *scabini* as collective assessors or judgement-finders.[37] Historians have sometimes wondered whether the *scabini* were a 'popular' institution: it must surely be taken that they were, in the Isidorian sense that they represented the *populus*, rather than the *plebs*. They were local landowners who ought to know the law and customs of their county and could therefore judge on its behalf. The object of setting up permanent panels of *scabini* seems to have been to secure a regular quorum of reliable judges, some at least of whose functions had been fulfilled earlier by the *ad hoc* appointment of *rachinburgii*. The new arrangement seems therefore to have involved no new juridical principle, and other 'good men' who were present in the *mallus* alongside the *scabini* still participated in judgement to some extent, if only by their approval and witness.[38] There is thus no need to adopt a narrowly diffusionist

[36] *Elenchus* [118], i. 424-5; Rimbert, *Vita Anskarii* [68], 57; Adam of Bremen, *Gesta Ham. Pont.* [4], 252-3.

[37] Althoffer, *Les Scabins* [218]; Ganshof, 'Charlemagne et l'administration' [431], 399-402; Byl, *Juridictions scabinales* [292], 1-13; cf. Kroeschell, 'Rechtsfindung' [514], 500-5, 514.

[38] Estey, 'Scabini' [399]. On 'good men': Nehlsen-von Stryk, *Boni homines* [605], 167-9, 345-8.

explanation of references to collective judgement in lesser courts in Francia, or in areas to which Charlemagne's reform did not apply—notably England and perhaps Saxony.[39] Here older forms presumably went on: the institution of *scabini* makes a well-attested starting-point for enquiry about the period after 900; it was not the starting-point of a revolutionary sort of judgement.

Thanks above all to the work of Duby, the old idea that the supersession of 'public' Carolingian courts by 'feudal' or 'private' courts ended collective judgements (except in England) can now be seen to be mistaken.[40] Quite apart from difficulties about defining feudal law and about the distinction between public and private,[41] a good deal of the evidence of law-suits during the tenth, eleventh, and twelfth centuries suggests that judgements were made in much the same way whatever the nature of the assembly. Assembly is a better word here than court: our understanding of law at this time may be enhanced if we recognize how indistinct was the boundary between it and politics or administration in general. Many assemblies which dealt with what we would call legal problems dealt with other sorts of business too. In England what historians call shire and hundred courts were generally called meetings (*gemote*) of the shire and hundred or, even more simply, 'pleas'.[42] Some of the problems about the status of particular assemblies and their judgements—or arbitrations—dissolve if one bears in mind the haziness of these categories.

The procedure for settling disputes peacefully, or for determining guilt, which seems to emerge from the surviving

[39] Robertson, *Anglo-Saxon Charters* [176], no. 5; cf. Cam, *Liberties and Communities* [303], 49-63; Althoffer, *Les Scabins* [218], 77-105; Bader, *Studien* [228], 347-9.

[40] Duby, 'Institutions judiciaires' [380] and *Société mâconnaise* [381], 102-4, 190-1; cf. Ganshof, *Tribunaux de châtellenies* [436], 65-6, 70-3, 85-7; Byl, *Juridictions scabinales* [292], 13-27; Fossier, *Picardie* [420], 478-90.

[41] Schlesinger, *Entstehung* [679], 110-29; Beumann, 'Entwicklung transpersonaler Staatsvortsellungen' [251]; Petot, 'Le Droit commun' [624], 415-16.

[42] Robertson, *Anglo-Saxon Charters* [176], index *sub* shire moot; Robertson, *Laws* [177], index *sub* burggemot, county, court, hundred; Liebermann, *Gesetze* [145], ii. 449, 552; Pollock and Maitland, *Eng. Law* [628], i. 535-6. Court seems as yet to have been used more for a king's or lord's court in the general sense of a dwelling or headquarters: Niermeyer, *Lexicon* [211], *sub* curia, senses 1-14. Cf. Seelman, *Rechtszug* [686], 174 n. 4, 184.

records of pleas that I have seen was this.[43] Assemblies normally (but not invariably) had a president, whether the king or lord himself or someone who represented him, or some respected layman or cleric to whom the parties had referred their differences. He directed proceedings and sometimes joined in making judgements. A hearing opened with statements from the parties (or an accusation) and culminated with a judgement, given either by all those present or by some of them, at the behest of the president. The judgement determined the issues to be proved and the method of proof—generally oaths, ordeals of water or hot iron, or battle—which should apply. Sometimes, however, the judgement was definitive, since examination of witnesses or charters, or simply the consideration of the pleas themselves, enabled the judges to dispense with further proofs.[44] Argument is seldom reported in detail, if at all, but there is enough information in some reports to show that judgement emerged from a discussion, even if it was a discussion in which fact and law were, by the standards of the later jurists, inextricably confused.[45] The boundary between our sort of witnesses to fact and the sort of witnesses who swore or fought for their principal—and indeed between either sort and the judges themselves—was also less clear than it would look in the later jurisprudence.[46] It is quite wrong to allow either these confusions (as they appear to modern lawyers) or the apparent irrationality of some of the methods of proof to cast a pall of irrationality over the whole procedure.[47] As

[43] For general accounts of procedure: Salvioli, *Storia della procedura* [672]; Pollock and Maitland, *Eng. Law* [628], ii. 598-611; Bongert, *Les Cours laïques* [264]; van Caenegem, in *La Preuve* [524], 710-53.

[44] Harmer, *Select Documents* [134], no. 18; *Chron. Ramsey* [16], 78-80; Robertson, *Anglo-Saxon Charters* [176], no. 66; Bigelow, *Placita Anglo-Norm.* [92], 17-18; *Gallia Christ.* [129], xi, app. col. 202-3; *Cart. de Redon* [108], no. 345; *Cart. de Saint-Aubin* [99], nos. 9, 106-7; *Chartes du Cluny* [100], no. 3821; *Cart. de Marseille* [132], no. 691; Ficker, *Forschungen* [416], iv, nos. 21, 43, 46; Muratori, *Antiq. Ital.* [163], iii, col. 643-6, 647-50.

[45] Harmer, *Select Documents* [134], no. 18; MGH Dipl. [156], i. Otto I, no, 398; *Cart. de Mâcon* [173], no. 10; cf. Milsom, 'Law and Fact' [588].

[46] Salvioli, *Storia della procedura* [672], i. 275-6; Ficker, *Forschungen* [416], iv, no. 46; *Cart. de Marseille* [132], no. 29; Bigelow, *Placita Anglo-Norm.* [92], 17-19; *Gallia Christ.* [129], xi, app. col. 202-3; *Chartes de Cluny* [100], no. 3685; *Leges Henrici Primi* [49], 134 (31, 8); *Documenti di Arezzo* [167], no. 370.

[47] Colman, 'Reason and Unreason' [335]. The cases cited here provide more

for formalism and rigidity, they are notable chiefly by their absence. All the evidence suggests that pleading was pretty informal. The only evidence that verbal precision was required at this period seems to concern oaths, and not all of them had to be taken in absolutely set form.[48] Oaths and ordeals took place not after mere 'declaratory rituals',[49] but after the issues for probation had been isolated and clarified through discussion. Ordeals may have helped to establish the results of consensus but they were not apparently the primary means of reaching it. That was done in the judgement which preceded them and which itself emerged from a discussion which was presumably no less rational than most human discussions.[50] In fact it was probably more rational than many, since it was conducted in solemn circumstances by responsible people who worked within an agreed framework of customs and values.

There were many variations in procedure. The authority of the president of an assembly or court was presumably greater if he represented a king or other lord with powers of enforcement than if he were simply an arbitrator chosen by the parties, but the difference between law-suits and arbitrations was otherwise far from clear. Where a political vacuum left noble disputes to be solved by what later jurists would call arbitration or mediation, the resulting judgements were hard to enforce, but the language of the records does not suggest that the procedures themselves were juridically distinct,[51]

evidence of argument than might be expected from e.g. Cheyette, 'Custom, Case-Law' [319], 367-70, or Brown, 'Society and the Supernatural' [286].

[48] Robertson, Laws [177], 233 (3 §2), 361; Leges Henrici Primi [49], 106, 202 (9, 6; 64, 1). For oaths sworn in precise form in customary law: Gellner, Saints of the Atlas [786], 106-25. Formulae which have been preserved in writing probably varied in practice: Goody, Domestication of the Savage Mind [791], 118. Cf. Harmer, Anglo-Saxon Writs [133], 89.

[49] The expression is Brown's: 'Society and the Supernatural' [286], 138.

[50] See n. 44, and MGH Capit. [154], i, no. 136; Asser, Life of Alfred [10], 92-3; Cart. de Mâcon [173], no. 10; Cart. de Saint-Aubin [99], no. 5.

[51] On 'arbitrations': Brunner, Land und Herrschaft [289], 425; Ficker, Forschungen [416], iii. 264-9; Duby, 'Les Institutions judiciaires' [380], 20-7; Bongert, Les Cours laïques [264], 97-111, 159-82. The distinction between compromise and judgement, made e.g. in Fulbert of Chartres, Letters [29], no. 86 (count Eudes's letter); Robertson, Laws [177], 68 (13 §3); Leges Henrici Primi [49], 164, 177 (49, 5a; 57, 1a), does not seem to coincide with that between an arbitration and a law-suit in modern terms. Judicia could be made by assemblies without established jurisdiction: e.g. Cart. de Saint-Aubin [99], no. 106,

or that the parties preferred this kind of procedure because it stressed reconciliation rather than normative justice. In many parts of France, where arbitration-like procedures have been particularly noticed,[52] they were not so much an alternative to more formal law-suits as the only kind of law-suit available. In any case the distinction between reconciliation and justice is artificial: all adjudication surely aims at both, and the absence of formal jurisdiction was the result of political conditions not of the absence of norms. The custom that guided arbitrators was in its way highly normative, but the less power of enforcement they had, the more necessary it was both that each party should be sent away with something to keep him quiet and save his face, and that justice in the widest sense should be seen to be done.[53] The lack of any firm line between the categories of law-suits and arbitrations is emphasized by the fact that the absence of a president, which may make a plea look less formal and more like some kind of arbitration or mediation, was not always the corollary of the absence of recognized authority. Late in the ninth century the early stages of an interminable case about Fonthill (Wilts.) were delegated by King Alfred of Wessex to a group of important nobles and 'more men that I can now name', who only called on the king (while he was washing his hands) when the accuser would not otherwise agree to their judgement that the accused should clear himself by oath.[54] What determined whether the president himself joined in the judgement is also uncertain. In 1139 Count Geoffrey of Anjou, presiding over a plea in the cloister of a church at Angers, made one of a group of laymen and ecclesiastics who deliberated privately in the chapter-house, and it was he who then pronounced their judgement to the parties and the rest of the assembly in the cloister. His father, on the other hand,

distinguished by its editor, but not in the text, as an arbitration. Other pleas of dubious status: *Actes de Philippe I* [172], no. 51; Lot, *Saint-Wandrille* [556], no. 37; *Cart. de Marseille* [432], nos. 702, 804. *Chartes de Cluny* [100], no. 3726 recounts two pleas on the same issue in superficially different sorts of 'court'.

[52] Cheyette, ' "Suum cuique tribuere" ' [320]; White, ' "Pactum legem vincit" ' [749].

[53] Cf. Richards and Kuper, *Councils in Action* [818], 8-9, 23-7; Gluckman, *Barotse Jurisprudence* [789], 10-17; Gellner, *Saints of the Atlas* [786], 114-15. On the validity of compromises: Robertson, *Laws* [177], 68 (III Ethelred 13. 3).

[54] Harmer, *Select Documents* [134], no. 18.

hearing a plea as king of Jerusalem at about the same time, told several knights to go away, make the judgement, and come back and report it.[55] It may be that this is yet another distinction that was not very significant at the time.[56]

Another range of variations was in the constitution of the panel of judges—whether they were permanent *scabini*, *judices*, or lawmen; whether they were appointed by the president *ad hoc*; or whether everyone present joined in. Permanent panels seem to have survived in some parts of the former Carolingian empire where governmental authority was strong. In other areas their disappearance may reflect that of the government that had appointed them. In England, which had never had *scabini* as such, judgements were sometimes apparently made by a general consensus of all, and in Germany there are references to both systems.[57] About 997, accusations in English wapentakes were ordered to be made by a panel of twelve,[58] and in both England and Germany, as indeed elsewhere, a special panel could on occasion be sworn in, generally by royal authority, to make a particular inquiry.[59] Legal historians have seen these royal inquisitions as intrinsically different in legal principle from other collective judgements, but to contemporaries they may have been just a way of discovering the truth which was most readily available to a president of high authority[60] and most appropriate for

[55] *Cart. de Saint-Aubin* [99], no. 9; Usāmah ibn Munqidh, *Arab-Syrian Gentleman* [77], 93-4. Cf. Bongert, *Les Cours laïques* [264], 271.

[56] It may be that the peculiarity of Lombard (and other Italian) procedures lay rather in the fullness, and therefore explicitness, of their reports of pleas than in the systematic participation of presidents of tribunals in judgement: cf. Salvioli, *Storia della procedura* [672], i. 330-3, and below, p. 32.

[57] Apparent general consensus: de Boüard, *Manuel de diplomatique* [270], pl. 21; Robertson, *Anglo-Saxon Charters* [176], nos. 44, 69, 78, 83; but cf. *Chron. Ramsey* [16], 78-80; *M.G.H. Dipl.* [156], i: Otto I, nos. 54, 78, 204; *Mon. Boica* [153], xxviii (2), no. 116; cf. Franklin, *Reichshofgericht* [425], ii. 127-9. *Scabini*: Ganshof, *Tribunaux de châtellenies* [436]; Byl, *Juridictions scabinales* [292], 13-65; *M.G.H. Dipl.* [156], i-iv, index *sub scabini*. On *judices*, cf. Fried, *Entstehung des Juristenstandes* [427], 24-36.

[58] Robertson, *Laws* [177], 64 (III Ethelred, 3. 1). For a more general duty of accusation alongside: Hurnard, 'Jury of Presentment' [484].

[59] *MGH Dipl.* [156], i: Otto I, no. 419; van Caenegem, *Royal Writs* [296], 62-7; Salvioli, *Storia della procedura* [672], 278-9. The authority to enrol a panel did not have to be royal: Bongert, *Les Cours laïques* [264], 271.

[60] Though Calasso, *Medio evo* [300], 207-14 sees proof of custom by inquisition as symptomatic of disintegration of authority. The link between Carolingian

issues which required special knowledge. If one or two respected witnesses could give adequate information that might do just as well. Some cases were by their nature suitable to the judgement of near neighbours,[61] while in others, in which a lord threatened the rights of his subject or vassal, the judgement of a man's peers would be the fairest.[62] To contemporaries the relative authority of all the sorts of judgement was, so far as the records of pleas seem to imply, much the same. Even the collective decision that made a preliminary accusation (as in the procedure laid down in England in 997) probably did not carry a very different legal authority from a judgement made in the course of a dispute. Both might need a subsequent proof and both involved solemn responsibilities and the possibility of perjury.

In practice the difference between all the differently constituted bodies of judges may have been decreased by the hierarchical temper of the times: if the number of judges was limited, then people of higher status would be more likely to be chosen, and if it was not, then they would dominate deliberations anyway. By the twelfth century the courts or assemblies of some lordships or provinces, and of some towns, in northern France seem to have had groups known as peers, who may have formed élites of judgement-finders rather like *scabini*.[63] Elsewhere the word 'peers' continued to be used to describe the equals of a litigant who were his natural judges:[64] it is not clear why some courts developed fixed bodies of peers or just what function they fulfilled. The tension between hierarchy and equity, deference and justice, posed eternal problems, and a permanent body of peers—like

and later 'administrative' inquisitions is accepted by Boulet-Sautel in *La Preuve* [524], 310.

[61] In addition to cases already cited: Harmer, *Anglo-Saxon Writs* [133], 253-4. As with arbitrations (above, n. 51) sources do not always distinguish as inquisitions processes described as such by historians (e.g. Ganshof, in *La Preuve* [524], 92), while the word *inquisitio* can be used quite loosely in the sources.

[62] Thietmar of Merseburg, *Chronik* [73], 342-3; *MGH Dipl.* [156], iv: Conrad II, no. 244; *MGH Const.* [160], i, no. 68 c. 4; *Leges Henrici Primi* [49], 134 (32, 3); Bongert, *Les Cours laïques* [264], 271; Cam, 'East Anglian Shire-moot' [103].

[63] Feuchère, 'Pairs de principauté' [414]; below, p. 246.

[64] There does not seem to be any reason to see judgement by peers as peculiarly 'feudal' as e.g. Fuhrmann, *Deutsche Geschichte* [429], 189.

a permanent body of *scabini*—may have offered some solution. Peers in this sense were those who were more equal than others.

Another advantage of a fixed panel of people of more or less equal status may have been to facilitate decisions when there was a difference of opinion. It is sometimes suggested that all collective decisions in the early middle ages had to be unanimous, and that the transition to acceptance of majority decisions was a sign of increased rationality.[65] This seems a little culture-bound.[66] It is also contradicted by at least one piece of evidence. Ethelred II of England ordered that if twelve thegns disagreed (perhaps in making the accusations of crime already mentioned) then the verdict of eight should stand.[67] We have no reason to believe that this was a new or unusual idea, but equal votes would make more sense in a small fixed number of equals than in a large and amorphous assembly. In the early twelfth century the author of the *Leges Henrici Primi* may be making this distinction when he says in one place that disagreements between equals (*inter pares*) are to be decided by majority vote (*vincat sententia plurimorum*), and in another that when the judges disagree the opinion of the better, which best accords with justice, should prevail (*vincat sententia meliorum et cum iustitia magis acquieverit*).[68] A preference for unanimity is not necessarily a sign of ritualistic irrationality. Obviously a unanimous decision is always best, and it must be particularly desirable when enforcement is going to depend on the support of public opinion, led by those who are themselves making the judgement.[69] In such circumstances the next best thing to unanimity is a consensus in which everyone is in the end prepared to join: hence, perhaps, the penalty imposed on the outvoted minority within the twelve thegns of Ethelred's law. If further confirmation is needed that early medieval people

[65] e.g. Ruffini, *Ragione dei più* [669], 12-17; Brown, 'Society and the Supernatural' [286].

[66] Bailey, 'Decisions in Councils' [772].

[67] Robertson, *Laws* [177], 68 (13.2, 3).

[68] *Leges Henrici Primi* [49], 86, 132 (5, 6; 31, 2): *iustitia* here seems more likely to mean abstract justice than (as the translation has it) a royal judge. Ibid. 134 (31, 3) also suggests that the views of the great should prevail.

[69] Richards and Kuper, *Councils in Action* [818], 8-10.

were as capable of appreciating the force of numbers as most people in comparable circumstances, then it might be supplied by, for instance, the rules of the Salic Law about how an immigrant might get permission to settle anywhere, or by the requirements for compurgation, which seems to have needed more oath-helpers for less respectable people or those accused of more serious crimes.[70] In practice, of course, the president of any assembly might often sway its decisions himself, so that the judgements would even be referred to as his, rather than everyone's.[71] That would not necessarily seem wrong. The crux was that any decision should seem to embody what everyone concerned—or as many as possible—would think was right and just.

Apart from individual cases where an assembly was dominated, willingly or unwillingly, by its president, there are two general classes of law-suit in which it might be suggested that the general rule of collective judgement did not apply. First, it is often said or implied that unfree peasants, unless or until they secured grants of liberties in the twelfth century or later, were judged by their lord or his deputy, whether mayor, *villicus*, or reeve.[72] Courts dealing with peasants were no doubt more subject to their lord's arbitrary will than most, and before records became more plentiful at just about the time when peasants began to get grants of customs, there is little evidence of what went on in most of them. Judgement in some, at least, however, was collective,[73] and belief in the validity of custom must have pushed others in the same direction. Although being less free meant being more subject to one's lord's will, there was often no hard and fast way to draw a boundary between free and unfree.[74] Even the

---

[70] *Lex Salica* [117], 202-4; Attenborough and Robertson, *Laws* [87, 177], indices *sub* oath.

[71] Bates, 'Origin of Justiciarship' [238], 3; Stenton, *English Justice* [696], 62, n. 46; Marchegay, 'Duel judiciaire' [150], 563 (though note *ab eo simulque omnibus rogatus*); *Gallia Christ.* [129], xi, app. col. 202-3.

[72] e.g. Pertile, *Storia del diritto* [622], vi (1), 161-2 (stating the rule but citing exceptions); Duby, 'Institutions judiciaires' [380], 193; Byl, *Juridictions scabinales* [292], 53-5. The same inference might be drawn from Lennard, 'Early Manorial Juries' [539].

[73] Vollrath, 'Herrschaft und Genossenschaft' [730]; Pertile, as previous note.

[74] *Ordonnances* [144], i. 3-4; cf. Aubenas, 'Inconscience de juristes' [226]; Bak, 'Serfs and Serfdom' [229].

distinction between slaves and serfs, which is often assumed to be self-evident, must have been hard to make in individual cases within the economic and legal systems of the time. Nor was there any clear dividing line between rights of government and rights of property which would exempt a lord's 'private property' as such from the usual norms of custom and equity.

The other possible exception to the general rule lies in the area of sub-Roman law. Here references to judgements by a single *judex* or only two or three *judices* occur. *Judices* could be very like *scabini*, if not identical with them, but some apparently spoke from a more esoteric and learned knowledge of the law. In the Romagna a single *judex* was often by the eleventh century nominated to hear a case, acting as both president and judge, and this practice, with other Roman or sub-Roman forms, began to spread to other parts of Italy. Nevertheless the more usual practice until the twelfth century, at least in Upper Italy, Tuscany, and Spoleto, was to have separate presidents and judges, with all those present approving the judgement, and this was not unknown even in the Romagna.[75] A recent account of procedures in Latium, moreover, confirms that, despite an apprent predominance of judges learned in Roman law, the 'good men' of local assemblies played an important part in eleventh-century pleas.[76] *Judices* learned in traditional Roman law may also have fulfilled a quasi-representative function in the towns of which they formed a civic élite. The use of Roman forms did not preclude the immanence of other values.

The argument propounded here is not that collective judgement was invariable, but that it was sufficiently common to imply the prevalence of a norm. In the mid twelfth century, just after my closing date of 1140, Otto of Freising remarked that if a noble (*aliquis ex comitum*) in Hungary offended the king, sentence on him was given by the king alone, not, *sicut aput nos moris est*, by his peers.[77] 'Our custom' looks as

[75] Ficker, *Forschungen* [416], iii. 83–4, 245–305; Checchini, 'I "Consiliarii" ' [316]; Leicht, *Scritti vari* [533], ii (1), 65–78, ii (2), 5–73; Salvioli, *Storia della procedura* [672], i. 330–3.
[76] Toubert, *Structures du Latium* [715], 1229–54, 1292–1303.
[77] *Gesta Friderici* [58], 50–1. On the actual practice of the German royal

if, in one form or another, and despite occasional breaches by masterful kings, it was common to all or most of western Christendom. If that is right, then some of the arguments about the origin of urban *échevins* (*scabini*) or jurats and of the English jury look overstrained. In a given town it may be possible to trace a continuity of titles among civic officers through the period when municipal independence was growing, but that does not tell us very much about the significance of the office. Nor, given the widespread use of oaths, the undifferentiated character of law, and the likelihood that a town's judgement-finders would also be its general decision-makers, is there any reason to suppose that references to *jurati* in towns necessarily betray the influence of revolutionary communes or *conjurationes*.[78] Oaths were constantly taken in law-suits, including oaths by quite large bodies of people: panels of judges may often have been sworn, like witnesses and compurgators, while one assembly of 'a good thousand' representing several counties is said to have sworn its judgement.[79] Sworn communes and *conjurationes* constituted the extension to new purposes of habits and procedures long familiar in the practice of law. Seen against the background of traditional procedures, moreover, the polarization of categories implied in Maitland's description of the origins of the jury as 'not English but Frankish, not popular but royal'[80] is, quite simply, unnecessary. Collective judgements, sometimes and perhaps often sworn, were traditional everywhere except perhaps in some areas of Roman law, and even there some signs of them appear. The jury of presentment and the petty and grand assises of later twelfth-century England constituted varieties of traditional procedure which were unusual only because they were given precise form and

court in Otto's time: Appelt, 'Kaiserurkunde' [221]. Otto may be ill-informed or tendentious about Hungary.

[78] See pp. 173–4, 176.

[79] Robertson, *Anglo-Saxon Charters* [176], no. 41. The men of two shires, on the other hand, who were to give a verdict in 1101, are not explicitly stated to be sworn (van Caenegem, *Royal Writs* [296], no. 138), though Turner ('Origin of Jury' [718], 7) calls them a jury.

[80] *English Law* [628], i. 142; cf. Hurnard, 'Assize of Clarendon' [484]; Turner, 'Origin of Jury' [718]; Campbell, 'English Government' [307]; van Caenegem, 'Public Prosecution' [295]; Milsom, *Legal Framework* [589], 11–13, 36–8, *et passim*.

rules of application by a monarchy with the power to enforce them. The English jury did not create collective judgement but preserved it long after the legal ideas which it had once embodied had been forgotten. The way that judgements continued to be recorded as made *per consideracionem curie* reflected the old ideas and practices, and the Anglo-American habit of referring to a single judge as 'the court' reflects them still. In other countries popular judgements sometimes secured preservation, though not for so long, by their enshrinement in charters of liberties and grants of customs. Here too the novelty lay in the formal record which inhibited occasional arbitrary action from above rather than in the norm of collective judgement as such. Demands for charters were stimulated by the economic changes of the time but their character was determined by the sense of community, the acceptance of collective responsibility, and the habit of collective deliberation which had long been fostered by traditional law.

Collective action at law

Just as the undifferentiated character of law made it easy to transfer legal habits to political activity, so the indeterminacy of its categories facilitated collective action. One example of this is the Peace of God which was promoted by the clergy from the late tenth century.[81] The successes of the Peace, and the associated Truce, of God may be better understood against a background in which collective oath-taking and some collective responsibility for law and order were already taken for granted.[82] Sworn associations of the peace seem particularly innovatory to historians who start from the assumption that law and order are normally the responsibility

[81] Surveyed by e.g. Cowdrey, 'Peace and Truce of God' [342].

[82] Brunel, 'Juges de la paix' [287], esp. 40-1. One reason for excluding peace associations from this book is that I suspect that their importance in the development of law, government, and collective activity has been exaggerated. The findings of Devailly (*Berry* [358], 428, 489-93) suggest that the use of popular armies has been overestimated. Their contribution to the change from feud to punishment looks less significant outside Germany (where peace ordinances were issued by kings) than Hirsch found it (*Die hohe Gerichtsbarkeit* [471]): cf. above, p. 20. Moreover, though the clergy gave the concept of peace a new holiness, they did not invent it. The maintenance of peace was always an objective of law and government and collective oaths were always one way to achieve it.

of governments, not their subjects, and that the 'right of association' is politically controversial and legally definable. One of the most striking examples of a distinction appropriate only to the later jurisprudence, however, is the difference between corporate and non-corporate groups. Without that difference the assumption that group activity is in any way peculiar—that groups need some special formality or authorization in order to engage in any activity which is already lawful for individuals—becomes untenable.[83] At this period all sorts of groups were allowed to act in a way that later centuries would associate with corporate status. Every community had its customs, which seem to have involved some hazy right of legislation—the making of by-laws in terms of the later English law of corporations.[84] Many villages or groups of tenants owned land or rights over land[85]—and this distinction is another which is more or less meaningless in terms of early medieval land-law.[86] Guild-halls, like the right to receive and administer tolls, or to be free of tolls, belonged to groups which were often exceptionally indeterminate even by eleventh-century standards: contemporaries seem to have hardly distinguished between the burgesses of a town, the inhabitants of a town, and the members of its guild, while all rules of membership seem as yet to have been very vague.[87] All sorts of communities sued and were sued and, however undefined their membership, were represented in a rough and ready way when they did so. Monasteries were represented by their abbots or advocates, villages by their mayors, syndics, *burmeister*, reeves, etc.—with or without other members in support.[88] Though grants of collective privileges were not yet as common as they would shortly become, all this suggests that collectiveness as such was not seen as creating legal problems. Collective privileges were no doubt seen in much the same way as collective responsibility, which was universally taken for granted, most unpleasantly in the

---

[83] For further argument, below, pp. 59-64.

[84] For the original meaning of by-law: *OED* [212], i. 1235-6.

[85] Below, pp. 111-12.

[86] Milsom, *Legal Framework* [589], 37-41; cf. Mair, *Social Anthropology* [805], 154-8.

[87] See pp. 167-8.

[88] Cam, *Law-Finders* [302], 159-75; below, pp. 92, 97-9, 112.

form of collective punishments. In England this is illustrated by the harrying of Dover, even before the Conquest, and by the *murdrum* payment after it.

Collective habits, then, worked both ways. Rulers could make use of them to punish, tax, raise forces, and police their lands. But they profited subjects too, and it is hard to avoid the conclusion that in some ways all the indefiniteness of customary law about groups and their rights and duties profited subjects more. It must have made it easy for them to put their customs of collective legal action to collective political use. We should not confuse the clarification of concepts during the twelfth and thirteenth centuries with a growth in the 'spirit of association'. Though it came to be embodied in new forms and to find new force thereafter, the spirit itself was old in 1140.

Conclusion

This chapter has argued not only that the practice of law between 900 and 1140 fostered collective activity but that it fostered intelligent collective activity. In what way the mental processes of people living in 'primitive' societies are different from the generality of those in 'advanced' ones seems to be a much more debatable issue today than it was when historians first started to study early medieval law.[89] It may be that people in small-scale, illiterate societies remain at a cognitive level which developmental psychologists could call pre-operational. On the other hand, it may be that the chief difference lies in the absence of the particular habits of thought induced by reading and writing. One reason that their superstitions and rituals look so strange to us is that they are strange—in the sense of unfamiliar. We have our superstitions and rituals too, which we take for granted or explain away. 'Primitive' people may, like us, operate on several levels of belief and reasoning: you do not have to believe that God intervenes directly in an ordeal in order to

[89] Gluckman, *Politics, Law and Ritual* [790], 264-5; Goody, *Domestication of the Savage Mind* [791]; Hallpike, *Foundations of Primitive Thought* [793]; Gellner, 'Actions before Words' [785]; cf. Needham, introduction to Durkheim, *Primitive Classification* [779], pp. xi-xii.

accept its result any more than you have to believe in the invariable fairness and rationality of juries in order to accept
theirs.[90] The more exact forms of reasoning in our society do
not spread far outside the specialized fields of their professional practitioners. If 'primitive' societies do indeed remain
at a fairly elementary cognitive level that does not necessarily
mean that we should treat their legal and other procedures
as all that remote from the ways we conduct our public affairs
in general. The historian who makes too big an imaginative
leap into the mind of the past may end up as far from it as
the one who makes no leap at all.

The problem about an imaginative leap into early medieval
law is that the interpretation of it as essentially formal and
ritualized depends on assuming that it must have been,
because primitive law must by definition be formal and
ritualized and because the early middle ages look primitive.
This argument is circular: the hypothesis about primitive law
is vindicated by ignoring the evidence of informative and
argumentative procedures. Trial by battle and trial by ordeal
were irrational, but they were not the whole of law. Intention may have been largely ignored in assessing degrees of
guilt (though it is not clear that it always was[91]), but then
intention is not quite so important to law as it is to morality.
If it was played down it seems unlikely that that was because
taking it into account was beyond the reasoning capacities of
early medieval people. Their apparent concern with the
injuries of the victim as opposed to the criminal's degree of
guilt seems in some ways more rationally constructive than
the concern of later law with retribution.[92] Above all, considering the scarcity of all sorts of evidence, that which
describes serious discussion of individual cases, and implies
serious concern to relate them to general ideas of equity and
justice, is impressive. We cannot make sense of the transformation of lay society and government in the twelfth and
thirteenth centuries if we start from the belief that people

[90] Gellner, *Saints of the Atlas* [786], 114-15.
[91] e.g. Attenborough, *Laws* [87], 70-84 (Alfred, 13, 17, 23.2, 26-8, 36, 42);
Robertson, *Laws* [177], 106, 208 (VI Ethelred, 52.1; II Cnut, 68.2-3).
[92] Beckerman, 'Adding Insult to Iniuria' [241]; cf. Radding, 'Medieval Mentalities' [640]. That the penitentials never ignored intention in assessing degrees
of sin seems clear from Frantzen, *Literature of Penance* [426].

then inherited a purely—or even largely—formalistic, rigid, and magical idea of law from their predecessors.

The idea of law is one thing. Its practical working is another. In the tenth and eleventh centuries, and even later, many people, particularly powerful people, who had a grievance, did not bring their case to a tribunal at all. They used force. If they did go to law the procedures and penalties might well involve cruelty and injustice. Even unanimous collective judgements, when made in an hierarchical society with a high regard for loyalty and a toughly punitive (though often flouted) moral code, were likely to produce some rather nasty consequences for any nonconformist plaintiff or defendant. Nevertheless, the evidence I have used has been largely derived from actual law-suits: the concern for justice —as then perceived—and for consensus—however forced or intolerant—cannot have been entirely theoretical. Law was custom—normative custom. With all its imperfections it gave people the habit of arguing and agreeing and acting together to maintain the peace and to fulfil their responsibilities to their rulers. It must have promoted not only their sense of community but their readiness and ability to act as independent communities on their own account.

2

Legal change, 1140–1300

There can be no doubt that the twelfth and thirteenth centuries began to bring important changes to the ideas and practices of law. The strengthening of government began to transform the law by emphasizing one source of its authority and enforcement among others. More and more crimes came to incur formal punishments, inflicted by the authority of the ruler, instead of being left to mutual negotiation by feud and wergeld. Although in practice the maintenance of law and order still depended in large measure on collective self-policing, it was now the king's (or sometimes the count's or duke's) peace which the law-breaker broke. The old amorphous assemblies were replaced by something more like modern law-courts, working within something more like defined jurisdictions, and these gradually began to be organized into hierarchies of superior and inferior authority.[1] Meanwhile the keeping of records reduced the flexibility of custom at the same time that the increasing pace of secular legislation, combined with religious reform and the extension of papal jurisdiction, started to cast doubt on its inherent validity. Finally, the academic study of law lifted the whole subject to a new intellectual plane: the relationships between law and custom, legislation and judgement, and between the different sorts of proof became matters for debate—and debate of a sort that threatened the old supremacy of unlearned, collective judgement.

How far all this affected the attitudes of laymen to law and politics, and in particular to collective decision and action, is not immediately obvious. To start with, just because the new jurisprudence was specialized, intellectual, and new, it did not permeate the lay world in the same way as the old

[1] See e.g. Duby, 'Institutions judiciaires' [380], 31–8 and *Société mâconnaise* [381], 575; Brunner, *Land und Herrschaft* [289], 180–96; Salvioli, *Storia della procedura* [672], ii. 1–22, 62-3.

had done. New procedures seeped down from the grander courts where professional lawyers practised to the humbler ones where they were rare, but that need not imply that the ideas which may have lain behind the procedures—and which some of the professionals themselves did not appreciate—travelled as far or as fast.[2] Further, it is important to remember that even the intellectuals approached Roman law, just as they approached Aristotle's *Politics*, from the presuppositions of their own society, not of ours. Some of their ideas look much less innovatory if they are seen in their contemporary context rather than as the first approximations to modern doctrines.[3] The real impact of their work came not from any revolutionary principles but from the clarity of the distinctions that emerged from their debates and the stimulus that such distinctions gave to further argument. First in Italy, then among Roman and canon lawyers elsewhere, and then more widely still, Roman concepts and methods helped to bring a new tone of critical analysis to the discussion of all sorts of legal problems.[4] Paradoxically, their effect could be far-reaching even when they were applied without understanding to situations which they did not really fit: according to Milsom's persuasive interpretation the later English common-law distinction between seisin and right, with all its consequences for what came to be called the 'forms of action', may derive, not from deliberate royal policy, but from Roman analogies afterwards perceived and immortalized by the author of 'Glanvill'.[5] In the same way, though the professionalization of law hindered the passage of the more esoteric new ideas to a wider lay public, the sharpness of a few Roman-law tags carried them through the barrier

---

[2] Gouron, 'La Science juridique' [446]; Coing, 'Römisches Recht' [333]; van Caenegem, 'Le Droit romain' [294].

[3] See pp. 319-29.

[4] Leicht, *Scritti vari* [533], ii (1), 65-78; Vaccari, 'Diritto Longobardo' [721]; Didier, 'Droit romain' [362]; Kuttner, *Harmony from Dissonance* [518]; works cited in n. 2 and other fascicules of *Ius Romani Medii Aevi*; Trusen, 'Zur Urkundenlehre' [717]; Thorne, introduction to Bracton, *De Legibus* [13], i, p. xxxiii; Acher, 'Le Droit savant' [213]; Chénon, *Droit Français* [317], i. 494-6; for different views of the importance of Roman influence: van Caenegem, 'State, Society, and Private Law' [297] and Kantorowicz, 'Kingship' [495].

[5] Milsom, *Legal Framework* [589], 36-41, 65-6, 165, 171, 176-86; *Glanvill* [37], 148.

on their own. Seen against the background of collective government in the tenth and eleventh centuries, the principle that what touches all should be approved by all (*quod omnes similiter tangit ab omnibus comprobetur*[6]) looks platitudinous, but in thirteenth-century conditions its succinctness may have helped to press the message home both to subjects summoned to agree to taxes and to rulers who, having first used the phrase as a platitude, may have begun to wish that they had never heard of it.[7]

Some of the changes in legal practice which took place may have come as much, or more, from the demand of governments for practical help from lawyers as from the supply of new thought and theory as such. The interplay of ideas and practice is inevitably complex, but there can be no doubt that governmental needs stimulated new legal and political thinking. Kings employed lawyers to argue their need of men and money, and clerks to record the results. Among the products of literacy, lists and accounts, and the habits of mind they engendered, had a more immediate impact on lay society than did new ideas about the nature of the state or of law.[8] An example of the way in which structures were changed more because of the logic of politics than because of the logic of explicit argument is the system of appeals, with all that it implies about the hierarchy of jurisdiction and authority. The church's need for correctness and uniformity in its law produced an articulated system of appeals very early. Then royal courts began to hear cases from the local secular courts too: it was a good method of exercising control. The lay systems look, however, as if they followed the canon-law pattern without any rethinking of the ideas about the source of law which were implied in collective judgements but were implicitly denied by appeals to higher authority. As a result the theory was maintained that appeals to royal courts were only permissible when there had been a default of justice lower down, but was often breached in practice. On this subject canon law offered a good system

---

[6] *Corpus Iuris Civilis* [19], ii. 231 (*Codex*, v. 59. 5).

[7] Below, p. 327.

[8] Clanchy, *From Memory to Written Record* [327]; cf. Goody, *Domestication of the Savage Mind* [791].

to be copied, not a new idea in jurisprudence to be thought about. The ecclesiastical hierarchy may also have helped lawyers towards the idea of a 'feudal hierarchy' of jurisdictions: the belief that the extension of royal jurisdictions in thirteenth-century France eliminated an earlier 'feudal hierarchy' of justice looks like a piece of later rationalization.[9] The task of professional and academic lawyers was to justify and explain the law as they found it or as their clients wanted it to be, not to investigate the real past or understand its different values.

Custom and law

The combination of much more argument on particular subjects with little change of large principles shows well in the discussions of custom. Because church reform and papal policy were so often frustrated by local customs, the canonists were at pains to distinguish custom on the one hand from right and law on the other.[10] Yet their attack on custom was very half-hearted, for they only questioned its validity when it contradicted the church's doctrines or needs. The Romanists questioned it even less,[11] so that, though in theory and practice custom by the thirteenth century needed to be formally proved and recorded so as to be safe from attack, it still formed the bedrock of all law.[12] To Aquinas human law must be not only right and just but also consonant with custom,[13] while less subtle and systematic writers still barely distinguished the categories at all. In practice, moreover, although formal legislation nibbled at custom from all sides, governmental activity in some ways strengthened it and its collectivist implications: not only were particular sets of customs now more often preserved by written record, but the first line of defence against any threat of oppression was

---

[9] Devailly, *Berry* [358], 451, 464. Below, p. 232.

[10] Le Bras, *Droit de l'église* [527], vii. 205-19, 533-57; Winterswyl, 'Neue Recht' [756].

[11] Calasso, *Glossatori* [299], 94-7.

[12] Calasso, *Medio evo* [300], 410-14; Chénon, *Droit français* [317], i. 489-92; Krause, 'Gewohnheitsrecht' [511].

[13] *Summa* [75], Ia IIae, q. 97; cf. Gratian, *Decretum* [38], pt. 1, dist. 1, dist. 4 after c. 3: following Isidore of Seville and Ivo of Chartres.

normally an appeal to custom, while the normal way to prove custom was to have it stated by a body of people who represented the community within which it applied.[14]

As governments became more effective, and in particular as they extended their control over properly constituted law-courts, so the major units of custom tended to be assimilated to the areas under particular governments. By the later twelfth century the law practised in the royal courts of England was being discussed as a single whole, and by the thirteenth century French lawyers (though not, oddly enough, English ones) were begining to speak in terms of a 'common law' of their whole kingdom.[15] Germans sometimes thought of Saxon, Swabian, and other provincial laws as separate, but sometimes of German law as one general body.[16] These developments were reflected in writings by canonists, who, in recognizing the traditional diversity of law, seem to have acknowledged the peculiar importance of kingdoms. Where the effective unit of government was a county, duchy, or town, it was seen in much the same way: every government was supposed to respect the customs of its subjects, who formed a *populus* to which the whole conglomerate of custom belonged. Their own custom was one of the most frequently cited marks of a people which claimed some sort of autonomy.[17] When these ideas came to be stated explicitly their formulation owed much to Aristotle, whose *Politics* stimulated academic political thinking in the thirteenth century much as Roman law had stimulated legal thinking in the twelfth. Nevertheless, the common thirteenth-century assumption that political autonomy was linked with peculiarity of custom was not derived from Aristotle. Like the analysis of the different kinds of law which Aquinas attached to his Aristotelian discussion of the state, it looks much more like the embodiment, face to face, of values that at an earlier

[14] Pertile, *Diritto italiano* [622], i. 390 n; Chénon, *Droit française* [317], i. 496-500; below, p. 130.

[15] Petot, 'Droit commun' [624]; Acher, 'Droit savant' [213], 168; Pollock and Maitland, *Eng. Law* [628], i. 175-6.

[16] Above, p. 18, n. 20; *Deutschenspiegel* [23], 75, 78, 110, 112; below, p. 292.

[17] Mochi-Onory, *Fonti canonistiche* [591], 82-139; below, pp. 256-61.

period can only be seen reflected darkly in the glass of traditional practices.[18]

The divergence of custom between kingdoms meanwhile became more noticeable in practice as the courts in different jurisdictions solved legal problems in different ways and as their respective legal professions developed their own mystiques and monopolies. The idea of separate but equally valid legal systems coexisting together had already become familiar from the development of canon and Roman law. In 1156-60 the Pisans codified their law in two divisions, one using written law (though it was at first more Lombard than Roman) and the other using customary law (*usus*).[19] North of the Alps, where Roman law did not take over secular courts, it seems to have preserved its position in lawyers' minds as a reserve of universally valid norms—all the more valid, no doubt, for being safely remote. The authors of 'Glanvill' and 'Bracton' seem to have thought of it as a kind of ideal type of law: it was presumably to it (and possibly canon law as well) that they referred by implication when they said that English law counted as law though it was unwritten.[20] If 'Bracton' really believed that England was the only country using customary law, and if his knowledge is representative of that of his professional colleagues, then English lawyers were remarkably ignorant of what went on over the Channel. The system of original writs had set English law on its insular course and Roman law would increasingly be seen as a dangerous threat to English law and lawyers. Suspicions may have been deepened at the end of the thirteenth century when some Scottish lawyers envisaged Roman law as an approximation to 'the natural law by which kings reign'.[21]

'Feudal law', which is sometimes referred to as if it was a distinct legal system, was not yet that, but it was becoming a distinct subject of study—the study of what one might call the law of property, or perhaps the law of free or noble

[18] Above, p. 19.

[19] Classen, 'Kodifikation' [331].

[20] *Glanvill* [37], 2; Bracton, *De Legibus* [13], ii. 19; cf. Pollock and Maitland, *Eng. Law* [628], i. 188. For *ius scriptum* apparently meaning canon law: Matthew Paris, *Chron. Majora* [52], ii. 593.

[21] Stones and Simpson, *Edward I and Scotland* [192], ii. 167, 205.

property. The composite treatise of the twelfth century which became known as the *Libri Feudorum* or *Consuetudines Feudorum* was widely copied and commented upon.[22] In the 1220s Eike von Repgow divided his work on Saxon law into two sections: *lantrechte*, which seems to cover the general customary law of the province, and *lenrechte*, which covers the customs of noble or military tenure.[23] 'Feudal law' in this sense flourished because the law concerning the property of rich men was profitable to lawyers. Another branch of law which was becoming more distinct was criminal law. That was profitable in a different way—not to professional advisers and advocates, but to those with jurisdiction. Its content and procedures remained relatively simple, but rivalry between jurisdictions, and the pressure of governments upon all subordinate jurisdictions, stimulated more systematic classification of types of criminal jurisdiction.

Whatever the classification of laws and the clarification of legal concepts, and whatever the varying jurisdictions under which people lived, everyone, lawyers and non-lawyers alike, still apparently believed that all law must conform to justice, that reconciliation was better than conflict, that wise and honourable men should be able to harmonize apparently conflicting interests, and that justice should therefore be attainable. Hence their continued recourse to arbitration. Arbitrations were now distinguishable from law-suits but they were not replaced by them. Cases were referred from courts to arbitrators and all sorts of political disputes were submitted to arbitration as if they were equally susceptible of solution.[24] The old values associated with the old traditions of customary law had not been superseded.

Legislation: kings and the law

The ruler's right to legislate and his relationship to law in general began to emerge into a slightly clearer light at this

[22] Lehmann, *Langobardische Lehnrecht* [48]; Kelley, 'De Origine Feudorum' [501].

[23] *Sachsenspiegel* [25]; cf. Erler and Kauffmann, *Handwörterbuch* [395], 1527-35, 1995-2001.

[24] *Curia Regis Rolls* [109], xv, index *sub* arbitration; below, pp. 212, 272; Artonne, *Le Mouvement de 1314* [224], 21-3.

time, as some of the problems of the old system of consultative government began to be recognized and discussed. As Frederick Barbarossa said to the Romans in 1155, according to the speech put into his mouth by Otto of Freising: 'I forbear to mention that it is for the prince to prescribe laws for the people, not the people for the prince.'[25] The new emphasis on the ruler's authority is generally associated with the study of Roman law: Ulpian's references to the prince as *legibus solutus* and to his will having the force of law were just the sort of tags that were suited to attract attention to new ideas.[26] In fact, however, Roman lawyers everywhere seem to have continued to interpret Ulpian's remarks in an entirely traditional way, making it clear that any prince was morally bound to conform to the principles of the law, that he still had to consult before expressing his will, and that his powers belonged to him as the supreme representative of his community.[27] The same goes for other writers who discussed law in general terms, from John of Salisbury, through John of Ibelin, 'Bracton', and Beaumanoir, to Aquinas and the Aristotelian writers of the thirteenth century.[28]

The real threat to traditions of collective legislation and the supremacy of law came less from theory than from the changing needs of government. Not only did kings often need to override custom in order to raise taxes and armies, but, as population grew, so government had to become more complex, and more laws and more enforcement were required. Legislation therefore became more frequent and more recognizable as such.[29] Though not all these pressures applied to ecclesiastical government, some of them did, and it was subject to extra pressures of its own. An essential condition for the

[25] *Gesta Friderici* [58], 138.

[26] *Corpus Iuris Civilis* [19], 1. 34, 35 (*Digest*, I. iii. 31, iv. 1).

[27] Carlyle, 'Relation of Roman Law' [308]; Calasso, *Glossatori* [299]; Lewis, 'King above Law' [548].

[28] John of Salisbury, *Policraticus* [46], i. 237-9, 241, 290-1 (iv. 2-3; v. 4); *Rec. Hist. Croisades: Lois* [63], i. 22-6; Bracton, *De Legibus* [13], ii. 19, 21, 305-6; Beaumanoir, *Coutumes* [61], §§ 1043, 1512, 1515; Aquinas, *Summa* [75], Ia IIae, q. 97, ad 3. Other writers are conveniently surveyed, with quotations, in Carlyle, *Med. Pol. Theory* [309], v. Despite Ullmann, *Principles of Government* [720], 205, Beaumanoir specifically mentions the need for *grant conseil* in § 1515; he is certainly no less clear on the point than 'Bracton'.

[29] Wolf, 'Gesetzgebung' [758], 520-7, and 'Forschungsaufgaben einer europäischen Gesetzgebungsgeschichte' [759].

pope's control of the church and its doctrine was that his power to bind and loose should be recognized and made effective. Despite the theoretical recognition of general councils, and despite a wide range of local variation and local autonomy, legislation in a reforming church had to come from above.[30] It would be reasonable to look for influence from the new model of ecclesiastical legislation on lay attitudes to the subject, but it is surprisingly hard to find. The ideas that churchmen developed about the revocability of papal grants and the delegation of authority from above do seem to have had wider influence,[31] but they did not affect the more serious issue of the ruler's right to legislate. The popes themselves do not seem to have attempted to govern their lay subjects in Italy with the same sort of authority as they governed the church. Though the people of Ravenna had occasion to remind a papal legate in 1294 that he could not legislate for laymen in temporal matters without their consent, there seems to be no evidence that any thirteenth-century pope seriously thought that he could or deliberately tried to do so.[32]

A few years after Frederick I told the Romans—or forbore to tell them—that he had the right to prescribe laws for his subjects, Roman lawyers at Roncaglia told him that all jurisdiction derived from the emperor and that as the living law he could do what he wanted. This suggests both that he and they were thinking in absolutist terms and that the inspiration came from Roman law.[33] Neither suggestion should be taken too literally. The lawyers' actual advice about the reclaiming of imperial rights in Italy was apparently based on law, not on claims to be able to override it, and their more extravagant remarks may have been intended, and received, as flattering hyperbole. Frederick's own predecessor over a hundred years before had made disrespectful remarks about the law without benefit—presumably—of Roman ideas of absolutism: the temptations of monarchy

[30] Le Bras, *Droit de l'église* [527], vii. 133-51, 433-4; Chodorow, *Christian Political Theory* [321], 133-53.
[31] Krause, 'Dauer und Vergänglichkeit' [510], 234-8.
[32] Waley, *Papal State* [735], 118-19, and 110-20, 304-6; cf. Martène, *Thesaurus* [151], ii, col. 445.
[33] Benson, 'Political *Renovatio*' [244]; cf. below, p. 172.

were not new. Frederick, however, though understandably annoyed with what would seem to him usurpation of royal rights, does not seem to have succumbed very far to the particular temptation of making and breaking law at will, let alone to thinking that he had the right to do so. At Roncaglia he legislated after due consultation and, apparently, after getting sufficient, if grudging, consent. Obvious as the problem of legislative authority may seem to us, therefore, it does not seem to have arisen either for him or for most kings of the twelfth and thirteenth centuries. Imperial legislation is not recorded as running into difficulties on this ground and nor is that of the kings of France. Beaumanoir, though he clearly thought that the king would and should consult, does not seem to have considered the point controversial. What increasingly aroused opposition in France was not legislation but taxation, and arguments about taxation did not need to go to the heart of the issue of the king's control of law or his subjection to law.[34] Difficult decisions of principle are seldom made before practical controversies make them necessary, and in most thirteenth-century kingdoms new laws were passed with enough consultation, and were sufficiently uncontroversial in content, for the relative contribution of king and community to remain undecided. So long as the king's exclusive right to make law was not at issue his more general duty to obey it could be hopefully assumed, however often individual kings might break or evade it in practice. Potentially shocking and worrying texts from Roman law were therefore glossed in an anodyne way and did no harm.

There was, however, one kingdom which peculiar circumstances made susceptible to Ulpian's virus. That was England. After Magna Carta and its revocation the issue of exclusively royal or exclusively baronial legislation was in the air, and Henry III's difficult relations with his subjects kept it there. Henry's claims to interpret and revoke charters and to choose his own servants[35] need not imply a considered claim to be absolutely above the law but we have other evidence that such a claim was under consideration. In 1235 Henry accused the bishop of Winchester of having made him deviate from

[34] Below, pp. 312-15.
[35] Clanchy, 'Did Henry III have a Policy?' [324].

justice, to the peril of his soul, by telling him that he should be able to deal with his subjects according to his will. In 1256 he referred in a similarly shocked tone to his belief that affairs in Castile were managed according to the sole will of the king.[36] In 1258 Henry's own barons accused his half-brothers of whispering to him damnably that a prince was not subject to laws, and a few years later the Song of Lewes accused his son Edward of thinking that whatever he wanted was lawful.[37] It must be noted that all these references were disapproving: we have no first-hand evidence that either Henry or Edward or even the bishop of Winchester really believed that kings ought to be absolute, though they may have done. In practice Henry's quarrels with his barons seem to have been conducted largely within the framework of traditional principles of subjection to law. There was enough room for disagreement there to make the theory of absolutism almost irrelevant.[38] Nevertheless the undoubted fact that people in England could envisage its dangers may explain the cautious ambiguities of the authors of 'Bracton' about the king's relationship with the law, as contrasted with Beaumanoir's unconcern. During Edward I's own reign the theoretical issue does not seem to have been revived. His troubles, like those of contemporary French kings, concerned taxation and military service rather than law-making, and little discussion of absolutism seems to be recorded.

Another place where the problem was confronted, though in a rather different way, was the Frankish kingdom of Jerusalem. Although outside the scope of this book it is relevant because it so closely mirrored western values, and because conflict between king and barons came to a head there while the emperor Frederick II was king. The arguments which upset the traditional balance between royal authority and the rights of subjects to be consulted were in this case those of the subjects, not the king, but their effect may well have been to make Frederick pay more attention to the attractions of absolutism.[39] It is indeed often claimed that

[36] *Royal Letters* [187], i. 468; *Close Rolls* [105], *1254-6*, 389-91. I owe these references to Dr D. Carpenter.

[37] *Annales Mon.* [7], i. 463; *Song of Lewes* [71], ll. 440-4.

[38] Below, pp. 271-2.

[39] Riley-Smith, *Feudal Nobility* [660], 137-44, 159-84.

Frederick's government of Sicily was absolute both in practice and in principle. The practice is doubtful so far as legislation is concerned, for some of Frederick's constitutions or assises were certainly issued at large assemblies and they all may have been.[40] That the initiative in making them came from above and that the consultation may have been formal was not exceptional and would not have imperilled their validity in thirteenth-century terms so long as their content seemed just. The account in the preamble to the Constitutions of Melfi of the transfer of law-making from the *quirites* of ancient Rome to the emperor, however, shows that Frederick and his advisers undoubtedly appreciated the crucial issue of absolutist legislation, that they associated it with Rome, and that they approved of it. In spite of this, and of the apparently conventional ideas of Frederick's subjects about politics, there seem to have been no repercussions: perhaps Sicilian magnates did not notice the dangers or thought they could not do much to avert them.[41] At any rate Frederick does not seem either to have made comparable claims in Germany or the rest of Italy or to have invaded his Sicilian subjects' rights much more than did contemporary kings who never claimed to be absolute. It was not absolutism for which he was criticized and condemned in his lifetime.

It can be no accident that the two western kingdoms (apart perhaps from those of Spain) where absolutist theories were explicitly mentioned were England and Sicily, which both had exceptionally powerful governments. Random acts of arbitrariness were a commonplace, but people would be most likely to consider the possibilities or the dangers of theoretical absolutism where the government had some hope of controlling the working of the law in practice. That condition may have been fulfilled both in England and in Sicily, but only in England was there the right combination of a powerful government which lacked the confidence of its subjects to force the issue momentarily into the open. Even then it was of marginal importance, for tradition was strong.

---

[40] Calisse, *Storia del Parlamento* [102], 298-304; cf. Ménager, 'Législation' [585], 483-5.

[41] Conrad, *Konstitutionen* [107], 44-6 (I. 31). For Sicilian political ideas, below, p. 300.

It is ironic, in view of the traditional interpretation of English history, that so far as the relationship between king and law in England was exceptional among other thirteenth-century kingdoms it was not because of English 'constitutionalism'. The resistance of people in England to any suggestion of absolutism was entirely normal and traditional. What was unusual was that absolutism should have seemed a dangerous possibility.

Meanwhile the boundary between legislation and judgement everywhere continued in practice to be vague and the power to legislate was still diffused. Local custom was now more liable to be overruled, while the principle that it could be overruled was implied in the recognition of kingdoms as the supreme secular communities and of royal courts as the supreme secular courts of appeal. In practice, however, subordinate communities continued to maintain and adapt their respective customs as a matter of course, with little reference to higher authority. Also taken as a matter of course were the means of consultation: rules about the proper constitution of assemblies, about those who should attend, and about how representatives should be chosen, remained very vague.[42] New laws at any level did not derive their validity from the identity of the individuals who happened to be present when they were promulgated: despite all the growing difficulties of reconciling theory with practice, they were valid because they became part of the just law and custom of the community.

Collective judgement

The practice of collective judgement that had lain at the heart of tenth- and eleventh-century law underwent some erosion in succeeding centuries. Wherever kings were powerful and professional lawyers were active the trend was away from it, and in the Roman and canon-law systems it was greatly reduced. Canon law was particularly influential because of its universality. Whereas in the eleventh century pleas between abbeys might be decided in much the same way as pleas between laymen, cases which came before the

[42] See pp. 144–5, 185–93, 302–19.

ecclesiastical courts of the classic age of canon law were
decided by judges who were appointed by bishop or pope,
and who were beginning to adapt the old forms of collective judgement to something more like the procedure
of witness laid down in the approved texts of Roman and
canon law.[43]

Where Roman law itself was used directly in secular courts
the trend towards judgement by a single presiding judge,
which had already been discernible before 1100, now became
dominant. Yet even in Italy not all elements of the old system
disappeared. Though the *consiliarii* or assessors whom judges
might consult were themselves to be *jurisperiti*, and though
some Italian legal historians deny that they represent any
'Germanic' principle,[44] their appointment may at first have
seemed particularly natural to those who were familiar with
the practices of traditional, unlearned law. Even now, when
learned and traditional systems began to diverge, the two
often coexisted side by side, as they did at Pisa from the mid
twelfth century. There the court which used written law had
three trained lawyers as judges, while the court which followed
customary law (and seems to have dealt particularly with
mercantile and maritime cases) had five judges of whom only
one was *jurisperitus*. A third court, which heard appeals from
both the others, had five judges (*cognitores*) of whom two
were *jurisperiti*. All the judges were appointed annually by
the consuls of the year. The whole arrangement seems to
subsume some of the old traditions of collective, representative
judgement.[45] Where the old traditions died, this cannot always
be attributed to direct, intellectual conversion to the principles
of pure Roman law. Another pressure came from the danger
of faction in the Italian cities and from the efforts to defeat
it by importing officials from outside. Wherever a *podestà*
came in, bringing his own train of subordinate judges, that
encouraged an acceptance of judgement by a neutral outsider

---

[43] Donahue, 'Proof by Witnesses' [371]; Le Bras, *Droit de l'église* [527], vii.
25-6, 167-85; Trusen, 'Urkundenlehre' [717], 197-8.

[44] Checchini, 'I "Consiliarii"' [316]; cf. Leicht, *Scritti vari* [533], ii (2),
24-7; Marongiu, 'Legislatori e giudici' [571].

[45] Classen, 'Kodifikation' [331]: the distinction here is between written law
(Roman and Lombard) on one side and custom on the other, not between Roman
and 'Germanic'.

which was foreign to the old traditions and may have paved the way to new ones associated with Roman law.

Meanwhile survivals of the old sort of judgement can be noticed here and there all over Italy, like judgement by peers in cases about landed property (*feuda*), and public accusations by *camparii* chosen from among the worthy landowners in the countryside or by lawful men elected by the whole community in towns.[46] In Sicily, where Frederick II reserved cases concerning counts, barons, and other military men (*ceteris militaribus viris*) to his own court, the judgements on them were to be made by the counts and barons themselves.[47] Fourteenth- and fifteenth-century urban statutes which replaced lay by learned judges for various purposes thereby suggest that some cases had remained under collective judgement until then.[48] Above all, jurisdiction in disputes among merchants and craftsmen was generally left, in Italy as elsewhere, to mercantile courts under special consuls or to the trade and craft organizations.[49] These courts used customary law and discouraged the employment of professional lawyers, so that learned law probably did not begin to impinge on them until relatively late. Occasional references in civic statutes, mostly from after 1300, show that the presidents of these tribunals were sometimes elected by the merchants themselves and that they generally delivered the more important judgements only after consultation with representative merchants. A great deal of their work—as in other Italian courts—was of the nature of what a more formal jurisprudence would call arbitration.[50] Thus, even while the old ideas of communal law, justice, and judgement may have become less perspicuous in the higher civic courts of Italy, they were preserved in those tribunals which were the most familiar of all to the ordinary citizen.

In northern Europe, where Roman forms were not yet

[46] *Liber Consuetudinum Mediolani* [89], p. 123; Leicht, *Scritti vari* [533], ii (2), 5-73; Salvioli, *Storia della procedura* [672], i. 167, 357-61, ii. 9-10, 12; Caggese, *Classi e comuni rurali* [298], i. 393-4.

[47] Conrad, *Konstitutionen* [107], 70-2 (Const. Melfi, I. 47).

[48] Lattes, *Diritto consuetudinario* [525], 84-6, 88.

[49] The twelfth-century Pisan court of customary law seems to be an exception to this, since it also dealt with other matters.

[50] Salvioli, *Storia della procedura* [672], ii. 95-102; Pertile, *Storia del diritto italiano* [622], vi (1), 169-70.

applied outside the ecclesiastical courts, collective judgement remained widespread until after 1300. In France the king's extension of his authority brought more people to attend his court and join in its judgements. In 1185 Robert of Boves did homage to Philip Augustus and then said to the count of Flanders, whom he hated: 'Hitherto, my lord count, I have been your man, but now, God willing, I have been made your equal and have to judge with you in the court of the lord king.'[51] It may have been this development which first prompted the greatest lords of the kingdom to describe themselves as peers of France and demand to be judged only by each other. They could have got the idea both from Carolingian legends of the twelve peers of France and from the bodies of peers already established in some provincial courts of north France.[52] On occasion during the thirteenth century those who were recognized as peers of France succeeded in being allowed to deliberate apart, but their exclusive position was never formally recognized.[53] What was recognized in principle in the royal court was that judgements were made by some sort of general consensus, even if (irrespective of the claim of the peers) the consensus was coming to be dominated more and more by the king's own authority and by the professional judges, lawyers, and officials who represented his interests.[54] The same traditional principle was observed in provincial and urban courts, though wherever a royal official presided the danger of his domination seems to have been felt.[55] According to Beaumanoir there were some places— not, apparently, within his direct knowledge[56]—where the bailiff rather than the holders of fees gave the judgements, but even there the bailiff still ought to take advice from the most wise. As for disagreements, Beaumanoir found it hard to decide what should be done in the evil case of disagreement between peers. He was prepared for majority verdicts

[51] Gislebert de Mons, *Chronique* [36], 185.

[52] Feuchère, 'Pairs de principauté' [414]; above, p. 29.

[53] 'Judgement by peers' could be referred to apparently in its more general sense in relation to the king's court as to other courts: Guillaume de Nangis in *Rec. Hist. de France* [64], xx. 398; cf. *Actes du parlement* [97], i, p. ccciii.

[54] Sautel-Boulet, 'Le Rôle juridictionnel' [676]; Chénon, *Droit français* [317], 696 n.; *Les Olim* [90], ii. 660–1.

[55] See pp. 285–8, for the grievances of 1314–15.

[56] *Coutumes de Beauvaisis* [61], § 24, 1883.

but uncertain between the weight of numbers and wisdom, and whether it would be better to secure agreements by delay, by imprisonment of those who could not make up their minds, or by asking for advice from a higher court.[57]

In England, although the system of writs and eyres enshrined a form of collective judgements in the civil assises and juries and in the collective accusations of criminals by grand juries, the swift development of royal jurisdiction brought a correspondingly acute threat to more traditional collective judgements. In 1215, like the French charters of a hundred years later, Magna Carta tried to restrict the power of royal justices and officials to judge unilaterally. It required the king to proceed against his subjects only by judgement of peers or the law of the land and to have financial penalties assessed by the neighbours of the accused, or in the case of earls and barons (whose neighbours would not be their equals and who would be tried for serious offences in the king's court) by their peers. These provisions were repeated in 1225 to become part of the permanent law of the kingdom,[58] but they were difficult to enforce, especially perhaps in respect of great men in conflict with the king. In 1233, when the other bishops reproached Henry III for exiling barons and nobles without any judgement by their peers, the bishop of Winchester retorted that there were no peers in England as there were in France. In England the king could choose whom he liked as his justices and it was they, *mediante judicio*, who exiled and condemned people.[59] The remark leaves little doubt that the significance of 'peerage' in both France and England was judicial, and that what the judgement of peers was primarily designed to prevent was autocratic judgement by kings and their officials and judges. Taken with Henry's condemnation of the bishop of Winchester a couple of years later for his wicked teaching about kings and the law, it confirms the erosion of collective judgement implied in Magna Carta. As Henry's volte-face also shows, however, royal policy was not consistently maintained.

[57] Ibid. §§ 1860, 1862-3 (and, in general, §§ 23-4, 26, 31, 36, 42, 44-5, 1507, 1883, 1888, 1898–1903, 1911). Cf. *Les Olim* [90], ii, p. 100 (9).

[58] Holt, *Magna Carta* [475], 322, 327 (1215, c. 20–22, 39), 353, 355 (1225, c. 14, 29).

[59] Roger of Wendover, *Flores Hist.* [70], ii. 58.

Though great men who were tried in the king's court were always liable to arbitrary treatment neither Henry nor his successors managed to destroy the principle that they ought to be tried by their peers. The protection that others received from the contemporary development of the criminal trial jury in lesser courts would have made the systematic denial to magnates of something comparable too anomalous. Thereafter, throughout the middle ages, criminal juries remained fairly independent of judges, while the survival of traditional collective judgements by the whole body of suitors in the county courts, and the amount of legal expertise which was to be found among the suitors there, combined to preserve the old habits and norms.[60] Decisions in county courts were still reached by the same compromises between consensus and majority voting as they probably always had been and as they seem to have been, to judge from Beaumanoir, in the comparable courts of France.[61] Juries, which seem to have worked at first in rather the same way, were, meanwhile, being increasingly forced into unanimity.[62]

In Germany collective judgements continued to be made in the traditional way in both royal and lesser courts.[63] Frederick I acted against Henry the Lion in 1179-80 with the agreement of his great men, and it seems highly probable that the 'just judgements according to the reasonable custom of their lands', which all those who held courts were to see done in them according to the Peace of Mainz in 1235, were to be made collectively.[64] The *Sachsenspiegel* allows majority verdicts among the neighbours who would judge in a property dispute, but Eike's slight concern with the matter suggests that he hoped or assumed that agreement would be possible on most issues.[65] By the fourteenth century the problem in Germany, unlike France or England, was no longer the softness of the law's nose in the king's iron hand. The decay of

[60] Green, 'Jury and Law of Homicide' [456], 489-91, 498-9; Palmer, *County Courts* [619].

[61] Below, pp. 246-8.

[62] Pollock and Maitland, *Eng. Law* [628], ii. 625-7 (though the reference to Bracton is not very convincing).

[63] Franklin, *Reichshofgericht* [425], ii. 127-9; Wohlgemuth, *Urkundenwesen des Reichshofgerichts* [757], 81, 83; Brunner, *Land und Herrschaft* [289], 425.

[64] *M.G.H. Const.* [160], i, no. 279, ii, no. 196, c. 4.

[65] *Sachsenspiegel* [25], i. 207 (III. 21 § 1).

royal authority was throwing the kingdom into rather the
same situation as France had been in three centuries before.
The remedies applied show how little fundamental ideas
about law and order had changed. Great men went to arbitration and made alliances to keep the peace. In Westphalia and
perhaps elsewhere free courts known as *Veme*, which were
set up to fill some of the jurisdictional gaps in the interests of
lesser people, seem to have used traditional procedures, with
judgements given by *Freischöffen*.[66] Many towns found
themselves without anyone to turn to outside for authoritative
judgements or legal opinions, and this probably explains the
emergence of what became known as *Oberhöfe* in the 'mother
towns'. These were not really courts so much as panels of
legal consultants, to whom problems could be referred from
the 'daughter towns' which followed the mother's customs.
The *Schöffen* of the mother towns, who comprised the *Oberhöfe*, thus found themselves converted from being representative judgement-finders in their own towns to being paid
expert advisers to people elsewhere.[67] These fourteenth-
century developments fall outside the scope of this book but,
however sketchily outlined, they suggest that the old traditions of justice and judgement were being changed more
because of varying political circumstances than because of
radical rethinking.

Everywhere, moreover, old customs survived most vigor-
ously in those courts where professional lawyers remained
rare—namely the humbler local courts and those which dealt
with commercial and craft disputes. Merchant law seems to
be better recorded in England than elsewhere. Cases in the
fair court of St. Ives in the thirteenth century were judged by
the merchants themselves: that is to say, in the old indeterminate way the assembled merchants either gave a definitive
judgement themselves or referred pleas to a sworn inquest.
Sometimes cases were respited until there should be a fuller
attendance of merchants.[68] Mercantile pleas which are
recorded in various English courts in the later middle ages
follow the same lines and, to judge from the apparently very

---

[66] Du Boulay, 'Law Enforcement' [374].
[67] Dawson, *Oracles of the Law* [352], 158-76.
[68] *Cases in Law Merchant* [184], ii. 39, 42, 44-5, 50, 52, 86, 87-8.

sparse records, there seems to be no reason to doubt that elsewhere much the same body of custom, and much the same procedures, were being followed.[69] In the kingdom of Jerusalem, the melting-pot of western custom, the *jurés* who gave the judgement in the court of the Chain and the court of the Funda or market were drawn from the seafarers and merchants who composed the one and the Syrian and Frankish suitors of the other.[70]

Not only in towns but in rural communities grants of privileges quite often included the right of people in the local community to judge themselves or to appoint their own judges. The usual emphasis on the novelty of such a right and its origin in special grants is, however, mistaken. It was normal in the English countryside, where charters of liberties are more or less unknown. During the later thirteenth century it came there to assume the characteristic form of the manorial jury of presentment and the inquest. The first was clearly derived from current practice in the higher English courts, but manorial juries were a replacement not for the single judgement of the steward but for the judgement of the whole court. In practice, of course, presidents of peasant courts everywhere, as of other courts, could and did take some decisions on their own, and peasants may have been particularly vulnerable to bullying, especially where they had not got their customs recorded. All the same, the evidence that the hard-edged categories of academic law had as yet deprived them of all their traditional rights in custom and law is more assumed than solid. Freedom and unfreedom were still hard to define and it was even harder to apply any definitions consistently to particular cases.[71] In that situation the less free profited from norms and values obtaining in the rest of society. In the kingdom of Jerusalem even the Syrians had their own court, under their *reis* with *jurés* who decided the pleas before him.[72] Collective judgement was under threat

---

[69] *London P. & M. Rolls* [195], *1381-1412*, pp. xxi-xxix; Morel, *Juridictions commerciales* [595] summarizes material from France and Germany.

[70] *Rec. Hist. Croisades: Lois* [63], ii, pp. 44, 45, 171; Prawer, *Latin Kingdom* [636], 152-5.

[71] Below, pp. 129, 141-3; Wunder, 'Serfdom' [766]; Bak, 'Serfs and Serfdom' [229].

[72] *Rec. Hist. Croisades: Lois* [63], i, p. 26; ii, p. 171; Prawer, *Latin Kingdom*

everywhere that governments were powerful or professional lawyers were assuming control of the law, but it was still cherished. As the citizens of London pointed out to royal justices in the thirteenth century, in much the same terms as Beaumanoir used and with the tone of those stating a well-known truth: 'And besides, it is the lord's court, not the lord, who ought to make the judgement.'[73]

Collective action at law: the idea of a corporation

The aspect of new legal ideas which is often supposed to have had most impact of all on lay politics in the twelfth and thirteenth centuries is the derivation from Roman law of the idea of groups with the legal capacity of individuals—what modern Roman law calls legal persons and English common law calls corporations. It seems to be supposed both that this enabled collective groups to achieve greater unity and power and that it enabled rulers to repress collective action by forbidding some groups to enjoy corporate status. There are various difficulties in this interpretation. Collective activity and governmental repression were matters of politics, not of legal conceptualization: long before academic lawyers had started to get interested in what Roman law texts said about *collegia* and *universitates* collective groups had been acting without legal impediment both to coerce their own members and to maintain themselves against outsiders, while kings had rewarded or punished them without legal inhibition. Moreover the Roman law texts did not actually define *collegia*, for the Romans themselves, according to one recent historian of the subject, did not have any clear concept of what their modern successors call legal personality.[74] The chief reason for the persistence of the belief that corporation theories developed in the thirteenth century seems to be the assumption that there is now a single, coherent, and self-evident concept of a corporate body, and that lawyers then were trying to find it. When Innocent IV, for instance, is found making a remark which sounds more or less compatible with modern

[636], 152-5.

[73] *Munimenta Gild. Lond.* [175], i. 66; *Coutumes de Beauvaisis* [61], § 1883.
[74] Orestano, *Problema delle persone giuridiche* [611].

ideas, he is applauded as if he were 'getting warm' in a game of Hunt the Concept. But the idea of Hunt the Thimble only makes sense if a single thimble is there all the time, if one is trying to find it, and if there is someone who has hidden it and knows where it is. Legal concepts are not like thimbles, to be found in inappropriate places. They exist only within appropriate legal systems. The concept of a legal corporation or legal personality can exist only within a legal system in which there are things which an individual or a corporate group can do and suffer at law which an unincorporated group cannot. It also needs circumstances in which people feel a fairly serious need to distinguish the responsibilities of individuals from those of the groups to which they belong.

Making these distinctions is not so much a matter of intellectual subtlety as of having the occasion to apply subtlety in a particular way. There seems little reason to believe that early medieval people could not distinguish, in a common-sense sort of way, between the rights of a church (or its saint) and the rights of its clergy as individuals, or between the rights of a town and its burgesses.[75] From the twelfth century philosophers and jurists began to skirmish around the difficult edges and implications of the common-sense distinction. Even then, however, the principles they tried to establish did not and could not amount to any definition of legal entities as such, any specifically legal concept of a corporate group. Innocent IV himself was chiefly concerned with the problem of collective sanctions and in particular with the justice or injustice of collective excommunication. At one point he alluded to the Roman-law dictum that *collegia* needed superior authority in order to exist, but since he allowed the authority to be tacit and did not say what they could do that other groups could not, that did not really amount to anything one could call a definition.[76] This vagueness was not the result of a failure to make a distinction which was always there but which people at the time failed to see or to express clearly. People did not 'confuse' the rights and responsibilities

[75] For their alleged incapacity to think in terms of public interest etc., above, p. 20, below, pp. 324-6.

[76] Rodriguez, 'Innocent IV and the Element of Fiction' [662]; cf. Gillet, *Personnalité juridique* [441], 61-168; Feenstra, 'L'Histoire des fondations' [410], 424-9.

of groups and their members: for most legal purposes the two were the same. Excommunication was a special case, for obvious theological reasons, but when it was a question of collective responsibility for debts or collective consent to taxes, although individuals sometimes tried to get out of their shares, there were no rules of law to assist them and no evidence that such rules were generally felt to be desirable. Beaumanoir suggests at one point that communes which go to law should record the names of those who have agreed or disagreed on the action, so that they will know who should share the loss or gain, but this may be testimony to his relative unfamiliarity with urban politics.[77] Generally speaking, the power of law-abiding collective groups to make their decisions in whatever way would best combine the needs of justice and order, and to bind their members to abide by such decisions, seems to have been assumed.[78] The more or less unlimited liability of members of groups for the group's wrong-doing or debts falls into the same pattern of collective assumptions. The hard cases which sometimes got into the records seem to have been dealt with on their merits—or on the merits of the political situation in the eyes of authority—without, apparently, prompting anyone to question in general terms either the obligation of an individual to the group to which he belonged or the possibility of distinguishing groups which could incur and impose obligations from those which could not.[79]

Throughout the thirteenth century collective nouns like *universitas, collegium, societas,* and *communia* (or *communio*), to which historians attach peculiar (though legally obscure) corporate force, were used so widely as to show that, even if there had been any concept of a corporate group as such, they did not express it.[80] *Universitas* might be used of a group which held property, had a seal, or litigated, but it could also be used in a phrase like *noverit universitas vestra quod nos . . .* at

[77] *Coutumes de Beauvaisis* [61], § 155; but cf. 155-7, 169, 171.

[78] For examples, below, chapters 5 and 6.

[79] *Placitorum Abbrev.* [169], 140; *Liber de Antiquis Legibus* [9], 80-2 and Williams, *Medieval London* [754], 233-7; *Les Olim* [90], i. 804-5; *Annales Mon.* [7], iii. 378-81; Dubled, 'Communauté de village' [372], esp. 22; Brown, 'Agency Law' [281]. On unlimited commercial liability: Sapori, 'Compagnie mercantili' [675].

[80] Below, index *sub* commune, *universitas*. Michaud-Quantin, *Universitas* [586] collects many examples.

the beginning of a deed addressed to *universis sancte matris ecclesie filiis*.[81] In parts of the north the word 'commune' acquired subversive connotations for a while as a result of some well-publicized urban revolts, so that a nervous English monk could say at the end of the twelfth century that a commune was 'a rising of the people, the fear of the kingdom, and the terror of the clergy',[82] but by then most rulers were both more robust and more practical in distinguishing different sorts of local group according to their usefulness or rebelliousness, rather than the words that were used to describe them. All sorts of group continued to act at law as they had always done. Henry III of England thought that villages could prosecute suits either through their lord or through three or four of their members.[83] When objections were raised it was because rulers feared subversion or saw practical profit to be made from quashing a particular association or making it pay for privileges. An obvious example is the quashing of communes in thirteenth-century France, which Petit-Dutaillis attributed to a new definition of the commune as *une notion juridique* which, he said, allowed royal lawyers to insist on royal authorization for the formation of a commune or, he implied, any other group with legal personality.[84] It is true that some communes were indeed quashed, that the existence of others was denied, and that the lack of a charter or other evidence of approval was sometimes alleged as a reason. But though better-educated lawyers may have liked to know that the Digest provided authority for this, the total lack of consistency in applying any such rule suggests that the rule itself was not the result of any conceptual advance.[85] The demand for royal warrant is more likely to be related to the contemporary acceptance of the idea that governmental functions in general could only be exercised by royal delegation. In this connection the English proceedings on Quo

---

[81] *Charters of H.T. Caen* [104], no. 18; cf. similar wording in 9, 14, 15, 17, and many other charters.

[82] Richard of Devizes, *Chronicle* [67], 49: for this reading, which has no warrant in the text for one of the words, see Reynolds, *Eng. Medieval Towns* [652], 104 n.

[83] Below, p. 140. On the canon-law view: Bader, *Studien* [228], ii. 415-16.

[84] *Les Communes* [623], 136-40.

[85] Below, pp. 168-83.

Warranto made no distinction between franchises held by individuals and those held by churches or towns.[86] In England, as in France and elsewhere, there was evidently no significant legal difference between collective and individual privileges. The difference was political. If the men of Lyon whose sealed proxy was rejected by the king's court in 1273 because they had *nec communia nec universitas nec aliquod collegium* had not been locked in conflict with their archbishop their collective activity would have been ignored. If they had been asked for a tax it would have been required. Petit-Dutaillis's use of this case to illustrate rules about the possession of seals derives from the understandable (and probably inevitable) propensity to interpret unexpected evidence in the light of familiar categories.[87]

Seals illustrate very well the danger of applying the distinctions of later jurisprudence retrospectively. There does not appear to have been any necessary connection at this period between having a seal and being what we should call a corporation, and no good reason, therefore, why the citizens of Oxford's lack of a common seal before 1191 should reflect their imperfectly corporate condition.[88] After all, groups which historians would consider indisputably corporate sometimes lacked seals too, like the Swiss nunnery which used its abbess's seal in 1259 because it had none of its own.[89] Not having a seal did not prevent Oxford from acting corporately. Use of someone else's seal shows no lack of legal capacity—just lack of a seal. About 1300 some Pisan prisoners of war in Genoa, appealing for release, used a seal inscribed *Sigillum universitatis carceratorum Pisanorum Ianue detentorum*.[90] One could hardly have a less incorporable body in modern terms than a group of prisoners. Such anomalies—

---

[86] Sutherland, *Quo Warranto* [709], 101-10, 115-16, 123, 159, and references there to *Plac. de Quo Warranto* [168]. This, however, at e.g. pp. 384, 385, 793 refers to claims to *have* a free borough (i.e. to have a privilege) not to *be* a borough (i.e. some sort of 'corporate' body). A distinction between individual and corporate liberties is, however, drawn, though obscurely, in *Eyre of Kent, 1313-14* [123], 130-1.

[87] *Les Olim* [90], i. 933; Petit-Dutaillis, *Communes* [623], 140.

[88] Davis, 'An Oxford Charter' [349].

[89] *Urkundenbuch Zürich* [120], no. 624.

[90] Manni, *Osservazioni sopra i sigilli* [149], 117-29 and sig. xii. For unfree peasants with a collective seal, below, p. 150.

as they appear to us—need to be noted alongside the cases which appear to foreshadow later principles.

By 1300 it is possible to look forward to guess at the origin of the later principles. Governments everywhere had become increasingly worried by the passage of land into the hands of the church and the loss of services that that could produce. Legislation to control or license grants was the result, and when that was extended to land held by guilds and chantries and even municipalities—all of which could shade into one another—then the need for rules and definitions appeared. Even so it seems to have taken a long time to work out the rules and even longer to produce any remotely consistent concept of a corporation to fit the rules.[91] As Maitland said: 'Now-a-days it is difficult to get the corporation out of our heads',[92] but if we do not, it is even more difficult to make sense of collective activities before 1300.

Conclusion

It seems impossible to avoid the conclusion that in 1300 many of the traditional practices of collective law and law-making survived in lay society and that the ideas that they reflected survived too. That is not to say that there were not plenty of new ideas around, particularly in the higher courts and the universities, but none that derived from the study of Roman or canon law seems to have ousted the traditional ideas of law from the minds of laymen at large. Most of the new thinking concerned reaches of law that impinged relatively little on most laymen: when non-lawyers think of the law they more often think of criminal law than lawyers do, and criminal law remained little affected by academic debates. The changes that it underwent came from the creation or development of defined jurisdictions, and these were the effect less of new thoughts than of new power. Theorizing came later.

Much of the usual emphasis on Roman law and on its

[91] Orestano, *Problema delle persone giuridiche* [611]; Ke Chin Wang, 'Corporate Entity Concept' [498]. I allude to a few of the problems of late medieval English developments in the notes to Reynolds, 'Idea of the Corporation' [651]. See also Blair, 'Religious Gilds' [260].
[92] *Township and Borough* [568], 15.

difference from traditional law seems in fact to derive from the teleology and insularity of traditional legal history. Because modern ideas of state sovereignty emphasize the dependence of law on the state, and because the law of the different states of Europe has evolved differently, legal historians have tended to read the differences back into the middle ages. Those who now use Roman law have been inclined to equate it with rationality and to contrast it with the primitive irrationality of 'Germanic' law or the class-ridden irrationality of 'feudal' law. There seems to be no doubt that the recovery of Justinian's law coincided with a great upsurge in debate and discussion of law, and it seems to have done much to stimulate it. But even if that had been the only stimulating factor at work—and it clearly was not—that does not mean that all change meant more rationality or that all rationality came from Roman law. Nor can rationality in this context be identified with the exact and consistent use of words which happened later to acquire peculiar legal significance.[93] The obsession of some legal and constitutional historians with defining words often ignores the 'fact that words were used outside the law too, and that the notions or concepts they represented may have been wider and more various than the legal records suggest and may well have changed through time. Writing brings more chance of consistency and definition, but only in the contexts of the documents. Recordkeepers and academics do not control the language used outside their records and treatises or the meanings which people in changed circumstances will find in what they have said.

Despite the apparent confidence of these assertions the conclusions drawn here have to remain tentative. There seem to be few specialist studies which discuss the relationship between academic law and law as it was practised in secular courts on the basis of any serious study of both the academic treatises and the records of secular courts. The two subjects are generally studied in isolation. To some extent, however, argument about the influence of academic law is irrelevant here. If it is accepted that the habits of collective deliberation, decision-making, and responsibility were entrenched in

[93] Milsom, 'Reason and Development of Common Law' [590].

traditional law from at least the tenth century, then the legal changes of the twelfth century, impressive as they were from other points of view, look much less important in the context of this book. Occasions for collective activity, and for conflicts between groups, multiplied in the twelfth and thirteenth centuries, but that was the result of demographic and economic growth and of the strengthening of government. By the thirteenth century conflicts between rulers and ruled, lords and men, as well as within lesser communities themselves, displayed a new clarity and sophistication of argument that (so far as it is not just a result of better record-keeping) probably owed much to the new clarity of the law, but there is little evidence that the conflicts themselves derived from new legal principles. There was nothing new about the 'spirit of association' and no new 'concept of the commune'. The effect of the intellectual development of jurisprudence was less to create new legal norms than to clarify the distinctions in the old ones. The new jurists came not to destroy the old law but to articulate it. Many of the beliefs about law which are recognized to lie at the heart of medieval political thought were already held, in however inarticulate and rudimentary a way, before the twelfth century. To borrow, through Maitland, the words of Browning:

> Justinian's Pandects only make precise,
> What simply sparkled in men's eyes before,
> Twitched in their brow or quivered on their lip,
> Waited the speech they called but would not come.[94]

[94] Browning, *The Ring and the Book*, lines 1781-4; see *Township and Borough* [568], 20.

3

Fraternities and guilds

Of all the forms of medieval community known to us, one of the oldest, most cohesive, and most universal was the fraternity or guild. Essentially this was a voluntary association of people who were not blood-relations but who used the analogy of brotherhood to express their solidarity. The use of the word guild[1] seems to have been simply a regional peculiarity which implied no essential difference of character, but associations described as guilds are, as it happens, relatively well attested early in the period. From the eighth century to the eleventh the words *gildonia, gelda,* etc. (or in Old English *gild, gegyld, gyldscipe,* etc.) were used in north-western Europe to describe a feast or *libatio* of a more or less religious character and the association of people who celebrated it.[2] The word guild is Germanic and the institution may have started in pagan times, so that it is easy to see why the clergy were for a while suspicious of it, the more so since guild members were sometimes—probably always—bound together by oath.[3] Gradually, however, the church took guilds over and tamed them, so that by the tenth and eleventh centuries the religious side of their activities seems to have been firmly Christian. The clergy indeed played a prominent part in the more pious sort of guild and by now seem to have objected to others only when they involved excessive drinking.[4] In addition to feasts the purposes of guilds included the provision of burial ceremonies—and in Christian times saying masses and prayers—for deceased members. They also provided a variety of mutual benefits for the living, such as

[1] On its spelling, below, n. 26.
[2] Coornaert, 'Les Ghildes médiévales' [338], remains the fundamental work on the early guilds and the nature of the guild-bond in general.
[3] *M.G.H. Epist.* [157], iv, no. 290; *M.G.H. Capit.* [154], i, p. 51 (c. 16), 64 (c. 26); Thorpe, *Diplom.* [196], 610–13.
[4] *P.L.* [60], cxxv, col. 778 (c. 16); Hefele, *Conciles* [136], iv (2), p. 1421 (c. 9); *Anselmi Opera* [8], p. 223.

prayers, masses, and in two relatively early references, mutual insurance against flood and fire.[5] Like other medieval communities they made their own rules and did justice among their members, generally imposing penalties for infringements by way of fine. At least from the ninth century some guilds —generally of the more pious sort—included women.[6]

This framework of voluntary mutual obligation, reinforced by oaths, ceremonies, and sociable feasting, looks capable of creating very cohesive groups which could be either useful or dangerous to the weak governments of the early middle ages. And so it was. In 884 King Carloman of the West Franks forbade villagers to form guilds against thieves, but in seventh-century and ninth-century Wessex guild members (*gegildan*) were recognized as able to take the place of kinsmen when one of their number, who had no kin, was involved in crime.[7] In the early tenth century a great guild to keep the peace (*friðgegyldum*) was formed in London with every appearance of legality. It was led by bishops and reeves and comprised a great number of people, both noble and nonnoble, from an unspecified area around.[8] Clearly this was a very different affair from the little guilds of entirely private and pious purposes that are recorded a century later in Devon and Dorset, yet it too provided for monthly dinners of its officers, a dozen at a time, and ordained that all members should make offerings and sing psalms at the death of any one of them.[9] About a century later a clerical chronicler remarked disapprovingly on the fierce behaviour and lawless judgements of the men of Tiel, who claimed imperial sanction for their independence. Their regular celebration of feasts by solemn drinking, financed from a common purse, makes them look rather like a guild.[10] If so, it was one which, in its relations with authority, falls midway between the

---

[5] *M.G.H. Capit.* [154], i, p. 51 (c. 16); Thorpe, *Diplom.* [196], 613–14.

[6] *P.L.* [60], cxxv, col. 778 (c. 16).

[7] *M.G.H. Capit.* [154], ii, p. 375 (c. 14); Attenborough, *Laws* [87], 40, 42 (Ine, c. 16, 42), 76 (Alfred, c. 30 § 1, c. 31); cf. Thorpe, *Diplom.* [196], 610–13. Gross's reluctance (*Gild Merchant* [457], i. 166–91, esp. 169, 177) to recognize guild members in *gegildan* derives from a narrow view of guilds which Coornaert has made untenable; cf. Whitelock in *Eng. Hist. Docs.* [119], i, p. 365.

[8] Attenborough, *Laws* [87], 156–68 ('VI Athelstan').

[9] Ibid. 162 (c. 8 § 1), 164 (c. 8 § 6); Thorpe, *Diplom.* [196], 605–10, 613–14.

[10] *Elenchus* [118], i. 424–5.

illicit guilds of vigilantes in ninth-century French villages and the highly respectable peace guild of the tenth-century English establishment in London.

Although the word guild is not found in the south, there is no need to polarize 'Germanic' and 'Roman' so as to assume that nothing similar existed there. In the north the words *confratria* and *consortia* were used as alternatives to *geldonia* by the ninth century, and by the eleventh and twelfth *fraternitas*, *religio*, and *caritas* are found describing the same sort of association.[11] Fraternities are also found in the south, and although too much should not be made of the vexed issue of continuity, here too some kind of link with pre-Christian *collectae* and *conviviae* is possible. The statutes of the confraternity of Sant' Appiano in Valdelsa, from about 1000, make it look very like the most pious sort of guild. It included clergy and laity of both sexes, offered masses and prayers for its dead, and had regular meetings and meals. It seems unusual in having no common funds: individual members acted as hosts for the meals, and the only penalty for offences was expulsion. The meals were unusual in other ways too, for the members were to eat in silence while listening to a reading.[12] Other Italian associations which are recorded rather later were not so quiet and abstemious, any more than were all of the northern societies which called themselves fraternities or confraternities rather than guilds. Perhaps some conformed to Hincmar's requirement that they should serve only single glasses of wine,[13] but most, even of those which included clerical members or were named after saints, were probably more convivial.[14] About 1200 a peasant fraternity at Castelfiorento in Tuscany, which was supposed to exist for the good of the local church, had become proverbial for having only a halfpenny left over after paying for its feast.[15]

Because guilds and fraternities were 'in terms of medieval

[11] *P.L.* [60], cxxv, col. 778 (c. 16); Meersseman, *Ordo fraternitatis* [152], 36-7; Le Bras, 'Confréries chrétiennes' [526]; Sicard, 'Notes' [689].

[12] Meersseman, *Ordo fraternitatis* [152], 60-5.

[13] *P.L.* [60], cxxv, col. 778 (c. 16).

[14] *Anselmi Opera* [8], p. 223; Hefele, *Conciles* [136], v. 1345 (c. 15); Le Bras, 'Confréries chrétiennes' [526], 354 n.

[15] Meersseman, *Ordo fraternitatis* [152], 19-20.

European society ... a form of association as unself-conscious and irresistible as the committee is today',[16] they served many and varied purposes. A guild or fraternity formed for one purpose could easily enough be turned by later members to another or could serve the different purposes of different members at the same time, just like a modern golf-club. One obvious use for such a body in the tenth and eleventh centuries is suggested by the case of the wild merchants of Tiel who have already been mentioned. In a growing town an association for mutual insurance and protection could readily become the body which campaigned for privileges for the town's traders and its mayor or alderman[17] might become the spokesman for the town as a whole. This seems to be the origin and explanation of the 'merchant guilds' (*gilde mercatorum, gilde mercatorie*) which appeared in some northern towns in the eleventh and twelfth centuries. Generally these guilds faded out as urban self-government became formally established and recognized, but in some cases the town guild or merchant guild continued in close relationship with the municipality.[18] Some merchant guilds included all a town's traders, down to the humblest craftsman-retailer or shopkeeper, while others were dominated by rich wholesalers and devoted to their interests. Some were open to non-residents.[19]

As towns grew, guilds and fraternities multiplied in proportion to the separate groups and interests which appeared in them. Because many guilds thus became connected with particular crafts, historians have compounded the problem of understanding them by seeing 'craft guilds', as they call them, as the quintessential form of guild. It is true that some of the first associations of craftsmen that we know of in the twelfth century were called guilds or fraternities in the sources, and that some of them secured monopoly control over their respective crafts.[20] On the analogy of the relations of merchant

---

[16] Martin, 'English Borough' [575], 126 (though referring only to guilds).

[17] Alderman: Gross, *Gild Merchant* [457], i. 26; mayor: *Actes des comtes de Flandre* [199], no. 52.

[18] Planitz, *Deutsche Stadt* [627], 283-4 and notes thereto; Reynolds, *Eng. Med. Towns* [652], 81-3, 115.

[19] Reynolds, *Eng. Med. Towns* [652], 75, 83; Ennen, *Europäische Stadt* [393], 108.

[20] Planitz, *Deutsche Stadt* [627], p. 464, nn. 12, 14; *Mun. Gild. Lond.* [175], 33; Leicht, *Scritti vari* [533], i. 372 (a *convivia* of tailors at Verona, 1131).

guilds with early town governments we may guess that this happened because guilds were such an obvious means of organization for any autonomous group which needed to protect its members and further their interests. Later, as municipal governments were established and assumed control of urban affairs, crafts as such were normally regulated by delegation of authority from the rulers of the town to leading members of the crafts. These were not necessarily or normally *ex officio* members of a guild. Some of the resulting craft organizations[21] took on the kind of convivial and charitable activities that characterized guilds and that came so naturally to medieval groups.[22] On the other hand there were towns where the formal organization of crafts as quasi-autonomous local government organizations occurred only long after the establishment of independent guilds or fraternities within some of the crafts. In Chartres formal craft organizations are not recorded before the fifteenth century, yet early in the thirteenth century confraternities of craftsmen presented windows to the cathedral.[23] It is not impossible that some of these associations survived to be absorbed in the later organizations, but fraternities probably came and went in the intervening period. There is no particular reason to connect those recorded in the cathedral windows with those which were recognized by the municipality over two hundred years later. Although examples can be recorded, moreover, where fraternities or guilds of craftsmen included all the practitioners of a craft, or just all the masters, they cannot be assumed to have done so. Where they did not, the outsiders would nevertheless still be subject to any municipal controls. An obvious example of this would occur when a highly select guild or fraternity of leading craftsmen succeeded in getting control of their craft and became its official governing body.[24]

Given the variety of relationships between crafts and their guilds it is not surprising that the sources do not always make them clear. In some towns the word guild continued to be used after the twelfth century for craft organizations, though

[21] Craft organizations as such are discussed on pp. 194-5, 200, 207-11.
[22] e.g. Planitz, *Deutsche Stadt* [627], 291-3 and notes thereto.
[23] Aclocque, *Corporations à Chartres* [214], 54-6.
[24] Veale, *English Fur Trade* [724], 101-32 analyses the relationship extremely clearly for a slightly later period.

whether that was because originally independent guilds had maintained control of the crafts or because craft organizations had taken on fraternal or guild-like functions is generally unknowable.[25] Understanding of the relationships is made more difficult by the tendency of historians to assume that most guilds were concerned with particular crafts, that the primary purpose of any of these was to regulate its craft, and that what historians call 'social and religious guilds' were a separate but minor phenomenon. English-speaking historians of Italy (where the word guild was, apparently, not used at all) even translate *arte* by 'gild'[26] and have taken over the nineteenth-century formulation 'gildsman' as a synonym for craftsman.[27] It would be easier to understand the various associations and the purposes to which they were put if the language of the sources were followed more accurately. Words like *ministerium*, *mesteria*, *officium*, the Italian *arte*, or the medieval German *amt* or *ambacht* no more meant 'guild' then than either 'work force' or 'trade' today mean 'union'. *Gildona*, *gelde*, etc. no more meant 'craft' than 'club', 'society', or 'union' mean 'work force' or 'labour' today. On the one hand no craft organization should be assumed to have had convivial or charitable functions, and, on the other, no guild or fraternity of craftsmen should be assumed to have had public functions of economic control, unless there is appropriate evidence either way. Neutral words like *societas*, *consortia*, *communitas*, *unio*, or *einung* (corresponding to modern German *Innung*) need supporting evidence for either interpretation; the French *corporation* and German *zeche* or *zunft* (and perhaps even *fraternitas* in some contexts) may come under this non-committal head too.[28]

What the sources suggest, if one removes the economic spectacles of modern preoccupations, is that economic motives

[25] De Boüard, 'De la confrérie pieuse' [271]; Czok, 'Zum Braunschweiger Aufstand' [346], 43.

[26] The variant spellings 'gild' and 'guild' have no significance. I have used guild because 'gild' seems to be a nineteenth-century historians' archaism which is particularly associated with the nineteenth-century concept of 'craft gilds'.

[27] Cf. also e.g. Mulholland, *Gild Records of Toulouse* [161]; the religious and fraternal elements in the regulations appear to be minimal: ibid. *passim* and pp. xxvii-xxx, xli.

[28] Planitz, *Deutsche Stadt* [627], 289-94 uses the word *Zunft* in a general way for all the associations but his notes illustrate some of the variations.

and interests were much less important to fraternities and guilds than historians—and especially economic historians—have generally supposed. Merchants might well use fraternal associations of any sort to further their trade, and craftsmen used them to protect craft interests, but these were not the prime objectives of guilds as such. The action that people took because they were guildsmen was first and foremost drinking, with some performance of religious ceremonies (especially burials) and charitable works thrown in for good measure. If they called themselves a fraternity there might be more emphasis on religion and charity and less on drinking, but that is by no means certain. Guilds proliferated in towns partly because so many people there were uprooted from their homes and families of origin and needed the warmth and sociability they offered. Of all the drinking and charitable clubs (in our terms) that they formed, the ones which are most likely to be known to us now are those which owned property, were involved in the government of the town, or were subversive. All these activities were, however, subsidiary by-products of their primary functions. We tend to assume that any association of craftsmen must have been designed to promote its members' economic interests and that any subversive activities it pursued were directed to that end too, but when guilds and fraternities got into trouble it was as often because their sworn fraternal cosiness made them dangerous politically as because of any connection that they had with particular trades or with perceived economic conflicts.

In the twelfth century guilds renewed their originally bad reputation with the clergy when town or merchant guilds led campaigns for self-government in episcopal or abbey towns, while the heretical nature of some fraternities widened the area of suspicion.[29] Thereafter, though church authorities used fraternities themselves to promote piety and withstand heresy, they still tended to fear all sworn associations for their independence and uncontrollability. Secular lords generally took a more robust line. Sometimes they fined or licensed guilds, presumably for financial profit: given the

---

[29] Below, pp. 167–8; Little, *Religious Poverty* [554], 113–34. The use in the modern literature of the word 'brotherhood' for these heretical groups creates a distinction of categories which may not have been noticeable to contemporaries.

absence of any concept of a 'corporate body' as such, they could not have meant that all guilds or fraternities really needed permission to exist or to own property. There were always some which were just as 'corporate' as others but did not have to get licenses because they were not thought dangerous.[30] If secular rulers tangled with fraternities more closely it was either at the behest of the clergy or because they too feared political subversion. Both reasons may have prompted Simon de Montfort the elder, setting up his government in the county of Toulouse in 1212, to forbid barons, knights, burgesses, or country people (*rurales*) to gather together under oath or make any *conjuratio* under pretext of a confraternity or other good purpose, except with the assent of their lord. The penalties were graded according to status, with barons to pay most and *rurales* least. Merchants and travellers who took oaths together to protect their company (*pro societate sua servanda*), presumably in travelling, were specifically excepted.[31] Much the same combination of motives probably lay behind Frederick II's condemnation of *cuiuslibet artificii confraternitates seu societates quocumque nomine vulgariter appellantur* in German towns a few years later.[32] The towns of Italy were by this time positively riddled with fraternities,[33] some of which were heavily involved in politics. In 1198, during the struggle between nobles and *popolo* in Milan, the Credenza di Sant' Ambrogio was founded by a mixed bag of craftsmen, and a few years later the nobles retaliated with a *societas de Galiardis*. The *credenza* had its own tower and banner, exercised some sort of jurisdiction, and even received a share of the civic funds. The name suggests that its members were bound together in a traditionally religious way.[34] About a hundred years later the Parisian fraternities seem to have been temporarily dissolved as a consequence of Philip IV's ban on meetings of more than five people—and perhaps partly too because of riots against a recoinage.[35]

[30] See p. 62.   [31] De Vic and Vaissete, *Languedoc* [201], col. 632 (c. 35).
[32] *M.G.H. Const.* [160], ii, no. 156; cf. nos. 62, 106, 108; Bohmer, *Acta imperii* [94], no. 945.
[33] Le Bras, 'Confréries chrétiennes' [526], 324.
[34] Ghiron, 'Credenza di Sant'Ambrogio' [438].
[35] Fagniez, *L'Industrie à Paris* [401], 51-2, 281-3, 293.

Inevitably municipal governments, like clergy and kings, distrusted independent guilds and fraternities at times. Fraternities which catered for poorer townsmen might seem most liable to suspicion, but *any* sectional association, and not merely those which were formed by people whose economic interests seem to us to have been most opposed to those of the town's rulers, could be seen as threatening the sometimes fragile unity of a town.[36] In 1306 some prominent citizens of York used an old guild or fraternity (both words are used in the records) as a cover for a conspiracy to dominate and corrupt the city's government, laying all the burden of taxes on the poor. Here one can see just what a good front-organization a fraternity made and how useful its oaths and rules made it for subversion. The ostensible purposes of the York guild were to hold an annual feast at Trinity *ad potandum*, to repair the dilapidated old *Domus Dei* on Ouse Bridge, and to maintain its chantry. They had the usual sort of officers—an alderman, a dean, two chamberlains, and a *bedeman*, but the *gildebrethere* or *confratres* were sworn to support each other against all outsiders whatsoever and to submit all their disputes to their own private court before the alderman and dean so that the guild and not the town got the profits of justice.[37] During the fourteenth century both inter-craft disputes and class conflicts were to multiply, but even then, when lay governments quashed or licensed guilds or fraternities or enquired into them, they probably did so for much the same reasons as their predecessors back to the ninth century. To judge from the English government's enquiries of 1388-9 they were perfectly capable of distinguishing guilds from craft associations and of taking separate action against both if they wanted.[38]

Some guilds were, and remained, above suspicion even to the most nervous clergy and rulers. After all, many of the values they sustained, and the means by which they sustained them, were those of all medieval communities. Even in monasteries feasting and the commemoration of the dead had

---

[36] See pp. 203-14.
[37] Sayles, 'Dissolution of a Gild' [181], 92-8.
[38] *English Gilds* [188], 127-30; cf. Le Bras, 'Confréries chrétiennes' [526], 359-60.

long gone together,[39] while the development of the doctrines of purgatory and indulgence in the twelfth century and after must have been an important stimulus to the formation of associations concerned to safeguard their members' souls after death. The same forces that produced fraternities which were deemed heretical produced others whose religious fervour was approved.[40] The third orders of thirteenth-century and later religious life were in a way one end of a spectrum of fraternity of which subversive or bibulous guilds were the other. Many fraternities, unlike the one at York, really did engage in genuinely charitable work, such as building or maintaining hospitals or bridges, while others from the later thirteenth century, celebrated the feast of Corpus Christi.[41] There must have been many which came and went, feasting, saying masses, and maintaining brotherly solidarity, without leaving any trace in surviving records. Many of them were probably in the countryside. Town guilds are better recorded not only because urban conditions may have stimulated fraternal associations but because town records are better. There may have been plenty of village guilds like the one at Binham (Norfolk) which is casually and obscurely referred to in a priory custumal.[42]

In the late twelfth century Walter Map told a fairy story set in the eleventh which was probably based on fact.[43] In the course of it he mentioned a *ghildhus* such as the English had *in singulis diocesibus* for drinking. Whether he meant bishoprics or smaller areas is uncertain:[44] although in Denmark some *gildi* are later known to have been coextensive with bishoprics, the guilds which were attached to the cathedral in eleventh-century Devon were scattered through the diocese.

[39] Jorden, 'Totengedächtniswesen' [492], 85 n., 89, 99; Bishko, 'Liturgical Intercession' [254], 57-8. The 'confraternity' of Cluny, however, involved no social links between its members: Cowdrey, 'Unions and Confraternity' [343], 162.

[40] Le Bras, 'Confréries chrétiennes' [526]; *M.G.H. Scriptores* [54], v. 453 (Bernold on lay communities).

[41] Reicke, *Das deutsche Spital* [644], 53-71; Boyer, 'Bridge Building Brotherhoods' [274]; Craig, *English Religious Drama* [344], 138-44; Le Bras, 'Confréries chrétiennes' [526], 320.

[42] Homans, *English Villagers* [479], 456, n. 17.

[43] *De nugis curialium* [80], 154-8; on the story, Reynolds, 'Eadric *silvaticus*' [650].

[44] Le Bras, *Hist. du droit de l'église* [527], viii (2), pt. 2, 223; on English parishes at this date, below, p. 84.

Another late twelfth-century story refers to a rustic drinking house (*domus potationis*) where prayers were customarily said during drinking, which suggests a guild-like character.[45] The common English use of the word guildhall to mean town hall, which occurs in some towns where no town or merchant guild is recorded, may be a relic of a time when many local communities had their own *ghildhus*.[46] Medieval law was casual about common property, and it would be easy for guildhouses or other guild property to have got lost or absorbed in other property which belonged to the parish or even to the lord of the manor.[47] In and around the Alps and central France many confraternities of the Holy Spirit have been traced which included the whole population of their respective parishes. Although their oldest statutes date only from the thirteenth century they may well be older. Their chief purpose was to hold an annual parish dinner at Pentecost and to distribute food to their members at the same time, but they also said masses for the dead and some carried out other religious duties.[48] These parish fraternities are good examples of the way in which such groups could bring together different classes in quasi-fraternal fellowship—though of course we do not have to believe that quarrels and differences of status were always forgotten within them. At the same time one can see how even a parish fraternity—*la paroisse consensuelle*, as Le Bras called it[49]—could be a rather dubious institution to the authorities of an established and all-inclusive church.

Lay fraternities and guilds illustrate well the strength and character of the medieval drive to association. Despite all their rules, and the coercive jurisdiction or trading monopolies which they might acquire, they relied first and foremost on affective bonds, modelled on the ideal of sibling relationship or monastic community, reinforced by oaths, and maintained by the collective jurisdiction over their members that all

---

[45] Thorpe, *Diplom.* [196], 608-10, 613-14; Coornaert, 'Les Ghildes' [338], 36, 43; Lennard, *Rural England* [541], 405.

[46] London's example may have been influential but London's guildhall is not the earliest recorded: Reynolds, *Eng. Med. Towns* [652], 82.

[47] See pp. 111-12, 150.

[48] Duparc, 'Confréries du Saint-Esprit' [388].

[49] 'Confréries chrétiennes' [526], 351.

collective groups tended to assume. The particular objectives of individual members, the degree of each one's individual piety, greed, or ambition, could transform the activities of any fraternity without depriving it of its essential character. That character was shared by many other associations which are not recorded as guilds or fraternities, but it was displayed with extraordinary constancy right through the middle ages by those which are. Just as modern associations will elect chairmen, keep minutes, and turn themselves into some kind of committee, so medieval ones shaped themselves into the form which is seen at its most characteristic in the fraternity or guild. Whether or not it used those names, any group which wanted to maintain and demonstrate its closeness would act in the way that seemed, from long tradition, to be the essence of brotherhood: they would drink together, swear solidarity, and pledge themselves to mutual good works. Above all, they would do for one another the one act of mercy that everyone needed, by giving each other honourable burial and a helping hand into the next world.

4

The community of the parish

It is tempting to take the community of the parish for granted as needing no explanation. If longevity is a sign of strength in local forms of community then medieval parishes were certainly strong. Parish churches may have been rebuilt or entirely demolished, but neither Reformation nor wars of religion shook the framework of parishes as such. In most of western Europe they steadily accumulated more duties over the centuries, and it was not until after 1800 that substantial changes were made in their boundaries. Even now parochialism is synonymous with localism and the parish pump remains the symbol of local concerns.

Presumably, since the parish was originally an ecclesiastical unit, its cohesion was originally derived from the church. Common recourse to a single church and common submission to the demands, whether spiritual, moral, or financial, of its clergy, must have promoted some degree of community. By the thirteenth century there is ample evidence that many parishes were in fact very effective communities. Yet it has to be acknowledged that the most effective of them were those that belonged to villages or towns which also enjoyed a purely secular unity.[1] Hard as it is, moreover, to say how far one sort of unity promoted the other or profited from it, one point seems to be clear: parish communities did not develop because of any particular encouragement from the hierarchy of the church. The parish as such received scant attention from canon lawyers.[2] To them a parish church was a matter of clerical concern, the object of clerical rights—or sometimes, regrettably, of the rights of lay patrons—and not a forum of local activity and a focus of congregational care. Paradoxically, however, clerical neglect may have favoured lay activity, by leaving the laity to get on with a good deal of

---

[1] Le Bras, *Hist. du droit de l'église* [527], viii (2), pt. 2, 236–41.
[2] Ibid. 219.

unofficial or semi-official business connected with the parish and its church. Certainly the larger territorial divisions of the church's ministry, which mattered much more to the hierarchy, had correspondingly little meaning for the laity.

The most important example of this is provided by bishoprics. Since cathedrals were normally built in centres of government and local exchange, and since dioceses were at first more or less coterminous with the regions dependent on such places, one might expect bishoprics to have won a corporate devotion proportionate to the lay solidarity which could develop in a lordship or province.[3] That does not seem to have happened. Some fraternities or guilds were attached to cathedrals,[4] some relic of collective lay participation in episcopal elections was preserved for a while in Italy,[5] and associations of the 'peace of God' were sometimes organized by bishops,[6] but none of these phenomena seem to have united the laity of their bishoprics for long: most of the evidence of genuinely diocesan fraternities is early; the most effective lay participation in elections was by kings and lords, not by the whole lay community as such; and diocesan peace armies were probably less popular and less diocesan than has sometimes been suggested. The wave of lay enthusiasm that provided voluntary unskilled labour for the construction of some twelfth-century cathedrals was not trammelled by diocesan boundaries, and when bishops and chapters succeeded in getting much money for their cathedral-building it seems to have come rather from their cathedral cities than from their bishoprics at large.[7] Some Italian cities indeed virtually took over the entire financial responsibility for their cathedrals, but for those living outside the city, though their cathedral might remain a focus of devotion, it was a place of only occasional resort. Parishes might send representatives to pentecostal or other processions, and Hostiensis maintained that laymen might on occasion attend diocesan synods, but the great objective of the religious reformers who initiated the regular holding of synods was to liberate the church from

[3] Below, pp. 243-4.   [4] Above, p. 76.
[5] Kurze, *Pfarrerwahlen* [517], 101-5, 108.   [6] Above, p. 34, n. 82.
[7] *P.L.* [60], cxc, col. 1133; Delisle, 'Lettre de l'abbé Haimon' [112], 121, 124; Kraus, *Gold was the Mortar* [509].

lay intervention and lay control. Without meetings of the diocesan laity a lay community of the diocese could hardly develop. In parts of southern France laymen occasionally met in diocesan assemblies in the twelfth and thirteenth centuries in order to provide for the keeping of the peace, apparently because the secular authorities were not preserving it, but in general by that period—which is also the only period for which we have reasonably good records—bishoprics had become too heavily dominated by the clergy for their lay populations to demonstrate much corporate solidarity.[8]

The formation of parishes

By the thirteenth century the most important ecclesiastical area from the point of view of the laity was the parish. This meant that, though a fair number of subordinate chapels survived in lesser villages or hamlets, the normal country church was a parish church; that is, it had its own priest, who was supported out of its tithes and endowment, had the responsibility of baptizing and burying the inhabitants of the parish, and in return enjoyed the corresponding dues. In practice, part at least of the endowment, tithes, and other dues was often alienated from him to a monastery, but all of it pertained in principle to the parish which he served. The compulsory payment of tithe, moreover, meant that parishes had to have defined boundaries which could be changed only with formality and, generally, with difficulty.[9] A rural parish consisted not merely of a settlement and its inhabitants (or several settlements), but of the dependent lands as well—the lands that paid tithe to the parish church.[10]

In principle the system by which the countryside of western Europe was divided into parishes of this kind dates from around 800. Before then the clergy who looked after

---

[8] Le Bras, *Hist. du droit* [527], viii (2), pt. 2, 11-14, 28, n. 118; Owen, *Church and Society* [615], 29, 41-2, 107. Some smaller bishoprics, which might otherwise have had more chance of solidarity, were subject to alterations of boundaries: Brentano, *Two Churches* [276], 62-4.

[9] Though see e.g. Reynolds, *Eng. Med. Towns* [652], 191 n. for references to changes in urban parish bounds. The *presumption* of unchanging boundaries is generally only that.

[10] Le Bras, *Institutions ecclésiastiques* [528], 204-11; Addleshaw, *Parochial System* [215].

people in the country had been based in relatively few 'mother churches' to which all dues, baptismal rights, etc. normally belonged. They might travel round to visit other churches or chapels in the country but most of these had no clergy of their own and no rights over people living around them. The reformers of the Carolingian age seem to have decided that full parochial rights ought to be more widely dispersed among local churches. Since the number of such lesser churches multiplied greatly during the next few centuries it has therefore generally been assumed that, within the area to which Carolingian legislation applied, most of them became full parish churches from the start.[11] It is recognized that that did not apply to England, where the two-tier system of mother churches and dependent chapels survived into the eleventh century or later, or, more surprisingly, to Italy, where it went on even longer. In towns everywhere, moreover, very few lesser churches achieved full parochial status until after 1100. These variations are slightly puzzling, especially when one considers that it was not until about 1100 that parishes anywhere began to show signs of really effective cohesion. The answer seems to be that they are an illusion. When one compares the evidence for the supposed earlier supersession of the rights of mother churches in France and Germany with that for their later survival in towns, in Italy, and in England, it looks very thin. The Carolingian reforms had less impact, and single-tier parishes were formed more slowly, than is generally supposed.

The reasons for asserting this may be more apparent if one takes the supposed exceptions first. In northern Italy most parochial rights in the countryside were reserved, long after the Carolingian age, to baptismal churches or *pievi*, each of which had dependent churches (*tituli, capellae*) scattered among the villages and hamlets around. Though the origin of the *pievi* is disputed their boundaries often approximated to those of lay authority and their churches were generally established in traditional centres of local government. By the tenth century most *pievi* were already old, but a new one

---

[11] Hauck, *Kirchengeschichte* [464], ii. 737–41, iv. 21–52; Ammann and Dumas, *L'Élise au pouvoir des laïques* [220], 266; Addleshaw, *Parochial System* [215], 1; Le Bras, *Hist. du droit de l'église* [527], viii (2), pt. 2, 219, 226.

was more likely to secure recognition if its church stood at the headquarters of a powerful lord. Most *tituli* were apparently built by lesser lords and fell more or less under their control, but their tithes still went to the *pievano*, who, at least in principle, also retained rights in the appointment of their priests.[12] It was not until after 1100 that any general transfer of parochial rights to the lesser churches even began to take place: in the diocese of Lucca the first recorded use of the word *parochia* in its modern sense occurs in 1118.[13] By that time, however, the development of canon law and of episcopal control was beginning to make it difficult to deprive any church of its customary rights without formality, so that the separation of parishes thereafter was slow and often contested. In the towns, though lesser churches began to acquire some parochial rights at the same time as in the countryside, they often failed to acquire all of them. A cathedral, towering over its city, was a potent focus of civic loyalty, and its symbolic function was shared not only by its *campanile*, which summoned the citizens to prayer, counsel, or defence, but also by its baptistery, where all continued to be baptized in the same font. Loyalty to the mother church, therefore, in addition to vested interests, explains the stunted developments of urban parishes. In the countryside the situation was rather different. Not only did greater intervening distances make the communities around lesser churches more distinct from each other, so that their lands could be delimited with fewer disputes, but many *pievi* had by the thirteenth century become collegiate churches which were too bedevilled by absenteeism to be centres of community for their own clergy, let alone for their lay parishioners. The records of litigation which accompanied the piecemeal transfer of parochial rights from them to the *tituli* suggest that the *pievi* retained their position through the entrenchment of their legal rights, rather than through the devotion of those subject to them. Many village churches were still without baptismal rights in 1300, but loyalties in the countryside look less divided than they were in the towns. It was the

---

[12] Nanni, *Parrochia* [604]; Boyd, *Tithes and Parishes* [273]; Castagnetti, *Pieve rurale* [311]; cf. Toubert, *Structures du Latium* [715], 855–63.

[13] Nanni, *Parrochia* [604], 56.

tituli which the laity felt belonged to them and to which they preferred to pay their dues. Rights in consequence trickled from *pievi* to *tituli* steadily from 1100 to modern times.

England, where the Carolingian reforms did not apply, is also recognized as a territory of late parochial development, though not so late as Italy. Here, as elsewhere, a great many village churches were built in the tenth and eleventh centuries, but it is clear that many of them did not rank at first as full parish churches. Tithes became compulsory in the tenth century and about 960 King Edgar ruled that they were normally to be paid to the 'old minsters'. These minsters or mother churches, despite the different history behind them, had a good deal in common with the *pievi* of Italy.[14] As the original bases for mission, quasi-monastic or collegiate in character, they had often been founded in centres of local government—the sort of places that have been described as 'primary towns'.[15] Edgar allowed any lord to divert a third of his own tithes to his own church, if he had one built on his own land with its own graveyard, but his tenants still apparently had to pay all their tithes to the minster.[16] This means that, though some parish boundaries were later to run along the lines of much older estate boundaries, few could have been drawn along those lines as yet.[17] During the next century or so Edgar's rule was presumably relaxed so that tenants' as well as lords' tithes were diverted to the lesser churches, but the Italian evidence reminds us that even when that happened it would not automatically mean that all parochial rights, apart from tithe, were immediately transferred to them. There is quite a lot of evidence from Domesday and even later to suggest that churches which in other documents appear as appurtenances of manors, and which are often assumed to have been full parish churches, still owed dues of various kinds to the old mother churches.[18] Their full ecclesiastical emancipation took place soon after.

Records of disputes from the twelfth century on suggest

[14] *Pievi* were sometimes called *monasteria* too: Nanni, *Parrochia* [604], 11-13.
[15] Everitt, 'Banburys' [400]; cf. Barrow, *Kingdom of Scots* [235], 7-68.
[16] Robertson, *Laws* [177], 20 (II Edgar, 1, 2).
[17] Cf. Cunliffe, 'Settlement Patterns' [345], 6-7.
[18] Lennard, *Rural England* [541], 297-319; Barlow, *English Church* [233], 183-208.

that the same processes of ecclesiastical control that fossilized the situation in Italy came into force in England at about the same time or not much later. After the mid twelfth century the formation of a new parish was more likely to be disputed: relatively few new churches or dependent chapels managed to secure full parochial rights after this. Here, however, the pattern had become set at a more advanced stage than in Italy, so that, though quite a lot of English parishes had some dependent chapelries (and some, for instance in parts of the north, had many), the characteristic village church had full parochial rights. So too, in contrast to Italy, did some town churches, even in the cathedral cities, though most secured them later than did the average country church. By 1086 there were many little churches in some of the bigger towns, some belonging to lords who had built them for their tenants, some belonging to the burgesses themselves or to groups of burgesses. Like the country churches attached to manors in 1086 these have sometimes been said to have had their own parishes already, but lay 'ownership' no more implied full parochial rights in a town than it did in the country.[19] As late as 1092 none of the churches in Worcester had any parochial rights, which were all reserved to the cathedral.[20] In Winchester some sort of parochial system had been formed by 1141, but in the thirteenth century the city churches were still listed as *capelle* in contrast to the *ecclesie* of the countryside, and they did not have baptismal and burial rights as a matter of course until even later.[21]

The interpretation of France and Germany as the classic territory of early parishes, where the old two-tier system was superseded from the ninth century, has been coloured by two dubious assumptions. One is that Carolingian legislation was immediately and permanently effective in overriding the rights of mother churches. The other is that there was a consistent and significant contrast between the 'public' character of mother churches and the seigniorial or 'proprietary' character of the rest. From this last belief was derived a further assumption that any church which came under seigniorial

---

[19] For the problems of 'ownership' in general, below, pp. 220-1.
[20] *Hemming's Cart.* [135], 528.
[21] Biddle, *Winchester* [253], 332.

control thereby automatically ceased to be 'public' and simultaneously became a separate parish.[22] To judge from the Italian and English evidence this seems *prima facie* improbable. Local people might use seigniorial churches for worship and yet at the same time owe part of their loyalty and dues to the mother church. The real contrast with Italy and England derives from the apparently small number of completely new villages founded in either of those countries after 900 compared with the large number founded in France and Germany.[23] Since it seems to have been agreed at the time that new churches in new settlements ought to receive all their own tithes and dues, a fair proportion of the new churches built in France and Germany in the eleventh and twelfth centuries automatically became full parish churches from the start. Their number may indeed have been a factor in establishing the norm of a single independent parish church for each village. Perhaps in modern times it has also distracted the attention of historians from the more obscure evolution of relations between greater and lesser churches in older settlements.

Obscure is what it is: but there seems to be even less evidence to show that single-tier parishes were already normal in old villages before 1100 than to show that elements of the two-tier system survived. In parts of southern France the change from the old system to the new seems not to have taken place until that time in the eleventh and twelfth centuries when the rural population was regrouped into *castra*.[24] Some of the evidence cited in studies of other areas to support the belief in early single-tier parishes looks ambiguous: the increased use of the word *parrochia* and the identification of people and their property by parishes have been cited to show a solidification of the parish community in the eleventh century,[25] but they may, more obviously, indicate the novelty of single-tier parishes as such. In Germany regional studies suggest regional variations. Mother churches in

---

[22] Above, n. 11.
[23] Below, p. 107.
[24] Font-Réaulx, 'L'Origine des villages' [419].
[25] Duby, *Société mâconnaise* [381], 230–3; Beech, *Gâtine of Poitou* [243], 26, 32; Devailly, *Berry* [358], 72–4, 91, 241–8, but note the implications of the canons of 1031, ibid. 148.

Lotharingia and other western and southern parts of the kingdom retained some of their rights over their dependent territories at least until the twelfth century. In Saxony and the east, evangelization was based on churches founded for lay units of settlement and government, and these seem to have had single-tier parishes from the start.[26] The large size of the original parishes and their lack of daughter churches is presumably to be explained by the relatively late conversion and even more by the sparsity of settlement before the twelfth century. In both France and Germany, as elsewhere, the assignment of separate parishes to town churches is known to be largely a phenomenon of the twelfth century or later.[27]

Hazy as it is, this sketch may nevertheless simplify too much, not least in its suggestion that the pattern of parochial organization varied between kingdoms rather than at a more local level. Nevertheless it may suffice to establish the point that in many areas, if not in all, parishes (in the sense of the basic units of ecclesiastical authority) were a good deal larger before 1100 than they were afterwards. It seems reasonable to suppose that where a parish, with or without dependent chapels, included a number of separate villages or consisted of dispersed settlement, it would be less likely to develop a strong sense of community. The division of religious functions between mother church and chapel, moreover, might weaken the pull of each on its people. To judge by the outcome it was the small unit which won the tug of war, but we should not conclude that mother parishes inspired no popular loyalty at all at the earlier stage, during the tenth and eleventh centuries. The frequent coincidence of mother parishes with lordships, traditional local government areas, and market regions suggests otherwise. Though reformers of the eleventh century and later deplored any lay control of churches, the bonds of lordship may sometimes have strengthened the hold of a church over its lord's followers and dependents. It was an age when the links of lord and man, and between the men of a single lord, were strong. Even if churches were 'proprietary'

---

[26] Feine, *Kirchliche Rechtsgeschichte* [413], 183-4, 187-90; Kauss, *Pfarr-organisation* [497], 143-4, 162-3.
[27] Le Bras, *Hist. du droit* [527], viii (2), pt. 2, 227-30.

(according to the rather artificial and anachronistic nineteenth-century concept) that does not mean that they were not the object of religious loyalties: evidence that a church was later regarded as the property of a lord is not evidence that his ancestors' tenants did not help to build it or regard it as also 'theirs'.[28]

Whatever we may try to guess about parish solidarities and activities before 1100, however, the evidence is almost entirely lacking. All we know is that the laity seem to have wanted more churches nearer at hand: most of the churches which got parishes assigned to them in the eleventh and twelfth centuries had probably been built by lay lords for their tenants or by groups of inhabitants for themselves. The achievement of parochial status must have been both an effect and a cause of increased communal feeling at local level. Social and economic historians have tended to argue that the motivating force was a new secular, economic solidarity, which breathed new life into a pre-existing ecclesiastical framework. Ecclesiastical historians, also assuming the pre-existence of single-tier parishes, have tended to attribute the new life to ecclesiastical reforms from above. Either way, the assumption of an old framework looks unjustified, but if it is right that the framework was established only during the eleventh century and later, then that is in itself further evidence of the strengths of the new forces to which both interpretations draw attention.

That these new forces were partly secular and economic is certain,[29] but the new single-tier parishes did not become the norm only because local communities were gaining secular solidarity. If that had been so it would be hard to explain why the old mother churches did not profit from the increased effectiveness of local government at the wider level, or from the increased activity of markets held in the 'primary towns'. One reason why they did not was that, as ecclesiastical historians have pointed out, they had been losing prestige since the tenth century in the face of the new reformed monasteries. The monasteries themselves, meanwhile, as more and more village churches were given to them, used their influence and

[28] Owen, *Church and Society* [615], 6.
[29] See pp. 122-38.

prestige to press for more independent control over their acquisitions, free of obligations to mother churches. Even in northern Italy, where the baptismal churches retained their rights for so long, and where their territories developed some communal institutions, the solidarities implied by the institutions do not seem to have owed much to religious loyalties. In so far as the development of the single-tier system of parishes was the result of religious changes which weakened the position of the mother churches, it cannot be explained in purely secular terms.

The traditional ecclesiastical interpretation, while providing necessary modification of that which stresses purely economic factors, itself needs amplification in so far as it implies that the pressure for ecclesiastical change came primarily from the monasteries and the hierarchy. The evidence suggests on the contrary that the formation of the parochial system in these centuries was largely the result of lay demands for local churches. Like the monastic movements themselves, it was not only the cause but the result of growing fervour among the laity. The dislike of taking babies or bodies long distances for baptism or burial, like a lord's desire to have his own church under his own control, may have derived from motives which look imperfectly religious, but that does not mean that they were not religious at all. Pious motives did not belong exclusively to the famous reformers. Indeed, so far as piety in this context included a concern for the welfare of lay souls, then the motives of lay lords were more pious than those of many religious. To the reformers of the time monastic ownership of village churches was infinitely preferable to lay ownership, but, judging from the struggles of later bishops to secure better care of churches appropriated or incorporated (according to the varying terminology of later lawyers) to monasteries, the cure of lay souls was not a high priority for monks.[30] It was not the monastic ownership—or even episcopal or capitular ownership—of churches, many of them built by laymen and only later given to monasteries, which produced all the developments in popular religion and lay education of the time. The important point here, however, is that, while lay people clearly wanted their own local

[30] Cf. Toubert, *Structures du Latium* [715], 881-94.

churches before the eleventh century, it was not until about that time that they began to secure the parochial organization that enabled their churches to harness their loyalties really effectively. Some of the pressures for change came from within the new parishes but some came from outside. The whole process needs much more exploration. It looks both more complex and more mysterious than has always been recognized.

The collective activity of parishioners

The untidy overlaps of secular and ecclesiastical units, combined with the apparent indifference of medieval people about the particular unit in which to act at any moment, often make it difficult to separate parish activity from the activity of villages or units of lordship.[31] In some circumstances, however, parishes fulfilled a role in secular as well as ecclesiastical matters which was distinctive and remains distinguishable in the records. Some of the settlements on the newly drained coasts of Frisia, for instance, were so scattered that it was the territories dependent on the churches, rather than the little hamlets within them, that formed units for the organization of common work on fields, drains, or roads.[32] Here the parish filled a gap left by the absence of effective village communities. Where the clergy tried to maintain peace through sponsoring sworn associations to keep the 'peace of God' the associations were sometimes organized in parishes under their parish priests.[33] A parish could also provide a forum for activity in an area split between several lords if, as often happened, there was one single church for the whole village or for the village and its hamlets. In England, on the other hand, separate manors within a single village sometimes had their own separate parishes so that the village remained fragmented ecclesiastically as well as seigniorially. At Reepham (Norfolk) the fragmentation took the bizarre form of three churches which each had its own parish though they all stood

---

[31] See p. 143.

[32] Feine, 'Kirche und Gemeindebildung' [412]; Stoob, 'Landausbau und Gemeinde' [700], 413-22.

[33] Fossier, *Picardie* [420], 27 n.; Brunel, 'Juges de la paix' [287].

in a single churchyard.[34] Since two of the parishes were related to lesser settlements close by, it looks as if the siting of the churches was determined by the holiness of the site. Despite their institutional separation, the geographical propinquity of the churches, with the market-place beside them, must have forged some kind of bond between the inhabitants of the three parishes and their settlements.

Urban parish churches—or urban churches which later secured their own parishes—could also serve to focus loyalties in various ways. Some were founded or taken over by sectional groups of different kinds, whether immigrants from a particular area or practitioners of a particular trade.[35] In some towns parishes served as subordinate units of local government.[36] In others the parishes were so small that it is difficult to envisage what purpose they served, or how they were supported, after the first enthusiasm which built them had died away. Nevertheless the more viable of them constituted attractively cosy units within the wider civic community. A new town, on the other hand, often formed a single parish, so that its church fulfilled the same symbolic function as the cathedral of an ancient city. Everywhere churchyards were liable to serve as market-places, church bells summoned people to secular as well as religious duties, and churches themselves doubled as warehouses or fortresses.[37]

The building of their own church was sometimes a task undertaken by settlers on new land in the twelfth and thirteenth centuries, while some churches in existing villages are known to have been endowed by contributions of land from the local lord and all his men—an acre of land, for instance, from each bovate or virgate.[38] Whether or not that kind of collective foundation is recorded, parish churches and churchyards were by the thirteenth century the property and responsibility of parishioners in many practical ways. It has even been suggested that in Picardy churchyards were the earliest common property of villages, though in most places

[34] O.S. Map 1/2,500 Norfolk, xxxviii. 6 (1886).

[35] Müller, 'Beitrag der Pfarreigeschichte' [601].

[36] Below, p. 194.

[37] Le Bras, *Hist. du droit* [527], viii (2), pt. 2, 298–301; Michaud-Quantin, *Universitas* [586], 297; Hartridge, *Vicarages* [460], 140–1.

[38] Stenton, *Documents of Danelaw* [191], p. lxi and no. 465.

common rights in woods and pastures, which in contemporary terms were equally common property, must surely have existed sooner.[39] However that may be, parishioners generally had to cover at least part of the cost of maintaining their church and its equipment. Thirteenth-century documents give the impression that this burden was only then being transferred from clergy to laity, but that is probably an illusion created by an increase in records, many of which were intended to define and limit clerical responsibilities. Custom varied and only began to be defined during this time: the arrangement which became traditional in England, by which the rector maintained the chancel and the parishioners maintained the nave, is referred to in 1250 though it was not yet consistently followed.[40] At about this time the men of Louvres (Oise) formed a *confratria* to build (or rebuild) their church and pay its debts as well as to repair their causeway and wells. In 1271 the parishioners of Merzé (Saône-et-Loire) sold a wood and a rent to Cluny so that they could pay the debts they had incurred in repairing their church.[41] By this time tithes, which had once gone partly to the poor or the church fabric, were generally reserved to the parish clergy (or to the religious or other lords to whom they had been diverted), so that parishioners had to organize themselves as best they could to raise money for repairs.[42]

Tithe was itself a matter on which parishioners felt their interests to be shared, and this community of interest and responsibility was accepted by the authorities, as for instance, when the *universitas villanorum* of Lampertheim (Hesse), represented by their *scultetus* and another villager (*villanus*), defended a law-suit for the tithe of hay.[43] The importance of tithe to the parish community, as well as to the clergy, is indicated by the permanence of parish boundaries even where they cut across more obvious social units. The villages of

[39] Fossier, *Chartes de coutume* [126], 26–35. For common property in general, below, p. 112.

[40] Le Bras, *Hist. du droit* [527], viii (2), pt. 2, 279–81; Hartridge, *Vicarages* [460], 137–40; Clément, 'Recherches sur les paroisses' [332].

[41] *Actes du parlement* [97], i. 138–9; *Chartes de Cluny* [100], no. 5167.

[42] Clément, 'Recherches sur les paroisses' [332].

[43] Wopfner, *Urkunden* [205], no. 176; cf. (for much earlier—955): *Urkundenbuch Zürich* [120], i, no. 203. Below, pp. 138, 143.

Iffley and Cowley (Oxon.) lay less than a mile apart and until the late twelfth century shared a church at Cowley. Then the lord of Iffley built the fine church which still stands there and, after some opposition from the Augustinians who held Cowley church, Iffley thus became a separate parish.[44] When the area was surveyed and mapped in the nineteenth century the parish of Iffley consisted of the village itself, clustered around its twelfth-century church, the fields immediately surrounding it, and nine other detached bits of land, some of them inhabited and geographically forming part of the village of Cowley and of another neighbouring village called Littlemore.[45] One of the detached pieces may date only from the seventeenth-century enclosure of the royal forest nearby, but the others almost certainly go back to the first formation of the parish, when the lord of Iffley had tenants who lived in Cowley and Littlemore, some of them presumably holding lands scattered through the open fields of Cowley.[46] In cases like this a common obligation to tithes and so forth must have created some sense of community between the inhabitants of a parish, but for many of them (particularly if they ceased to be part of a single lordship) their sense of parish solidarity may have been weaker than their solidarity with neighbours who lived in the same village but in different parishes.

The most striking manifestation of parochial activity was the election of parish clergy by the parishioners. Town councils sometimes made elections to town churches by permission of the patron or because they had acquired the patronage for themselves but, apart from this more expectable arrangement, election by the parishioners as such was customary in some places during the twelfth and thirteenth centuries. Evidence of it is fairly widespread in parts of Italy and Germany though not in France or England.[47] Not surprisingly it ran into opposition from the clergy, but even canon lawyers seem to have accepted it as an Italian custom in the thirteenth century, and both there and in some places in Germany it survived into the later middle ages. Depositions

[44] *Oseney Cart.* [180], vi. 135-6.
[45] *O.S. Book of Reference to Iffley* [812].
[46] *V.C.H. Oxon.* [728], v. 76, 189, 191, 197, 201, 210.
[47] Kurze, *Pfarrerwahlen* [517] surveys and discusses the evidence.

in a law-suit of 1197 show with unusual detail how it had
been working until then at Santa Maria Novella in Florence.[48]
In the twelfth century the church of Santa Maria served as
a suburban retreat for the cathedral canons to whom it
belonged, but it also had its own priest, who was called the
chaplain or rector. For some time before 1197 it had been
customary for the people to choose a priest and then go to
the provost (*prepositus*) and canons to report their choice.
The provost then invested the candidate with the temporali-
ties and received his promise of obedience, and the bishop's
deputy invested him with the spiritualities, all in chapter and
in the presence of the people. How far the popular election
technically required the provost's licence seems, in 1197, to
have been uncertain, but on one recorded occasion the
people had said: 'We want the priest Gerard for our rector'
and the provost had replied: 'I let you have him with pleasure,
for he is a good clerk.' The troubles which culminated in
1197 seem to have started when this good clerk Gerard got
the church into debt. Thereupon the people chose two of
their number as *rectores* to look into the matter, and Gerard
answered their enquiries defiantly: 'Who are you to try to
supervise me? When the prior and canons, on whose behalf
(*pro quibus*) I hold this church, ask me about it, I shall
answer to them.' The efforts of another priest, Paul, to repay
the debt at the same time as getting himself elected in Gerard's
place seem to have aroused suspicions of simony. That may
be why the provost and canons, together with only a token
representation of the people (one or four according to different witnesses), then elected yet another priest to replace
Paul. The people, however, re-elected Paul, rang the church
bells, and fortified the church tower against his rival.

Santa Maria Novella was unusual not only because some of
its elections are so vividly recorded but because it soon afterwards passed into the hands of the Dominicans so that the
right of election disappeared. Elsewhere, in Italy and in
Germany, both in town and country, as well as elsewhere in
Europe outside the scope of this book, it went on. How and
when it had started in the first place is unknown. Before

---

[48] Arch. di Stato, Dipl. S. Maria Novella 29 aprile 1197 [3]; related documents are summarized in Brown, *Santa Maria Novella* [285].

1100 there are Italian examples of the election of *plebani*, generally by clergy and people together, but evidence on the whole is very sparse. Some of the parishes which later elected their clergy, especially those in Germany, may not yet have been in existence. It is possible that at this early and relatively unrecorded stage some elections took place in France and England although they did not continue long enough to become part of accepted and recorded custom. The groups of burgesses in East Anglia, for instance, who owned churches in 1086 may well have elected their priests, and if they did it would be hard to say whether they did so as joint patrons or as parishioners. So far as England is concerned, from the twelfth century on the rights of the people in ecclesiastical elections, which were always recognized, however vestigially, by canon law, were abrogated because the royal courts kept control of litigation about presentations. As a result, advowsons were treated simply as property, which town councils, for instance, might acquire, but in which parishioners as such had no legal rights. Nevertheless in 1250 the inhabitants of Wellow, within the mother parish of Edwinstowe (Lincs.), agreed with the dean and chapter of Lincoln that they would provide (*ad inveniendum*) a chaplain to be presented to the dean and chapter to minister to them in the chapel at Wellow. It is clear that they were to choose him for themselves, as well as choosing and supporting a clerk, providing ornaments and lights, repairing the chapel, and keeping up their contributions to the mother church of Edwinstowe.[49] In 1291 the parishioners of Haxey, in the same county claimed unsuccessfully that they and not their vicar should appoint the holy-water carrier in their church.[50] These cases suggest that there may have been others in England, and perhaps in France too, where the interest of parishioners in choosing their clergy was at least expressed, even if it was not decisive or if the record of it has not been preserved. The phenomenon seems to be one of the many matters on which medieval custom varied from place to place for reasons which are now obscure. It certainly does not, for instance, fit into the boundaries drawn by much traditional historical writing

[49] *Reg. Ant. of Lincoln* [127], 311-13.
[50] Owen, *Church and Society* [615], 117.

between 'Roman' and 'Germanic' practices. Presumably, at Wellow and in a good many places in the Netherlands and further east in Germany, it could be a corollary of the building of their church by the local community. Whatever the origin and explanation of the custom in each place, however, we shall probably understand it best if we remember that it was only one manifestation of something much more widespread—the collective activity of parishioners in looking after their church.

Building and repairing their church, paying tithes, and electing their clergy were all activities which properly belonged to parishioners as such. Just, however, as records sometimes described those who undertook these duties not as parishioners but as inhabitants of a village, so parishioners are often described as acting for entirely secular purposes. The identity or overlap of parish, village, and lordship, together with the prominence of the church as a place of assembly, must often have led people to think in terms of parishes when they would have been hard put to it to say if they were acting as parishioners, tenants, or inhabitants of a settlement. Charters of liberties and declarations of custom quite often say that they were granted to parishioners, and this may be one reason why historians have sometimes envisaged rural parishes as forming essentially peasant communities.[51] In one sense they obviously were: their parishioners were predominantly those whom we now describe as peasants.[52] Where a lord was non-resident or had his own private chapel the parish church must have seemed the preserve and headquarters of his tenants. In 1256 the lords of Domvast (Somme) insisted that when the men of the village had rebuilt the church its tower was to be used only as a refuge in case of need, not as a fortress for rebellion.[53] One can imagine that many other churches and churchyards saw a good deal of peasant grumbling and agitation, if not of open revolt. Nevertheless lords did not always worship in private chapels or stand apart from their parishes, and not all charters, whether granted specifically to

[51] Prou, 'Coutumes de Lorris' [171], 445-57; Chartes de Cluny [100], no. 4205; Dubled, 'Communauté de village' [372], 24; Bader, Studien [228], ii. 182-234; cf. Duby, Société mâconnaise [381], 232.

[52] Below, pp. 139-41.

[53] Fossier, Chartes de coutume [126], 483-4.

parishioners or not, were the result of open conflicts.[54] Even where parishes appear to have served peculiarly peasant interests it was (except in cases of tithe) as tenants or subjects, rather than as parishioners, that peasants felt their grievances. We have to keep remembering that documents often refer indifferently to parishioners or inhabitants or just 'the men' of a place: the use of the word parishioners is no guarantee that it was the parish bond that most united people in any way that was especially relevant to the particular transaction. In the country, as in towns, parishes did as much to bring together diverse groups and classes of laymen in some sort of association as to provide a forum for conflict and confrontation. The desire to consolidate this sort of superficial unity was presumably what led some parishes to form parish fraternities or guilds to feast together each year and promote brotherly fellowship.[55]

The structure of parish government

Parishioners did not need any formal act to constitute themselves into a community capable of acting together either at law or in other ways. The men of Louvres formed a *confratria* or *communitas* when they needed to raise money, but that was because they were for secular purposes under the authority of the mayors of Gonesse, nearby, and were simultaneously involved in a protest against them.[56] In this semi-rebellious situation the bond of a fraternity, which they tried to make all the inhabitants join, made very good sense. In references to *universitates* or *communitates parrochianorum*, however, the collective nouns have no particular significance: they are just a convenient way of describing the local community when it was acting together.[57] 'Acting together' was, moreover, just that. There was no legal difference between, for instance, an endowment of a church by a whole parish or one made by each of the parishioners individually contributing his share.[58] Some more formal institution of a collective

---

[54] Below, p. 00. [55] Above, p. 77.
[56] *Actes du parlement* [97], i. 138-9.
[57] Bader, *Studien* [228], ii. 182-3, 217-21, 415-16.
[58] Stenton, *Documents of Danelaw* [191], no. 465; cf. B.L. Add. MS. 6040 [1], no. 16. I owe these references to Dr W. J. Blair.

entity may perhaps lie behind some of the thirteenth-century Italian *comuni di pieve* which developed quite elaborate institutions, such as a college of consuls acting under the presidency of a *rector*. Nevertheless even these *comuni* seem to have evolved gradually. Their statutes, like charters of privileges, did not so much create communities as give them more authority or define more exactly an authority which was already exercised.[59] There was no particular authority, privilege, or constitution which was connected with the use of any particular collective noun or with the use of a collective noun at all: the records show that parishioners, like other groups, could engage in much the same sort of activities whether they were described explicitly as a collectivity or simply as the inhabitants, named or unnamed, of a parish.[60]

For some purposes the parish priest would be the natural leader or representative of his flock. The *communitates patrie parrochiarum* which Louis VI called out to help in his war against brigands seem to have served under their priests.[61] In many circumstances, however, parochial responsibilities were by definition those of the laity, so that lay officers might be needed. In Pirano (now Piran, Istria) the tithe of oil was collected by two men, one appointed by the clergy and one by the laity.[62] By the thirteenth century fabric funds are known to have been managed in some places by laymen, and in some English parishes these look very like the later churchwardens.[63] Where there was a parish fraternity or guild whose property was not distinguished from that of the parish we may suspect that its priors, *rectores*, or aldermen were sometimes the effective wardens, masters, or treasurers of the church—or *vice versa*.[64] Similarly where a parish was more or less coextensive with a town or other unit of government its affairs might be dominated by the civic or other officers. That would not necessarily involve any usurpation of authority.

[59] Santini, *Comuni di pieve* [673].

[60] e.g. 'Coutumes de Lorris' [171], 445; below, pp. 141-4; cf. privileges secured by agreements between lords: Devailly, *Berry* [358], 342-3.

[61] Suger, *Vie de Louis VI* [72], 138; Orderic Vitalis, *Hist. Eccles.* [57], vi. 156; cf. *Cart. de Mâcon* [173], no. 632.

[62] *Chart. Piranense* [128], pp. 22-33.

[63] Owen, *Church and Society* [615], 115; Le Bras, *Hist. du droit* [527], viii (2), pt. 2, 279-81; le Picard [625].

[64] Duparc, 'Confréries du Saint-Esprit' [388], 358.

Rather, it would be a manifestation of the acceptance of normal authority within what was in effect a single community, various as its functions might be. A good example occurs in the series of law-suits waged between the bishop of Capodistria (now Koper) and the people of Pirano between 1201 and 1205.[65] The Piranesi were doggedly resisting the bishop's claim to the tithes of oil, which they maintained had always been used to light the churches of the town, and to the *quartese* of the other tithes, which they said traditionally went to the poor and the church fabric. Their proctors in court were appointed by the *gastaldio* (or *podestà*), *judices*, consuls, and all the people.[66] Town and parish were one.[67] On this occasion even the local clergy stood solidly beside their parishioners. They appointed their own proctors but did so at the same meeting as the laity appointed theirs. They denied the bishop's accusation of leaguing improperly with the laity against him,[68] though they admitted that they could not desert their friends and relations. Such local solidarity between clergy and laity on a matter of tithes must have been rare, but it illustrates the universally ready recourse to collective action and the ease with which solidarities were formed and adapted to the needs of any occasion.

Elections of clergy were sometimes made in a way which reveals the characteristic medieval desire to reconcile respect for authority with popular participation. In one twelfth-century appointment of a parish priest in the diocese of Lucca the patrons were to make their choice *cum accordamento vicinorum* and in the early thirteenth another shows a system of election being devised by which the number of *vicini* participating was to be the same as the number of patrons:[69] votes were therefore being counted as equal. Sometimes the wish for consensus seems to have been met by indirect elections, with the *podestà* or other person or persons of authority,

---

[65] *Chart. Piranense* [128], pp. 10-81.

[66] Ibid. pp. xxix-xxx, 10-11, 12, 22-31.

[67] In this case a *pieve* (mother-parish).

[68] *Nullam societatem fecerunt cum parrochianis suis in causa ista nec in alia contra episcopum suum vel honorem suum*: ibid. p. 23. Cf. p. 43 where the bishop accused them of making a *coniurationem et conspirationem* with the laity against him, and pp. 47-50, 57.

[69] Nanni, *La parrochia* [604], 161-2. For the significance of *vicini*, below, pp. 103, 154.

sometimes explicitly after full consultation of the whole community, choosing a panel of electors to choose the priest.[70] On many occasions, both in parishes which elected their priests and in the far more numerous ones which did not, parishioners no doubt made their collective decisions by the usual amorphous consensus in which we may guess that the richer and more senior of them took the leading part. *Parrochiani meliores et antiquiores* can be found representing their parish just as the *seniores et meliores de villa* represented a village.[71]

---

[70] Kurze, *Pfarrerwahlen* [517], 491-531.
[71] Bader, *Studien* [228], 285.

5

Villages and rural neighbourhoods

Medieval historians talk a good deal about 'the village community' but the concept is one which needs some examination before the manifold evidence of collective activity in the thirteenth-century countryside can be evaluated.[1] To start with, we need to consider how much of the rural population lived in villages rather than in more scattered settlements, and in particular, how many of them lived in the typical medieval village of the textbooks: a firmly nucleated settlement with its own church and single manor-house in the middle, and its open fields and common pastures spread round about. The terminology both of the sources and of the modern literature is unhelpful here. *Villa*, for instance, could mean either a settlement or an estate or lordship,[2] and sometimes it even meant a unit of local government which might comprise a number of separate estates and settlements.[3] A good many historians have written as if all these sorts of unit were identical. Sometimes they were, and medieval documents, for good social and legal reasons, are apt to read as if they were, but it is difficult to make sense of those same documents without recognizing that this was not always the case and that, if it were not, then the nature of the bonds between neighbours would vary.

The first set of problems that we must consider therefore concerns the pattern of settlement. In the classic village the sheer proximity of dwellings would presumably promote some degree of solidarity, which would be increased if people had to co-operate in labour services at hay-making

---

[1] Beckerman, 'Customary Law' [242], 234–41 contains a cogent criticism of some uses of the expression.

[2] I use this word for any unit subject to a single lord. In this chapter that means typically the sort of unit of exploitation and jurisdiction known in English contexts as a manor. The word and concept are discussed on pp. 219–20.

[3] Bader, *Studien* [228], i. 20–37; Winchester, 'The Medieval Vill' [755]; Niermeyer, *Lexicon* [211], 1101–3; cf. 1104–5 for *villare, villata, villatica*.

and harvest or in the working of a regulated open-field system. How far did people who lived in scattered settlements or practised less co-operative systems of agriculture nevertheless act as some sort of local community? So far as nucleated villages are concerned, if, as the evidence suggests, a fair number of thirteenth-century settlements were of this kind, can we assume that the same holds good for the tenth century? If not, was the change a cause or a result of increased local solidarity?

Secondly, through what means did groups of neighbours, whether in villages or not, function as communities? Many of the assemblies which appear to have regulated local affairs were the courts of lordships. How far could such a court act as a forum for the community of subjects or tenants, and how far could a village function as a community if it were not under a single lord? Similar problems arise from the relationship of village to parish. So far as the community of the parish can be separately discerned it has been discussed in the previous chapter, and the community of higher and wider types of lordship will be dealt with in chapter 7, but so far as lordships carried powers of local government at village or neighbourhood level they will have to be discussed here. A local community might or might not be a parish, but it is the contention of this book that an essential attribute of any local group which was perceived as a group was the right and duty to participate in its own government. The extent to which any locality was a unit of lordship and local government was thus an important measure of its cohesion. This chapter will therefore have to attempt to sort out some of the ways that the demands of lord and church strengthened the bonds of neighbourhood and how far the instititiuons of lordship and parish provided a framework of neighbourly activity.

Thirdly, it is often difficult to know whom the 'village community' is supposed to have included. Leaving aside women, living-in servants, and, of course, children, do we envisage the effective community as one which included all the inhabitants, only the landowners, or only the peasant landowners? If we see it as essentially a peasant community, was it united primarily by the dues owed to the lord or lords and consequent common interests against them, and how far did the free and unfree, the richer and the poorer—however we define all these categories—form one community? Who dominated its deliberations?

Lastly, we should consider the relations between this local community and the outside world. How far were peasant conflicts with lords, or the charters of liberties that peasants sometimes won, influenced by the better-known and more sensational demands and achievements of townsmen? Or, if 'village communities' were 'peasant communities', does that mean that they were those closed, mutually hostile communities to which people belong 'in a way in which they belong to no other social group', and which Macfarlane has characterized as the essence of a genuinely peasant culture?[4]

It ought to be the purpose of this chapter to solve these problems, as well as to answer more profound questions about the working of local communities. In practice medieval records, even from the relatively rich period after 1200, are inadequate to say much about the personal relationships which underlay and determined such collective activities as did get recorded. Nevertheless, even if it is pointless to pose many of the questions one would like to have answered, and even though this chapter will do little more than scratch the surface of both sources and literature, some problems must be confronted if only to see what one is talking about.

To start with there is the terminology. The subject must be the community of neighbours (*vicini*) as well as the community of villages as such. Ideally it might be sensible to avoid the word village altogether unless one were sure that the sources refer to a nucleated village or to its inhabitants acting as a whole. The word 'vill', which is quite often used by those who write about medieval England, has some attractions, particularly if it could be used consistently in the sense in which Maitland defined it. He used it to translate *villa*, meaning a territorial unit consisting of a settlement (or a settlement and its dependent hamlets) with its lands, and contrasted it with township, as a translation of *villata*, which he maintained was used in the sources to mean the community which

---

[4] Macfarlane, *Origins of English Individualism* [560], 31-2.

inhabited a vill.[5] Unfortunately, though Maitland had good evidence for saying that medieval Englishmen sometimes seem to have made the same distinction between *villa* and *villata* as he did, in many contexts the two would have come to much the same thing for them, and it is difficult to keep the two senses distinct in practice. 'Vill' therefore is liable to turn into one of those pseudo-technical archaisms, usually left undefined in the modern literature or given conflicting definitions, which do so much to make medieval history impenetrable. It also has the further disadvantage of implying that there is something peculiar about English villages which needs to be expressed in a peculiar word. It would surely be better to make such a suggestion explicit, and try to substantiate it comparatively than to assume it by the use of an insular translation of a term used all over Europe. The search for a precise vocabulary is in the end bound to fail. Words were used in different senses in different places and at different times, and the connection between words, concepts, and social phenomena is too complex and variable to be represented by any consistent terminology. The best solution seems to be to translate *villa* and *villani* by village and villagers where the Latin words seem to mean more or less what would be suggested by the normal popular usage of these words in modern English, and to try to distinguish the different sorts of community under discussion, and the different sorts of bond which united neighbours, as clearly as possible without relying on *ad hoc* definitions.

The pattern of settlement

The history of rural settlement, like that of field systems and of medieval agriculture in general, is an enormous subject of great complexity which cannot possibly be tackled here. What would be useful would be a crisp summary of current scholarship so that we could consider the framework within which local societies functioned as communities. Unfortunately it is a subject on which new work is being done all the time in many places, and there seems no possibility of making a summary which would be much crisper than a cold

[5] Pollock and Maitland, *History of British Law* [628], i. 563-4.

pancake. Before the twelfth century the evidence is, as usual, sparse, and its interpretation depends as often as not on procedures like reading social relationships into place-names or arguing backwards from the later period, with all the dangers of circular arguments that such reasonings involve.

Traditionally the pattern of rural settlement has been traced back to the barbarian settlements or, in the south of Europe, even further to Roman or pre-Roman times. More recently evidence has been adduced to suggest that open-field systems developed later and more gradually than used to be thought,[6] and that, in some areas at least, the nucleated villages which are associated with open fields were not the original pattern of settlement. According to what threatens to become a new orthodoxy of late villages and late open fields, the early middle ages were a time of hamlets and farm-steads rather than of large villages. In parts of Italy and southern France, for instance, there seems to be no doubt that between 900 and about 1150 a significant proportion of the rural population moved into new walled settlements called *castra* or *castell(a)e* in Latin (Italian: *castelli*). The evidence of a consolidation of settlement in parts of Germany at much the same time is also apparently good. How far the change in each area was a defensive measure, a sign of the troubles endured by those who lived in dispersed settlements, and how far it was a sign of growing population and pros-perity, and of the desire of lords to profit from it, is debated.[7] Either way, some people in southern France, for instance, already lived in relatively large, nucleated villages, while others went on living scattered outside the new walled villages.[8] It would, in any case, be wrong to generalize these findings too widely. In many other areas of western Christen-dom, particularly in forest or upland regions, a good deal of the rural population remained dispersed in farmsteads or

[6] Hoffmann, 'Medieval Origins of Common Fields' [472]; and below, p. 110.

[7] *Cam. Econ. Hist.* [304], i. 356; Fasoli, *Studi ezzeliniani* [407], 17-20; Toubert, *Structures du Latium* [715], 303-13, 325-8, 367-8, 473-9; Baratier, 'Communautés de Haute-Provence' [231], 237-9; Font-Réaulx, 'L'Origine des villages dans le sud-est' [419]; cf. Devailly, *Berry* [358], 302-11.

[8] Higounet, *Paysages et villages neufs* [468], 373-97; Gramain, 'Villages et communautés en Bas-Languedoc' [449], 121-2, and 'Structures féodales en Biterrois' [450].

small hamlets throughout the middle ages and beyond.[9] In Picardy, on the other hand, recent and detailed study has confirmed the stability of predominantly village settlement from well before 900.[10] The same might hold good for other areas which have not yet been investigated or where enthusiastic adoption of the revisionist thesis has cast doubt on traditional ideas without very much evidence being cited (or, perhaps, being available) either way.[11]

That is not, of course, to deny that the pattern of rural settlement changed significantly between 900 and 1300 in many areas outside those already mentioned. The foundation of castles and churches quite often attracted people to new sites and the rise of population provoked the foundation both of new villages and of new hamlets and farmsteads. In England, and particularly lowland England, the chief time when entirely new settlements were established seems to have been relatively early, and may have been over before the eleventh century. Outside the north, where a good many villages were probably founded or refounded when the countryside recovered from William I's harrying (1069-70), there seem to have been few whole villages which were not in existence by 1086 or perhaps a hundred years earlier, and many hamlets which were not mentioned in written records before the twelfth or thirteenth century may nevertheless have existed then too. Nevertheless the pattern of settlement was not rigid, and throughout history villages have been less fixed on their sites than one might imagine. Some of the isolated Norfolk churches, for example, can be explained by the way that villages have moved, sometimes gradually or in a series of steps, to new sites within their own territories.[12]

---

[9] Bader, *Studien* [228], 25-36; Hoffmann, 'Medieval Origins of Common Fields' [472], 35-8, 42-3; Higounet, *Paysages et villages neufs* [468], 159, 373-97; Hoskins, *Provincial England* [480], 15-52.

[10] Fossier, *Picardie* [420], i. 163, 345-55.

[11] Duby, *Économie rurale* [377], 58-9; see e.g. Taylor, *Cambridgeshire Landscape* [713], 54-66, 71, 75, 92-3, citing no evidence before 1086. The articles cited by Taylor in 'Aspects of Village Mobility' [712], though full of interesting hypotheses, contain no hard evidence of a change from dispersed to nucleated settlement or of entirely new villages (as distinct from those which moved, mostly within their own territory).

[12] Sawyer, *From Roman Britain to Norman England* [677], 132-67; Aston, 'Postscript' [225]; Arnold and Wardle, 'Early Medieval Settlement Patterns'

Some of these shifts, of course, represent the geographical displacement of a community rather than a change in its character, and a good many of them came after 1300 and fall outside the scope of this book.

In France the pattern varied widely. In some areas, in addition to many new hamlets and farmsteads which were inserted between older villages or spread into the forests and hills, whole new villages were still being established. Colonization in the Auvergne had started by the tenth century but in most of the regions which have been studied it seems to have begun rather later. New villages appeared throughout the twelfth century and, in smaller numbers, in the thirteenth, under a variety of names—*villes neuves* (Latin: *ville nove*), *bourgs*, *sauvetés*, *castelnaux*, *bastides*, in addition to the *castra* or *castelle* which have already been mentioned. In the Netherlands and along the North Sea coast of Germany new settlements were appearing on land reclaimed from the sea and marshes by the eleventh century, some of them as proper villages but more as small hamlets and farmsteads. In Italy the resettlement in *castelli* seems to have been accompanied or succeeded, where land remained available, by entirely new settlements in the same form. By the mid twelfth century, however, the original trend was reversed in some parts of the country and people began to move out from the defended sites once more.[13]

Clearly therefore there were many variations between regions and even within regions throughout the period. No area can ever have been without nucleated settlements and few can have been without some people living in smaller groups. One cannot start an account of local communities either from the premise that nearly everyone throughout the period lived in nucleated villages or from the premise that nucleated villages were a new phenomenon whose appearance explains the characteristic village community of the twelfth and thirteenth centuries. It is tempting to guess that the way

[223]; Roberts, 'Village Plans in County Durham' [661]; Wade-Martins, 'Origins of Rural Settlement in E. Anglia' [732].

[13] Duby, *Économie rurale* [377], 153–65; *Cam. Econ. Hist.* [304], i. 295–6, 357, 393–5, 463–4; Higounet, *Paysages et villages neufs* [468], 235–42, 373–97; Ennen and Janssen, *Deutsche Agrargeschichte* [392], 164–78; Settia, 'L'Incidenza del popolamento' [688], 267.

that new villages were planned, and that people settled into them and established their customs, implies that both lords and settlers had an ideal type or model of a village in their minds from the start. They may have had, but there were often other reasons, like defence, for putting settlers into villages, and the way that some settlers continued to establish themselves in isolated farmsteads shows that not everyone found the model irresistible. Nevertheless, when all qualifications are taken into account, far more people lived in bigger and more densely populated places after 1100 than before: many a classic village of the thirteenth century had probably been a small cluster of houses with no church—or no parish church—in the tenth.[14] The ideal type must have been altered and reinforced by the growth of population as well as by the economic, social, and administrative developments which accompanied it.

Local communities in the tenth and eleventh centuries

A hundred years ago most historians believed that the active rural communities which they found recorded in the twelfth and thirteenth centuries derived their cohesion from the 'mark communities' of free Germanic settlers who had first taken possession of the north European countryside hundreds of years before—or, in the case of Italy, from rural communities which had survived from Roman times. More recently it has been argued or implied that there was little or no real local community at peasant or village level in the tenth and early eleventh centuries.[15] Quite apart from the doubts which have been cast on the existence of nucleated villages it has been argued that (at least in some areas) there were as yet no regulated open-field systems and no lands common to all the inhabitants of a locality. Meanwhile the division of local populations both between kinship groups and between free and unfree was exacerbated by the disintegration of Carolingian government, which replaced the collective activity of

---

[14] See pp. 81-90.
[15] Duby, *Société mâconnaise* [381], 122-4, 227-33; others imply rather the same thing by discussing the formation of rural communities with reference to the period after *c.*1100.

'public' courts by arbitrary seigniorial control in 'private' courts. It also seems to be agreed by many historians that the pressure of lordship on the peasantry as a whole became heavier around the twelfth century, and that it was this which moulded peasants into coherent local communities. This section of the chapter will try to weigh the evidence on these matters, though it must be confessed at once that so little is known about them all that *a priori* opinion tends to loom large in any interpretation.

To take the last point first, the idea that lordship became in some way stronger and more oppressive during this period has been around a long time. In the nineteenth century it took the form of theories of free, equal, and independent 'Germanic' settlers who were only gradually subjected to 'feudal' lordship.[16] Since then, a good deal of the evidence of early freedom and equality has evaporated under closer scrutiny, but the idea of gradually increasing control and oppression of peasants by the upper classes has not been abandoned. It is certainly true that as government became more systematic and as rulers got more control of legislation and law-enforcement, so lords found ways of exacting their dues more consistently. The parcelling out of the countryside into defined jurisdictions during the twelfth and thirteenth centuries helped, as I shall argue, to define the communities within which peasants acted. Nevertheless, defining the boundaries of actual communities is not the same as creating the sense of community in the first place; an increase of records of seigniorial oppression and collective peasant resistance is not the same as increased oppression and resistance; and more systematic and effective government after 1100 was not merely or entirely a weapon of class conflict. The evidence, such as it is, suggests that most small-holders in the early middle ages were subject to some sort of control and oppression by their social superiors. The harsh and hostile views which clerical writers often expressed about peasants suggest that some degree of class solidarity was established well before 1100 and even before 900.[17] Peasant

---

[16] On 'Germanic' settlers: Reynolds, 'Medieval *Origines Gentium*' [653]; on 'feudal' lordship: below, pp. 220-4, and Brown, 'Tyranny of a Construct' [284].

[17] Duby, *Early Growth* [378], 31-47 and *Economie rurale* [377], 97-107,

rebellions and conspiracies were no novelty.[18] Poor as the records are, moreover, we none the less have some evidence of local groups of peasants negotiating collectively with their superiors about matters which—so it appears—concerned them all.[19] So far as local solidarity depended on oppression and conflict between lords and men there was probably as much scope for it before 1100 as after.

Other pressures towards peasant solidarity, however, did not operate, or did not operate so strongly at this stage as they did later. These include matters of agricultural practice. For this period it is easier to find evidence of newly cleared land in separate ownership than of furlongs being cleared co-operatively, and then divided and allocated to individuals, in the way that the model of an aboriginal open-field system requires. There seems in fact to be no unambiguous evidence of open fields subject to common rotation or common grazing on the fallow before the twelfth century. In some places which later had such systems, crops were being rotated so haphazardly in the eleventh century, and even as late as the thirteenth, that any common and regulated use of the arable would have been impossible.[20] The cumulative evidence that field systems became regulated only after the great period of population growth is therefore strong. Whether that means that agriculture in the tenth century was in general particularly individualistic[21] is another matter. In some areas there was—and always remained—a good deal of scope for individual enterprise. In the villages of Latium, for example, everyone could cultivate his bits and pieces of ground in his own way. Yet, though the later fragmentation of holdings complicated the pattern further, holdings here were intermixed from the start.[22] Even though they were not subject to

117-29; Aston, 'Origins of the Manor' [225]; James, *Origins of France* [490], 73-6, 196.

[18] *Leges Langobardorum* [91], 73 (Rothari, c. 279-80); for a conspiracy of c.1000: William of Jumièges, *Gesta Norm. Ducum* [40], 73-4.

[19] Duby, *Économie rurale* [377], 118, 122; *Urkundenbuch Zürich* [120], i, no. 203; below, pp. 111-12.

[20] Dodgshon, *British Field-Systems* [364], 1-38; Hoffmann, 'Common Fields' [472]; Fossier, *Picardie* [420], i. 331-44.

[21] Hoffmann, 'Common Fields' [472], 33-41; Dodgshon, *British Field-Systems* [364], 75-6.

[22] Toubert, *Structures du Latium* [715], i. 290-3; *Cam. Econ. Hist.* [304],

common rights, that must have necessitated a fair degree of interaction between owners and, in this particular area, of co-operation over irrigation. Like the later fragmentation, the original layout was the product of a society to which at least a modicum of collectivity was acceptable. The same applies in many other regions which probably did not yet have regulated systems of open fields but which seem to have had some or all of their arable holdings intermixed. It has recently been suggested that in England between about 950 and 1300, or a bit earlier, villages may have periodically reorganized their arable so that newly cleared land, at first cultivated separately, was incorporated into the open fields. The only reason for supposing that they did not make such reorganizations before the tenth century seems to be the belief that lordship was then becoming firmer and that only superior authority could have achieved these reorganizations.[23] The argument looks circular. Equally circular, but equally plausible, would be one which postulated that regular rearrangements of arable were an example of the kind of collective control which is attested even where lordship was weak. Collective action on this interpretation would have been a cause as well as a result of the gradual evolution of field systems.

Collective use of non-arable land may also have been quite widespread. Everywhere common rights in woods and pastures were less strictly controlled in the tenth and eleventh centuries than they would be later, but they nevertheless existed and, as the law of the time allowed, they were enjoyed and perceived in very much the same way as other property rights.[24] They were in fact, in contemporary terms, the collective or corporate property of the local population.[25] In 970 Otto I granted to certain tenants (*incensiti*) of Santa Maria in Organo, Verona, who lived in Azzago (Veneto), all his royal dues for pasture and pannage (*herbaticum et escaticum*) in full ownership (*iure proprietario*) for ever, along with i. 368-70.

[23] Dodgshon, *British Field-Systems* [364].

[24] Bognetti, 'Beni comunali' [263]; Maitland, *Domesday Book and Beyond* [567], 142-4, and *Township and Borough* [568], 11-36; Duby, *Société mâconnaise* [381], 123, 227-30; for rather later, Fossier, *Picardie* [420], 713-14.

[25] Above, p. 35.

the right to cut wood, plough, and pasture beasts in some woods nearby. In 996 his grandson heard a plea about a meadow, an island, and various lands which were disputed between the people of four other places near Verona.[26] The rival claims could perhaps be interpreted in the terms of the 'primitive communism' attributed to 'mark communities' by nineteenth-century historians but are more likely to be analogous to later disputes between parishes about their boundaries. One fact is clear: the local inhabitants in these places had, and were recognized to have, collective interests in their lands. Such interests only needed to be referred to—and perhaps only envisaged as property—when they were disputed or conveyed. Though references as full as the two cited seem fairly uncommon there are sufficient allusions to suggest that this sort of common property was quite usual, though probably less so in areas of scattered settlement.[27] Charters conveying whole estates to new lords sometimes imply that woods and pastures were to be seigniorial property, but in other documents it looks as if lords' rights to their use were more or less on a par with everyone else's. Churches and mills, though used by all, were normally referred to and disposed of as seigniorial property but, despite the overriding subjection of individual peasant holdings to seigniorial government and dues, rights over territory which was exploited jointly were sometimes envisaged as belonging to some sort of local community which might or might not be coextensive with a lordship.[28]

One argument for the relative weakness of peasant communities before the later eleventh century is that the division between free and unfree within them precluded any effective unity. References to *terra francorum* in Burgundy, for instance, have been adduced to suggest that the community which owned or controlled common rights and land was a community of free men rather than of all inhabitants.[29] The significance of this depends on the definition of free and

[26] *M.G.H. Dipl.* [156], Otto I, no. 384; Otto III, no. 227.

[27] For slightly later examples: Muratori, *Ant. Ital.* [163], iii, col. 647-50 (1098); Dubled, 'La Communauté de village en Alsace' [372], 1 (1126); *Layettes* [194], i, no. 314 (1182); cf. Bader, *Studien* [228], ii. 175-6; iii. 1-3.

[28] *Chartes du Cluny* [100], no. 2959; Fournier, *Basse Auvergne* [423], 105.

[29] Duby, *Société mâconnaise* [381], 123.

unfree; the question which peasant landowners in tenth-century Burgundy would have been excluded from the *terra francorum* is not easy to answer now and might not have received very clear or consistent answers from local people then.[30] In any case, as we have seen, rights over territory were in some places envisaged as belonging to all the inhabitants. Presumably that came to much the same thing as saying that they belonged to landowners, and the more substantial among the landowners are likely to have dominated local groups anyway. The difference between all these sorts of shared or common rights may well have been less clear and significant to contemporaries than to later legal historians.

It is also sometimes suggested that such local communities as existed at the beginning of the tenth century were units of kinship rather than of settlement. In areas of scattered settlement the units of settlement as of tenure were 'manses' (or part-manses) which were held by family groups, free or unfree, which had little connection with each other. Again, the argument is not totally convincing. There is certainly evidence of scattered settlement, as we have seen, and there is also a good deal of evidence that land was held by families or kin-groups, but some of the evidence adduced to show kin-based settlements seems to be nothing more than the formation of a place-name from a personal name.[31] Place-names do not keep their meanings for ever and places can be named from people without implying that all the inhabitants, even at the time the name is formed, are blood relations. Moreover, though a household may be thought of as a family, exogamous households—or families—will presumably be in contact with their neighbours from time to time. Even manses which are described as free and unfree in seigniorial documents may sometimes have differed from each other only in respect of their obligations to their lord: they may have shared woods and pastures and their inhabitants must surely have interacted in other ways.

The most important way in which one would expect local people to have worked together, according to the norms of medieval society and government, would be in doing justice

---

[30] See pp. 31-2.
[31] Fournier, *Basse Auvergne* [423], 85-7; cf. Fossier, *Picardie* [420], 262-73.

among themselves and being responsible to higher authority for their own local government. Law-codes and Carolingian capitularies alike had for long imposed duties of judgement and policing on neighbours (*vicini*). The Salic law went so far as to ordain that no one could settle permanently in a *villa* unless everyone agreed. If one or two of the *vicini* persisted in objecting then the matter could be referred to the *mallus*. Once the newcomer had stayed for a year and a day unchallenged then he could stay permanently *sicut et alii vicini*.[32] It is often argued that by the tenth century collective responsibility had been eroded in areas where government was breaking down, and that an increasing number of peasants were falling under the exclusive jurisdiction of their lords. This looks possible, but on the other hand the similarity of rules and forms of government before and after—like this rule about a year and a day's residence, for instance—makes it tempting to guess that some of the old customs, and the collective solidarities that they reflect, had survived through the virtually unrecorded interim period. This argument obviously relies on the retrospective use of later evidence, but so, as we shall see, does the argument which it counters. The only way to avoid the danger is to look at what strictly contemporary evidence there is, bearing the arguments in mind. The material for England is relatively good and it may be helpful to start there. The English evidence may even help us to understand what was happening elsewhere, even though political conditions were different.

During the tenth century the West Saxon kings legislated about local government as they gradually extended their control over the whole of England. Shire meetings here, like the meetings of the *mallus* or county in the former Carolingian empire, were probably attended only by the most substantial of the peasantry, but a relatively large number probably went to the hundred.[33] The duty to attend the hundred regularly may have been restricted to free men but it seems improbable that humbler peasants were outside the hundred jurisdiction. Many of the provisions of the tenth- and eleventh-century laws would have been useful only if they had applied to the

[32] *Lex Salica* [117], 202-4 (tit. 80 = 45 § 1, 2, 4).
[33] Below, pp. 225-6.

rural population at large, including those who owed heavy services to their lord and came under his authority for many purposes. Edgar's laws imply that from the king's point of view hundreds were divided into villages (*tunas*) and tithings, not into lordships. The men of a village had the duty of informing the head of the hundred (*þam hundrodes ealdre*) if anyone acquired cattle without proper witnesses, while parallel or particular responsibilities also lay on the heads of tithings. By the eleventh century, and probably before, all men over twelve were supposed to be in tithings, which seem to be groups of surety and mutual responsibility very like the later frankpledges.[34] From the early eleventh century geld was collected by villages, not by lordships, and would presumably have been paid by all landholders, both free and less free.

It seems improbable therefore that local communities in England were normally divided by a wide gulf between the free who went to the 'public' or 'communal' assemblies and the unfree who may have been justiciable for some or many purposes by their lords. The boundary between public and private, free and unfree, cannot always have been clear, for some hundreds were probably always under 'private' lords from the time when they had superseded older and less tidy units of local jurisdiction. Sokemen who went to hundred meetings might nevertheless owe service and dues to their lords, and, even if the lord was also lord of the hundred, they might pay them locally, not at the hundred itself.[35] While the more substantial inhabitants of a village may have felt part of the wider community of the hundred or even of the shire, and the less substantial may have felt more enclosed within a lesser lordship or manor, the village itself and its tithings had some responsibilities which they all shared. It would be wrong to exaggerate the import of this. We know too little; but what can be discerned tends to suggest that, where villages existed, the community of habitation and perhaps of common rights gained some reinforcement from public duties. Tithings may also have lent a modicum of

[34] I Edgar, c. 2, 4; IV Edgar, c. 3, 8 (Robertson, *Laws* [177], 16, 32, 34, and see index *sub* hundred, tithing); Morris, *Frankpledge System* [599], 1–41.
[35] Davis, *Kalendar of Abbot Samson* [110], pp. xxxi, xxxvii, xlvii.

collective feeling to people who lived in scattered hamlets or homesteads.

Virtually nothing seems to be recorded about the lowest level of local government in the kingdom of Germany before the twelfth century. Later there was a variety of units— *burschaften*, *heimgerede*, *honschaften*, *zendereien*, whose distribution corresponds partly to varying patterns of settlement and partly also to regional variations of law, though it became complicated by migration and colonization.[36] A document of 1211 refers to an agreement made by the abbot of Deutz around 1025 with *quatuor vinciniarum hominibus que vulgo geburscaf vocantur*, which may justify putting *burschaften* at least back into the eleventh century.[37] Like the other units, *burschaften* were small and presumably consisted mainly of fairly humble people. The four *burschaften* of 1025 were all in one parish[38] and in 1211 they were rearranged from four to six: since they belonged to an area of dispersed settlement such rearrangements were no doubt easy and may have taken place before. *Burschaften* may therefore not have been very cohesive units, and nor may the other similar areas, while, effective as was the German monarchy at a higher level, it may not have been directly concerned with communities of this small size or imposed many duties on them.[39] All the same, like the English hundreds, *tunas*, and tithings, they look like collective bodies with some kind of quasi-public function. The fact that, like hundreds, they may sometimes have been under seigniorial control, so that local lords appointed their officers and received the profits of their justice, would not, of course, have robbed them of their collective character: it simply reveals the same tension between lordship and collectivity that pervades all medieval government.

The post-Carolingian disintegration of local government was most serious in parts of France and Italy, though the argument that this caused a wholesale collapse of local

[36] Ennen and Janssen, *Deutsche Agrargeschichte* [392], 178–86 surveys and gives references to recent literature.

[37] Steinbach, *Collectanea* [695], 581.

[38] Though for the large size of parishes at this date, see p. 87.

[39] Though *rustici* were mobilized *per . . . centenias* in civil war in 1078: *M.G.H. Scriptores* [54], v. 312. And see Bosl, *Frühformen* [268], 425–39.

communities has not been applied to Italy as forcefully as to France. In Italy, as counties became fragmented so lordships dependent on *curtes* or *castra* replaced the old hundreds and *sculdasiae*. As usual, little is known about the working of the new lordships before the twelfth century, but since they were often based on units of settlement, and were also sometimes coextensive with older areas, they are likely to have preserved some of the old customs and cohesion.[40] The diplomas of Otto I and Otto III to groups of inhabitants in the Veneto which were mentioned above both said that half the penalties which would be paid for infringements should go to those same local communities. Evidently the emperors recognized them as permanent associations which administered their own funds. They may well have also had some public responsibilities.

For France a series of impressive regional studies shows the structure of local government collapsing around the end of the tenth century and—their authors often suggest—such feelings of local solidarity and collective responsibility as there were collapsing with it.[41] Some historians suggest that such feelings were already weak, since free and unfree peasants shared so few burdens and duties. In some places *vicairies*, *voieries*, or *vigueries* (Latin: *vicariae*) fulfilled rather the same functions during the tenth century as the English hundreds, sometimes still having their judgements made by panels of *scabini*. Whereas in England, however, the hundreds gained duties as the monarchy extended its power, in much of France the vicariates decayed with the declining authority of king and count. Where effective superior authority was absent, local lords—the castle owners or castellans—were able to wield their powers more arbitrarily than their opposite numbers could do in England or Germany. Thus, it is thought, they subjected the dependent peasantry ever more completely and drove an ever deeper wedge between them and the free men, who perhaps still maintained some sort of local

---

[40] Vaccari, *Territorialità* [722]; Fasoli, 'Castelli e signorie rurali' [404]; Toubert, *Structures du Latium* [715], 1191-1313.

[41] Duby, 'L'Évolution des institutions judiciaires' [380] and *Société mâconnaise* [381], 106-8, 186-90; Beech, *Gâtine of Poitou* [243], 25, 107-113; Devailly, *Berry* [358], 109-23, 168-87; Fournier, *Basse Auvergne* [423], 311, 389-90; cf. Fossier, *Picardie* [420], 480-534.

collectivity on the basis both of their attendance at the
'public' assemblies of the vicariate and of their control of
common property. During the eleventh century the functions of the vicariates were more or less absorbed by tribunals
under castellans, and it was not until the *châtellenies* themselves were broken up into smaller parish or village lordships
that government structures really began to reflect and en-
hance popular solidarities.

This summary is very simplified and lacks many of the
local variations that historians have revealed. In Flanders, for
instance, the count kept good control of his dominions, while
in Picardy, although the counties became fragmented, comital
power was maintained, with no subordinate vicariates, and
was only gradually delegated to viscounts and castellans.
There is much in the general picture, with the greater nuances
which are shown in regional studies, that cannot be denied.
But it may nevertheless be too gloomy. If that is so, then it is
all the more important to consider the arguments carefully
because views of French 'feudal anarchy' have traditionally
had a great influence on ideas about the rest of Europe. The
belief that local communities in general were formed only
after about 1100 (so far as it does not derive simply from the
improvement of the evidence then) probably now derives
largely from the fact that French historians have put such
a strong case for it in relation to France. We need not only
to compare the evidence about French conditions with that
about other countries in order to evaluate the arguments
about France itself, but also to consider how much we are
applying models which particularly fit those French conditions to parts of the west where conditions were quite different.

One reason for suspecting that the French evidence may
have been interpreted too blackly is that so much of it comes
from the great churches, which were interested in the grass-
roots of local government only when it affected their interests, and whose members' attitudes to Law and Order were
characteristic of those who lived in disciplined and privileged
enclaves in a more fluid society. The very collapse of law
and order was, however, itself a stimulus to collective action.
The 'peace associations' which the churches supported are

one illustration of this.[42] They were formed first in France, and in those areas of France where conditions were worst, but they could not have succeeded as well as they did if some local cohesion had not survived, unrecorded, at the grass-roots even when formal enforcement of the law was at its weakest. Another illustration comes from Champagne, where the monks of Saint-Thierry, Reims, were driven by the difficulties of protecting their village of Villers-Franqueux (Marne) to let its inhabitants look after themselves and elect their own protector—until he became too rich and powerful for their liking.[43] The negative view which historians take of local cohesion at this time may also have been affected by two arguments or assumptions which need a closer look, not least because, if they were correct, they might affect our view of conditions outside France too. The first is the belief that the division of jurisdiction over the peasantry between 'public' and seigniorial courts, and between a mass of different seigniorial courts, separated local communities. The other is the belief that seigniorial courts were not places of collective judgement. Both may have some truth in them, but they owe more to traditional views of 'feudal anarchy' than to documentary evidence from the period.

We do not know how deeply, so long as the public tribunals survived, the peasantry were divided between those who attended them and those who did not. Many peasants everywhere, in England and Germany as well as in France and Italy, owed heavy dues to their lords and were presumably, *de iure* as well as *de facto*, more or less under their authority. The difficulty is that what that 'more or less' means is totally obscure. A significant proportion of the population *may* have been so unfree as to be completely under seigniorial justice, both before and after castellans took over the public tribunals, but just how many, and just how far that affected local solidarities, is unknown. In France the free who still attended surviving 'public' tribunals or castellans' courts may nevertheless have come under the authority of lords for some purposes, as they did even in England, where royal authority was strong, so that their fellow-feeling with the less free may have been fostered by some shared interests. As in Italy,

[42] Above, p. 34.   [43] Bur, *Champagne* [291], 347.

moreover, a good many of the new lordships were more or less coextensive with the old areas and others started off with some sort of transference of authority from them. As yet, while the population was relatively small and scattered, a relatively large proportion of it may have attended the meetings of these relatively large areas, and such areas may have formed the most cohesive local units that there were. However oppressed, peasants may have known a fair amount about what was going on. William of Jumièges, writing soon after 1070, described a peasant revolt of about seventy years before in terms that, if he is to be trusted, suggest rather effective communications over quite a wide area. He says that the *rustici* of Normandy met in *conventicula*, claimed the use of woods and waters according to their own laws, and sent a pair of deputies from each gathering to a central *conventus*. Their organization did not ensure success, for the revolt was fiercely suppressed, but it sounds like something more than a mere riot.[44]

As well as not knowing how divisions of jurisdiction affected local solidarities, we are almost entirely ignorant of the procedures followed before the twelfth century in lords' courts for their peasant tenants. Later grants of customs and liberties show that the arbitrary and uncollective judgements of seigniorial courts were resented, but they also show that peasants regarded the rule of custom and collective judgement as right, if not as automatically *their* right. It was an essential attribute of unfreedom that one was more completely subject to one's lord's will, but that does not mean that all justice over unfree peasants was as a matter of course assumed to be autocratic by right. The pressure towards collective judgement which was exerted by custom and by general social values and norms would presumably be reinforced in local lordships by the often collective character of peasant dues and obligations, which were themselves subject to customary contraints. Where a lord had assumed any part of his jurisdiction by a transfer or usurpation of the work of an older tribunal, moreover, then his court may have continued some of the old procedures. In Flanders and Brabant *scabini* gave judgements in seigniorial courts as they had in the *mallus*.

[44] Guillaume de Jumièges, *Gesta Normannorum Ducum* [40], 73-4.

The more closely the procedures in lords' courts for their peasants reflected those of other tribunals, the more those subordinate to them may have perceived themselves as some kind of collective group and the smaller would be the gulf between them and those who were justiciable elsewhere.[45]

Altogether, then, battered as many French peasants were by the troubles of the countryside during the tenth and eleventh centuries, and little evidence as we have of their communal activity, we cannot assume that they felt no sense of local cohesion before the new seigniorial jurisdictions appeared, or that the new jurisdictions created cohesion merely by their new uniformity of oppression. Humble people who lived in the most troubled areas of the countryside were doubtless those who suffered most from oppression, but the similarity of the economic conditions and the burdens of peasant life, as of legal norms, everywhere in the west suggests that the absence of records need not imply that people in the most troubled areas lacked all the collective customs and duties that obtained elsewhere.

Almost everything that can be said about neighbourhood communities before 1100 is speculative, and it may be that because my subject is collective activity I am exaggerating the faint hints of its existence. But it still seems fair to conclude that the arguments that deny it in general terms are unproven. Wherever we have record evidence, as opposed to lamentations about disorder, we have evidence of collective activity of some sort. It may be that in England local cohesion was greater because a powerful government first maintained and then increased the duties imposed on local communities. In fact, however, we do not know that cohesion was greater there—or anywhere else—or, if so, why it should have been. In the tenth century royal government was more remote from the valleys of Switzerland and the villages of Italy than it was from southern England, but the inhabitants of the valley of Uri negotiated collectively about tithes and several Italian villages are known to have managed their own common lands and held their own funds.[46] We cannot assume that when the evidence starts to improve in the twelfth century it

[45] Above, p. 31.
[46] *Urkundenbuch Zürich* [120], i, no. 203; above, pp. 111–12.

was because new structures of government had united local communities for the first time, so that a new 'spirit of association' had appeared, any more than that it was because people were then living in entirely new forms of settlement.

The consolidation of the local community

The collective habits and responsibilities which I have tentatively ascribed to earlier local communities begin to appear much more clearly in the records between about 1050 and 1200. Partly, as I have suggested, that is simply because the records themselves improve, but the process was more complicated than that. First of all, the improvement of the records was part of a general development of literate administration and law which tended to fix, define, and standardize duties and relationships more exactly. That could in itself have consolidated hitherto informal communities. Meanwhile other changes were taking place in the countryside which also combined to make people work together more regularly. Pasture and arable were being more strictly regulated, new settlements were being founded, local jurisdictions were being consolidated, liberties and customs were being granted or confirmed, and more villages were acquiring their own parish churches. These processes were not equal and autonomous causes of greater local solidarity: they are interrelated phenomena which seem to suggest that something important was going on. If there was one single underlying cause for them all it must have been the growth of population and of the economy, which left the old settlements larger and more densely populated than before and brought a variety of new ones alongside them. In itself this confirms the presumption that the change was not a simple and sudden one, for the growth of population was something that had been going on for some time before its effect made much impact on surviving records. At this stage, however, it seems best to leave underlying causes on one side and instead to describe in turn each of the various processes that offer evidence of increased collective activity in many parts of the countryside of western Europe.[47]

[47] Parish churches are discussed above, pp. 82-8.

The stricter regulation of land-use is one phenomenon which (even if one is not primarily concerned with causes) seems to be directly connected with the pressure of population on resources and with a consequent need to use them more intensively. Disputes between neighbouring communities about their woods and pastures are quite often recorded in the thirteenth century,[48] while communities ready to sell their commons seem to have found willing buyers.[49] The early thirteenth-century Customs of Milan held that where commons were to be divided between the lord of a village (*domino cuius est totum districtum*) and the *vicini*, then the lord should get half and the *vicini* half.[50] The English Statute of Merton (1236) allowed lords to appropriate woods and pastures to their own use provided that they left enough to the other commoners, and in 1291 King Rudolf of Germany ruled that lords could allocate bits of common land (*communitatem*) to individuals if that was the local custom, but that men of a village (*villae*) could not appropriate adjacent common without the lord's consent.[51] Clearly the need to make the most of land was sharpening the sense of common property and the conflicts it induced.[52] The same pressures bore on arable land with even greater effect. If crops were rotated regularly and uniformly over intermixed holdings then pasture rights could be established on the stubble and fallow. By the twelfth century evidence of this begins to appear so that we can see the classic open-field system taking shape on the lowlands of northern Europe. In Picardy the first evidence of regular rotations comes from lords' own lands about 1100 and the first rotations common to whole villages are recorded in the thirteenth century.[53] In

[48] Fossier, *Chartes de coutume* [126], pp. 75-7, no. 85; Dubled, 'Communauté de village' [372]; *Urkundenbuch Zürich* [120], iii, no. 1024; Bognetti, 'Beni comunali' [263], 472-3; Neilson, *Terrier of Fleet* [164], pp. xli, 77-8; Bader, *Studien* [228], ii. 180.

[49] *Annales Mon.* [7], iii. 378-81; *Urkundenbuch Zürich* [120], ii, nos. 624, 1070; *Urkundenbuch Basel* [202], iii, p. 365-6; Dollinger, *L'Évolution des classes rurales* [367], 491 n.; *Chartes de Cluny* [100], no. 5167.

[50] *Liber consuetudinum Mediolani* [89], p. 108 (21. 15); for *districtum*, below, p. 128.

[51] *Statutes of the Realm* [190], i. 2-3 (c. 4); *M.G.H. Const.* [160], iii: Rudolf, no. 458; cf. *Freiburger Urkundenbuch* [137], i, no. 167.

[52] Fossier, *Picardie* [420], 713-14; Bader, *Studien* [228], iii. 1-3.

[53] Fossier, *Picardie* [420], i. 336-45; above, p. 110.

some places a change from a two- to a three-field system can be detected rather later, though in much of southern France, for instance, a two-course rotation apparently survived because it was more suited to the soil and climate. Some fields there were subject to common rights and some were not.[54] Regional variations in field patterns remained numerous and within regions there was more variation than has always been acknowledged.[55] Some places which would later come to have fully regulated systems were still without them in 1300,[56] but the norm was becoming sufficiently well established in some people's minds for them to take it with them when they went to settle new territories.

Common rotations and common grazing on fallows and stubble required a great deal of organization, co-operation, and supervision. They were most likely to be established where people were predominantly engaged in arable farming, where they lived close together with their arable holdings already more or less intermixed, and where they already had institutions through which to make and enforce agricultural regulations. In England manorial courts often served the purpose, and on the English evidence it has been argued that strong lordship and an unfree peasantry were preconditions of a 'farming community' with regulated open fields.[57] This is a bit over-simplified. Because many English lords continued to exploit their lands directly through reeves or bailiffs they kept a direct interest in village agriculture and so the manorial court of a village with only one manor was the natural forum for regulation. Manorial courts, however, were not entirely subject to seigniorial will, and where there were several manors the parish may have provided the necessary bond for villages to organize their farming. This does not seem to be recorded before 1300 in England, but that may be because the records of village or parish activity, unlike the records of manors, were either not kept or have

---

[54] Miller and Hatcher, *England, 1086–1348* [587], 90; Faucher, 'L'Assolement triennial' [409].

[55] Campbell, 'Regional Uniqueness of Field Systems' [305].

[56] *V.C.H. Middlesex* [728], iii. 23; Miller and Hatcher, *England, 1086–1348* [587], 95.

[57] Dodgshon, *British Field-Systems* [364], 666–75. Cf. Harvey, 'Planned Field Systems' [461]; Yelling, 'Rationality in the Common Fields' [767].

not survived.[58] What happened in other countries where direct seigniorial exploitation had largely been abandoned before cropping became regulated suggests that lordship and servitude were not essential to the introduction of highly co-operative farming. Fossier connected the introduction of common rotation to Picardy with the concurrent development of autonomous peasant communities, while Duby suggested that at Saint-Ambreuil (Saône-et-Loire) common rotation and common pasture on the fallows were combined both with weak and divided lordship and with rather scattered settlement.[59] That may be exceptional: regulated fields were apparently always most common in areas of predominantly village settlement. Nevertheless some of the partial and untidy-looking systems which are recorded at this period— and Saint-Ambreuil looks like one of these—might be explained as the product of smaller groups within a locality (whether inhabitants of a hamlet or sharers of an inheritance) regulating their part of the arable on their own. Everything that we know about the overlapping communities of lordships, settlements, parishes, fraternities, and so forth, suggests that people were prepared to act collectively at many levels and that there was no universal trend from one sort of community to another. Whether regulated fields were the fields of a manor, of a more or less autonomous village, or of a smaller group within either, they were the product of local societies that had already become prepared to impose controls of considerable complexity on farmers and were able to organize the details. Any group that had, by whatever method, gradually or at once, achieved a system of common rotation and common grazing on the arable, needed to maintain its unity and collective authority to enforce the system. The move towards the classic open-field system, where it occurred, was therefore both a cause and a result of increasingly close community.

New settlements, another obvious result of population growth, appeared, as we have seen, at many dates and took

[58] For a later example of such village action: Wake, 'Communitas Villae' [733].
[59] Fossier, Chartes de coutume [126], 66; Duby, Société mâconnaise [381], 288–93.

many forms. A significant number of them consisted of nucleated settlements, which had their own parish churches,[60] a bank or wall around the houses, and a defined territory assigned to them outside the defences. When foundations like this were recorded it was usually because they were made by lords who wished to exploit their lands more fully. When and where a lord first decided to attract settlers by offering them advantageous terms is unknown, but early in the twelfth century the archbishop of Hamburg made an agreement with six Hollanders, including a priest, who proposed to settle on uncultivated marshland (Hollerland, near Horn, Lower Saxony) in his diocese. Rents and tithes were fixed; the archbishop granted a tenth of the tithe for the maintenance of the priests who would serve the parish churches; and the settlers granted one manse from each of the prospective parishes for its priest. In return for an annual payment the settlers were allowed to decide their disputes among themselves; they were to refer greater matters which they could not resolve to the archbishop, who would come to hear them at their expense. Two-thirds of the profits of justice were to go to the settlers and a third to the archbishop.[61] During the twelfth century grants of liberties to new settlements, as to old, became increasingly common. Variations were endless and there were no liberties exclusive to the new villages, but many of them had at least some of their rents and dues fixed, and their rights of inheritance specified, while some secured a measure of autonomy. This usually included the holding of some or all of their own pleas, as in the Hollerland charter, and some of the legal procedures which would be followed might be laid down. Sometimes settlers, like other villagers, were allowed to choose their own local officials to preside over their assemblies and collect their dues.[62]

Charters tend to give an impression that settlements were more recent and had been more planned and organized from above than was often the case. Some charters which purport to establish new villages really only conferred privileges on

[60] See p. 86.

[61] Inama-Sternegg, *Deutsche Wirthschaftsgeschichte* [139], ii. 13 n.; Deike, *Entstehung der Grundherrschaft* [354], 14–16, 35, for commentary and reference to other printed texts.

[62] See below.

people who had already made their own spontaneous settlement, had presumably formed themselves into some kind of community, and may have taken the initiative in asking the lord for a charter.[63] Many new settlements remained without any special privileges, particularly of course many of the new homesteads and hamlets that were built on the edges of woods and commons between older villages. Although some Italian *castelli* were—to judge from the seigniorial documents—certainly founded on seigniorial initiative, others were built by groups of *vicini* apparently acting on their own.[64] New settlements, and particularly new villages, developed new solidarities of their own but there does not seem to be much evidence of immigration by the sort of isolated individuals from far away who would need to be welded into entirely new collective forms. People who had moved into the *castelli* of tenth-century Latium had normally come in groups of kinsmen or of several associated families, and most came from fairly nearby. *Incastellamento* there does not seem to have been directly connected with changes in family structures.[65] Nor perhaps were later migrations. According to a rather scornful monastic chronicler the Franconian settlers in the diocese of Merseberg at the beginning of the twelfth century came each with his own little household (*cum famili-olae suae contubernio*), cleared the land by his own labour, and gave his own name to the settlement (*villa*) which he founded.[66] Later in the century things became more organized, and lords in the east began to employ property developers or *locatores* to bring people to the east and lay out the villages and lands they were to occupy.[67] Many of the settlers came from far away, but, to judge from the way that they brought their customs with them, they came in fairly homogeneous groups. The contribution of new settlements to the development of local solidarities was not so much therefore that they created entirely new kinds of solidarity, or that their liberties were peculiar or unprecedented. Rather, they may just have

[63] Fossier, *Picardie* [420], 349-51; Ennen and Janssen, *Deutsche Agrargeschichte* [392], 185.

[64] Fasoli, 'Castelli e signorie rurali' [404], 553-4.

[65] Toubert, *Structures du Latium* [715], 325-6.

[66] *M.G.H. Scriptores* [54], xvi. 247.

[67] Ennen and Janssen, *Deutsche Agrargeschichte* [392], 165-9.

helped to establish a new norm of nucleated village, consisting of houses gathered around its own parish church, and forming a separate unit of jurisdiction and administration. At the same time a much less dramatic expansion of settlement was going on at the edges of old cleared land. Some settlers in forests or mountain valleys may have deliberately rejected village life and developed an individualism analogous on a small scale to that of the American frontier, though doomed to be unrecorded by Hollywood.

Relations with lords also helped to consolidate peasant communities in various ways. Outside England local jurisdiction and government gradually became consolidated in the hands of lords, who thereby, in the terminology of later lawyers, came to hold both high and low justice—became holders of the ban or *districtus* (*districtum*, *districtio*). Their authority extended over all peasants (whether free or unfree, including tenants of other lords and those who held land without paying rent or dues to a lord) who lived within their ban, *districtus*, or *potestas*. The process involved disputes between lords, of which early signs appear in eleventh-century complaints about 'evil customs' imposed on church lands by the lords of castles, while later stages are reflected in some of the enquiries and agreements about customs which were recorded in the following centuries. As these suggest, overlaps of jurisdiction were not eliminated entirely, and many churches retained immunity for their lands and tenants, but the general trend was towards a correspondence between the boundaries of jurisdiction and the boundaries of parishes—and thus, where people lived in villages, between the boundaries of jurisdiction and the boundaries of village territories.[68]

In England villages did not become units of jurisdiction in the same way since virtually all jurisdiction over serious crimes and over free land was reserved there to the crown. In some villages, however, the chief manor claimed view of

[68] Duby, *Économie rurale* [377], 482-4 and *Société mâconnaise* [381], 232-3, 440-4; Fournier, *Basse Auvergne* [423], 389-90; Devailly, *Berry* [358], 317-29, 335-49; Fossier, *Picardie* [420], 510-33, 687-700; Dubled, 'La Notion du ban' [373]; Bader, *Studien* [228], ii. 90-102; Schlesinger, *Mitteldeutsche Beiträge* [680], 272-4; Vaccari, *Territorialità* [722], 53-72; Tabacco in *Storia d'Italia* [710], ii. 150-67.

frankpledge and other petty rights over everyone and the royal government used the unit of the *villa* or *villata* for various of its own ramifying purposes.[69] Where people did not live in villages, or where the villages were too small to make practical units, they were grouped together to fulfil their duties in areas which were reckoned for the purpose as *ville* and sometimes described as *ville integre*.[70] Although these uses of the word suggest that settlements as such were thought of as normal units of government, it nevertheless remains true that the trend towards the coincidence of lordship and village that is found elsewhere did not occur in England. Here the manor remained the most important instrument for the exercise of seigniorial power: because manorial lords maintained their interest in direct exploitation and therefore their right to labour services, they were able to keep a considerable measure of control over the lands and persons of their unfree tenants (those too unfree to claim the protection of the royal courts) through their manorial courts.[71] Since the boundaries of manors more often than not failed to coincide with those of villages, this meant a village seldom had a single court in which all its inhabitants or landholders would meet as a matter of course.[72] Parish churches may sometimes have provided the missing forum, but for many peasants the jurisdiction of their manorial court and the duties it imposed must have been more real and more burdensome than any other authority. Perhaps therefore the community of the manor and its court sometimes equalled or outweighed the community of a village or hamlet that did not have its own church.

One result of seigniorial pressure upon local communities, as lords sought to increase or maintain their incomes, was to increase conflicts between peasants and lords—both those lords who exercised rights of higher jurisdiction and those whose powers were more purely economic. The sharpening of

---

[69] Cam, *Law-Finders and Law-Makers* [302], 72-4.

[70] Lees, 'Statute of Winchester' [530]; Winchester, 'Medieval Vill' [755].

[71] Miller and Hatcher, *England, 1086-1348* [587], 204-24; Bridbury, 'Farming Out of Manors' [277]; Hyams, *King, Lords and Peasants* [485]; Hatcher, 'English Serfdom' [463]; cf. Duby, *Économie rurale* [377], 469-72.

[72] Kosminsky, *Studies* [508], 73-80; on the overlaps, see *Fleta* [27], 442-3 (v. 51).

conflict with a single lord could be both a cause and an effect of local unity, though equally the division of lordship may sometimes have stimulated a village to develop its own institutions.[73] Even without conflict, institutional development was a potent force for solidarity, and one which resulted directly from the growth of both seigniorial and governmental power. I have already suggested that lords' courts sometimes employed collective procedures of inquiry and judgement before 1100. As the twelfth and thirteenth centuries advance we have increasing evidence that they often did so, although on occasion they were overruled by the representatives of their lords. Not all the examples of collective decisions come from places with special grants of privileges:[74] the development of all government in medieval conditions led inexorably to the development of collective institutions both to ratify decisions and to carry them out.

As local government became more effective so records were made of customs, and grants of new liberties were issued—whether in the form of custumals, *chartes de franchises*, *Weistümer*, or *statuti*. All these sorts of document should be seen as the natural concomitant of government, produced often out of conflict but also as part of the general trend towards record-keeping. Charters are significant not only as evidence that some communities secured exceptional liberties but as testimony to the customs and rights which all communities wanted and which many may have enjoyed, at least intermittently, without grants. Statements of custom range from agreements between lords about their respective rights over a group of peasants, through records which may or may not contain novelties, like the German *Weistümer* or the Italian *statuti*, to charters which purport to grant entirely new liberties. It is generally impossible to tell whether a grant to an existing settlement really bestows anything new or whether it merely confirms and records in writing customs that were already supposed to be observed. Some charters and many custumals were intended to record customs as

---

[73] Bader, *Studien* [228], ii. 75, 94.

[74] Beckerman, 'Customary Law' [242], 30-100, 177-8; 'Cartulaire de Gorze' [138], ii. 317-18; *Documenti de Arezzo* [167], no. 370; *Chartes de Cluny* [100], no. 4523; Brunner, *Land und Herrschaft* [289], 360.

much or more for the lord's benefit as for that of his subjects.[75] For all these reasons it would be impossible to say
when lords first started granting liberties, even if all the documents had survived, which of course they have not. An early
example, however, is the agreement which the abbot of
Nonantola (Emilia) made with all the inhabitants of Nonantola in 1058. In return for their undertaking to build three-
quarters of the wall around the *castrum*, while he saw to the
rest, he promised that neither he nor his successors nor their
servants would arrest, assault, punish, or slay any of the
inhabitants; nor would he take their goods by force or dis-
traint; nor demolish any house, except according to law and
saving the rights of justice of his lordship.[76] For any English
medieval historian the evocation of Magna Carta clause 39
must lend support to the argument that thirteenth-century
ideas of corporate liberty were not a new creation of current
political conflicts or academic political theory. Conflicts
stimulated theorizing and sharpened the need to have rights
recorded, but the rights had long been valued. In 1058 the
abbot went on to grant the people of Nonantola and their
successors rights of inheritance to their individual properties,
within stated bounds, and all his lands, woods, and pastures
in the same area. The penalties laid down for infringements
of the agreement—£100 on the abbot or his successors, £3,
£2, or 20s. respectively on any of the greater, middling, or
lesser of the people—suggest either that the people had
funds of their own, like the tenth-century Veneto communities, or that there was some common fund which
belonged to them and the abbot together.

During the twelfth and thirteenth centuries grants of
liberties multiplied, except, apparently, in England, with old
settlements getting very much the same sort of customs and
privileges as new—that is, more or less defined rents, dues,
and rights of inheritance; exemption from more burdensome

---

[75] Schneider, 'Chartes de franchises' [682]; Perrin, 'Chartes de franchise'
[621]; Caggese, *Classi e comuni rurali* [298], i; Fasoli, 'Castelli e signorie rurali'
[404], 558-63.

[76] ... *audeat vel presumat aliquem hominem ... apprehendere, neque assalire,*
vel percutere, aut occidere, neque sua bona per vim ei tollere, vel pignorare,
neque domum aliquam frangere, nisi secundum quod lex precepit, salva tamen
donnicata justitia: Muratori, *Antiq. Ital.* [163], iii. col. 241-3.

legal procedures; and sometimes the right to elect their own officials.[77] As early as 1116 the people of Guastalla (Emilia) had the right to elect twelve men as consuls who governed the affairs of the lord and the people and without whose consent the lord should not alienate the *castrum* and *curtis*.[78] In France particular sets of customs became well known and were granted to many communities. Louis VII gave customs to the inhabitants of the parish of Lorris (Loiret) in 1155 which later spread to other places under royal control; Nicholas, lord of Avesnes, granted laws, commune,[79] dues, rents, and liberties (*leges et communiam et pactiones et redditus et libertates*) in 1158 to the *burgenses* of Prisches (Nord) which were afterwards copied at some thirty other places in Hainault and Vermandois; and in 1182 the archbishop of Reims gave the mayor, *jurati*, and other men of Beaumont-en-Argonne (Ardennes) customs and liberties which were later enjoyed by hundreds of places in Champagne, Burgundy, and Luxemburg.[80] In fact the differences between the various sets of customs were often less significant and more haphazard than this may suggest. All these three, incidentally, included the rule about free residence after a year and a day which has generally been associated with new urban liberties but which had probably originated in rural custom long before.[81] In practice the particular terms of any grant depended on the varying interests of lords in particular places as well as on the particular points of custom which may have been in dispute there.

[77] For regional surveys: Faraglia, *Comune nell'Italia meridionale* [402]. Caggese, *Classi e comuni rurali* [298]; Perrin, 'Chartes de franchise en Lorraine' [621]; Schneider, 'Chartes de franchises' [682]; Higounet, *Paysages et villages neufs* [468], 383-5; Ourliac, 'Villages de la région toulousaine' [614]; Werkmuller, *Weistümer* [742].

[78] *Regesto Mantovano* [197], no. 173.

[79] For the significance of communes, below, p. 135.

[80] Prou, 'Coutumes de Lorris' [171], 445-57; Prou's evidence for a previous grant from Louis VI is not strong, but Louis made other grants: Higounet, *Paysages et villages neufs* [468], 235-42 and *Ordonnances* [144], vii. 444-5, xi. 184. Verriest, 'Charte-loi de Prisches' [200], 337-49; Teulet, *Layettes* [194], i, no. 314; cf. Walraet, 'Chartes-lois' [737], though the *Layettes* text does not support his reference to Beaumont as a *villa nova*.

[81] Above, p. 114, and Perrin, 'Chartes de franchise' [621], 37, 38 n. For seigniorial limitations on the rule, e.g. *Ordonnances* [144], xi. 184, and Homans, *English Villagers* [479], 331-2. It was also marginally limited at Prisches: Verriest, 'Charte-loi' [200], 346 (c. 45).

The free election of officials—whether they were called reeves, mayors, *villici, sculteti, syndaci, judices* or anything else—was clearly valued. Sometimes elected officers replaced the old ones, sometimes the community inserted their own representatives alongside or under the lord's: there seems to be no consistent significance in the names used and it is often pointless to agonize whether mayors in any region, for example, were seigniorial or 'popular' officials. The free election of officials was probably at first valued more because it would avert oppression by corrupt officials than because of any general desire for free elections as such. When there were fierce disputes, of course, one motive would turn into the other, but peasant officials appointed by lords must always have had divided loyalties anyway. The inhabitants of a village, or the tenants of a manor or lordship, could act collectively —could be a community—without having exclusive rights to elect their officials. Some groups were actually *required* to elect officials by their lord: in the thirteenth century the men of Cadland (Hants), embattled in resistance to the services demanded by their lord, the abbot of Titchfield, tried to get out of having a reeve at all. Early in the next century they varied their tactics by doggedly refusing to elect one, while the abbot apparently felt inhibited about appointing one himself unilaterally.[82] Some charters and customs also refer to the judgements and decisions of *jurati* or other groups of counsellors. The casual nature of many of the references suggests that the appointment—or election—of such groups did not generally constitute an innovation.[83] The supreme objective in seeking a charter was not any particular constitution or even perhaps any particular degree of autonomy, since local communities seem to have been required to do so much self-government anyway.[84] It was to secure exemption from oppression and arbitrary extortion. That was what the villagers (*villani*) of Burgbernheim (Franconia) won when Frederick I allowed them, in return for an annual rent, to possess their *villa* free from all lordship, so that they would

[82] Watts, 'Peasant Discontent' [740], 126-7.

[83] e.g. Verriest, 'Charte-loi de Prisches' [200], 345-7 (c. 41, 46); Feigl, 'Entstehung der Weistümer' [411], 431-3; cf. Beckerman, 'Customary Law' [242], 30-47; and below, p. 145.

[84] Below, pp. 148-52.

live under the protection of his imperial highness safe from all tyranny.[85]

Some charters and *Weistümer* were no doubt the product of oppressions and conflicts which are now unknown. Other struggles did not end so happily, but their length and bitterness is poignant testimony to the solidarity of the local communities which carried them on. The serfs of Rosny-sous-Bois (Seine) sued their lords off and on for over fifty years in a way later lawyers would think only a chartered corporation could do, and even had the worldly competence to send proctors to Rome about it on at least one occasion.[86] As in this instance, or that of Cadland, it was often ecclesiastical lords who were most reluctant to give anything away. All the clergy, in addition to having a particularly strong ideological bias towards due order and hierarchy, were under an obligation not to alienate the rights and property of their churches. When it came to a dispute, moreover, a religious house probably had more internal cohesive force (as well as carrying more legal and political clout) than the most determined village. It is, however, impossible to work out rules about the sort of lords who granted liberties and the sort of places which got them: there was, after all, little correlation between the formality of a grant and the degree of independence any community enjoyed.[87] In England, where there were no rural charters of liberty as such, manors were none the less being farmed out to their tenants from the eleventh century, and the terms in some cases conveyed more corporate autonomy and freedom than some French villages got from their charters of franchises.[88] In the same way, the pope's seigniorial rights were being granted to local communities from the eleventh century, and in the twelfth some of the north Italian villages that enjoyed various degrees of self-government did so by custom rather than by any recorded grant.[89] Customary

---

[85] *Mon. Boica* [153], xxix (1), no. 522.

[86] Bloch, 'Serfs de Rosny' [261].

[87] Collin, 'L'Administration des villages lorrains' [334].

[88] Hilton, *A Medieval Society* [470], 153-4; Cam, *Law-Finders and Law-Makers* [302], 79, and note the request for 'certain special liberties' in *Royal Letters* [187], i. 381-2; Ault, 'Village Assemblies' [227], 18-22.

[89] Partner, *Lands of St. Peter* [620], 126; Vaccari, *Territorialità* [722], 112-13.

privileges were vulnerable and leases could be ended, but charters were not proof against withdrawal either. Although they give an impression of steady expansion of liberties that is partly because later on more was recorded and more records survive. Some of the inhabitants of *sauvetés* in southern France had lost some of their liberties by 1300, and so had some of the archbishop of Hamburg's Dutch settlers, while the thirteenth century may have seen some erosion of liberties in the Italian countryside when the great cities extended their control over their *contadi*.[90] Just as formal liberties were not necessary to establish a close sense of local community, however, so their withdrawal did not necessarily weaken it.

The charter of Prisches which has been mentioned above gave Prisches a *communia*, whereas the grants of otherwise similar liberties to Lorris and Beaumont did not use the word. It is a difficult one which has been much discussed. Most discussions start from the belief that it had (or ought to have had) a consistent legal and constitutional meaning which was connected with a new distinction between groups of people who had or did not have legal personality. I have already argued that there was no room for this distinction in any legal system of the period and that it was therefore not envisaged by anyone.[91] I also maintain that there is no reason to suppose that *communia* and its variants (*communio, communa, communantia*, etc.) should, either jointly or severally, have had any consistently exact constitutional or legal meaning, and that they did not in fact do so. Words, after all, are often used in a variety of senses in real life, not least when they are current in political contexts which vary from place to place and from time to time, so that the word picks up new connotations from its varying surroundings. *Communio, communia*, and *communantia*, for instance, were all used to mean (among other things) common rights or common property as well as a group or association of people.[92] In the twelfth century the various forms of the word came to be used so generally in so many areas for local political associations

[90] Ourliac, 'Villages de la région toulousaine' [614]; Deike, *Entstehung der Grundherrschaft* [354], 89–92; Caggese, *Classi e comuni rurali* [298], ii. 5–84, but cf. Bowsky, 'Medieval Citizenship' [272].

[91] Above, pp. 59–64, and below, index *sub* commune.

[92] Niermeyer, *Lexicon* [211], 219–223.

that one of its meanings came to be a collective group that enjoyed, or that wanted, some measure of autonomy. Whether a commune was defined essentially by its oath is very doubtful: members of such groups might well take an oath, but then so did many groups which were not communes. That was hardly a defining characteristic.

As time went on, communes began to need special authorization in the sense that, because governments were establishing their authority, it was becoming difficult for either individuals or groups to claim any special degree of autonomy without permission. Because of the common use of the word for groups claiming autonomy, therefore, a government giving or withholding permission might do so by saying that a group might or might not form a commune. In 1252 the papal rector of the March of Ancona allowed the men of Penna San Giovanni to form a *communantia*. In fact they had formed it four years before: what he was really doing was recognizing it and agreeing that, under certain safeguards, the people of Penna should run their own affairs while he kept control of the castle.[93] His charter went on to spell out the liberties they would have, for merely allowing a town or village—or a hamlet, or a parish, or any other local group— to form a commune did not define its degree of liberty.[94] The particular liberties enjoyed by any commune—or a group which did not happen to be called a commune—depended on grant or custom, or a combination of both, not on the word which was used to describe it. On occasion the grant of a charter to one part of a locality might divide an existing community in two for the purposes of local government,[95] but most groups of country people who secured a charter must already have been fairly effective communities and their charter simply consolidated their unity. By getting a charter to themselves and their heirs they became something pretty like a modern corporation whether or not the charter happened to refer to them as a commune, but many groups of country *vicini* organized their corporate life in much the same way without ever getting a charter.

[93] *Liber Censuum* [116], i. p. 563-4; Leicht, 'La "carta di libertà" di Penna San Giovanni' [532].   [94] Cf. Bader, *Studien* [228], ii. 3-29, 177, 190.
[95] Devailly, *Berry* [358], 543.

The foregoing account of the changes which promoted peasant solidarity in the twelfth and thirteenth centuries has begged the question where peasants got their new ideas from. That is because, so far as I can see, the ideas which inspired them were not particularly new. It is often suggested that people in the country took their ideas of liberty from the towns, and it is indeed likely that news of some of the struggles and victories of townsmen stimulated their rural neighbours. Nevertheless peasants were not significantly later than townspeople in demanding confirmations of good custom, and they presumably learned from each other as well as from the towns. What both sets of people were asking for at first was simply good custom: they perceived the liberties which they wanted as old. That is not, of course, to say that there had necessarily once been a time of greater peasant freedom or, if there had, that they remembered it. Custom was often ambiguous anyway. The changes that occurred came not because values changed, but because increasing pressures on custom from all sides—increasing for economic and demographic reasons—made the fulfilment of traditional values at once harder and more desirable. Each struggle—each victory—in the countryside, as in the towns, must have stimulated others. One striking exception to the apparently general prevalence of traditional ideas deserves to be mentioned. This comes in the liberties granted to Rocca d'Orcia (Tuscany) in 1207, so that it was apparently the lord rather than the peasants who expressed it. Guido Medico opened his charter by declaring, at some length, that Rome, the head and mistress of all the world, had grown through equity, justice, and liberty, and that no land could flourish without these qualities. Here at Rocca affairs had gone from bad to worse, because of inequity, injustice, and servitude, so Guido, on behalf of himself and his kinsmen, now wanted to put matters right. This he could do only by reducing the services of the men of Rocca to regular annual amounts and laying down what they should be. Then everyone on both sides would live in equity, justice, and liberty, and Rocca (*Arx*) would flourish among the other *arces* of Italy. This evocation of the glories and values of ancient Rome in a seigniorial document from a rural lordship would have been unenvisageable before the educational and academic advances of the twelfth century. Yet all Guido's splendid antiquarian grandiloquence is the preamble to clauses which deal with customs and dues of a traditional sort in an entirely traditional way. Allowing for variations in local custom, they could have applied to any north European village at the same time.[96]

The character of local communities

So little is recorded about local communities before about 1100 that it seems pointless to pile speculation upon speculation by saying more about their character and government at that period. The rest of the chapter will therefore relate to the twelfth and thirteenth centuries, not because the character, structure, and activities of local communities then were necessarily in all respects different from what they had been before, or, on the contrary, because it is safe to argue back from the later period to the earlier, but simply because it is only at this time that the evidence seems to be good enough to be worth discussing further.

The first point to make is that there was no one sort of group which acted collectively. The people of a whole village, or of a manor or lordship, or of a parish, or of several villages or other settlements, might all act together on occasion. Their behaviour was strongly and frequently collective, not because each person belonged to any single close community (outside the household), but because people seem to have been ready and able to act collectively in any group that had common interests in the matter in hand. Any of these groups might be described quite loosely as a *universitas* or *communitas*. Many people must have thought of themselves (if they thought consciously about the subject at all) as belonging to overlapping groups within their immediate locality and also to layers of collective activity beyond it. The consuls of the *comuni di pieve* in north Italy were generally elected by the separate villages or quarters within the *pievi*, mountain valleys developed communal organizations uniting several villages or settlements, while the scattered farmsteads of the North Sea marshes were united in *Bauerschaften* which were

[96] Zdekauer, 'La *carta libertatis* della Rocca di Tintinnano' [206].

themselves grouped into parishes.[97] Different places under the same lord shared interests in so far as he treated them the same way, for good or ill.[98] During the thirteenth century the inhabitants of the villages in the Val di Sieve (Tuscany) which belonged to the Bishop of Florence repeatedly resisted the officials he appointed and the dues and services they demanded. Borgo San Lorenzo seems to have been the administrative and market centre of the area and also the centre of resistance, but it looks as if the bishop's subjects throughout the whole valley were acting at least intermittently in concert.[99] Few villages can have been cut off from the outside world. Everywhere peasants went to market, some served in armies, and some went to courts in nearby or distant towns. So far as collective behaviour and loyalties are concerned Macfarlane is right therefore when he denies that English country people were peasants of his ideal type, living in 'largely identical but mutually antagonistic and bounded territorial groups, segmented "into units of high similarity and low mutual interaction" '.[100] But nor were the country people of other parts of western Europe: they were all highly collective in their habits and attitudes but very flexible about the units in which they acted.

These small local communities of *vicini* or *villani* were peasant communities in the looser sense that their membership was largely composed of non-nobles who (we may deduce), though many of them had servants of their own, themselves did physical labour on their own holdings and made their livings from the land. Many of the more dramatic pieces of information about them show them acting in groups over against their lords, whether because the lord was granting them privileges or otherwise ordering their activities, or because they were in conflict with him. Everywhere there were disputes, or agreements which presumably resolved disputes, over the level of rents and dues, over the lord's right to

[97] Santini, *Comuni di pieve* [673], 194, and *Comuni di valle* [674], 8–10, 164–5, 188–96; Vaillant, 'Les Habitants des communautés briançonnaises' [723]; Baratier, 'Communautés' [231]; Stoob, 'Landausbau und Gemeinde' [700]; Mayer, 'Vom Werden der Landgemeinde' [583], 485–7.
[98] Kuhn, 'Zur Kritik der Weistümer' [516]; Lennard, review of Homans [540].
[99] Lami, *Monumenta* [142], ii. 793–822 (at foot of pages).
[100] *Origins of English Individualism* [560], 32, quoting T. Shanin.

arbitrary tallage, or, in England, over labour services.[101] When rising population caused wages to fall, and rents and prices to rise, the conflicts may have got worse, though to some extent this may be an illusion created by improving documentation: when peasant revolts became widespread in the later fourteenth century they seem to have fitted a Tocquevillean rather than a Marxist model. In any case to look only at the documents which reveal or imply class conflict is to beg the question: local communities although predominantly composed of peasants, and although quite often in conflict with their lords, did not owe their solidarity *merely* to that conflict. Some of the most independently active local groups, like the coastal marsh or Alpine valley communities, seem to have been active precisely because lordship was weak or divided and they were left to get on with it. The development of lordship and government united local communities not only by oppressing them into unity but by providing the framework within which they fulfilled normal public duties. In this aspect of their relationship with their lords most peasants may have seen little cause for conflict, provided the lord observed custom. The mayor or reeve who collected dues and enforced obligations may have been liable to turn into an enemy, but he was also one of the natural representatives of the community to the outside world.[102] Just as for some purposes a priest might speak for his parish, though for others their interests would be opposed, so a lord or his official was often seen as the natural representative of his tenants or subjects. Outside authorities seem to have been equally ready to deal with a deputation appointed directly by them, provided of course that they were not acting against the lord. In 1254 Henry III of England reminded the archbishop of Canterbury that *villate et communitates villarum* had the right to prosecute suits through three or four of their number. The archbishop should therefore allow the tenants of Imbert de Pugeys, one of the king's favoured courtiers, to

[101] Hilton, *A Medieval Society* [470], 154-61.

[102] Cam, *Law-Finders and Law-Makers* [302], 81-3; Schlesinger, *Mitteldeutsche Beiträge* [680], 222; for a village sharing the guilt of a (seigniorial) *villicus* who was accused of homicide: Dubled, 'Communauté de village' [372], 22; for a lord's treaty binding his subjects and their successors: Calasso, *Ordinamenti* [301], 226 n.

prosecute or defend cases *pro communitate sua* in his court so that Imbert would not need to be bothered.[103] Not surprisingly, although there was much concerted resistance to lords, communities did not always manage to maintain a united front against them,[104] and some directed a good deal of their hostility against their neighbours instead—or as well. In the mid thirteenth century the parishioners of Louvres (Oise) made a unilateral declaration of independence against the mayors of neighbouring Gonesse, who had authority over them, while gang warfare broke out on several occasions between the men of Clent and Halesowen (Worcs.), probably being provoked by disputes over common rights.[105] Solidarities were as flexible as the groups which felt them.

Charters, statements of custom, and law-suits give the impression that local communities thought of themselves as including everyone. Charters were granted indifferently to the men, or good men, or inhabitants, whether of parishes or of places whose names are given with no qualification, description, or boundaries. In the case of the French settlements known as *bourgs* the word *burgenses* is commonly used, while Alsatian charters, for instance, refer to *universitates rusticorum* or *villanorum*.[106] All these words and many others seem to be used in a fairly loose way and do not imply any particular legal status. Charters of liberties did not automatically turn serfs into free men in any way which would have been consistently recognized at the time. Some charters may have made them much more free, but normally in the sense that the recipients were to be free from certain dues, rather than that their whole social and legal position was deliberately being transformed. The concepts of freedom and unfreedom were less simple and uniform in the twelfth and thirteenth centuries than they became in the eyes of later historians.[107] Nicholas of Avesnes apparently envisaged his

---

[103] Cam, *Law-Finders and Law-Makers* [302], 79–80; cf. Bader, *Studien* [228], ii. 182–3, 217–21, 408–16, and records of law-suits, *passim*.

[104] *Curia Regis Rolls* [109], vii. 343; *Placitorum Abbreviatio* [169], 140; though cf. Hilton, 'Peasant Movements' [469].

[105] *Actes du parlement* [97], i, no. 1560a; Homans, *English Villagers* [479], 328–9.

[106] Dubled, 'Communauté de village' [372], 14, 30 n.

[107] Cf. e.g. *Actes de Philippe Auguste* [111], no. 541, and Prou, 'Coutumes de

charter to Prisches as applying to both *liberi* and *servi*, for he promised that both would be free from arbitrary arrest.[108] In England common lawyers notoriously found it hard to draw the boundary between freedom and villeinage around individual people, and general prosperity, rather than legal status, was what determined a man's standing among his neighbours.[109] Though the co-operation, as well as the discontents, involved in regular labour services, may have made villeins into a community within a community, and though court rolls sometimes mention separately the consent of free and unfree to manorial ordinances, as yet both categories of people seem to have attended the same courts.[110]

For many purposes the 'everyone' whom the community included would be the resident householders: to enjoy liberties and customs one would need to be a fully paid-up and responsible member of the community to which they were granted. Some charters made this clear.[111] Some, granted to new foundations, guaranteed the right to come and settle freely, while in many places settlement would have been controlled by the lord's court, and thus subject to some element of collective decision.[112] One way this worked was through the fixing of entry fines for new tenants. For the unfree, departure from the community was also controlled, though on this point one may suspect that seigniorial restrictions less often enjoyed collective support.[113] In Halesowen the manorial court sometimes declared a poor person *persona non grata*, thereby in effect banishing him or her from the manor, though some of these unfortunate people hung on for

Lorris' [171], 542 (c. 1); Gouron, 'Affranchisement' [447]; Chomel, ' "Francs" et "rustiques" ' [323]; Buchda, 'Dorfgemeinde' [290], 17-20; Vaillant, 'Les Origines d'une libre confédération' [723], 326-8.

[108] Verriest, 'Charte-loi de Prisches' [200], 345 (c. 40).

[109] Hyams, *King, Lords and Peasants* [485], 233-68 *et passim*; Hatcher, 'English Serfdom' [463]; Cam, *Liberties and Communities* [303], 124-35; Homans, *English Villagers* [479], 241-50.

[110] Homans, *English Villagers* [479], 76-82; Beckerman, 'Customary Law' [242], 248-50; cf. Duby, *Société mâconnaise* [381], 612 n. Though note the Carlton ploughing competition, apparently restricted to free men: below, p. 151.

[111] e.g. Prou, 'Coutumes de Lorris' [171], 546-7.

[112] Homans, *English Villagers* [479], 331-2; above, p. 130.

[113] Hatcher, 'English Serfdom' [463], 15-18, 29-33; *Select Pleas in Manorial Courts* [186], 90 (concealment of flights).

a while as servants.[114] In practice a local lord and his family, even if permanently resident, would have stood outside the community for some purposes, and so might other inhabitants. In Italian *castelli*, for instance, there might be groups of nobles who filled a rather different position in local society from the normal local lords, since they were divided from the more prosperous of their neighbours more by their traditional ethos and life-style than by having any great jurisdictional or other rights over many of them. The relationship of groups like this to their neighbours presumably varied from place to place and from time to time. In Penna San Giovanni they joined in a *communantia* with everyone else in 1248, having previously been apart, and at the same time they renounced dues from various people in return for lump sums.[115]

From our point of view the most baffling of the many puzzles involved in defining those who fell under collective authority seems to be that which would arise from the overlaps of lordships, settlements, and parishes. Where privileges were at issue, geographical boundaries were sometimes carefully drawn, so that French villages which might otherwise have remained single communities became divided and are still separate communes to this day.[116] In other cases one may suspect that things were more rough and ready. Villagers divided between separate lordships or manors may have put on their parishioners' hats to regulate their common affairs, but the haphazard way that groups are described makes one wonder if they often noticed and bothered to change hats at all. It is quite possible that manorial courts in England sometimes handled matters which the royal government thought of as the responsibility of *ville*.[117] Unsatisfactory as all this vagueness may be to us, it illustrates an important point: the effective membership of local communities varied according to the structure of the local economy, society and

---

[114] Razi, *Life, Marriage and Death* [642], 78-9, 82.

[115] Leicht, 'La "carta di libertà" di Penna' [532]; for clergy and *milites* and the commune (though it should probably be classified as urban) of Roye (Somme): *Actes de Philippe Auguste* [111], no. 541; cf. Vaillant, 'Libre confédération' [723], 310, 315-26; Le Roy-Ladurie, *Montaillou* [543], 34-9.

[116] Devailly, *Berry* [358], 543.

[117] On the distinction, above, p. 129.

polity. This may seem blindingly obvious, but it needs to be said, because modern discussion of medieval village communities has tended to be distorted by a mass of anachronistic legal and constitutional technicalities which would have confounded contemporaries. Country people do not seem to have needed nicely defined categories for their collective activities.

Information about decision-making is sparse. The general impression is that the ideal was unanimity or consensus, in which, in the absence of any special liberties, the lord would have the first voice and the most substantial and senior of his subjects the next. Some historians have complained that the content of supposedly 'popular' liberties or statutes betrays seigniorial influence,[118] but in medieval terms that was perfectly reasonable. Just as kingdoms were supposed to be ruled by kings, by and with the advice and consent of their counsellors, so villages were supposed to be ruled by their lords with the advice and consent—however humbly and respectfully given—of the villagers. If a lord wanted to give them liberty to act without him he could; and then, ideally, both he and they should take part in devising the terms of the grant. In the absence of such a franchise the classic formulation for the making of statutes or by-laws would be something like *Ordinatum est per dominum ex assensu omnium tenentium.*[119] Meanwhile, just as villagers were supposed to be humble and respectful, stewards of courts were supposed to be polite: the thirteenth-century treatise on the *Court Baron*, which deals with the sort of matters which would arise in an ordinary manor court, makes the steward address the suitors as 'fair friends' or 'fair sirs' (*beus amys* or *beus seignurs*) when he asks for their views on a case—though it also makes them reply by asking him to give his opinion.[120] Many uncontentious bits of everyday business in a local court would often, no doubt, have been left to the suitors to decide as they wished. That no more abrogated a lord's right in theory than it did when a king left a matter to his

[118] Kuhn, 'Zur Kritik der Weistümer' [516]; Lennard, review of Homans [540].
[119] Beckerman, 'Customary Law' [242], 244; cf. Caggese, *Classi e comuni rurali* [298], i. 336-8.
[120] *Court Baron* [21], 48-9.

magnates,[121] but the accumulation of this kind of custom must have accounted for a good many subsequent disputes.

Although the appointment of officials led to many conflicts, procedures for elections were left as vague as everything else. The *Sachsenspiegel* seems to allow for a straight majority vote if necessary,[122] but most texts assume that choices will be unanimous. In practice some *villici* or mayors farmed their offices and others inherited them, which would preclude choice—and may explain some of the popular wish for elections.[123] One possible procedure in the absence of special privileges was for the people to choose someone (or perhaps more than one) and present him (or them) to the lord. At Montegemoli (Tuscany) the *rector*, elected annually by the people, was to be chosen *de amicis et ad honorem comitis*.[124] The variety of titles given to officials does not seem to reflect significant variation in their functions and method of appointment, however much it may reveal of the varied origins and 'families' of local customs. Single chief officers seem most usual, but some country communities, like some towns, were ruled by a college of mayors, *scabini*, or consuls.[125] In addition to other lesser officials, like harvest reeves, haywards, woodwards, watchmen, and so forth, who carried out the various duties which might be necessary, many places had permanent or occasional bodies of judgement-makers or counsellors.[126] These were sometimes called *jurati*, sometimes *scabini*, but were sometimes simply referred to as so many 'good men'. There does not seem to be any justification for assuming that these bodies were new or for seeing them as a mark of liberty: autonomous, privileged communities are more likely to have elected their *jurati* freely, but many other places had them,

[121] e.g. above, p. 22.

[122] *Sachsenspiegel* [25], i. 175 (Landrecht, II. 55); discussed by Buchda, 'Dorfgemeinde' [290], 7.

[123] Collin, 'Administration des villages lorrains' [334], 398-400; Fossier, *Picardie* [420], 717-20; Buchda, 'Dorfgemeinde' [290], 20-1.

[124] *Placitorum Abbreviatio* [169], 140; Watts, 'Peasant Discontent' [740], 127; *Regestum Volaterranum* [183], no. 424; Bader, *Studien* [228], ii. 68.

[125] *Actes du parlement* [97], i, no. 1560a; *Regesto Mantovano* [197], no. 173; Santini, *Comuni di pieve* [673], 194.

[126] Collin, 'Villages lorrains' [334], 397; Byl, *Les Juridictions scabinales* [292], 44-62; Fossier, *Picardie* [420], 720-3; Devailly, *Berry* [358], 342-3, 542; Bader, *Studien* [228], ii. 285-6, 347-53; Caggese, *Classi e comuni rurali* [298], 380-5.

in one form or another, and probably accepted them as representative. The 'better and older' or 'better and more discreet' no doubt often found themselves serving again and again as *jurati* without anyone making any very agonized decisions about it.[127] In English manors the use of juries spread so that by the mid fourteenth century, in Beckerman's words, 'community participation had given way to village government by committee'.[128] Though the tenants may not have noticed or objected, he sees the change as benefiting lords rather than people.

How all this worked in practice, and how much internal conflict it caused in communities, is largely undiscoverable. The richer records of urban self-government reveal much oppression and conflict, but then towns had a wider range of wealth and more independence than most villages, so that both the temptations and the opportunities for peculation were greater. The consensus may thus have been easier to maintain in the country than in towns—that is, of course, among the peasants themselves. No doubt the more prosperous often looked after their own interests, but the fact that they did better than their fellows is not evidence that they were unjust by contemporary standards. This applies as much to autonomous communities as to others: the winning of corporate liberties was not intended to introduce a democratic revolution (let alone to equalize wealth), and there was no hypocrisy or betrayal if thereafter the poor continued to come off badly. The normal and just maintenance of custom was insufficient to protect the poor against the troubles of poverty, especially when the pressure on land and wastes increased. Razi says of the yardlanders (that is, those with relatively large holdings) who dominated the manor court of Halesowen that 'like members of other ruling elite groups in other periods they were grasping and aggressive', and points to the way that they actually committed more offences than other people.[129] Grasping and

---

[127] Lennard, 'Early Manorial Juries' [539], 517; Gramain, 'Villages et communautés' [449], 125; Bader, *Studien* [228], ii. 271–88; Fossier, *Picardie* [420], 725–7; Byl, *Juridictions scabinales* [292], 74–85; Razi, *Life, Marriage and Death* [642], 78–9.   [128] Beckerman, 'Customary Law' [242], 100.

[129] *Life, Marriage and Death* [642], 77–82, 87, 94–8; cf. Fossier, *Picardie* [420], 724–5.

aggressive they may have been, but Razi's information shows that the yardlanders were being duly prosecuted for their offences: the system was therefore not, by its own standards, totally corrupt. In Louvres, moreover, those who formed the *confratria* or *communitas* were said to have tried to get everyone to join, including apparently both employers of labour and employed. The document leaves it unclear which group initiated the movement, but both were involved.[130] The thirteenth-century charter of Mennetou-sur-Cher (Loir-et-Cher) included a clause providing that poor people could complain of unjust dues (*censa*) to the annually elected council of twelve good men (*probi viri*). This of course threw them back on the mercy of the relatively substantial, but it is not inconceivable that the substantial sometimes included men of probity.[131]

There is, it must be admitted, more guess-work than hard evidence in all of this. It is, indeed, sometimes argued that we know nothing of what peasants thought about their collective duties and rights, or about anything else, because the documents were not written by them: even charters of liberties reflect what lords would give rather than what their subjects wanted. This is true but only partly true. Seigniorial records are full of the evidence of collective discontents and so are the records of law-suits. Depositions of witnesses, in particular, are unlikely to have been entirely distorted by the clerks who wrote them. So far as we can trust the ample evidence of discontent, the most stubborn struggles of country people were for ideals which were pretty well in accord with what the rest of society thought right—though of course some people in the rest of society would have denied that *rustici* had any right to have those ideals fulfilled in this world and most would have agreed that *rustici* were always wrong to rebel against their masters. No doubt peasants concealed many of their true feelings from clerks and chroniclers, but even if they did, they were more likely to have shared the norms and values of their contemporary superiors than those

[130] One allegation was *quod ipsi subtrahebant communionem suam illis qui non erant de confratria et quod illis nolebant conducere operas suas* and witnesses said that those in the community *non locent operas suas* to those outside it: *Actes du parlement* [97], i, no. 1560a.

[131] Devailly, *Berry* [358], 542 n.; cf. Homans, *English Villagers* [479], 332-3.

of modern socialists and liberal democrats. Many of their collective activities, although undemocratically organized for inegalitarian ends, probably seemed right and reasonable to most of them, provided they conformed with custom.

Collective activities

Some of the collective activities of country people have already been referred to in passing during the course of this chapter, but it may be useful to summarize here the main sorts of activity that seem to have been undertaken. Once again it should be noted that to call an activity 'collective' or 'communal' here does not mean that it was necessarily decided on by the unfettered will of the villagers, or that it was as 'villagers' that they acted. In the first place, to put the matter in terms of English conditions, people acted collectively in their capacity of tenants of manors as well as in their capacity of villagers. One cannot polarize the 'seigniorial' manor court, with its imposed regulations, against the 'popular' or 'communal' village or parish meeting, with its collective local customs. In the second place, collective activity was not the prerogative of villagers in the sense of people living in nucleated settlements. Villagers, in this sense, were those most likely to regulate their arable farming collectively, but policing, church-building, and other public works were undertaken by all sorts of local groups.

It is impossible to draw a line between collective duties imposed from above and activities which local people organized for themselves. For instance, they often had to send representatives to higher tribunals, like the four men from English *ville*, sometimes accompanied by their priest and reeve, who had to attend shire and hundred meetings and coroners' inquests, but they also, on their own initiative, sent representatives to law-courts whenever they wanted to prosecute or defend their common interests at law.[132] Similarly in military and policing matters. Many charters specify and restrict the military service, along with the other services, owed by privileged communities, and suggest, by doing so,

---

[132] Cam, *Law-Finders and Law-Makers* [302], 71–84; cf. Schlesinger, *Mitteldeutsche Beiträge* [680], 241. Also above, p. 92.

that peasant communities were generally liable to provide soldiers for outside duties from time to time.[133] Inhabitants of new settlements sometimes built their own defences, whether on their own initiative or their lord's, and Fasoli has suggested that the building, maintenance, and use of the walls of Italian *castelli* was an important factor in turning older neighbourly solidarities into the *comuni* of the twelfth and thirteenth centuries.[134] When villages in the Auvergne began to get both liberties and defensive walls, the inhabitants, after some conflict with their lords, generally took charge of their walls for themselves.[135] In England, we know that people were grouped in tithings for mutual surety and policing from the tenth century; from 1233 each *villa* had to appoint at least four men to keep watch; and from the late thirteenth century local units—probably the same *ville integre*[136]— were choosing the men they had to supply to royal armies through commissions of array.[137] Meanwhile, in the civil war of the 1260s, the hundred of Wirksworth (Derbys.)—that is, a rather larger unit, comprising a number of villages— taxed its landowners to raise money to buy off a ravaging royalist army, while the Leicestershire village of Peatling Magna fought against another royalist detachment which was passing through and which the villagers accused of going against the welfare of the community of the realm and against the barons.[138]

Church-building and other public works were also partly obligatory and partly voluntary. The obligation to build, repair and equip parish churches has been mentioned elsewhere, but it should be noted here too, if only because the church and churchyard must so often have served as the meeting-place of the local community and its refuge in time of war.[139] The most impressive public works apart from

[133] e.g. Verriest, 'Charte-loi de Prisches' [200], 339 (c. 12); Teulet, *Layettes* [194], i, p. 137; Fossier, *Chartes de coutume* [126], pp. 81-3.

[134] *Studi ezzeliniani* [407], 21.

[135] Fournier, 'Chartes de franchises' [422].

[136] *Close Rolls* [105], *1231-4*, 309; Lees, 'Statute of Winchester' [530]; above, p. 129.

[137] Cam, *Law-Finders and Law-Makers* [302], 71-2; Prestwich, *Law, Politics and Finance* [637], 101-2.

[138] *Annales Mon.* [7], iii. 230; *Select Cases without Writ* [185], 42-5.

[139] As at Peatling; also above, p. 96.

churches were probably those undertaken by the often scattered populations which reclaimed their lands from the sea, kept them drained, and built roads and causeways across them.[140] Some Italian villages, on the other hand, maintained complex systems of irrigation in order to keep their lands wet.[141] Magna Carta refers to the customary obligations of *ville*, as well as of individuals, to repair bridges, while the men of Louvres apparently set themselves to repairing their own causeway.[142]

From a medieval point of view churches and roads were common property and so were woods and pastures. They were sometimes managed through official village or manor courts, but more autonomous-looking groups of parishioners or inhabitants are found selling or defending common property.[143] In 1295 the customary tenants of Bromham (Wilts.) had to pay a fine to their lord for having a common seal made. Presumably they wanted it in connection with their common property, and it is, incidentally, worth noticing that the lord did not apparently object to them having a seal, provided that they got—and paid for—his permission.[144] It is from the thirteenth century that the 'mark communities', which were once thought of as the earliest 'Germanic' peasant communities, really date. They seem to have been associations of villages (not of individual people) which shared woodland and pasture between them, in the same way as groups of English villages did at the same time.[145] In addition to sales of common land, at least one purchase is recorded: in 1241 the inhabitants of Saint-Paul-de-Vence (Alpes Maritimes) bought a whole lordship which seems to have been largely uninhabited and served them as extra pasture ground.[146] As for arable farming, that involved endless co-operation, from ploughing agreements between groups of neighbours to the complexities involved in working a regulated system of open fields, which have been mentioned earlier.[147] While open

---

[140] Stoob, 'Landausbau und Gemeinde' [700].
[141] Toubert, *Structures du Latium* [715], 237-40.
[142] Holt, *Magna Carta* [475], 323 (c. 23); *Actes du parlement* [97], i, no. 1560a.
[143] Above, p. 123.   [144] Homans, *English Villagers* [479], 332.
[145] Bader, *Studien* [228], ii. 174-82.
[146] Dufour-Antonetti, 'Forêt de Roquefort' [383].
[147] Homans, *English Villagers* [479], 78-81; above, pp. 123-4.

fields were beginning to absorb more collective attention in parts of northern Europe, however, they were being divided and enclosed for purely individual use in Lombardy.[148]

Local communities, as property-owners and property-managers, held funds of various sorts. The liberties some of them secured entailed the making of collective payments, and, even when taxes or dues were not owed collectively they often had to be assessed and collected by local panels of one sort or another.[149] Autonomous rights of jurisdiction meant the receipt of monetary penalties, and all kinds of groups probably taxed their members on occasion, as there was nothing in contemporary law to stop them.[150] Sometimes they may have done this through guilds or fraternities, which were also particularly associated with promoting solidarity through conviviality[151]—though the Louvres *confratria* imposed penalties on those who sold or drank wine after curfew, and many places may have enjoyed feasts and jollification without formal fraternities or guilds. At Headington (Oxon.) the lords, St. Frideswide's abbey, provided food and drink to their tenants on St. Frideswide's day, while the bailiff and reeve had dinner with the prior, until about 1293, when the custom was abandoned amid conflict and recrimination.[152] At Carlton (Notts.) there was said to be an annual ploughing competition on the morrow of the Epiphany, which was attended by the lord, the parson, and all the free men of the village and which was used to share out part of the common each year among the free men who competed.[153]

Examples of collective action could probably be multiplied and varied almost indefinitely. Whatever activities any particular local group undertook, however, there was one which any group which really deserves to be called a community was then bound to undertake: the holding of meetings to regulate its affairs through collective counsel and collective

---

[148] *Cam. Econ. Hist.* [304], i. 369-70.

[149] Homans, *English Villagers* [479], 332-3; Devailly, *Berry* [358], 342-3.

[150] Duby, *Société mâconnaise* [381], 607; *Actes du parlement* [97], i, no. 1560a.

[151] Above, chapter 3.

[152] Madox, *Firma Burgi* [147], 65 n.

[153] Homans, *English Villagers* [479], 361-3.

judgement. From our point of view there is a difference in kind between the law-courts of manors, lordships, or autonomous communities with legal jurisdiction on the one hand, and the mere meetings of parishioners or guildsmen or unprivileged villagers. To contemporaries courts and meetings were different in degree rather than in kind: courts dealt with general political and administrative business as well as with law in the narrow sense, while meetings, even of voluntary associations, were apt to make rules and impose penalties on their members. Both made their decisions, or were supposed to make them, either by general consensus or through juries or other panels, which, however chosen, were supposed to represent the whole community. Much of our evidence of village communities either comes from the records of courts or meetings of this sort or it implies that such courts or meetings lay behind the action that is recorded.

Conclusion

This chapter has not answered all the questions posed at its beginning, but it has discussed them, and some answers of a sort seem to have emerged. By the thirteenth century there is enough evidence available to show that the west European countryside, or quite a fair part of it, was a network of communities in the sense that it contained a mass of local groups, often overlapping with each other, which acted collectively in running their agriculture, their parish churches and fraternities, their local government, and perhaps a good deal more besides. Many of the groups seem to have consisted of peasants, both free and unfree, who were partly united by their subjection to the same lordship, but partly by their common rights and duties as farmers, parishioners, and neighbours. *Mutatis mutandis*, this applies to areas of scattered settlements as much as to nucleated villages. Some of the activity was new in the twelfth century, while the ideals and values it reflected must have become clearer to people from that time on through repeated statements of them and conflicts about them. Nevertheless not all the activity was new and none of it seems to have reflected entirely new ideas.

It is difficult to know how to assess the trend towards

collectivity. There was, after all, a contemporary trend towards more individual activity too: the growth of the economy, of towns, of education, and of government, however little scope for personal advancement they gave to most peasants, at least gave some of them more chance to farm for the market or to get out of their villages altogether. Communities probably overlapped more in 1300 than in 900 and that may have given some individuals a chance to influence or manipulate them in one way or another. It is worth noting too that, though more people lived in bigger and more densely populated villages in 1300 than in 900, settlement patterns may imply a growing scope for individual choice in some places. Although topographical evidence can never reveal the motives or methods of decision making, the movement of small nucleated settlements from one site to another before 1000 looks as if it was more the result of corporate decisions than were some of the later movements of population which, for instance, left some Norfolk churches so strikingly isolated. There are problems here which could only begin to be solved by enquiries which would go far beyond the scope of this book. For present purposes it remains clear that small neighbourhood communities seem to have been very active, and very varied in their activities, in the twelfth and thirteenth centuries, and that they had probably been active, though less varied in their activities, in the tenth and eleventh.

There must have been much unwilling and unhappy submergence of individuals within peasant societies, but in no part of western Europe about which I have read does collective activity appear to have been organized in rigid categories which excluded all choices on the part of the community itself. Because village custom was so largely unwritten it was more flexible and gave more scope for change—for instance in field systems—than contemporaries themselves recognized. That does not mean that I argue that medieval villages were places of democratic harmony or collective consensus. Lords had oppressive powers and sometimes used them arbitrarily, while within peasant society itself communal activity must often have borne hard on nonconformists and underdogs. Nevertheless the ideal—an ideal which peasants, so far as the evidence of their feelings goes, seem to have shared—was harmony, and a harmony which involved much collective activity. To judge from the casual way that groups often defined themselves and referred to their rules, all this activity required a large measure of voluntary co-operation. Words like *vicini* and *villani*[154] suggest that one of the bonds—perhaps one of the most important bonds—between country people was that they were neighbours. Neighbours were not in reality always good neighbours, but charters and customs seem to assume that most people will submit to collective decisions and will be more or less willing to undertake a good deal of co-operative work. Whether or not most settlements had ever really been inhabited predominantly by kinsmen, the belief in old, inherited customs, together with the occasional use of expressions like 'the blood of the village',[155] suggests that villages may have sustained their consensus by some kind of vaguely articulated myth of common descent. To medieval people the ideal type of medieval village was perhaps not merely a nucleated settlement, with its church, standing among its own fields, pastures, and woodlands, but one which, like a miniature kingdom, was also a unit of descent, custom, and government.

[154] Cf. also *gebur*: K. Stackmann and G. Köbler in Wenskus, *Bauer* [741], 164-7, 243-5.
[155] Homans, *English Villagers* [479], 122, 216; cf. Razi, *Life, Marriage and Death* [642], 29-30, 120-4.

6

Urban communities

No one who has read the preceding chapters on law and on the rural community will be surprised to find that this chapter argues that some of the distinctions usually drawn between urban and rural communities are false. Once the force of collective habits in medieval life in general is recognized, then the need to search for the origin of town communities in the 'communal movement' of the twelfth century, or to argue whether it derived from any particular institutions—either guild, commune, or consulate on the one hand, or the forms of seigniorial government on the other—is eliminated. The basis of urban community, like the basis of community in nucleated agricultural settlements, was geographical propinquity, fortified by the traditional practices of law and local government. Towns did not win new liberties in the twelfth and thirteenth centuries because of new movements of association, or new ideas about politics, but because of new economic and political conditions in which values and habits of association which were already established in both rural and urban life were translated into a new range of institutions. The most striking of these was the more or less autonomous town government, but neither townsmen nor the bitterest of their critics and opponents seem to have seen independent municipalities as embodying quite the same sort of novelties as historians have attributed to them. Self-governing towns were not, for instance, perceived as having any particular degree of legal or political unity that was different in kind from that of other local communities. They were simply more independent, which gave their rulers more freedom of action. The powers deriving from independence reinforced the stimulus given both to solidarities and to conflicts by economic and social change, so that towns became at once the focus of intense civic patriotism and the scene of fierce civic dissension.

At first sight, with their republican constitutions, mercantile rulers, industrial conflicts, and personally free populations, towns seem an anomaly in the monarchical, seigniorial, and agricultural middle ages. Nevertheless, even if in the long view of historical development they may be seen as embodying an economic antithesis to feudal society (in the Marxist sense of 'feudal'), closer inspection of the society and values of medieval townsmen makes them look much less anomalous in their own age than one might expect from the remarks of historians like Pirenne, Rörig, or Postan—or of Marx himself.[1] The new institutions evolved in towns bore a strong resemblance to those outside. Even in the most independent, rich, and splendid cities of Italy very few revolutionary ideas about society and politics seem to have been produced before the fourteenth century. It is the purpose of this chapter to describe the way that townspeople acted collectively, so as to substantiate these suggestions. At the same time I shall try to distinguish what was old and traditional from what was undoubtedly new and distinctive in the forms and character of their activities.

As usual it is necessary to start with a definition. The primary difference between the sort of place considered in the last chapter, and those which I call towns and consider in this one, is that people living in the first were predominantly engaged in farming and other closely related occupations (or lived off the work of those who were), whereas a significant proportion (if not always a majority) of those in the second lived off a variety of quite different occupations, notably trade, manufacturing, and administration of various sorts. In order to distinguish a town from a barracks or a monastery with its dependent workshops, one should add that the work of towns is normally pursued in a number of separate enterprises. The second mark of a town derives from the first: both the inhabitants of a town and those who live in the countryside around recognize them as separate and different. Townsmen form a social unit which, however internally divided, they and their neighbours feel to be distinct.

None of this means that everyone at the time is certain

[1] Pirenne, *Les Villes* [626]; Rörig, *Europäische Stadt* [665]; *Cambridge Econ. Hist.* [304], ii. 172; Marx and Engels, *Communist Manifesto*.

whether he lives in a town or a village, or that later historians can assign every settlement to one category or the other. Some of the *castri* or *castelli* which I referred to in the last chapter, and even some places called simply *ville* in the sources, may have hovered for short or long periods on the boundary between categories. That is in the nature of the phenomena and does not invalidate the definition. Even if some individual places have been misplaced between this chapter and the last, the general classification which results from my working definition reflects social realities more accurately than do the traditional definitions based on constitutional forms, topography, or size of population. Constitutional definitions—the possession of liberties, charters, or guilds, the use of particular words like commune or borough —have often attracted medieval historians in search of exactitude, but any which they find is spurious, for it creates a mass of anomalies. The resulting arguments tend to drown any ideas about the character of medieval urban society in a bog of anachronistic legalism. Topographical criteria—the possession of walls or market-places—seem no more satisfactory, while the modern inclination to think in terms of the size of population is clearly inappropriate to a period in which urban functions were exercised and urban characteristics enjoyed by many places which were no bigger than some agricultural settlements. To deny them the title of town would be obviously nonsensical.

What this chapter is concerned with, therefore, is not any particular constitutional, topographical, or demographic category of settlement, but that sort of place which, however it was governed and however small its population, fulfilled the functions which are normally implied by the modern use of the word 'town' in British English, 'city' in American English, *ville* in French, *Stadt* in German, and *città* in Italian. As the variety of all these words—not to mention all the derivatives of *urbs* and *burgus*—suggests, medieval usage did not distinguish urban settlements consistently.[2] Partly this

[2] Verbruggen, 'Castrum, castellum' [725]; Schlesinger, 'Stadt und Burg' [681]; Köbler, 'burg und stat' [506]; Banti, ' "Civitas" e "commune" ' [230]; Lombard-Jourdan, 'Oppidum et banlieue' [555]; Reynolds, *English Medieval Towns* [652], pp. ix-x, 24, 31, 96-100, 112, 114; Le Goff, *La Ville médiévale* [531], 59-83, 103-41; cf. Schütte, *Wik* [685]. Following tradition I sometimes refer to cathedral

was because different languages adopted different words from the Latin and vernacular vocabularies available to them, and partly it was because medieval people were not always preoccupied with the sort of definitions and distinctions that have worried historians. The settlements to be considered include both great independent cities and small seigniorial towns, provided only that I have evidence that they formed the sort of social and economic category that I have described. It is the collective activity of lay people, in all these sorts of places that I consider to be towns according to this functional and social definition, that is the subject of the chapter.

The origin of urban communities

With a starting point of 900 it is unnecessary to devote much time to the 'continuity question'—that is, to discussing how much of medieval urban culture survived from the cities of Rome and how much was new. By 900 the society and institutions of former Roman towns, like Roman law itself, had become so much adapted to current conditions that Roman inheritances were matters of antiquarian interest and pride rather than real determinants of civic practice.[3] Nevertheless urban life had certainly been at a low ebb in the early middle ages, and how much of it there was anywhere in Europe by the tenth century has been much debated. Currently the answer seems to be that there was some, even if towns everywhere, even in Italy, were few and small compared to what they would be by 1300. In other words, the ideas of town origins associated particularly with the name of Henri Pirenne (1862-1935), which dominated medieval urban history for so long, have not withstood the test of all the archaeological and documentary investigations that have been made in the past thirty years or so. Pirenne believed that medieval towns (in effect he meant northern towns) appeared by a sort of spontaneous generation with the revival of long-distance trade in the eleventh century.[4] It now seems, however, that

towns (which included many in Italy) as 'cities', but this is not intended to suggest that they formed a separate category of any wider significance.

[3] For Roman revivals, below, pp. 170, 174, 216-17.
[4] Pirenne, *Les Villes* [626], i. 45; cf. Lestocquoy, *Études* [545], 39.

long-distance trade never entirely disappeared, either in the Mediterranean or the north, during the Dark Ages. Even before the tenth century, and even in the non-Roman north, there were some permanently inhabited ports and trading-places which look very like towns or 'proto-towns'. So, for the matter of that, do some of the defended sites which served as centres of government inland, many of them again, even outside Roman territory, standing on sites which had been inhabited for centuries as the nodal points of regional networks of routes and settlements. These were the 'primary towns', as Everitt calls them,[5] which were ready to develop when the societies to which they belonged developed a need for urban services and functions. Then, from the tenth century, archaeological and documentary evidence of trade and urban life begins to grow, and what is most striking about it is its wide distribution throughout Europe and throughout a mass of places, many of which never attained any great size or status. It looks as if towns were not growing only as centres of long-distance trade, injecting enterprise and wealth into the countryside from outside, as used to be envisaged, but as part of a much more widespread change. Population and wealth in the countryside were growing and it was above all that which stimulated urban growth, by increasing the demand for goods and services which towns could provide. The lowest level of need could be met by the proliferation of weekly markets, many of which never turned into permanent trading places with resident traders and craftsmen, but some places in Flanders and Germany, for instance, which were destined to become great and privileged centres of long-distance trade, seem to have made their first discernible steps towards dramatic urban growth when tenth- or eleventh-century lords or bishops founded markets in them.[6]

So long as long-distance trade was considered the one necessary and sufficient cause of urban development, and so long as it was considered to have been virtually non-existent

---

[5] Everitt, 'Banburys of England' [400].
[6] Ennen, *Die europäische Stadt* [393], 73–104; Fasoli and Bocchi, *La Città* [408], 27–30; Reynolds, *English Medieval Towns* [652], 16–45; Nicholas, 'Structures de peuplement' [608]; Le Goff, *La Ville médiévale* [531], 40–141.

in the ninth and tenth centuries, it was natural for historians to doubt the economic function of the walled settlements of the time. Even those which later became towns must, it seemed, have been mere seigniorial or ecclesiastical fortresses before the eleventh-century revival of trade came to give them the kiss of urban life. According to Pirenne and his followers a little marginal trade was carried on, but only by wandering traders who met together in unwalled trading-places which had few or no permanent inhabitants. Some of these places were, it is conceded, next door to the walled fortresses, but even so the 'topographical duality' of fortress and suburb reflected a significant social and economic division. It was not until the eleventh century, when the wandering traders settled down to become the mercantile 'patriciate' of the medieval town, and when new walls were built to enclose fortress and suburb in a single circuit, that the two sorts of community were united to form truly urban societies. Given the way that political, ecclesiastical, and economic forces are now seen to have combined to promote towns, this model looks implausible, and both documentary and archaeological evidence suggest that it is at best over-simplified. As towns began to grow they took different shapes according to local topography. Where existing walls enclosed space for markets, then markets might be held inside from the start, but sometimes trade converged on a more convenient sub-urban area like a waterfront on which boats could be beached or moored.[7] Sometimes buildings were grouped in several nuclei, and some of these might start with separate walls, but there is little evidence that the walls embodied important social barriers. There is in fact no evidence at all of any regular or significant duality: those who lived within walls and those who lived in suburbs did not normally form separate communities; if and when they did, it cannot be shown to be because of any clearly distinguishable economic functions.

If all this is right, then it seems reasonable to abandon the presuppositions of an earlier generation of urban historians, that we should be looking for a moment at which either

[7] Lestocquoy, *Études* [545], 13-19; Kaiser, 'Cologne' [494]; Reynolds, *English Medieval Towns* [652], 26-7; Le Goff, *La Ville médiévale* [531], 91-101.

'pre-urban' fortresses or 'pre-urban' trading-places became towns and their populations changed from servile or semi-servile rustics or wandering traders into a new class of townsmen. Although relatively few places fulfilled urban functions in 900 and all of them were small compared to the greatest towns of 1300, let alone later, it is reasonable to look for evidence that there were some settlements even at the beginning of the tenth century which contemporaries perceived as possessing the sort of characteristics that I have associated with towns. It is, after all, important to remember that records improve steadily from the late eleventh century, just when they start to depict lively and assertive urban communities all over the place. Some of those communities are likely to have been consolidating themselves slowly over the years in order to get so quickly into the records when political and administrative conditions allowed.

In Italy the great majority of towns stood on Roman sites and had been continuously inhabited ever since, so that some traditions of civic solidarity probably always survived even while the culture in which they were expressed was transformed. Those who lived within the towns were, sometimes at least, recognized as a distinct group to the extent of being distinctively described as *urbani* or *cives*. This may not mean much, but urban historians have for long stressed the late appearance of the characteristic Latin word used to describe a townsman in northern Europe (*burgensis*) as an argument for the late development of urban life there.[8] It is not very clear why that one word rather than another should be significant, but it may be significant that townsmen should be given a separate name at all. Such collective loyalties as early medieval *urbani* and *cives* in Italy felt are likely to have been fostered by the continued existence in some—perhaps in many—*civitates* of a core of lawyers and notaries who probably saw themselves as guardians and repositories of civic tradition. Local solidarity was also promoted by the church. Because Italian dioceses were small many towns had their own cathedrals which were important symbols of protection

[8] Pirenne, *Les Villes* [626], i. 137 n.; Mayer, *Studien* [582], 140-1, 149-50, 164-8, 286, etc.; Le Goff, *La Ville médiévale* [531], 103; Tait, *Medieval English Borough* [711], 9.

and unity. Some bishops secured comital powers over their cities together with a wider or narrower area around. Elsewhere their governmental powers were limited even within the city, but there was a general tendency during the troubled years of the tenth and eleventh centuries for bishops to turn from being the natural leaders and protectors of their cities to being their most effective if not their sole governors. In so far as government over a town remained more effective than government over the surrounding area, or became entirely separated from it, the separate solidarities of the townspeople would tend to be enhanced. By 900, moreover, the same forces were promoting similar solidarities in towns which did not themselves have any Roman traditions to preserve. Some ideas and traditions passed from old to new towns, some were developed according to local circumstances. Venice had many peculiarities which derived from the peculiar circumstances of its birth, but it would be folly to argue that its lack of ancient roots left it without the will or ability to create an effective community or develop a competent administrative class.[9] Meanwhile, at a humbler level, market towns were growing because they were the headquarters of rural lordships—or lords were making their headquarters at growing market centres. Since these settlements were also often the sites of *pievi* or mother churches,[10] they served simultaneously as places for judicial, religious, and commercial assemblies—assemblies in which townspeople must have been present if not predominant.[11]

Outside Italy, and especially where any ghost of Roman civic tradition was absent, one might expect to find fewer and later signs of collective solidarity. The signs are certainly fewer, but they are not totally absent and sometimes they occur in surprising places. Canterbury, although a former Roman town, could not claim any significant continuity with Romano-British culture, never enjoyed much long-distance trade, and never produced a large or privileged population. It

[9] Sestan, 'La Città communale' [687]; Fasoli, *Dalla civitas al comune* [405], 57-60, 70-6, 80, 121-6; Schumann, *Authority and the Commune* [684]; Wickham, *Early Medieval Italy* [750], 80-92, 174-5.

[10] Above, p. 82.

[11] Goertz, *Origini dei comuni* [444], 25-31, 41-4; Vaccari, *La Territorialità* [722].

was, of course, the first and most important cathedral city of England, yet what makes it look an exceptionally early town may be due less to that than to the luck that preserved some of the cathedral's early charters which refer to the town. From them we know that even before 900 the inhabitants were known variously as 'boroughmen' (*burgwara*), 'portmen', or *urbani*. The first word derives from Old English *burh*, which was by then starting to change its meaning from 'fortified place' to 'town', while the second comes from the Latin *portus*, meaning a place of trade. If the three words alike all imply that people at Canterbury were recognizable as a distinct group, then those who lived at places of equal or greater population and trade, like London, York, or Southampton (*Hamwic*), were no doubt equally recognizable too, and the non-appearance of the Latin *burgensis* in English sources before 1086 looks insignificant. English towns were not yet separated from their counties by royal grants to bishops, but town law (*burhriht*) is referred to in the early eleventh century. By then, if not before, sheriffs were probably holding separate assemblies for at least the larger towns and were collecting their dues separately from those of the rest of the county.[12]

In France and Germany the documentary evidence is both slight and patchy, but excavations in German towns leave little room for doubt that towns there had been growing for some time before the so-called 'communal movement' of the eleventh and twelfth centuries brought them into the written sources.[13] Flanders and the Maas–Mosel region, although they produce evidence of early development, were perhaps less exceptional at this stage than they later became. If grants of markets and tolls were more numerous in Germany and Flanders than in France that was probably because royal government in France was too weak to make royal charters worth having. It does not mean that there were no markets. Market law is referred to in both kingdoms in the eleventh century and in both the government of many larger towns had by then become effectively separated from that of the countryside round about.[14]

[12] Tait, *Medieval English Borough* [711], 9; Reynolds, *English Medieval Towns* [652], 28-9, 93.
[13] Barley, *European Towns* [232], 127-57, 355-71.

[See p. 164 for n. 14]

With the exception of Venice, which from the seventh century needed to make no more than a few polite bows in the direction of Byzantium, towns had of course no formal independence as yet. Nevertheless any town was by its nature well-fitted to make the most of the opportunities for autonomy which medieval methods of government and judgement gave to all local communities.[15] In the troubled times of the tenth and eleventh centuries the normal governmental assemblies were most easily held on defended sites, which generally meant within towns. Even where an assembly was meant to have jurisdiction over a wider area those who lived within the shelter of the town walls would be the most likely to attend in force. Town assemblies are best attested in Italy,[16] but that may be, not only because town communities were well-established there, but also because the tradition of record-keeping was better preserved. When tenth-century kings of Italy told bishops to consult townspeople about the line of walls to be built or about the fineness and weight of money to be coined they were only reminding them of the universal norms of good consultative government.[17] Town assemblies of one sort or another were a fact of town life—even its most obvious characteristic: the publicity of transactions in towns was presumably the reason why tenth-century English kings tried to restrict buying and selling to them.[18] A rash and overbearing lord of a town who failed to summon a formal assembly or overruled it too crudely might find an awkward informal assembly gathering in the market-place.

Relatively large populations concentrated in relatively small and well-defended areas were thus peculiarly well fitted both to maintain old customs and to develop new ones. Among the former may have been the inhabitants' right to control immigration into their settlement. Although an immigrant's right to become a burgess or citizen of a town, free from outside claims, after a year and a day's residence there, is generally considered a characteristically urban

[14] Planitz, *Die deutsche Stadt* [627], 71; Endemann, *Markturkunde in Frankreich* [391], 91-5; Le Goff, *La Ville médiévale* [531], 144-55.

[15] Above, pp. 19, 32-3, 35-6.

[16] Goertz, *Origini dei comuni* [444], 26, 34-5.

[17] Schiaparelli, *Diplomi* [182]: *Berengario I*, nos. 43, 47; *Lotario*, no. 1.

[18] Reynolds, *English Medieval Towns* [652], 32.

liberty and an achievement of the 'communal movement', it more probably derives from much older rural custom.[19] Just as the protection of his men was the duty of any lord, so protection of its members was the duty of any community. That presupposed some right to control membership, and that in turn meant controlling settlement—which was what some Frankish villages had done long before. The full implications of the old rule may, however, have been first worked out in towns, where frequent immigration gave it peculiar importance.[20] If that was the case then it illustrates the way that the same characteristics that made towns good preservers of custom also enabled them to adapt and change it as necessary. Many of the distinctive features of urban custom and law as they developed in this period were presumably responses to the common needs of growing towns. Almost everywhere urban land was more freely transferable than land in the country, rents were paid chiefly if not exclusively in money, while rules and procedures were developed and adapted to cope with commercial cases and with visiting traders who might have different customs of their own.[21]

Urban growth in the tenth and eleventh centuries ensured that as towns developed their peculiar customs so they developed the confidence and the bargaining power to try to protect their members' interests. In 958 the Genoese secured royal confirmation of their customs, by the eleventh century the men of Tiel (Gelderland) claimed imperial authority for the way they made their judgements among themselves, and from the early twelfth century many towns got confirmations of customs that were increasingly often spelt out in some detail.[22] Among them were likely to be

---

[19] Above, p. 114.

[20] Ennen, *Frühgeschichte* [394], 243–5, especially on the early Spanish examples. The need both to attract immigrants and to form and record local custom would be urgent in Spain. On the significance of the rule in general medieval terms: Strahm, 'Stadtluft macht frei' [701].

[21] *Borough Customs* [96]; Keutgen, *Urkunden* [141], 90–219, and cf. Planitz, *Die deutsche Stadt* [627], 79–81, 334–42, though German scholarship tends to stress differences between 'families' of urban law; Ennen, *Frühgeschichte* [394], 234–47, 261–7. Much of Italian urban custom looks similar (e.g. above, pp. 52–8), but the general difference of tenure as between urban and rural land does not seem to apply there.

[22] *Cod. Dipl. Genova* [106], no. 1; *Elenchus* [118], i. 424. For collections

rules of inheritance and rules of pleading (including exemption from trial by battle), the right to have all cases against
townsmen tried in the town courts, the immigrant's right of
protection after a year and a day, and, of course, freedom
from a whole range of varying dues and tolls. Tolls mattered
not only to merchants but to all town-dwellers. Once most
of a town's inhabitants were no longer farmers then they
depended on getting food from outside; they all needed free
passage on the roads leading to the town from nearby, while
merchants hoped for peace and protection further afield as
well. Consequently some of the earliest charters concerned
tolls as well as more general customs. The early grants of
markets were intended to benefit churches, not towns as
such, by giving the church the tolls from local markets, but
townspeople could benefit from a church's care of its market
just as they benefited from a grant which exempted its tenants
from paying tolls elsewhere. As early as 781 the bishop and
inhabitants of Comacchio (Romagna) co-operated to secure
concessions on the tolls they paid in Mantua.[23] By the
eleventh century—and probably long before—the cumulative effect of toll privileges was the general recognition that
inhabitants of different places might have different obligations to pay tolls anywhere.[24]

The tolls townsmen paid or from which they were exempt
thus consolidated their common interests. So might other
common dues. In England geld and military service were owed
to the king from all over the kingdom by the eleventh century. Though we do not know that they had charters to prove
it, and very likely they did not, several towns seem to have
had their geld or service modified by 1066. By 1086 the burgesses of at least two paid a lump sum for their local mint.[25]

of charters: *British Borough Charters* [88], Keutgen, *Urkunden* [141], and
Elenchus [118], i (Germany, Belgium, Netherlands, Scandinavia to *c.*1250) are
particularly useful. There are no comparable collections for France or Italy but
see Dollinger, *Bibliographie* [370]; Leicht, *Scritti vari* [533], i. 535–42; *Libertés
urbaines et rurales* [314].

[23] *M.G.H. Dipl. Karol.* [155], i, no. 132.
[24] Robertson, *Laws* [177], 72 (Ethelred, 2.5–8); 'Honorantia civitatis Pavia'
in Solmi, 'L'Amministrazione' [189], 21–4.
[25] Reynolds, *English Medieval Towns* [652], 6; *Domesday Book* [114], ii.
107b. On collective negotiations about coinage (though not generally by individual towns, apparently): Bisson, *Conservation of Coinage* [256].

This suggests that they had their own collective funds. London had its civic fund by the beginning of the century, for part of the penalties imposed for breaches of the peace and of toll regulations there went to the citizens.[26] The men of Tiel had a common purse from which they may have paid their imperial dues (*vectigalia*) as they did the costs of their riotous drinking sessions. The Tiel arrangements look very like those of a guild, and later references to the affairs of other northern towns show that before their municipal governments were formally established some of them were looking after some of their collective interests through associations variously called guilds, guilds of merchants, or hanses. It is, however, noteworthy that when they did so the documents often confuse the property and privileges of the guild with those of the town as such. Neither rulers nor townsmen seem to have found it necessary to distinguish the groups and their memberships;[27] it is hard to see them agonizing over the difference between the 'personal' association of the guild and the 'territorial' association of the town in the way that modern historians have done.[28]

Where there was no merchant or town guild, or even where there was, collective activity may have been initiated and controlled in the assembly which was likely to be meeting regularly in the town to do justice. Without a guild there would, presumably, be no alderman to act as spokesman in negotiations, and the lead would be taken by one or more of the *scabini* or other leading townsmen—the portmen, 'good men' of the town, or whatever they were called—who gave judgements in the assembly.[29] In practice the difference would be minimal: the richer merchants of the guild would be pretty much the same as the 'better and more discreet' of the town. There is no evidence that when towns began to press for liberties they did so as the result of any internal revolution, or that they thought that they were making constitutional advances, first by turning their attention from law to more general matters and then by negotiating with

---

[26] Robertson, *Laws* [177], 74 (Ethelred, 3.3, 4.2).
[27] Above, pp. 18, 35, 70.
[28] Ennen, *Die europäische Stadt* [393], 106-9.
[29] Above, p. 33.

their rulers about them. Alpert of Metz makes it sound as if the exceptional readiness of the men of Tiel to complain was what enabled them to bargain with the emperor at such an early date. We may guess that their negotiations were facilitated by their wealth and their comfortable distance from the centre of imperial power, but not by their enjoyment of any particular kind of unity as the result of having a guild.

According to contemporary law and politics, all the collective activity which we can dimly perceive going on in the eleventh century—and even more dimly in the tenth— needed no special authorization. Once townspeople had the common interests, the confidence, and the influence to negotiate with their rulers or with anyone else, then they could do so on whatever subject they wanted, asking for confirmation of their customs, restriction of their dues, or even, if they were ambitious enough, for entirely new privileges. What would limit the success of any town community, whether it worked through a guild or through its normal assembly, would not be its lack of formal constitutional machinery or legal standing but its lack of political and economic muscle.

The coming of municipal self-government

The twelfth century, as is well known, saw many old towns acquire a more complete independence and a more formal recognition of what they acquired, while many of the numerous new towns which were now founded were granted a comparable degree of independence from the start. Obvious as it is, however, that they would never have achieved so much if the growing wealth of their leading citizens had not given them a new confidence and determination to run their own affairs for themselves, there is very little evidence that townsmen were motivated by any new political ideology. They do not seem to have recognized that they represented a new social phenomenon which therefore needed a fundamentally new sort of government. Nor did the different ways that towns acquired privileges or the different degrees of liberty which they won apparently reflect either different ideologies or fundamentally different underlying circumstances.

They look much more like the result of differing local circumstances of a fairly superficial kind. Traditionally German and Italian historians have seen the 'Investiture Contest' as providing the crucial opportunity for towns to seize power for themselves, just as English historians have often connected the granting of urban privileges with the Norman Conquest. Consideration of what happened in all these countries, and in France too, suggests that each case may be one of *post hoc* rather than *propter hoc*. The exceptional degree of independence which the cities of Italy achieved in the twelfth century, and those of Germany later on, was certainly in part a result of the vacuum created by imperial weakness, but the initial movement towards civic autonomy looks much too general to be explained by any of these particular local causes.

For Venice the twelfth and thirteenth centuries could bring only a more explicit recognition of its independence, together with an increasing elaboration of government and of controls on the doge and his subordinates.[30] Elsewhere in north Italy some cathedral cities took over powers from their bishops, and from viscounts and other lay lords, by slow stages which often allowed them to remain on good terms throughout. The result is that it is very difficult to say when independence was really achieved: in some cases one can note the landmarks of decisive actions taken, or of privileges formally granted when a town became embroiled in the conflicts of popes and emperors, but charters did not always give entirely new liberties and not all the gains in moments of stress were thereafter sustained. In 1081 Henry IV, needing the support of Pisa, promised not to interfere in the city in various specified ways, confirmed various customs, and even agreed not to appoint any marquis in Tuscany unless twelve representatives of the city gave their consent in an assembly summoned by the town bells (*sine laudatione hominum duodecim electorum in colloquio facto sonantibus campanis*).[31] The rights of the archbishop and viscount were not affected. The twelve men may have been an ad hoc group, but those chosen would probably overlap, at least, with the *sindici* or good men of the city who are referred to

[30] Lane, *Venice* [519], 4-5, 91-101.
[31] *M.G.H. Dipl.* [156], vi, no. 336 (printing *laudationem*).

at other times. More independence, however, meant more responsibility and more prestige, and may explain the use of a new title—*consul*—which is found at Pisa soon after Henry IV's charter and in many north Italian towns before 1150. Like the earlier good men and *sindici*, consuls varied in number and function, carrying out a wide range of representative, consultative, judicial, and executive duties.[32] Their Roman title symbolizes a new sense of the dignity of their office but it does not imply any close knowledge, let alone inheritance, of Roman government. It was a piece of antiquarianism which would have occurred to no one if it were not for the prevalence of consultative methods of government and for the consequently common use of words like *consulere* and *consilium*.[33]

By the mid twelfth century another word was coming into use to describe town communities and their governments, and this was 'commune' (Latin: *communio* or *communia*).[34] Apart from its obvious connection with the very common word *communitas* and from the frequent use of phrases like *in commune consilio*, its use in urban contexts may derive from *communia*, meaning common property: not only walls and streets but also cathedrals and churches were increasingly regarded as the responsibility and therefore the property of the civic community. Their rights and liberties were also their common property which it was their responsibility to maintain. Common usage soon made *communio* (and later its Italian equivalent, *comune*) into the standard word for any collective unit of local government that enjoyed a measure of autonomy, but at first the word had no exclusive or special significance: in early twelfth-century Genoa *compagna* was used in much the same sense. The facts that we have some information about the way that successive Genoese *compagne* were ordered and that they had apparently peculiar local features does not mean that the different name of

[32] Goertz, *Origini dei comuni* [444], 47–97; Hyde, *Medieval Italy* [488], 49–51, 100.

[33] Leicht, *Scritti vari* [533], i. 377–83; Fasoli, *Dalla civitas al comune* [405], 142–4.

[34] Fasoli, *Dalla civitas al comune* [405], 144–5; Michaud-Quantin, *Universitas* [586], 153–66 collects examples. For uses outside towns: below, index *sub* commune.

the Genoese *compagna* made it significantly different from a *comune* elsewhere. As leading citizens in each town took more duties and powers upon themselves, so rules were elaborated, institutions took shape accordingly, and the words used to describe them accumulated new meanings.

As a rule, these changes took place with no more than occasional conflicts between town communities and their bishops or other local lords. The most obvious exceptions to that are provided by Milan and Rome. Ever since the tenth century the archbishops of Milan had had intermittent trouble with their subjects. Conflicts there over church reform in the eleventh century were exacerbated by the determination of popes and emperors to retain control of the most important city of Lombardy. Some of Milan's troubles came from the fact that, as the rich and populous centre of a rich and populous region, the city had a more mixed upper class, economically and socially, than did such great commercial centres as Pisa and Genoa.[35] Milan's internal conflicts do not seem to have either hastened or delayed its progress towards independence, but they may explain the separate election of consuls there by the upper, middling, and lower orders of society (*capitanei, vavassores, plebs*) which seems to have been in force in the mid twelfth century.[36] Rome, of course, was always entirely exceptional. Existing to support a clerical bureaucracy and their visitors, it housed a population of lay nobles and hangers-on which formed even less of a community than that of Milan. Any effort to unite the laity and win them any degree of self-government was doomed. A commune of any kind in Rome could not but be revolutionary.[37]

By the 1150s Frederick I, coming south to restore imperial power in Italy, was confronted by a host of urban republics which, whatever their lack of formal privileges and the variety of their internal constitutions, were outside his control. By now they were well entrenched. Their policies were determined

[35] Hyde, *Medieval Italy* [488], 74-6, 154-6, and 'Faction and Civil Strife' [486].

[36] Otto of Freising, *Gesta Friderici* [58], 116 applies this to Lombardy in general but it is most likely to apply to Milan: cf. Renouard, *Les Villes* [646], ii. 415.

[37] Benson, 'Political *Renovatio*' [244].

by their own interests and they refused to pay over to him the imperial dues and services which they had been appropriating and to which they now felt entitled by custom. Frederick's need of naval forces induced him to confirm the virtual independence of Pisa and Genoa,[38] but the towns of Lombardy, and in particular Milan, were another matter. All his efforts to coerce them and then, in his frustration, to destroy Milan entirely, first united the Milanese and then brought most of their neighbours and rivals into a league against him. In 1183 the Treaty of Constance recognized the *status quo*, including the right of the cities, places, and persons belonging to the league (. . . *vobis civitatibus locis et personis societatis* . . .) to fortify themselves and to renew their league. A clause obliging the cities to receive a 'consulate' from the emperor every five years, except where consuls were appointed by the bishop, in effect provided a formulation for imperial recognition of the consuls whom the cities appointed anyway.[39] What the treaty did not say was that the emperor was recognizing cities as constituting any new or special sort of community or governmental authority. The word commune was not used, and there is no reason to believe that it was deliberately omitted because its use would have implied any extra surrender of power. The recognition of the Lombard League did not imply that a *societas* was a new or special kind of entity either: all that happened was that, as part of the deal by which Frederick conceded hitherto debated rights to local communities which had proved too strong for him to crush, he also recognized this particular *societas* which they had originally formed to resist him. He used lawyers, including Roman lawyers, to argue his case, and they may have found in Roman law a neat formulation of the truism that collective groups needed imperial sanction, but there was nothing to explain what sort of groups that meant or for what actions they needed sanction.[40] It cannot have been much help in dealing with the realities of the situation in Lombardy.

[38] *M.G.H. Const.* [160], i, no. 205; *Cod. Dipl. Genova* [106], i, no. 308.

[39] *M.G.H. Const.* [160], i, no. 293; Fasoli, *Scritti* [406], 229-55; Waley, *Italian City Republics* [734], 122-8.

[40] The *conventicula* and *conjurationes* condemned in the Peace of Roncaglia, c. 6 (*M.G.H. Const.* [160], i, no. 176) were obviously defined by their political subversiveness not their legal capacity: cf. above, pp. 47, 59-64.

The reality was that from now on the emperors had lost any effective power-base in north and central Italy and, more important still, that custom, prescription, and royal authority were now behind the urban governments. Civic independence spread in consequence, except in the kingdom of Sicily and wherever greater towns were able to conquer and control lesser ones. By the thirteenth century even the papacy was prepared to concede a measure of purely local autonomy to outlying towns in the papal state and to use the word commune when doing so. In Rome itself, after the twelfth-century revolt was crushed, first a 'senate' and later a single 'senator' remained as a token concession to lay aspirations.[41]

In describing the growth of civic independence in Germany historians have often emphasized the conflicts between bishops and their cities which seem to mark its earlier stages more noticeably than they do in Italy. In 1074 the arch-bishop of Cologne provoked a riot in his city by requisition-ing a ship belonging to a rich merchant.[42] This is traditionally seen as foreshadowing the formation of a *conjuratio* at Cologne in 1112, *conjurationes* or sworn associations being seen as equivalent to 'communes' and the spearhead of urban liberation. In support of this view one could point to the commune or *conjuratio* sworn by the people of Cambrai when they rebelled against their bishop in 1077 and to Frederick I's quashing of a commune 'which is also called a *conjuratio*' at Trier in 1161.[43] The people of Cambrai, however, may have learnt the word commune from their French neighbours just to the south, while Frederick had by then met it in Italy: it was not often used in Germany before the thirteenth century.[44] To treat it and *conjuratio* as normally interchangeable, and then to look for formal sworn associations as the basis on which German towns regularly established their collective liberties, is misleading.[45] There is

[41] Partner, *Lands of St. Peter* [620], 178-87, 219-21, 226, 238; Waley, *Papal State* [735], 35-40, 68-80.

[42] Lampert of Hersfeld, *Opera* [47], 186-93.

[43] Vermeesch, *La Commune* [727], 88-98; *Elenchus* [118], i, p. 128-9.

[44] *Mittellateinisches Wörterbuch* [210], ii. 995, 1003.

[45] Planitz, *Die deutsche Stadt* [627], 297, 102-11; cf. Ennen, *Frühgeschichte* [394], 165-79; Bosl, 'Entstehung der bürgerlichen Freiheit' [267].

in fact no evidence that the people of Cologne took collective oaths either in 1074 or 1112: the oath that may have been taken at Cologne in 1114 (rather than 1112) had no apparent connection with any urban revolt.[46] In any case if towns-people there or anywhere else took oaths of mutual support in moments of stress that did not mark them off from many other groups both law-abiding and subversive, urban and rural, clerical and lay. Associations bound by oaths were commonplace and not in themselves subversive.

Furthermore, though the rebels at Cologne in 1074 complained of the harsh and tyrannical rule of their lord, and though the people of Cambrai succeeded in getting theirs to grant them concessions, there is no evidence that either group thought of overthrowing their governments permanently— let alone that there were any links between the grievances and objectives of the Cambrai rebellion of 1077 and another which had taken place there nearly a hundred years before. German towns did not all rebel against their lords as part of a single movement with constant long-term objectives. Nor were all lords, even all ecclesiastical lords, uniformly hostile to collective action by townsmen: though one archbishop of Trier got the emperor to quash a commune, his predecessor had recognized it and made use of it. Many lords allowed the new towns they founded considerable freedom of action. The independence which some German towns won in the twelfth century was achieved by the piecemeal accumulation of local government functions, and this was a process, as it was in Italy, to which slow encroachments in periods of relative harmony contributed as much as did either victories in open conflict or the formal concession of charters.

During the thirteenth century the word *consules* came into use in Germany for the members of the councils which appear as the ruling bodies of many towns. The title indicates influence from Italy (or southern France and Burgundy) and therefore no doubt brought with it exciting ideas of municipal liberty. The appearance of consuls is therefore a useful pointer to a fair degree of independence.[47] Although the senior

---

[46] Kaiser, 'Cologne' [494].

[47] Planitz, *Die deutsche Stadt* [627], 297; cf. Ennen, *Die europäische Stadt* [393], 135-8; Rabe, *Der Rat* [639], 89-102.

citizens of many towns had been acting as effective rulers and councillors for the best part of a century, and although some sort of consultation was older still, the new word came into use just when external dangers were threatening. The new aspirations it implies combined with external dangers to lift the more fortunate of German towns to a new level of liberty. Danger came first from civil war at the turn of the century and then from the new ruler, Frederick II, who was ready to buy—or try to buy—episcopal support by siding with any bishop who was alarmed by the unruliness of his urban subjects. In 1218 the emperor's court, through the mouth of the archbishop of Trier, declared that the people of Basel (and, by implication, of any town) could not have a council or any other new custom without their bishop's consent. In 1226 the citizens of Cambrai were prohibited from holding assemblies at the sound of their bell and jurisdiction over them was returned to their bishop. In 1232, finally, the emperor quashed and removed the communes, councils, masters and rulers of citizens, and other officials (*comunia consilia magistros civium seu rectores vel alios quoslibet officiales*) that had been set up by any urban community (*ab universitate civium*) against the wish of archbishop or bishop in any German town, and also all fraternities or societies of craftsmen by whatever name they were known.[48] This sort of thing must have helped to make civic freedom into a principle and words like commune and consul into something like slogans. Towns were beginning to band together: a league of a few towns around the Rhine was formed in Frederick's reign and enlarged during the wars after his death, while further east a series of alliances between other towns foreshadowed the Hanseatic League of the later middle ages. Meanwhile, at the same time that some towns were starting to establish their position as what later constitutional lawyers would call imperial free cities, others, in the absence of any effective central government, were slipping back under seigniorial control.[49]

Political circumstances were different again in France. Here there was no conflict between king and pope, or between

---

[48] *M.G.H. Const.* [160], ii, nos. 62, 106, 156; cf. no. 108.
[49] Planitz, *Die deutsche Stadt* [627], 180–3; Dollinger, *La Hanse* [368], 65–8.

king and lords, to create a sudden new opportunity, but the weakness of the monarchy before the thirteenth century left towns in very different, and often difficult, situations in different parts of the kingdom. In some areas the problems of collective self-defence were even more acute than in Italy, since towns were smaller and weaker to start with, and since some bishops and lay lords seem to have been at best ineffective and at worst tyrannical. Some of the rebellions that were to deceive later revolutionaries and historians into interpreting medieval communes as premature modern democracies took place in French towns where local lordship was by the standards of its own time unjust, ineffective, or both.

In 1070 the people of Le Mans, trapped in a seigniorial dispute over the control of Maine, formed a conspiracy which they called a commune (*facta itaque conspiratione quam communionem vocabant*) against their oppressive governor. They bound themselves together by oath, forced some of the local lords to join them, raised an army—apparently from both town and country—and marched forth behind bishop, priests, and crosses against a recalcitrant castellan. They probably thought of themselves as the kind of association for the defence of peace and punishment of peace-breakers which the clergy of France had been encouraging for nearly a century.[50] At Saint-Quentin, Beauvais, and Noyon, all close together to the north of Paris, communes were formed about 1081, 1099, and 1108 respectively, and they seem to have been formed along the same lines. All were recognized by outside authorities to a greater or lesser degree and all look pretty unrevolutionary. Nevertheless one commentator called the Beauvais commune a *turbulenta conjuratio factae communionis*, and it is easy to see that the more popular any sworn association became, however innocent its founders' intentions, the more likely it was to get out of control. If that happened, and if an ecclesiastical lord were to be the subject of communal complaints, then the clergy would think twice about encouraging any popular association to keep the peace. The commune formed at Cambrai in 1077, just outside the kingdom but very close to the three last mentioned, was one dangerous example. Then from about 1109 to 1112

[50] Above, p. 34.

Laon, still in the same area, was torn by riots and rebellions against its bishop in the name of a commune.[51] As the bishop was in the service of the king of England and called in the king of France to crush the rebels the whole affair received much publicity. The new and detestable word commune (*communio autem novum ac pessimum nomen sic se habet*), as Guibert de Nogent called it,[52] was beginning to evoke fear in the clergy and severity in kings. Yet Guibert's vivid and horrified account probably exaggerates the impact of events at Laon: although some kings and bishops did thereafter repress urban revolts, and some did not use the word commune even when they made concessions, attitudes both to the demands of townspeople and to the word remained variable. Even in north France revolutionary movements which called themselves communes were a small and temporary feature of the urban scene.[53]

Whether or not they were called communes, towns in the kingdom of France which secured liberties did so in the usual unsystematic way, apparently acting rebelliously only when they claimed to have been governed unjustly and against custom. In the south many found themselves in a power-vacuum during the eleventh and twelfth centuries and developed municipal institutions accordingly. The word consul, probably arriving along with Roman law from Italy, came into use here during the twelfth century as the characteristic description of independent municipal officers.[54] In the west Norman and Angevin rulers provided firmer government but allowed towns some measure of autonomy, no doubt because they were worth conciliating as military bases against the king of France and any rebels he might recruit. By the later twelfth century some towns in the Angevin dominions were allowed to call themselves communes.[55] Elsewhere in northern France the king and other lords granted or quashed liberties

[51] Vermeesch, *La Commune* [727], 81-113.

[52] *Histoire de sa vie* [39], 156.

[53] See Packard's review [617] of Petit-Dutaillis, *Les Communes françaises* [623]; Grand, 'La Genèse du mouvement communal' [451]; cf. Le Goff, *La Ville médiévale* [531], 164-75, 263-74.

[54] Gouron, 'Diffusion des consulats' [445]; Wolff, *Toulouse* [760], 72-5; Grand, 'La Genèse du mouvement communal' [451].

[55] Deck, 'La Formation des communes' [353]; Higounet, *Bordeaux* [467], iii. 33-4.

in much the same apparently pragmatic way as the Angevins, if with rather less control over the result.[56] Government in Flanders was more like that in Normandy: until the murder of Count Charles the Good in 1127 the counts maintained firm control while fostering and protecting their towns. The war of succession which broke out in 1127 demonstrated how much solidarity had by then developed within and between the great towns and how ready they were to turn it to collective advantage.[57] That very year one of the rival claimants confirmed the customs of Saint-Omer and ordered that the commune which the burgesses had sworn should not be dissolved.[58] The advance made then, however, was not consistently maintained. Once the counts had re-established their power their charters did not always give much, if anything, away, and when the great towns began to be riven by internal conflicts in the thirteenth century both king and count (or countess) retained enough authority to be called in on opposite sides.[59]

From the reign of Philip Augustus onwards the monarchy steadily extended its authority over towns all through the kingdom. That does not mean that urban liberties were crushed any more than it means that the royal government particularly favoured them. Collective local government, like any other local government, was allowed if it maintained order, custom, and law. Beaumanoir divided towns (*viles* or *bones viles*) into those with communes, which had their own mayors and *jurés*, and those without, which did not, but both were, in his view, subject to their lords' supervision.[60] Louis IX issued an ordinance about the financial administration of *villes*, *bonnes villes*, and *communes*, in which communes seem to be very vaguely, if at all, distinguished from the rest for the purposes of the ordinance. Mayors were to be elected at the end of October and the new and old mayors, with four

---

[56] Le Goff, *La Ville médiévale* [531], 175-6; Pacaut, *Louis VII* [616], 42, 62 n., 145-9, 163-5.

[57] Ganshof, 'Le Droit urbain' [433]; Dhondt, 'Les Solidarités' [361]; Galbert de Bruges, *Histoire* [31], 84, 138-40, 142, 148, 151.

[58] Espinas, 'Privilège de Saint-Omer' [121], 46 (c. 12).

[59] Ganshof, 'Deux chartes de Philippe d'Alsace' [432]; Berger, *Littérature et société arrageoises* [247], 63-6.

[60] *Coutumes de Beauvaisis* [61], §§ 154-73, 1516-32.

other responsible men, were to come to Paris to submit their accounts at Martinmas each year.[61] Saint-Riquier (Somme) was acknowledged to be a commune but in 1268 the king forbade its men to elect one particular burgess as mayor because he was thought to be a trouble-maker (*de turbacione ville esset suspectus*).[62] The best opportunity for French towns to claim real independence, if they had ever wanted to, was now past, but only those with exceptionally repressive ecclesiastical lords found it impossible to get recognition of any collective autonomy at all. In 1208 and 1273 archbishops of Lyon were still hotly denying that the Lyonnais formed any kind of community, but the archbishop of 1208 had to allow guilds to be established and the legitimate oaths customary in mercantile associations to be taken.[63] As for the king, St. Louis was evidently quite ready to let communes run their own affairs and elect their mayors, provided he could blackball undesirable candidates.

Thanks to the power of the English monarchy, English towns never had much opportunity for independence, but they seldom had very acute need for it either. Royal government might be oppressive and royal taxes heavy, but at least most kings maintained the peace and order that townsmen valued, and maintained it over a wide area, which was useful for trade. Nevertheless, Domesday Book shows that towns had begun to bargain with the king for more autonomy even before 1066,[64] and by the twelfth century their ambitions were rising. As a result they began to secure the right to raise and pay into the royal treasury the annual lump sum of dues that they owed (the borough farm or *firma burgi*).[65] Towns were prepared to pay for this privilege no doubt largely because it carried with it the right to elect the responsible officers, but the unusually good government records serve to remind us how difficult it is to be sure that we can tell from less full documentation which officials represented a town's interest and which represented its lord's. When the central

[61] *Ordonnances* [144], i. 82-4; cf. Mauduech, 'La "bonne ville" ' [580].

[62] *Les Olim* [90], i, p. 732; cf. *Ordonnances* [144], iv. 548.

[63] Kraus, *Gold was the Mortar* [509], 91-6; *Les Olim* [90], i, p. 933.

[64] Above, p. 166.

[65] The following paragraphs are based on Reynolds, *English Medieval Towns* [652], 102-17, and works cited there.

government appointed sheriffs at London it sometimes chose Londoners, who might be expected to feel solidarity and sympathy for their fellow-citizens, whoever chose them. Elected sheriffs (or, in other towns, bailiffs) would, on the other hand, still remain responsible to the king and might be closely supervised by his exchequer. Paradoxically, moreover, while one imagines that in Italy, for instance, municipal institutions profited from the weakness of the monarchy, in England they were developed partly because town officials, however appointed, were kept busy raising royal taxes.

Little as we hear of urban revolts in twelfth-century England, we cannot assume that English towns were without any aspirations to greater freedom of action. In two periods of the twelfth century when the government was vulnerable London formed a commune, and Henry II quashed communes in two other towns. The word here thus signified aspirations rather than any particular level of independence. In 1191 the Londoners' commune received (apparently short-lived) authorization, but exactly what that implied is not clear: one acceptation of the word commune in England at this time may have been as one which was suitable to describe a sworn association of a particularly public and important kind, but at least one monk still regarded it as synonymous with rebellion and mayhem.[66] In the next century it lost general currency in England.[67] Meanwhile, however, it had brought over with itself from France the title of mayor, which had long been used there for local officials of a normal seigniorial kind and had recently been taken over by some of the more independent communes of northern France.[68] It must have been in imitation of this new urban usage that the people of London had elected a mayor when they formed their second commune about 1190. Other English towns, some of them already enjoying authorized liberties and some without, soon followed suit. Most of the mayors who appear in English records during the thirteenth century must have been chosen by their fellow burgesses to represent their collective interests and stand for their liberties.

[66] Above, p. 62, below, pp. 269-70.
[67] *Dictionary of Medieval Latin* [207], 397-8, 399.
[68] Niermeyer, *Lexicon* [211], 628; Vermeesch, *La Commune* [727], 155-67.

During the thirteenth century the *modus vivendi* between monarchy and municipalities became reasonably well established in England as it did in France. Most of the larger towns were by now appointing their own officials to pay over their farms and were exercising an increasingly standardized selection of liberties under regularly renewed charters. Not all was gain and harmony, however: royal charters could and did limit as well as extend liberties and could be revoked. Quite a few towns suffered suspensions of their liberties for short or long periods and all had to be prepared to prove that they exercised them by royal delegation. However difficult that was in practice, since many of their functions had been assumed in less tidy ways than thirteenth-century governments liked to believe, there is no record that any town objected to the political theory that underlay the legal proceedings of Quo Warranto.[69]

In the effort to avoid the anachronistic teleology which traditionally permeates accounts of the 'communal movement' the foregoing account probably exaggerates the un-revolutionary, gradualist, and uncontentious way in which towns assumed power. Some towns were confronted by oppressive lords who resisted their demands and others by lords who simply wanted to make a larger profit out of urban wealth than townsmen wished to concede. There were in fact inherent conflicts of interest which became more obvious and more difficult to reconcile in customary ways as towns grew and as the necessities of government transcended old customs. What the contemporary accounts and records suggest, however, is that it was only gradually that the demands of townspeople went beyond the remedy of grievances and the confirmation of cherished customs. The idea that in forming communes under oath townsmen were forming a new sort of collectivity which could then—with authorization—own property, exercise jurisdiction, and so forth, is anachronistic. Townsmen already formed communities which already had the legal capacities which we associate with corporations or legal persons.[70] The word commune had no legal significance and its political significance was more variable than historians

[69] Below, p. 327.
[70] Above, pp. 59–64.

have always been willing to recognize. By the thirteenth century the various words which they translate as commune could be used according to context to cover the whole community of government and people together, or just the government, or just the community of people whom the government governed.[71] Frustrating as it may be for legal historians this colloquial flexibility is as comprehensible as similar usages are today.

What townspeople wanted when they formed communes and took oaths, then, was not a new 'right of association' but better protection for themselves, individually and collectively, against oppression. Inevitably that meant asking for greater freedom to run their communities, but since all government was supposed to be consultative, since officers were supposed to be appointed with the consent of the governed, and since towns tended to develop autonomy as they grew in population and wealth, the first demands to appoint their own officials may not always have seemed very revolutionary. The degree of revolution depended more on the attitude of lords to the first, often modest, demands that towns made than on the nature of the demands themselves.

Where order was already relatively well maintained then the lord could often allow a town more freedom without loss, particularly if his interests extended outside it. A king, for instance, might find it well worth his while to grant a new town considerable liberties, or to surrender some of his rights over an old one, in return for political support, obedience, and specified dues. A lord whose whole income and prestige came from a single town would think differently. It was the very closeness of the bond between a bishop, chapter, or abbey and his or its town which sometimes made it so hard for ecclesiastical lords to surrender their rights. The church's teaching on hierarchy and obedience was also a factor, but that does not seem to have prevented concessions at first. It was the weakness and ineffectiveness of their government as well as its oppressiveness that made ecclesiastical lords in some north French towns, for instance, so vulnerable to attack and therefore so hostile. Once conflicts had occurred

[71] Hyde, 'Faction and Civil Strife' [486], 279-82; Reynolds, *English Medieval Towns* [652], 132-6.

then attitudes hardened: sermons were preached on texts like 'Servants, be subject to your masters with all fear',[72] and clerics began to work out all the arguments for submission and obedience. Meanwhile, as more towns won more independence, the ideal type of town to contemporaries began to be the autonomous community—what was known in some (but only some) areas as a commune. More lords might begin to think that the only way to stop their towns from getting out of hand was to deny them any right to act collectively and independently at all—as the archbishops of Lyon tried to do. Some succeeded: there were plenty of small towns and some quite big ones that remained firmly under seigniorial control until 1300 and long after. The greater definition of the liberties that were granted in thirteenth-century charters may look like further evidence of this growing caution, but that is probably only partly true. More detailed charters were one manifestation of a general trend towards legal exactitude, better record-keeping, and more explicit recognition of the need for formal delegation of authority. They were of course used to preserve or recover royal and seigniorial rights, but not all of them were deliberately intended to reduce the liberties of subjects, let alone those of towns in particular.

Just as some lords learnt to adopt more deliberately repressive policies and others learnt to draw their own benefit from making concessions, so townsmen's ideas grew too. It looks as if by the mid twelfth century self-government had turned from being a means to being an end in itself. Whether because opposition and oppression made them stubborn, or because success made them ambitious, the demands of townspeople rose. That does not imply that they stepped outside traditional political and social ideas in any dramatic way. Urban liberties remained perfectly compatible with hierarchy, order, and customary government. It may have pleased, and still pleases, modern liberals and revolutionaries to see medieval townspeople as their political ancestors, but the process by which towns won their varying degrees of liberty offers little evidence to support this view.

---

[72] 1 Peter 2:18: see Guibert of Nogent, *Histoire de sa vie* [39], 177 (III. 10).

The structure of municipal government

Town liberties were normally granted to all the men, all the burgesses, or all the citizens of a town. Sometimes the same meaning was expressed by referring to them as the *universitas*, *communitas*, or commune of the town, but the distinction was immaterial.[73] Either way, the question arises: who counted as burgesses, citizens, or indeed men? By the thirteenth century it was clearly not the adult male population: quite apart from women, children, and living-in servants, who would presumably never have expected, or been expected, to participate in government or collective decision-making of any kind, there were quite a large number of people in all the larger towns who did not rank as members of its community. Whether a charter had been granted to burgesses, citizens or men, made no difference: all three words, like the collective nouns, by now came to the same thing. 'Men' in a town charter was evidently a synonym for citizens or burgesses, citizen (*civis*) being more often used of someone who shared the privileges of a cathedral city or former Roman town, and burgess (*burgensis*) of someone who shared the privileges of any other, but the distinction was not consistently maintained.[74]

Given the quite significant proportion of urban populations which were excluded from the citizen or burgess franchise, it is important, if one is to talk about town communities, to know why this was. In effect that must mean asking what were the qualifications for the franchise and whether they were narrowed after the *universitas* or *omnes homines* or *burgenses* acquired collective liberties. Oddly enough the subject has not received very much attention. Some historians have bypassed it because they are sure that political power within towns was so far monopolized by a 'patrician oligarchy' that the rights of everyone else were irrelevant.[75] A few have gone so far as to suggest that only the patricians ranked as burgesses or 'full burgesses',[76] but the references to burgesses

[73] Above, pp. 59–64, 138.

[74] Maschke's argument (below, nn. 76 and 108) that *burgenses* and *cives* formed mutually exclusive categories seems to me to rest on unreal assumptions about the use of language and the purposes of constitutional arrangements.

[75] e.g. Le Goff, *La Ville médiévale* [531], 343–7.

[76] Pirenne, *Les Villes* [626], ii. 27–39; Dollinger, 'Patriciat noble' [369];

or citizens in contemporary documents do not seem to support this. Some, like the complaints of 'lesser burgesses' against their rulers, surely belie it. Other historians have made town franchises look more deliberately restricted than they may have been by interpreting references to possible or sufficient qualifications as *necessary* qualifications.[77] I suggest that the reason for all this is that the medieval approach to the issue was so different from what we would expect that it is hard for us to appreciate all the implications of what the documents say—or, even more important, do not say.

As the charters of liberties and the common rule about a year and a day's residence show, it was at first generally assumed that anyone who lived in a town and paid his share of its dues would be a member of its community.[78] The payment of dues suggests, as might be expected, that this 'anyone' normally meant householders and probably permanent residents at that. As early as 1086, however, Domesday Book shows that these assumptions did not always fit reality: at Norwich 480 'bordars', who were presumably householders, could not pay their dues and therefore seem not to have ranked as burgesses.[79] During the twelfth century many new houses—and hovels—were built in many towns and immigrants poured in, so that everything became much more complicated, especially for those who now had to rule their own towns and decide who should be entitled to share in their new privileges. In so far as economic competition became fiercer in the thirteenth century that gave further edge to the issues, and in some places there are signs of restrictive attitudes as a result. On the whole, however, the occasional enunciations of more precise regulations which appear in the sources look less like the results of consistent policies than like responses to particular problems—the usual attempts to define old custom more exactly so as to suit individual cases and changing circumstances, which thus produced the usual anomalies and uncertainties for the future.

Maschke, 'Verfassung und soziale Kräfte' [579] and 'Continuité sociale' [578].

[77] e.g. Reynolds, *English Medieval Towns* [652], 125-6, where words like 'restricted' are used misleadingly and where the introduction of craft qualifications outside London is dated too early, partly because it is unjustifiably assumed that craft qualifications were necessary qualifications.

[78] Above, p. 165.   [79] *Domesday Book* [114], ii. 116b.

In Italy the position was especially complex because of the size and mobility of town populations and the ambiguous state of the inhabitants of the dependent *contadi*. For Siena we have what appears to be the one study of the subject that begs no questions.[80] It shows that by the late thirteenth century Siena had a mass of ill-defined categories between the full citizens and those who visited the city or even lived in it but shared none of its economic or political privileges— though some of them had to pay taxes and even do military service just the same. Though a new immigrant might be able to buy himself in, length of residence was the main criterion of citizenship. The citizens themselves were for a while divided into several categories according to the length of time they or their forebears had been in the city, though these gradations do not seem to have made much difference in practice. To judge from the difficulties which fourteenth-century jurists had with the concept of citizenship, the position in Italy remained unclear for some time, though lines were probably drawn in other towns in much the same way as at Siena.[81]

In England custom turned in rather a different direction, though it had only just started to do so before 1300. The change seems to have started in London, where by 1275 the franchise had been extended to those who had served a seven-year apprenticeship under a citizen. Whether this was really intended to apply to former apprentices who were not house-holders or masters, seems doubtful: the difference between the possible categories seems never to have been discussed and the only class of candidates for the franchise whose claims seem to have been contested in general terms were those who bought themselves in.[82] Perhaps in an age of high immigration apprenticeship was specified because it was a convenient way of measuring the length of residence, es-pecially for an aspirant to the enjoyment of trading privileges. Meanwhile the old vague assumptions continued to prevail in other English towns: though a link with apprenticeship and

[80] Bowsky, 'Medieval Citizenship' [272].

[81] Riesenberg, 'Citizenship in Late Medieval Italy' [659]; Luzzatto, *Dai Servi della gleba* [558], 421-4.

[82] *London P. and M. Rolls* [195], *1364-81*, pp. xviii-xxx; Reynolds, *English Medieval Towns* [652], 133, 171-2.

membership of a craft became more common later in the middle ages, it may well be that, when it did, the citizen or burgess franchise was being used as a means to freedom to trade rather than vice versa.[83] Political rights—like the right to vote—were apparently not at issue. In German towns definitions seem to be equally lacking, though the link between payment of dues and the franchise seems to be dominant.[84] The same may have applied in France.[85] In Douai five years' residence or marriage to the daughter of a burgess, followed by residence, were required in 1250.[86] The general impression everywhere is that everyone thought they knew what being a burgess or citizen meant and what sort of people were or ought to be burgesses or citizens. Individual cases might be tricky but the general principles were uncontroversial just because they were not thought out.

It seems that what preoccupied people when difficulties arose were not any political rights that the burgess franchise conferred but its economic and legal rights—the right to trade free of toll and sometimes the right to sell retail; the right to be tried in the town courts according to town custom; and the right to be protected from courts and claims outside. There was doubt and conflict on occasion about the right to trade and about the evasion of dues, but not about the right to vote. Again and again documents which set out the complicated systems of voting which will be mentioned below say absolutely nothing about who will participate at the first stage of voting in—presumably—town or ward assemblies.[87] Odd as this may seem to those who start from the premises of liberal democracy, the matter was unimportant to those who were interested primarily in collectivities and consensus. Few people outside the franchise can have felt themselves aggrieved at their lack of political rights. They could presumably go to the big open meetings which ordinary burgesses attended and could shout there with the rest. The sort of poor wage-earner who could not have become

---

[83] Reynolds, *English Medieval Towns* [652], 125-6, 171-2, though see above, n. 77.

[84] Planitz, *Die deutsche Stadt* [627], 255-6, 275; Erler, *Bürgerrecht* [396].

[85] Beaumanoir, *Coutumes de Beauvaisis* [61], §§ 1529-30.

[86] Espinas, *La Vie urbaine* [397], iii, no. 127; cf. i. 279-80, 387-91.

[87] Below, nn. 96, 99, 101.

a burgess even if he wanted would hardly have thought himself entitled to do more than that, while better-off people who remained outside the franchise presumably did so by choice. From the point of view of the community, provided that a good proportion of solid citizens turned up to assemblies and provided that not too many rank outsiders or hooligans turned up too, then a just decision for the good of all ought to be attainable.

The town assembly, open to all and summoned by the town bell or horn, was the fundamental institution of urban government.[88] In 1154 the consuls of Pisa claimed to draw their authority from the whole people (*cunctus populus*) gathered in their assembly (here called both *publica concio* and *parlamentum*, and at other times *arengo* or *arenga*) and shouting '*Fiat, fiat*'.[89] Despite their new name the consuls of Italy look much like the élites—*scabini*, portmen, peers, *jurati*, or simply 'good men'—who took the lead in urban assemblies everywhere and had probably done so long before towns became autonomous.[90] Towns which had not been separately governed before they became independent, and therefore had to set up entirely new institutions, followed the patterns they observed elsewhere. In 1200 Ipswich (Suffolk) secured the payment of its own farm direct to the exchequer and thereupon the whole town (*tota villata burgi Gippeswici*) met in the churchyard one Thursday and unanimously elected two bailiffs, who would be responsible for paying the farm, and four coroners. They then agreed by common consent (*per commune consilio*) to meet again the following Sunday to elect twelve portmen 'as there are in other free boroughs of England'.[91]

Who presided over these assemblies in place of the lord's representative is often unclear. Except in Venice (with its doge), French communes (with their mayors), and some towns where the alderman of a town guild may have taken the

---

[88] Mochi-Onory, *Fonti canonistiche* [591], 130 n.; Michaud-Quantin, *Universitas* [586], 297-8.
[89] Bonaini, *Statuti di Pisa* [95], i. 18.
[90] Above, p. 33.
[91] Gross, *Gild Merchant* [457], ii. 116-17. *Villata* should perhaps be translated 'township': see p. 103. It had no urban connotation but *burgus* did: Reynolds, *English Medieval Towns* [652], 100, 112.

lead, the first municipalities must often have been acephalous, just because they were now in effect lordless: in an age of seigniorial government they had become republics and lacked *ex officio* presidents for their assemblies. Some seem to have remained like that, but the appearance of mayors in northern France and England and single *Bürgermeister* in some German towns suggests that others felt that there was a gap to be filled.[92] In Italy unity of direction became imperative in order to surmount internal conflicts, and from the later twelfth century many Italian towns began to superimpose a single officer, called a *podestà*, on their administrations. The earliest *podestà* or *rectores* were emissaries of the emperor and resented accordingly, but soon many communes saw the advantage of having a single chief judge, chairman, and executive. Quite often he had to be an outsider who would remain strictly insulated from all local contacts and feuds during his short, fixed term of office. The podestate illustrates well the medieval tendency to assimilate politics to law and to believe that a wise and impartial outsider must be able to find a just solution to any political problem. In the end the podestate turned out to be too closely connected with the ruling élites, while the conflicts between rulers and ruled, as well as among the rulers themselves, turned out to be too deep for any *podestà* to resolve. As a result the great Italian towns began during the thirteenth century to develop extremely complicated systems of officers and councils to represent the ruled—the *popolo*—alongside the institutions of the commune itself.[93] In a political culture which continued to value harmony and disliked admitting that conflicts of interest were real and irreconcilable the Italian constitutions of the thirteenth century were a confession of failure. No one seems to have described them as if they embodied any new ideal: they were intended rather to circumvent what seemed to be new impediments which sin and greed had put in the way of the old ideals.[94]

[92] Le Goff, *La Ville médiévale* [531], 274; Reynolds, *English Medieval Towns* [652], 120; Planitz, *Die deutsche Stadt* [627], 323-4.

[93] Hyde, *Medieval Italy* [488], 100-18; Waley, *Italian City Republics* [734], 69-73.

[94] Hyde, 'Faction and Civil Strife' [486], 276-83, 300-7, though not referring directly to the constitutions. Cf. *Cod. Dipl. Cremonae* [86], i, pp. 215-17.

Important as open assemblies were as the ultimate source of authority when town governments were set up, they were not intended to embody a Rousseauesque democracy of equal individuals. The elections at Pisa and Ipswich were both parts of more complicated processes.[95] The elections of the portmen at Ipswich started with the bailiffs and coroners, who had already been elected, choosing four worthy and lawful men from each parish. These then chose portmen from among the better, more discreet, and more powerful men of the town. Indirect elections of one sort or another, sometimes involving elements of co-option, were common everywhere.[96] One reason was that they avoided domination by demagogues and mobs such as London suffered in the 1250s and 1260s. Consultation of aldermen and discreet men of the city was then superseded, according to an ex-aldermanic chronicler, by open meetings including 'the sons of divers mothers, many of them born outside the city and many of servile condition', who yelled 'ya, ya' or 'nay, nay' in answer to the proposals put to them.[97] An equal danger which indirect elections might equally avoid was that of cliques and corruption among the great. This was most acute in Italy and consequently the most complex systems are to be found there, reaching their finest flower in the method of electing the doge of Venice which was introduced in 1268: it went through eleven stages of election and lot-casting.[98] What all these systems show is the high value placed on unity. If unanimity was impossible then some kind of consensus was second-best: the object of elections was not to give individuals the right to express an opinion but to represent the whole community. Straight numerical majorities were a poor third best, and only suitable when the numbers were fairly small and countable and the voters seemed reasonably equal. The many committees and councils which town government spawned consisted of

[95] Consuls were elected indirectly at Pisa by 1164: Bonaini, *Statuti di Pisa* [95], i. 30.

[96] Ruffini, *La Ragione dei più* [669], 243, 272-92; Planitz, *Die deutsche Stadt* [627], 310-11; Reynolds, *English Medieval Towns* [652], 122-3; Wolff, 'Les Luttes sociales' [761], 450; Lestocquoy, *Les Villes de Flandre et d'Italie* [546], 69-71; Le Goff, *La Ville médiévale* [531], 275-6.

[97] Arnold fitz Thedmar, *Liber de Antiquis Legibus* [9], 36, 55; cf. Boncompagni, cited by Ruffini, *La Ragione dei più* [669], 237.

[98] Lane, *Venice* [519], 111.

members who were considered in the context of their municipal duties as equals, and a great deal of straight majority
voting therefore went on in them. Towns developed voting
systems not because they were more democratic or more
theoretically egalitarian than non-urban society but because,
firstly, they lacked lords who succeeded by hereditary right
and could thus resolve conflicts by their obvious authority,
and secondly because those who voted in towns were in
practice relatively equal, at least in their obligations to the
community of which they were members. All the methods of
voting, from the noisy acclamations of open assemblies to the
quiet co-options of councils, were designed to express the
will of the community as a whole in conformity with law and
custom.

By the thirteenth century full assemblies were being superseded in many towns, especially the larger ones, by councils.
These often consisted of twelve or twenty-four or some other
round number of members, rising in the larger Italian towns
to several hundreds. Councillors were sometimes elected by
full assemblies, sometimes by quarters or parishes, sometimes
by assemblies of different crafts, but more often by some
indirect system or by the retiring councillors. Sometimes
there were concentric rings of councils, the inner ring meeting most frequently to advise the officers (or the original
panel of *scabini*, portmen, peers, or consuls), and the outer
serving as a surrogate for the full assembly when further consultation was needed.[99] Until very recently almost all historians
have seen the establishment of councils as an oligarchical
ploy designed by the dominant patriciate to entrench its
power and close the system against intervention by the
poorer burgesses. This interpretation derives from a belief,
which medieval townsmen do not seem to have shared, that
government by the few rich must always be corrupt and that
the many poor must be frustrated if they are not able to
exercise their democratic rights.[100] It can be sustained only
by ignoring or explaining away such passages in the documents

[99] Waley, *Italian City Republics* [734], 62-5; Celli, *Origines du pouvoir populaire* [313], 31-9; Planitz, *Die deutsche Stadt* [627], 311-13; Le Goff, *La Ville
médiévale* [531], 274-5; Tait, *Medieval English Borough* [711], 337.
[100] On 'patricians' and oligarchy, see below, pp. 203-4.

as those which explain that innovations have been made necessary by past corruption or poor attendance, which prohibit the immediate re-election of councillors or the election of near relatives, or which require accounts to be regularly presented to well-attended meetings.[101] Provisions for the election—or nomination or co-option—of councils seldom abolished full assemblies and sometimes they required them to continue for important elections or the hearing of accounts. When full assemblies were abolished, first-stage elections by crafts or parishes were sometimes preserved, or subsequently introduced, in order to ensure an element of wide participation.

The documents suggest that the main purpose of replacing assemblies by councils, apart from the avoidance of mob-rule, was to ensure that the officers were regularly supervised and advised and to involve a good number of the most worthy citizens in the process. Regular meetings of councils were more practicable than regular open meetings, and councillors whom their fellow citizens thought to be the best and most responsible could be made to take oaths to attend them. It was accepted as in everyone's interest to get the rich and prominent to do most: the better, more discreet, and more powerful citizens or burgesses were those who, in medieval terms, had the duty as well as the right to take the lead in running their communities. When poor men were made *Schöffen* (*scabini*) at Andernach (Nordrhein-Westfalen) in the twelfth century they were unable to stand up for themselves and the law. At the request of the town, and with the advice of his clergy and the local nobility, the archbishop of Cologne therefore appointed fourteen new *Schöffen* from among the most prudent, better, and more powerful of the townsmen; required them to serve until death, poverty, or age incapacitated them; laid down rules for a quorum; and ordained that in future they should be replaced by co-option.[102] Co-option is to us so different from popular election, or even from

---

[101] Compare Espinas, *La Vie urbaine* [397], i. 310-19, 324, with text in Espinas, *Privilèges* [122], i, pp. 225-7; Planitz, *Die deutsche Stadt* [627], 310-11, 330-1 with 313, 314-15 and with footnotes, especially p. 311 n. 13, 331 n. 1; Bertelli, *Il Potere oligarchico* [248], 94 with Lane, *Venice* [519], 95, 111-14 and Chojnacki, quoted below, p. 208.

[102] *Elenchus* [118], i, p. 137; cf. Keutgen, *Urkunden* [141], 10-11 (c. 10).

indirect election, that it is tempting to see its introduction at Andernach as a characteristic piece of ecclesiastical conservatism, but co-option was not always imposed on towns from without. Perhaps, until sad experience taught otherwise, everyone assumed that those who had already been chosen as the better and more discreet would choose others like them and that all would have the interests of the community at heart. When an amended constitution was introduced at Ghent in 1301 the four electors who were to choose the *échevins* and councillors were themselves to be chosen the first time round by the *bonnes gens* of the town and then thereafter each year by the retiring *échevins* and councillors.[103] The difference between the two methods was presumably not thought to be significant. If closed systems facilitated corruption then stricter accountability by a wider group of citizens might be tried, but democracy was not. The Italians, with most experience of discord and trouble, opted for the complexity of checks and balances: their indirect elections avoided the worst results of co-option without losing the weight which it gave to seniority and experience.

All the systems, whether co-optative, indirect, or popular, seem to have been intended to get the same sort of people to take the chief posts, whether on councils or as executive officers—the two being often more or less indistinguishable. In practice some of the rich townsmen whom all the systems made into rulers betrayed their trust—though we have, incidentally, no reason to assume that they all did. Some of their fellows who were not considered sufficient or discreet enough no doubt resented it, but there seems to be little in the record of urban conflicts at the time to suggest that those who advocated more popular participation did so because they wanted the humble to be put in equal or greater positions of power.[104] It seems reasonable to believe that most if not all of the successive reorderings of urban constitutions that are recorded in this period were honestly intended to achieve the objectives they imply or declare—namely to ensure adequate consultation and prevent peculation.

Some towns were divided into quarters or wards for various

---

[103] Diericx, *Mémoires sur Gand* [113], i. 179-82.
[104] For conflicts, below, pp. 203-14.

purposes, including policing and the election of councillors. Parishes might serve as quarters, but not always. In London, for instance, a good deal of work was done in the twenty-four wards, each with its own wardmote over which presided the alderman who also represented the ward in the city's governing body, the husting. In 1298 the wards each sent six men, under their respective aldermen, to help elect the city's representatives in parliament.[105] The London wards were larger than the parishes, of which there were over a hundred, and while some of their boundaries coincided, others over-lapped in the untidy way so characteristic of medieval juris-dictions. In London the wards, and in Cologne the parishes, acted as collective witnesses to transfers of property. In both cities these units were older than the autonomous municipal government, and while the London wards, because of their links to the centre through their aldermen, may have been envisaged as exercising a delegated authority, the Cologne parishes seem to have been quite independent entities.[106] The distinction is unlikely to have worried contemporaries, even in the thirteenth century, when ideas of delegation were beginning to be worked out at higher legal and political levels.

By then, in another characteristic untidiness, some towns were using associations of craftsmen rather than territorial units to provide some of the necessary infrastructure. The degree to which crafts were integrated into civic government varied, but where independent guilds or other associations already controlled a craft before the town government was established they seem to have been suppressed or taken under municipal control so as to ensure that the community's wel-fare, as perceived by its rulers, took precedence over sectional interests. Town governments thereafter controlled the crafts by making ordinances for them or authorizing those they made for themselves. They might also either appoint wardens or inspectors or allow the craft to elect its own. These varia-tions became significant only in moments when the interest of any particular craft appeared to conflict with that of the town or its ruling citizens: normally the wardens or inspectors

[105] Jeffries Davis, 'Parliamentary Election' [348].

[106] *London P. and M. Rolls* [195], *1413-37*, pp. xxiv-xli; Strait, *Cologne* [702], 46-58.

of a craft would be its leading members, however they were chosen, and few craft ordinances betray obvious signs of sectional interests.[107] Where crafts were used for more general municipal purposes, such as providing the first-stage voting constituencies, there is no reason to believe that they were, or were intended to be, either more or less 'democratic' than wards or parishes, though, like them, they may have served to avoid the disadvantages of large open meetings. Sometimes (though more frequently after 1300 than before) constitutions, instead of making crafts into first-stage constituencies, reserved a certain number of seats on the council to their representatives. In such cases the choice of the other members may have been made in effect by the councillors, but that does not mean that no craftsmen could ever take part.[108] Giving the crafts extra representation was a good way of ensuring that the rank and file were not ignored by possibly corrupt or oppressive councillors. As no one was starting from one-man-one-vote individualism, the overlaps and possibilities of plural voting did not matter—though the system, like the Italian parallel constitutions, was an admission of discord and a general confession of sin.

In large towns, especially those with extensive liberties, officials multiplied alongside multiplying courts, councils, and craft organizations. It would, however, be wrong to picture them as bureaucracies. Even in Italy, where some posts were reserved to professional lawyers, an enormous amount was done by unpaid citizens, serving singly or on panels or committees.[109] Moreover, though the rich were considered the most suitable to bear the heaviest responsibilities, which often involved collecting money and withstanding all sorts of potentially corrupting pressures, all this amateur,

---

[107] Coornaert, ' "L'Origine" des communautés' [340], *Les Corporations* [337], and 'Les Corporations parisiennes' [339]; Desportes, 'Droit économique' [355]; Le Goff, *La Ville médiévale* [531], 280-91; Lane, *Venice* [519], 104-9; Leicht, *Scritti vari* [533], i. 337-76, 431-53; Planitz, *Die deutsche Stadt* [627], 289-94; Reynolds, *English Medieval Towns* [652], 165-8; *Cambridge Econ. Hist.* [304], iii. 198-206; Mulholland, *Gild Records of Toulouse* [161]. Also above, chapter 3.

[108] For an opposite interpretation: Dollinger, 'Patriciat noble' [369]; Maschke, 'Verfassung und soziale Kräfte' [579]; above, n. 74.

[109] Lane, *Venice* [519], 100; Waley, *Italian City Republics* [734], 73-5, 107-9.

part-time service by a wide range of burgesses or citizens demonstrates the degree to which they were all considered to be capable of exercising their judgement and to be equally obliged to do so when required. It accords ill with any picture of manipulative and resented oligarchies. In small towns, meanwhile, open assemblies often remained supreme or, in unenfranchised towns, remained the forum in which lord and community worked together as best they could.[110] In 1287 a *parlamentum* or *concio* of the people of Macerata (Marche) met there at the sound of the bell, trumpet, and voice of the herald, to decide how to pay for the town hall they had recently built.[111] A number of meetings were needed, one of them breaking up in disorder, but in the end, after a series of votes (made by standing up and sitting down), and with the help of outside arbitration, they devised a method of assessment to raise the money, *nemine discordante*. At Wallingford (Berks.) the merchant guild remained in such close symbiosis with the town that freedom or full membership of the two was identical and was enjoyed, in return for an annual subscription, by many people from the countryside who came to trade in the town, as well as by most of its inhabitants. Whether all of these joined in the government, or whether that was reserved for those who commuted their subscriptions by paying a lump sum, is not clear, but there is no evidence that anyone who wanted to make the down payment was excluded.[112]

The final impression left after an attempt to compare urban constitutions in different parts of western Christendom, and to set them against a background of contemporary law and politics outside towns, is that they are much more similar than one would gather from reading the histories of towns country by country. Vocabularies differed, and so did the degree of complexity, but the framework of councils and offices, rotating part-time service, assemblies, elections, and audits was very much the same. Some of the similarities were

---

[110] On the working of comparable rural communities, above, pp. 114–18.

[111] Zdekauer, 'Il Parlamento cittadino' [768], 115–22; the 'general council' of Macerata (ibid. 105) consisted of one representative from each house and so looks like the *concio* under another name.

[112] Reynolds, *English Medieval Towns* [652], 124.

the result of conscious copying. The consuls of southern France and Germany, like the mayors of England, show that, as do the many charters which granted one town the customs of another. Nevertheless simple diffusion tells only half the story. The way in which councils proliferated and regulations burgeoned shows that they were responses to problems. Where the problems were most acute the solutions were most complex, but the nature of the complexities shows that the problems were evaluated by much the same standards everywhere. All town communities took much the same view of what their rulers were supposed to do or not do. In the thirteenth century Brunetto Latini of Florence wrote a great encyclopedia in French of what seemed to him useful knowledge, and included in it passages about the government of cities, how their rulers were to be chosen and how they were to behave. Early in the fourteenth century extracts from these passages were copied into the *Liber Custumarum* of London. The copyist changed words like *seignor* or *sires* to *soverain, governor,* or *meire,* but that seems to have been all he thought necessary to make prescriptions for the government of Florence appropriate to the government of London. Looking at what Brunetto says, and looking at the constitutional arrangements of the twelfth and thirteenth centuries, one can see why: Brunetto concentrates on morality—the traditional morality of justice, reverence, and love. Burgesses and subjects must revere and love their rulers, rulers must love and watch over their subjects. Twelve qualities are required in a ruler: he should be of a fair age, noble in manners and life, a lover of justice, intelligent, strong and brave, uncovetous, eloquent, not a spendthrift, slow to anger, rich, free from the burden of other government, and faithful to God and man.[113] With such requirements, it is not surprising that Brunetto thought that rulers should not be chosen by lot but by full provision of wise and careful counsel. He thought that towns were peculiar in having annually elected rather than hereditary rulers, but he makes the ideals of urban government very like those of all government. Given that they shared so much of the moral and political values of

---

[113] Brunetto Latini, *Li Livres dou tresor* [14], 575-620; *Munimenta Gildhallae Lond.* [175], ii. 16-24 (= pp. 575-81, 611-14, 608-11 of Brunetto).

the outside world it is perhaps only to be expected that townsmen shared even more with each other.

One further point needs stressing here. Neither Brunetto nor any of those, either in Italy or elsewhere, who studied Aristotle's *Politics* in the thirteenth century seems to have applied Aristotle's classification of constitutions to the towns of their own day or followed him in worrying about the rights and wrongs of democracy and oligarchy. No one seems to have attacked urban governments as oligarchies, and no one seems to have defended them as aristocracies.[114] Despite all the admiration for Aristotle and all the effort to adopt and make sense of his teaching on the origin and purpose of the state, his concentration on the varieties of constitutions and their relative justice was not imitated. Only monarchy and tyranny were discussed, the one to be approved and the other, which seems to have been taken to be equivalent to any lawless government, condemned.[115] It seems reasonable to conclude that the principles which determined the structure of urban governments were controversial neither to townsmen nor to thoughtful observers from outside.

The activities of municipal governments

The scope of a town government's activities was determined by the extent of its liberties. The great Italian cities conducted independent foreign policies for themselves, sending out embassies and waging war in defence of themselves, their trade, and their expanding territories. By the thirteenth century they were raising mercenary forces to help with this, but citizens still formed the core of most armies.[116] Lesser towns, meanwhile, looked after their external interests on a humbler level, enquiring about each other's customs when doubtful points came up in the courts, negotiating with each other about conflicting liberties, and sending deputations to royal or other courts outside to plead on behalf of their interests. In addition to enduring the audit of their accounts

---

[114] For Marsilius' brief remarks: *Defensor Pacis* [51], 28-9, 31-6, 58 (I. 8, 9, 13).

[115] Below, pp. 328-9.

[116] Waley, *Italian City Republics* [734], 110-63.

and general supervision of their affairs by their king or other lord, they might also have to carry out a good deal of work on his behalf, raising taxes and forces within the town and carrying out his orders in general.[117] Lack of independence did not necessarily mean less work, only less freedom of action. By the thirteenth century even less highly privileged towns were beginning to exercise influence in provincial or regnal affairs: provincial assemblies in the papal state, for instance, were dominated numerically by representatives of the towns. Restricted as were the liberties of papal towns, they knew enough to limit their representatives' powers to bind them to unwelcome decisions. As Ravenna told the papal legate in 1294: 'You cannot make constitutions against the common laws nor legislate in temporal matters against laymen without their consent.'[118]

Any town with any liberties at all exercised some kind of jurisdiction. During the thirteenth century the meetings in which this was done began to be organized into something more like regular law-courts and in larger towns became subdivided to deal with different sorts of case. Where Roman law was practised professional judges and lawyers took over, so that law-courts were clearly distinguished from other kinds of meeting, but elsewhere collective judgement still reigned supreme, so that the citizens or burgesses who were gathered to do justice may sometimes have turned to administrative matters and dealt with them at the same time. Even in Italy mercantile and craft disputes were still decided in the traditional way. Everywhere a large number of townsmen must have been involved from time to time in judicial or quasijudicial business of one sort or another.[119] The multiplication of disputes between individuals, which we would consider legal, and of wider disputes, which we would consider political or economic, stimulated the recording of old customs and the making of new statutes or ordinances. Pisa codified its law very early, in the mid twelfth century, and by the thirteenth,

[117] Le Goff, *La Ville médiévale* [531], 303-15; Reynolds, *English Medieval Towns* [652], 129.
[118] Waley, *Papal State* [735], 118-19, and 110-20, 304-6; cf. Brown, 'Representation and Agency Law' [281].
[119] Waley, *Italian City Republics* [734], 107-9; Lane, *Venice* [519], 100-1; Reynolds, *English Medieval Towns* [652], 119; above, pp. 51-9.

even in the north, some towns were beginning to keep court records, accounts, lists of admissions to guilds, and other miscellaneous archives.[120] The story of the establishment of municipal government at Ipswich in 1200 was written down, as Martin has shown, after the town clerk had absconded in 1272, taking with him 'the roll of laws and customs called *le Domesday* and many other rolls of pleas'.[121]

Since one of the main functions of any town was to supply goods and services to the countryside around it, all towns were centres, large or small, of trade and industry. Even the smallest market-town had its metal-workers, leather-workers, and cloth- and clothing-workers, whether or not they were organized formally in craft associations: it is fallacious to deduce absence of a craft or trade from the lack of any record of a craft association—what historians call a 'craft-guild'.[122] One of the most urgent tasks for any town, and one which gave it much trouble, was the regulation of trade and industry. All government was assumed to have the right and duty to enforce justice in all aspects of life, including the economy. The reasons the subject loomed larger in towns than elsewhere were that the maintenance of their food supplies was often more difficult, their economies were more complex, and the varied interests within them were very hard to reconcile. To start with, markets had to be regulated, tolls fixed and collected, weights and measures inspected, and prices controlled. The provision of food in sufficient quantity, sufficiently fresh, and at a reasonable price, was a constant anxiety: some municipalities actually made bulk purchases of grain themselves, some contented themselves with fixing maximum prices. They also fixed wages—generally maximum wages—and issued and enforced regulations to control conditions of work and quality of goods in manufacturing and other trades, sometimes directly and sometimes by delegation to associations of craftsmen. All this caused a great many disputes, as well it might. It was extremely difficult to keep both wages and prices at what seemed to everyone—or

[120] Classen, 'Kodifikation' [331]; Planitz, *Die deutsche Stadt* [627], 323, 341; Le Goff, *La Ville médiévale* [531], 311–12; Espinas, *La Vie urbaine* [397], i. 961–3; Martin, 'Origins of Borough Records' [576].

[121] Martin, *Early Court Rolls of Ipswich* [574], 9.

[122] Above, pp. 70–3.

everyone who mattered—a just and reasonable level, and to protect the town's own traders at the same time as attracting business from outside. Difficulties did not only come from confrontations between well-marked sections of the community. Many individuals must have had divided interests, while town councils or assemblies must often have found the search for prosperity and economic justice as perplexing as do modern statesmen. Nevertheless the rulers' right to interfere constantly in all aspects of the economy was clear, and as a result councillors, wardens or inspectors of crafts, collectors, clerks, and panels of good and lawful citizens must have spent a great deal of time trying to implement what Pirenne called 'une sorte de socialisme municipale'.[123]

Public health and public works were another important and time-consuming preoccupation. Dirty as medieval towns were, their rulers did their best to keep them clean, to control noxious trades, and to provide adequate water-supplies. They also built walls, paved roads and market-places, built town halls, bell towers, market halls, mills, bridges, conduits, and even public baths and latrines. Some dug harbours and diverted rivers.[124] In Italy some cities assumed virtually full responsibility for their cathedral buildings, and outside Italy, if relations between city and clergy were good, the city might make considerable contributions to the cost of new buildings. Other churches were sometimes the responsibility of separate parishes, but the pattern of parishes varied greatly and the division of responsibility for churches varied even more: many small churches could for one reason or another become the object of municipal care and control.[125] Many towns established hospitals for the sick and old, and Bologna, for instance, paid a doctor to give medical treatment to citizens at fixed rates and to the poor for nothing.[126] Even quite small towns provided or supported schools for children, while

[123] *Les Villes* [626], i. 197; cf. *Cambridge Econ. Hist.* [304], iii. 156–81. For consequent disputes, below, pp. 207–12.
[124] Waley, *Italian City Republics* [734], 99; Le Goff, *La Ville médiévale* [531], 294, 362–4; Reynolds, *English Medieval Towns* [652], 128.
[125] Guasti, *Santa Maria del Fiore* [131]; Kraus, *Gold was the Mortar* [509]; above, chapter 4.
[126] Reicke, *Das deutsche Spital* [644], 196–251; Le Goff, *La Ville médiévale* [531], 349, 370–5; Martin, 'Church Life in Leicester' [573]; Waley, *Italian City Republics* [734], 100.

Bologna and Padua supported their universities.[127] Some of these religious and charitable activities were technically the work of fraternities or guilds rather than of the town government itself, but in medieval conditions the distinction was often unreal. While some fraternities and parishes would be distinctly separate entities, carrying on their activities quite apart from the town authorities (though always liable to be interfered with by them), many would have included some of the same leading citizens as dominated the government. Funds and accounts were not always kept apart.

The same applies to the social and religious ceremonies which underpinned municipal solidarity: some would be organized by the town itself, some by guilds or fraternities, parishes or crafts. This, however, is largely guesswork. We know much less about urban festivities and ceremonies in this period than we do in the later middle ages. Nevertheless it seems fair to deduce that the proliferation of guilds and fraternities is evidence that the usual medieval tendency to foster affective bonds through sociability and worship was well developed in towns.[128] Fraternities and guilds, feasting and fun, must have done much to encourage and sustain townspeople in the mass of unpaid duties so many of them had to undertake on behalf of the community.

In spite of unpaid service town governments needed money for their buildings, lawsuits, wars, and charities. All towns with liberties would have received some profits of justice and some tolls, and most had property of some sort which might bring in some money. To judge from the frequent records of disputes over them,[129] many also raised direct taxes—far more than the few which received formal permission to do so in their charters. The permission may in fact merely indicate that levies had been made or attempted in the past and had been resisted. Here as elsewhere charters give a misleadingly limited impression of urban activities.[130]

---

[127] Orme, *English Schools* [612], 167-84; Le Goff, *La Ville médiévale* [531], 370-1; Fasoli, *Statuti di Bassano* [124], 95-6; Kibre, *Scholarly Privileges* [503], 18-64.

[128] Above, chapter 3.   [129] Below, p. 211.

[130] Le Goff, *La Ville médiévale* [531], 296; Planitz, *Die deutsche Stadt* [627], 318-19; Erler, *Bürgerrecht* [396]; Reynolds, *English Medieval Towns* [652], 129.

Urban conflicts

Towns became notorious in the middle ages for their discords and oppressions,[131] and the feuds and factions of the great Italian cities of the time have been famous ever since. Italy probably suffered worst because the independence and wealth of the great towns there made the political stakes higher, but urban oppression and corruption seem to have been matters for complaint almost everywhere in the thirteenth century. Many historians have attributed these troubles to inherent conflicts of interest between the 'patrician oligarchies' who ruled the towns and those whom they ruled. In recent years it has often been pointed out that many of the conflicts were not really class ones in a Marxist or other readily definable sense: they were not between employers and employed, since the wage-earners, as predominantly non-burgesses (or non-citizens), were largely excluded from discussion or concern. Nor did landed nobles and bourgeois traders constitute mutually exclusive groups whose economic interests were straightforwardly aligned against each other, and the same goes for merchants and artisans. Nevertheless the words oligarchy and patrician continue to be used, and are often associated with either mercantile or landed interests, while craftsmen continue to be seen as a predominantly humbler category of people who, until they forced their way in, were excluded from power by the oligarchical patriciate.[132] My contention is that, though conflicts of economic interest and misuse of governmental power abounded, most of the categories in which they are now discussed are misleading, since the words used are ambiguous and carry a lot of inappropriate connotations. It is impossible to understand the conflicts of medieval towns until one examines the concepts now implied by these words and considers how far they correspond to the concepts implied in the words used at the time.

It has already been pointed out that the word oligarchy

---

[131] Beaumanoir, *Coutumes de Beauvaisis* [61], §§ 1522, 1525; Rymer, *Foedera* [179], i. 478; D'Avray, 'Sermons to the Upper Bourgeoisie' [351]; Giry, *Documents* [130], 58–62.

[132] Ennen, *Die europäische Stadt* [393], 168–9; Bertelli, *Il Potere oligarchico* [248]; Le Goff, *La Ville médiévale* [531], 329.

was not apparently used of medieval town governments before 1300—and perhaps not before 1500, either, for that
matter.[133] If medieval townsmen had applied Greek classifications to their constitutions they might have said that they
were aristocracies, or at least intended to be aristocracies, but
they did not use either word. The context of their discussions
seems to be different. Nor did they use the words patrician or
patriciate, which only began to be applied to medieval town
rulers in general rather later. From the sixteenth century,
under humanist influence, individual leading townsmen in
Italy and Germany began to be described sometimes as *patricii*,
but the use of 'patriciate' to describe town rulers collectively
may not have become current until German historians brought
it in during the nineteenth century. It seems to have been
applied first to the more or less closed and hereditary élites
of merchants or landowners which ruled Venice and some of
the imperial free cities of Germany in the later centuries of
the *ancien régime*. When the words patrician and patriciate
have since been applied to the middle ages it has been because
historians have thought that town governments then, as later,
were dominated or monopolized by the same sort of people
in the same sort of way.[134]

The first trouble about this is that sometimes the patriciate
is defined as the rich bourgeoisie who participated in government, sometimes as the rich bourgeoisie who dominated
government, and sometimes as the rich bourgeoisie who
monopolized government. There are important distinctions
between the three formulations, but the use of the word
patrician encourages historians to slip from one to another,
thus assuming points which need to be proved. How far the
patricians are to be proved or assumed to be merchants is
another uncertainty, and so is the degree to which any patriciate was interrelated by kinship and marriage. It is too easy
to find relationships between some councillors and then to

[133] Above, p. 198.
[134] On *patricius*: Kramm, Lahrmann, and Hirschmann in Rössler, *Deutsches
Patriziat* [666], 127-9, 140, 198, 267. I have not found any further discussion of
the history of the use of 'patriciate'. Grimm, *Wörterbuch* [208], vii. 1503, cites
the fourteenth-century Nuremberg chronicle, but the reference is to the commentary, not the text: *Chroniken: Nürnberg* [17], i. 214-22, especially 216 ('Das
eigentliche, später sogenannte Patriciat').

assume that all of them formed a charmed circle from which critics or opponents were deliberately excluded—and that everyone outside it was a critic or opponent. The unexamined assumption is that power *needed* to be monopolized—that contemporaries did not want the rich and powerful as rulers, and would, without firm control and manipulation by the 'patricians', have ousted them from power. Civic revolutions may seem to provide evidence of this, but only if we assume that those who came to power in them were not 'patricians' —and that is only too easily done by making the definitions and identifications fit. It seems impossible to use the words patrician and patriciate without falling into this kind of circular argument, and it therefore seems better to start, not by trying to define them, but by looking at the words which contemporaries themselves used to describe their rulers, and then trying to connect what they seemed to mean by those words with what we know about their civic constitutions and their grievances.

The first rulers of Italian towns are generally thought to have been different from those in northern Europe because they included noble families who had moved into the towns as well as mercantile families of urban origins. There is some truth in this, but the formulation incorporates several ana-chronistic categories, notably that of the nobility as consti-tuting the sort of legally defined, landed class or estate that it did in the last centuries of the *ancien régime*, from which an urban, commercial élite could be neatly distinguished. It has, however, been abundantly shown that this polarization does not fit the twelfth and thirteenth centuries.[135] Those who ruled Italian cities were rich and powerful men, so that it was natural for their contemporaries, and especially their fellow-citizens, to apply a word like *nobilis* to them, but it did not then imply any precise economic or political status. Nobility was a matter of 'reputation and prestige'[136] and, although the thirteenth century saw a good deal of snobbery about ancient lineage and *nouveaux riches*, nobility was not thought to be incompatible with the more dignified sort of trade.

---

[135] Sestan in Salvemini, *Magnati e popolani* [671]; Violante in Volpe, *Studi* [731].

[136] Hyde, *Padua* [487], 62.

Another word used of the great men of Italian towns was *magnati*. This had more closely political connotations: some-one who was described as a magnate—a great or important person—was, before the late thirteenth century, likely to be one of the rulers of his city or at least one of the sort of well-established, well-off citizens who seemed to be eligible for office. Whether his wealth came from land, trade, or manu-facture was irrelevant—provided, of course, that he did not himself do any very demeaning work with his own hands, which would in any event be unlikely for anyone rich enough to qualify for office.[137] In fact we do not generally know whether twelfth- and early thirteenth-century magnates belonged to craft associations or fraternities: craft attribu-tions were seldom recorded at that stage, perhaps because they were not politically controversial. Most of the *poten-tiores* and *discretiores* whom contemporaries would see as magnates, or potential magnates, were likely to come from families which were well established in their towns, but there is no reason to believe that they anywhere formed a closed group. The fact that some bore the same surnames, or even are proved to have been related to each other, does not prove that all or most were bound together by kinship or affinity. Prima facie it may be more likely that, when towns were growing fast and new fortunes were being made, new men could gain acceptance quite easily among the rest.

Politically, the magnates soon became very divided. There were difficult and dangerous questions of external relations to be decided, complex conflicts of economic interest to be resolved, and pleasant pickings to be found in local govern-ment. Differences of policy or interest soon hardened into faction, leading in some towns to the formation of *consorterie* or alliances of families which shared the extraordinary towers from which they fought their rivals and which still dominate the urban landscape that they created. To judge from the complaints made against them, which outside observers and arbitrators seem to have considered at least partially justi-fied,[138] the rulers of some towns had by the thirteenth century

---

[137] Hyde, *Padua* [487], 57–92; Waley, *Italian City Republics* [734], 22–44; Reynolds, 'In Search of a Business Class' [649].

[138] *Cod. Dipl. Cremonae* [86], i, p. 215–17; Ghiron, 'La Credenza di Sant'Am-

indulged in a good deal of oppression and peculation. Many a commune which had once seemed to represent the whole people of its city now seemed to represent only the magnates. Magnates and people (Lat. *populus*, Italian *popolo*) seemed to be mutually exclusive,[139] and so the people began to organize themselves in self-defence and protest, while the magnates began to close ranks accordingly. The bond of a fraternity was useful in such conditions: a single fraternity could unite the whole opposition, or wards or neighbourhoods could form separate associations, or craftsmen could work through their crafts—what anglophone historians call their 'gilds'.[140]

It is the last of these forms of organization that has attracted most historical attention, thanks to the nineteenth-century belief that the crafts were democratic institutions which represented the hard-working middle class if not the real working class as well. To some extent they did. Craft associations came to represent the humbler and poorer among the citizens just because those were the ones who needed to unite against oppression, but they were not primarily associations of underdogs: authority within them, after all, was normally exercised by the members who were considered most discreet and respectable. Particular crafts might have grievances against the city's rulers, if they thought the rulers were keeping down prices unfairly or monopolizing trade, but economic conflicts arose just as often between different crafts and involved the government only because it had to adjudicate in them. In any case it does not seem to have been any of these economic interests and disputes which brought the crafts as such into political conflict on a grand scale. If and when they became important vehicles for popular agitation it seems to have been primarily because people were already organized for various purposes along craft lines, so that these associations offered a convenient forum for political activity and protest.

When the *popolo* won a share in government, or took it

brogio' [438]; Bohmer, *Acta imperii* [94], no. 945; Keutgen, *Urkunden* [141], no. 147. Cf. Reynolds, *English Medieval Towns* [652], 131-5.

[139] *Cod. Dipl. Cremonae* [86], i, p. 215; for the ambiguities of the word *populus* see Ranieri da Forli, quoted by Bertelli, *Il Potere oligarchico* [248], 65, and Giacomo de Arena quoted (*via* Bartolo) by Hyde, *Padua* [487], 84.

[140] Above, p. 72.

over entirely, craft constituencies for elections were sometimes combined with territorial divisions like quarters or
parishes: the object was to secure wider representation, not
to represent any particular class or economic interest. Some
members of the *popolo* were in any case as rich as some of
the magnates and some belonged to families which had been
as long established in the town. Faction, however, had bred
faction, so that though the *popolo* started by voicing genuinely
popular grievances, its objectives and its effective membership soon became a matter of party alignment.[141] The various
revolutions or compromises which produced the complicated
new constitutions were not social revolutions, and even as
political revolutions they were pretty limited: their effect
may have been a wider participation in government, but the
link of cause and effect is not very firm. In Venice the crafts
did not win representation in the council but craftsmen participated in civic life and administration in other ways. In the
fourteenth century, according to Chojnacki, 'the leading
families' domination of the major governmental councils was
an indication less of oligarchical monopoly than of a more
general imperative of political participation, of bearing their
share of the patrician responsibility to man the government'.[142] Elsewhere, moreover, even where *magnati* became
a word to describe not those in power but those excluded
from it,[143] where particular local policies were changed to
suit particular local factions, and where new snouts were now
in the civic trough, the pigs, like those of Animal Farm, were
much like the old farmer. Unlike Orwell's animals, however,
the revolutionaries of the Italian cities seem to have started
without any egalitarian ideas: to judge from their recorded
demands they just wanted honest farmers.

Revisionist writing about patricians and about craft movements against them before 1300 does not seem to have gone
so far on the towns of northern Europe as on those of Italy,[144]

[141] Hyde, 'Faction and Civil Strife' [486].

[142] 'In Search of the Venetian Patriciate' [322], 69; Lane, *Venice* [519], 100,
104-9.

[143] What Bertelli calls Bartolo's definition of *magnates* is, however, only a
definition of those magnates whom it would be fair to exclude from government:
Bertelli, *Il Potere oligarchico* [248], 81.

[144] Though see Mollat and Wolff, *Ongles bleus* [592] for the period after *c.* 1280.

but a superficial survey of recent work on some individual
towns suggests that some of the old concepts are getting a bit
threadbare. There was always movement into and out of the
governing class at Cologne. The word *geslechte*, or in Latin,
genera, was used of great families in the city in the thirteenth
century, and, since the families which were to monopolize
the closed councils of German towns in later centuries would
then be called *Geschlechter*, some historians tend to imply
that the word already carried the same connotations.[145] This
sort of retrospective reasoning is not convincing. In the twelfth
century, at least, it is clear that rich and long-established
families, though prominent, did not monopolize power. They
also had much less exclusively mercantile interests than has
sometimes been supposed.[146] At Brunswick, on the other
hand, as probably at other Hanse towns, the ruling class was
indeed largely composed of long-distance traders and finan-
ciers, but here too it was not a closed class: Reimann's study
of its conflicts led him to conclude that while the term
'patriciate' might have meaning elsewhere it had little at
Brunswick.[147] Further west, the patriciate seems to be in
retreat even in Pirenne's own Netherlands. In 1945 it was
possible for Lestocquoy to introduce his study of the patricians of Arras by saying that a simple glance through lists of
échevins was enough to demonstrate patrician monopoly of
power, but Berger's closer examination shows that under half
the *échevins* recorded at Arras in the thirteenth century came
from eighteen 'lineages' while a good many of the rest came
from families which did not apparently belong to the first
rank. Once again the conclusion is that while 'great bourgeois
dynasties' may have monopolized power elsewhere they did
not do so in the town which has been studied.[148] The evidence
for London is also less good than it once appeared: most of
the 'patrician dynasties' rest on rather optimistic identifications, while the proportion of aldermen who actually belonged

---

[145] e.g. Ennen, *Die europäische Stadt* [393], 168-9.

[146] Strait, *Cologne* [702], 74-137.

[147] Reimann, *Unruhe und Aufruhr* [645]; cf. Czok, 'Zum Braunschweiger
Aufstand' [346].

[148] Lestocquoy, *Dynasties bourgeoises* [544], 14; Berger, *Littérature et
société arrageoises* [247], 95, 97; on sources of urban wealth in Flanders in
general: Nicholas, 'Structures du peuplement' [608].

to such 'dynasties' is not yet established—nor, perhaps, ever could be.[149] In London, as in Cologne and Arras, the boundary between wealth from land and wealth from commerce or craft seems to dissolve on close inspection. If 'nobles' were not such a feature of urban society in the north as they were in Italy, that was rather because most northern towns could not provide wealth or status on a grand enough scale than because all urban wealth was derived from trade and industry rather than from land.[150] As for the smaller towns of France and England, with their smaller pyramids of wealth and status and their consequent lack of a distinct class of great merchants, the concept of a patriciate seems prima facie inappropriate for them, beguiling as the word has been to recent writers.

As in Italy, however, the apparent absence of a closed governing class was not incompatible with plenty of discontents, and discontents which were often expressed through craft associations. The same background of political values, the same habits of association, produced similar discontents which were expressed in similar ways. Because the rulers of northern towns were more supervised from outside than were those in Italy, as well as because most of their towns were less temptingly profitable to rule, serious conflicts do not seem to have come to a head so soon, and craft representatives were generally not incorporated into councils before the fourteenth century.[151] It was in the cloth towns—as it probably was in Italy—that conflicts of economic interest were most fierce, since the range and complexity of the cloth trade made it easy for cloth merchants to abuse the influence which their wealth secured them, for instance by excluding weavers and fullers from the borough franchise.[152] In Arras one thirteenth-century weaver felt so aggrieved that he was alleged to have wanted to become an *échevin*.[153] It should, however, be noticed that the structure of most medieval

---

[149] Reynolds, 'Rulers of London' [655] and *English Medieval Towns* [652], 78.
[150] For nobles in south French towns: Le Goff, *La Ville médiévale* [531], 333-5.
[151] Mollat and Wolff, *Ongles bleus* [592], 37-41, 62-75; Maschke, 'Verfassung und soziale Kräfte' [579].
[152] Carus-Wilson, *Medieval Merchant Venturers* [310], 223-38.
[153] Berger, *Littérature et société arrageoises* [247], 239-49.

industries divided merchants and craftsmen much less than did the cloth industry, and that in many towns the rich would have had less temptation and opportunity to oppress whole crafts in the way that the cloth merchants did. Moreover, to judge from the content of the grievances that were formulated, both in the cloth towns and in others, and from the constitutional changes which were made in response to them by the 'craft revolution', the pretensions of the Arras weaver were neither widely shared nor fulfilled. They may indeed have been exaggerated or invented by the upper-class poet who recounted them in order to pour scorn on the pretensions of horny-handed sons of toil. In most towns outside Italy, as within it, the craft associations acted as vehicles for expressing general discontent with government more than specific class discontents.[154]

Everywhere, in Italy and elsewhere, the fundamental conflict was political and not economic—or was not then perceived as economic in class terms. It was primarily a conflict between rulers and ruled, not between merchants and craftsmen. Of course rich rulers could use their power for economic purposes, as when they monopolized or forestalled markets or when they discriminated against particular crafts. Above all, however, what people complained about was judicial malpractice and fiscal oppression—and the last perhaps most of all. Town taxes were notorious for unfair assessment and collection.[155] Town wealth was peculiarly difficult to assess, town rulers were both assessors and judges, and at first there were few rules and customs to guide them. Abuse was too easy. But it was the abuse, not the structure, that was the object of complaints. There seem to have been no conflicts of principle. Modern historians have been transferring the preoccupations of their own time into the middle ages when

---

[154] Wolff, 'Les Luttes sociales' [761]; Mollat and Wolff, *Ongles bleus* [592], 35-6; Le Goff, *La Ville médiévale* [531], 324-33; Reynolds, *English Medieval Towns* [652], 79-80, 130-9.

[155] Beaumanoir, *Coutumes de Beauvaisis* [61], §§ 1520-2, 1525-9; Rymer, *Foedera* [179], i. 478; Keutgen, *Urkunden* [141], no. 147; Lane, *Venice* [519], 106; Salvemini, *Magnati e popolani* [671], 59-65; Reimann, *Unruhe und Aufruhr* [645], 129-34; Berger, *Littérature et société arrageoises* [247], 76-8; Le Goff, *La Ville médiévale* [531], 328-9; Mollat and Wolff, *Ongles bleus* [592], 20-32, 42-5; Reynolds, *English Medieval Towns* [652], 131-5; *Cambridge Econ. Hist.* [304], iii. 196-206.

they have imagined that townsmen argued about the Right of Association, about Free Trade or Protection, or about the extension or restriction of the right to vote. The right of association was a right so basic that it could not be contested or even discussed—but associations must not be subversive; tolls and customs duties were imposed to produce income, not to protect home industries—but local craftsmen needed fair prices; all paid-up members of the community had the right and duty to participate in government according to their station—but there was no register of electors and no precise counting of votes except in councils and committees. Those who protested against abuses were of course primarily the poor and they were of course protesting primarily against the rich, because it was the poor who suffered most from heavy taxes and it was the rich who ruled and further enriched themselves by doing so. But the protestors do not seem to have proposed taking over the government, let alone expropriating wealth. All they asked was punishment of the guilty, proper consultation, and full accountability. Outside arbitrators and even some of the rulers themselves seem to have thought these demands reasonable. In so far as town rulers did not consult or account properly, and resisted demands to do so, then they can fairly be described as oligarchs, as they so often are,[156] but it is worth noticing that we have no evidence that any of them formulated any theory to justify their abuses or, apparently, attempted to disfranchise their subjects formally. It is shocking that an unscrupulous tycoon like Jehan Boinebroke of Douai could serve repeatedly as *échevin* and stifle criticism until after his death, but the nasty stories that then came out were obviously felt at the time to be discreditable.[157] Boinebroke offended against the avowed standards of his age as well as of ours, and his age was not the only one in which a rich man could make nonsense of the law.

Perhaps it would have been easier to correct injustices if ideals and values had changed. Arbitration, compromise, consultation, and stricter rules could not prevent conflict of

---

[156] I have also discussed this usage in Reynolds, 'Medieval Urban History' [654].

[157] Espinas, *Sire Jehan Boinebroke* [398], 15, 43; cf. ibid. 194, 210-13.

interest between urban rulers and ruled, as the fourteenth century was to prove. Perhaps, on the other hand, unity was less fragile than the abundant evidence of dissension allows us to see. Though contemporaries worried about the divisiveness of subordinate associations, the way that households, workshops, crafts, fraternities, parishes, and even the factions of Guelf and Ghibelline enmeshed so many people in a mass of associations may rather have helped to bind populations of immigrants into communities. Modern social anthropologists are less sure than medieval townsmen (or than Rousseau and his followers) that a multiplicity of loyalties weakens public spirit.[158] Medieval towns, moreover, had myths which could transcend the facts of immigration. As early as 1149 the people of Cologne and Trier concluded an alliance which was to make them into one people (*ut unus essemus populus*).[159] The word *populus* was a collective noun, not a plural: medieval towns, particularly those which had a fair amount of autonomy, thought of themselves as constituting whole peoples. Peoples were normally assumed to be of common descent, and it is highly significant that many towns in the twelfth and thirteenth centuries were beginning to claim that they had been founded by the Trojans or by some other ancient people.[160] They were not simply doing it so as to claim an honourable and ancient foundation; they were claiming a shared and single ancestry. So much was the single descent of town populations taken for granted on one level, however well aware individuals were of their immigration on another, that one explanation of the interminable conflicts of the Florentines was that they were descended from two peoples. How could descendants of the noble and virtuous Romans and the rude and warlike Fiesolans be expected to live together in amity?[161]

The acceptance of disunity was, I submit, the biggest change in political values which can be found in towns, even the towns of Italy, before 1300. Not only had majority votes, and even the casting of lots, become tolerable as an alternative

---

[158] Gluckman, *Custom and Conflict* [788], 10–26; cf. below, p. 330.

[159] Ennen, *Frühgeschichte* [394], 205.

[160] Borst, *Turmbau von Babel* [266], 589, 623; Clark, 'Trinovantum' [329].

[161] Villani, *Croniche* [78], i. 21 (I. 38); Rubinstein, 'Beginnings of Political Thought' [668]; on the idea of a 'people', below, chapter 8.

to dissension, but something like a system of estates was also developing.[162] When *capitanei*, *vavassores*, and *plebs* elected separate consuls, or great, middling, and lesser burgesses each elected a proportion of a council, that was not a manifestation of traditional hierarchy. It was a new and shocking admission that the great were too ready to oppress the humble and could no longer represent them.

Conclusion

This survey has had to be superficial, skimming the surface of a mass of learned and controversial literature, and largely ignoring many of the primary sources which the long continuities of civic life and the pride of civic patriotism have preserved. Many towns, even whole regions, have had to be passed over, and the rich variety of the rest has been squeezed into crude national categories. The economic foundations of urban life have also received very cursory attention, though that has been more deliberate: medieval communities and collective activity were shaped by medieval perceptions. Although some individuals, including many townsmen, pursued their own economic interests in a highly rational way, people do not seem to have applied much economic analysis to social and political structures. In contrast to the situation in modern Europe, it may be that economic inequalities were less glaring, or at least less resented, in towns than in the country. So long as the old ideas of hierarchy survived, the loyalties of craft and working household, however poorly requited, may have offset inequalities, especially for those workers who no longer had any home but their master's. Political conflicts on the other hand were endemic just because the old political ideals were so powerful: the ideals were impossible to achieve in the fast-changing economies of twelfth- and thirteenth-century towns, but all failures were horribly obvious to the citizens or burgesses and were perceived as the effect of sin and greed.

It may well be that I have exaggerated the traditional side of town life and have played down the innovations. If so it

[162] Below, pp. 316–18.

has been at least in part deliberate, because I felt that the corrective was necessary. No one needs to be told that two centuries which included the building of the cathedral, campanile, and baptistery of Pisa, the formation of the constitution of Venice, and the birth of Dante produced something distinctive in the way of urban life. Even in the north the digging of a new river channel at Bristol and the start of the great town hall and bell-tower at Bruges were no mean achievements of civic communities. Yet another argument of the chapter, which I hope has not been exaggerated, is indeed that even the greatest cities of Italy on the threshold of the renaissance had more in common with the small towns of the foggy north—and with the little market towns that Italian historians classify among the *comuni rurali*—than is generally recognized. They all shared, and shared with the rest of their contemporaries, an inheritance and tradition of collective judgement and law, of fraternal and neighbourly solidarity, and of respectful, voluntary submission to wealth and status. They were republics, but republics almost by accident, in which the idea of monarchy as the norm of government had not been replaced, and in which a new civic ideology was only just beginning to grow. They were probably places of relatively fast social mobility, but not of social equality or, apparently, of much aspiration towards political equality. The freedom that they won from seigniorial burdens and jurisdiction for their citizens was highly valued, yet poor people and servants can have found few opportunities and little effective freedom within them. Towns were not places of peculiarly communal values, the result of a communal movement that was peculiar to them, nor did they become communities by winning liberties. They won liberties because they were already particularly strong communities of a traditional sort. This chapter has had to be long not because towns were the closest of medieval lay communities but because we have such good evidence of the way in which they worked out the implications of universal ideas and assumptions about collective behaviour.

Medieval towns are sometimes said or implied to have been centres of some kind of new rationality. Having learnt to count money townsmen also counted votes.[163] Vote-counting, however, was a sign less of a new sort of rationality than of the need to use ordinary human rationality in a new way. As republics they needed to vote more than people who were ruled by kings, though not more perhaps than did village republics. Village records, however, are too poor for us to know how they voted. If, as seems probable, they used less complex systems, that was rather because they suffered less from faction than because they were less rational. Rationality is hard to evaluate, even harder to explain. Was it greater rationality that made the Venetian instructions to their ambassadors in Byzantium in 1197 into a model of clear sequential drafting, while those to the Genoese and Pisan ambassadors at about the same time were, like most medieval documents, a jumble of disconnected clauses?[164] It is easier to admire the Venetian achievement than to explain it, but the explanation may have more to do with unity of direction (perhaps even a draft worked out slowly on parchment by one brain?) than with fundamental cognitive differences. The Genoese and Pisan instructions are the camels which resulted from a committee's attempt to design a horse. In becoming republics towns did not automatically promote the better use of reason in every department of life.

Some historians attribute what they see as the greater rationality of urban life in general to the study of Roman law. That is an exaggeration, for Roman law was less different from other law and less pervasive in its impact than is often suggested. The real impact of ideas about the Roman past was more general and more diffused: they provided a splendid articulation for the civic patriotism and public spirit that were growing already in growing towns. It was probably early in the twelfth century that a Roman named Nicholas decided to try to revive the glories of Rome in his own house.[165] He built it of the usual brick but put round it segmental brick columns, supported by the wall in which they were buried, so that they appear rather like pilasters.

[163] Ruffini, *La Ragione dei più* [669], 13-17; Murray, *Reason and Society* [603], 189-94, 199-200, 206-7. Cf. below, p. 319, n. 176.

[164] Brand, *Byzantium Confronts the West* [275], 201-2, 217.

[165] Krautheimer, *Rome* [513], 197-8, 354-5; Kitzinger, 'Arts as Aspects of Renaissance' [504], 639, 649 n., 650 n.

Above is a fair attempt at an entablature, constructed from bits of ruins interspersed with new carvings. There were, of course, people alive at the time who could construct arcaded buildings on a grand scale, but Nicholas's enthusiasm for ancient Rome did not make him one of them. His house is at first touching rather than impressive, but the enthusiasm behind it was real: the same enthusiasm which later led the revolutionary Roman senate to put a preservation order on Trajan's column. The spell of Rome was not restricted to towns, as the charter given to Rocca d'Orcia shows,[166] but it was stronger there, because towns were places of greater education and literacy. The universities of medieval Europe would be unenvisageable without the towns in which they were founded. Inspiration from ancient history was not restricted to areas of Roman law either: in the 1170s a London-born cleric drew heavily on classical allusions in the praise of his city: its constitution was similar to that of Rome, its schoolboys' disputations were Socratic, its women were Sabines.[167] All this, however, does not alter the fact that the society and government to which classical architecture and classical allusions had to be fitted, whether in Italy or in England, were not classical. Roman phrases were an inspiration for the better formulation of medieval concepts.

In the end perhaps the greatest social achievement of towns in this period was that they offered a way of life that was attractive. People flocked into them and, though many must have died soon and died poor, they went on coming. Towns must have been extraordinarily impressive physically, with their walls, their huge cathedrals and churches, their paved and sometimes regularly laid-out streets and market-places. Many immigrants must have gone to them to see Life and they certainly saw more of it—ceremonies, festivities, riots, and all—than they would have seen in the country, even if they saw it only from their master's work-bench or kitchen. Nor should we fall into the fallacy of evaluating life according to the headlines. Abundant as is the evidence of conflict and corruption, public spirit did not disappear. For every Jehan Boinebroke there may have been as many

---

[166] See pp. 137-8.
[167] William fitz Stephen, *Vita S. Thomae* [82], 2-13.

or more *Schöffen* who gave legal advice to people in their
daughter-towns for modest fees because they thought it was
their duty.[168] Exclusive and unequal as was the cohesion of
medieval urban society it seemed real and valuable to townsmen. Sectional guilds and 'communes' were not prohibited
merely so as to protect mercantile interests, but so as to
preserve the unity of a town, to bind its people into 'one firm
fellowship and one true friendship'.[169]

[168] See p. 57.   [169] Gross, *Gild Merchant* [457], i. 227.

7

Provinces and lordships

This chapter is concerned with the collective aspect of units of government or lordship, whether royal, seigniorial, or acephalous, which occupied the intermediate ground of status and geographical extent between the local communities of chapters 5 and 6 and the kingdoms of chapter 8. They form a large and amorphous subject which will be surveyed even more briefly than the smaller local communities. If any justification for that is needed, beyond the sheer difficulty of covering so many sorts of collectivity, then the best one may be that communities of this kind encompassed less of their members' lives. They were communities primarily of judgement, government, and sometimes warfare, whose participants interacted with each other less often and in fewer ways than did peasants who lived in the same village and had to co-operate in its fields, or townspeople who tried to regulate their own economy and met regularly in the market-place and town hall.

The word 'provinces' is intended to cover such of the intermediate areas of local government as are usually thought of as 'public'—that is, areas, often stable over long periods and preserving traditions of solidarity, in which governmental authority was maintained actually or nominally by delegation from the king or other superior ruler. The early medieval counties are an obvious example. Lordships are more difficult to define, for the word is a vague one and only some of its meanings and connotations are relevant here. Vague as it is, *dominium*, its most obvious Latin equivalent, is even vaguer. It was used in this period for everything from the government or dominion of a king, or even of God, down to the domain, which we might now call private property, of anyone who had tenants or subjects under him. Much the same range of meanings seems to be covered by *dominatio* and *dominatus*, and some of them by variants like *dominicum*, *dominicatus*, *domanium*, and *demanium*.[1] Nowadays historians distinguish some of the senses in their terminology: we all distinguish government from property without thinking about it, while in French, for example, *la réserve* or *la réserve seigneuriale* is used for what English historians call the 'manorial demesne'. 'Demesne' is a pseudo-technicality of the worst kind, for it is inexact, arcane, and has not even the merit of being genuinely medieval. It covers both what a lord kept back from his peasant tenants within a manor—that is, *la réserve*—and those whole manors which a lord kept back for himself rather than granting to subordinate lords. The peculiar spelling, which looks technical and is especially confusing when it produces the pronunciation 'demean' and gets connected with 'mesne' (or intermediate) lordships, derives not from medieval usage but from seventeenth-century lawbooks.[2]

In the earlier middle ages few if any of the distinctions implied by all the varieties of modern terminology would have been recognized. This was not because medieval people were muddle-minded, but because their government and law did not need them. Both domains (or demesnes), as what we would call property, and dominion, as what we could call government, entailed rights over others which were subject to the constraints of custom and law. So long as there was no effective land-market and no closely structured system of government, any perceived difference between them was a difference between their real or supposed origins rather than between their structure or character.[3] To picture one as a 'feudal' lordship, which was essentially hierarchical and structured by the vertical bonds between lord and man, and to polarize it against an egalitarian, acephalous, and somehow more popular community of the shire or *Volksversammlung*, is to distort the medieval understanding of government. Both sorts of group depended on collective solidarity but neither was egalitarian.[4] The successful exercise of any sort of authority

---

[1] Niermeyer, *Lexicon* [211], 318, 349, 351-3, and cf. the related adjectives; Latham, *Revised Word-List* [209], 155. Cf. Maitland, *Collected Papers* [566], ii. 255. As was explained in the introduction, communities of seigniorial households, councillors, and immediate followers are excluded from consideration.

[2] *O.E.D.* [212], iii. 177-8; cf. iii. 592, vi. 369.

[3] Mair, *Social Anthropology* [806], 154-8 is particularly suggestive.

[4] Schlesinger, *Beiträge* [678], i. 9-52.

required collective activity and that created solidarity, so that the feudal or private lordship of one generation became the public province of another. Equally the existence of a traditional unit of local government would tempt an ambitious man to extend his authority over it but would tend to set its own limits to his ambitions. The province of one generation would thus become the lordship of the next. Shifts of boundary, meanwhile, tended to get forgotten in the retrospective creation of precedents for the *status quo*. Because lawful government was by definition government according to custom its units were characteristically perceived as ancient and natural communities of common custom and even of common descent—what are now sometimes called nations or tribes.[5]

Between the tenth century and the thirteenth the market for agricultural produce and for land itself became more active and kings began to control government more closely, so that a distinction between property and government began to emerge. Some lords secured a defined jurisdiction over everyone living within a solid block of territory and thus became effective rulers of it, even if their jurisdiction was to some degree subject to a superior one and their authority was rationalized as being the result of delegation from above. Other lords, who failed to acquire significant jurisdiction, became in effect mere landlords. All these distinctions, however, only became clear when lawyers got to work on the concepts and terminology of property and jurisdiction. The resulting definitions and rationalizations were full of inconsistencies, both between and within the emerging legal systems of different kingdoms, since the circumstances of individual disputes affected local decisions differently and made varying impacts on attitudes outside the legal profession. Most people seem to have gone on believing that any authority exercised according to custom was lawful authority, while that still needed consent and co-operation from the governed. Moreover, even where governmental authority and jurisdiction over a province were delegated through centrally appointed officers, there was still scope for lords within the province to exercise some separate authority and jurisdiction over their

[5] Below, chapter 8.

own tenants and subjects. Authority could be exercised, and rightly exercised, over all sorts of group. It naturally and rightly came in layers, and sometimes in overlapping sections, from the authority or dominion of the king over his kingdom down to the authority or dominion of the head of a household over his wife, children, and servants. If everyone behaved loyally and lawfully then all the layers and sections would coexist and would only create such conflicts as could be perfectly well sorted out by law. Naturally that did not always work out in practice, but the overlaps of types of authority were no more anomalous than those between, say, nationalized industries and private enterprise, or public and voluntary services, today. The containment of conflict between layers and types of authority seems to be a problem in all governmental systems, even where elaborate theories of sovereignty purport to eliminate it.

The lordships and provinces of this chapter include layers and types of authority which run from great provinces or principalities like Bavaria or Normandy down to the little county of Rutland or the lordship of the abbot of Bury over eight and a half hundreds of Suffolk. The Bury lordship gets in because its subjects were knights of sufficient standing to fight in the king's army, but hundreds in general, and other such small and subordinate units of government, are excluded: their working community seems to have been a largely peasant one and something was therefore said about them, though very briefly, in chapter 5. It seems, in the end, to be easier to classify the different sorts of lordship and province by their size and the status of their members than by the mutually exclusive 'public' or 'feudal' characters given to them in traditional historical writing. The higher the layer of government and the bigger the area it covered, then the higher the status of the members of the community that embodied it. Those who presided over the lordships or provinces considered here characteristically formed the core of the community of the kingdom, while many of their subjects would be lords of the local communities of chapter 5—or even, in some cases, the city fathers of chapter 6. Some of the subjects, however, would themselves also be active in the politics of their kingdoms and some might be more or less subject to village or local lords themselves. Status and duties were very loosely correlated and status seems to have derived more from wealth and style of life than from position in anything one could call a feudal pyramid of tenure. Today words like vassal and knight, fealty and homage, have much more precise connotations of what historians call feudalism than *vassus*, *vavassor*, *miles*, *fidelitas*, or *homagium* seem to have done in the middle ages, particularly before the thirteenth century.[6] As for *homo* and *fidelis*, they were, of course, often used in entirely different contexts. It cannot be right to consider only apparently convergent usages and then fix them with a technical meaning. The word noble was another vague and variable one, denoting an equally vague and variable concept. The privileges and obligations of nobility were not legally defined. Any privileges and respect which an individual enjoyed were the corollary of his wealth and life-style rather than of his proven descent from noble ancestors.[7] In the same way, at the bottom of the scale, the boundary between free and unfree, *liberi* and *servi*, shifted according to the economic and legal context in which the words were used.[8]

The communities of lordship and province to be discussed here consisted of those who are often described as vassals and vavassors (though neither word was much used at the time), along with some other free men, but who might better be called the lower nobility with some of the higher peasantry, in varying proportions according to the size and status of the lordship or province. Although they were all free men, that need not imply that all those who did not form part of them were *ipso facto* ignoble or unfree or held their land in some entirely

[6] Niermeyer, *Lexicon* [211], 423–4, 491–3, 1063–5, 1065–7, though note the way that words like 'vassalic' in the definitions strengthen the connotations of ideal-type feudalism. Among much recent writing on nobles and knights see e.g. essays in Reuter, *Medieval Nobility* [648]; Harvey, 'Knight and Knight's Fee' [462]; Duby, *Chivalrous Society* [375].

[7] e.g. *Miracles de Saint Benoît* [53], 218–21 (VI. 2); Rogozinski, 'Ennoblement' [664]. The loss of service when a non-noble acquired a fee, referred to by Rogozinski, was a potential loss *if* he could not do the service: *Ordonnances* [144], i. 746 (c. 6). Those summoned for service in *Ordonnances* [144], i. 546, 371 apparently needed to be defined by wealth as well as by being described as nobles. I do not see any reason to deduce from *M.G.H. Const.* [160], i, no. 140, c. 12 that *rustici* were normally and in principle debarred from carrying arms. Any such rule is difficult to reconcile with the conditions and ideas of the time.

[8] Above, pp. 31, 141–2.

different way. The basic qualification for active participation was that one was free enough to be able to attend courts and perform duties at some distance from home. One needed to be free enough to have free time. Some who qualified may have performed some physical work on their own land but they must presumably have had servants to do most of it. Most of them were the sort of people who carried swords rather than staves and were better at riding than at any agricultural skill. The service they owed to their king or their lord was honourable service, and they were free enough, or noble enough, for their service to be thought of in contractual terms.

The evolution of provincial government

The simplest way to summarize the evolution of provincial government seems to be to take it kingdom by kingdom. This will tend to obliterate local variations within kingdoms unduly but it has the advantage of demonstrating how a fairly homogeneous pattern of lordship and local government in the tenth century, derived as it was from common ideas about government and law and common difficulties of communication, was gradually broken up thereafter. Changes which are sometimes seen as the product of deeprooted national differences or inevitable tendencies either to unity or division may thus be revealed rather as the result of political conditions which happened to prevail in each kingdom at the time when jurisdictions were becoming fixed and established in custom.

Over much of western Europe provincial and local government in this period developed out of the Carolingian framework of counties (Lat. *comitatus*, sometimes *pagi*), which were subdivided into hundreds (*centenariae* or *vicariae*) and, in some areas, were themselves grouped together within larger units. Some of these larger units had once been kingdoms themselves but had since been relegated to the status of duchies.[9] Paradoxically this Carolingian pattern can be seen particularly clearly in non-Carolingian England, where it was gradually but quite systematically introduced by the kings of

[9] Ganshof, *Frankish Institutions* [435], 26-34; Schulze, *Grafschaftsverfassung* [683].

the tenth and early eleventh centuries.[10] Here and there, notably in the north, where counties arrived late, or where an ancient church was allowed to keep its old and special jurisdiction over the surrounding area, traces of an older arrangement have been found in the records: royal dues had, it seems, formerly been collected at royal estates from surrounding districts which had probably also served as units of general government and law. The name *scir* or shire seems to have been transferred from these older units to the new counties as the Old English equivalent of *comitatus*, while some of the old *scire* were slotted into the new system at a lower level as hundreds, or as groups of hundreds that continued to be managed together.[11] One obvious reason for introducing the new, two-tier system would have been the greater size of the new kingdom of England, compared with the old kingdoms it replaced, and the greater complexity of governing it. In the tenth century, when counties in some areas were new and in others had not yet been formed at all, authority over larger regions was exercised by nobles called ealdormen. Since some ealdormanries corresponded fairly closely to former kingdoms they may well have been a potentially dangerous focus of local loyalties, and that may explain why Ethelred II broke them up at the end of the century.[12] At all events, though his successors restored some large ealdormanries (under the newer name of earldoms), most were by now subdivided into shires. It was the shires which were to prove the more stable and enduring units. Although in 1051-2, for instance, the men of earl Godwin's and his sons' earldoms supported their rebellion, the boundaries of earldoms were too variable, and the opportunities for their constituent shires to act together were probably too rare, for them to retain or develop much cohesion.[13]

It is sometimes suggested that the shire reeves or sheriffs who begin to be mentioned, apparently as officers subordinate to earls, in the eleventh century, were more under royal

[10] Campbell, 'English Government' [307]; Warren, 'Myth of Norman Efficiency' [739].

[11] Barrow, *Kingdom of the Scots* [235], 7-68; Cam, *Liberties and Communities* [303], 64-105; Everitt, 'Banburys' [400], 30-2.

[12] Stafford, 'Reign of Aethelred' [694], 17-19, 29.

[13] Below, p. 265.

control than were the earls themselves. There seems to be no evidence to support this contention, nor is there any reason to suppose that a sheriff would be less likely to want to pass on his office to his son than would an earl. All such offices everywhere tended to become hereditary unless kings were careful, but a tough king could dismiss unsatisfactory ministers whether or not they had succeeded their fathers. Even an ealdorman, earl, or reeve who had succeeded his father seems to have presided over his shire as the king's deputy. Whatever his title to office, moreover, he would have to carry with him in his decisions and actions the other lords and landowners who were present. The laws do not distinguish those who had to attend shire meetings from those who went to hundreds, but presumably it was the more prosperous who went most regularly to the shire and dominated its judgements. Shires normally met twice a year and virtually all serious crimes, as well as pleas about land, were tried in their meetings. There is little evidence that pleas were held regularly anywhere else, except in the king's court and the hundreds, or in those few archaic quasi-shires which remained under church control. Great men may sometimes have adjudicated disputes among their immediate followers elsewhere, just as all lords probably dealt with those of their humblest tenants, but this kind of private jurisdiction does not seem to have detracted seriously from the business of shires.[14] Those who attended shire meetings, rendered their judgements, and occasionally served in the forces which the king, through the earl or sheriff, raised from them, may thus have come to form quite cohesive communities.

Though the Norman Conquest is often said to have enlarged the scope of seigniorial or feudal jurisdiction to the detriment of that of the shire, it did not really change the position much. Large earldoms disappeared, but shires or counties stayed, with some more being added until, by the later twelfth century, a network was formed which was to last until the twentieth.[15] Any strengthening of the bonds of lordship outside it was both accidental and temporary, deriving from the hostility which the conquest aroused. For a while William I

---

[14] Hurnard, 'Anglo-Norman Franchises' [483].
[15] Warren, 'Myth of Norman Efficiency' [739].

probably felt that he might need to raise soldiers exclusively from those who had come with him; he and they had to build—or get their subjects to build—forts to hold down the country; and they were no doubt unwilling at first to submit their own quarrels to collective judgements in county assemblies that included Englishmen. It was probably this sort of pressure—the effect of being an occupying army in a hostile land—rather than any wholesale importation of new and distinctively 'feudal' practices and ideas, that explains the much debated changes in military service and jurisdiction after 1066. Norman and English customs in warfare and litigation differed, but the recorded differences do not look structural.[16] At all events, military service now began to be levied by units of tenure—that is, by lordships, through their lords—rather than by shires, through their sheriffs. By the early twelfth century disputes between the *vavassores* of a tenant in chief were being decided in their lord's court, though disputes between the *vavassores* of different lords still went to the county.[17] The overlap of new and old units of jurisdiction was untidy and probably no one at the time looked at it in such a way as to analyse the difference between 'feudal' and 'public' (or 'communal') systems. Orderic Vitalis, writing in the early twelfth century about the years immediately after the conquest, does not seem to notice the distinction at all, describing grants of land as if they were grants of office over or within counties.[18] On the Welsh march, from which his best information came, the free hand in their counties that William gave to his first earls must have made such distinctions even more unreal than they seemed elsewhere.[19] In the long run, however, counties, with rare outlying exceptions, remained more or less under royal control, and it was the counties which retained all serious criminal jurisdiction.

If the concessions made by King Stephen in the mid twelfth century had lasted, counties might have turned—or been broken up—into hereditary lordships, but Henry II's accession

---

[16] Below, p. 265, n. 32. [17] Robertson, *Laws* [177], 286.
[18] *Hist. Eccles.* [57], ii. 262-6.
[19] Hurnard, 'Anglo-Norman Franchises' [483], 314 and *Lanfranc's Letters* [143], no. 31. For a possible, shortlived unit of several shires: Wightman, 'Palatine Earldom' [752], though cf. Alexander, 'Alleged Palatinates' [217].

prevented that. It has recently been pointed out that the compromise which Henry made with the great men of the realm produced a new distinction of principle between earldoms, baronies, and other landed estates, which remained hereditary, and sheriffdoms and justiceships, which did not.[20] It was the sheriffs, moreover, not the earls, who now controlled county government. The separation between land and office—between the private hereditary property of the lordship and the public office of the shire government—became the distinctive mark of English provincial government. There was the notable anomaly that lords still had some jurisdiction over their tenants, and some of them were later to secure more, but most of these rights (such as the view of frankpledge, the assizes of bread and ale, and even the right to a gallows) did not amount to very much in practice and, besides, were chiefly exercised over peasant tenants. From Henry II's reign on, the jurisdiction which lords had hitherto exercised over civil pleas between their free tenants was steadily eroded by the extension of royal justice.[21] From the eleventh century, moreover, if not before, lordships—honours, or baronies, as they came to be called—were normally scattered and often shortlived, while many men above the rank of peasant held land from several lords.[22] Real armies in the field had never consisted entirely of those who owed knight service, and under the Angevins the proportion of paid soldiers became even larger. Tenants in chief still recouped their scutage payments from their tenants, and this, together with royal demands for special rights and dues from those who held in chief, kept alive a moderately accurate memory of the hierarchy of tenure, but the bonds seem to have become more technical than affective. Ties of tenure, like ties of kinship and affinity, played some part in determining political alignments in the troubles of the thirteenth century but they were not decisive.[23]

---

[20] Clanchy, *England and its Rulers* [325], 121.

[21] Above, p. 55, below, p. 267.

[22] Le Patourel, *Norman Empire* [542], 307-15; Davis, 'What Happened in Stephen's Reign' [350].

[23] Holt, *Northerners* [476], 61-78; Blair, 'Knights of Durham' [93]; Powicke, *Henry III* [633], 510 n. and cf. *Calendar of Inq. Misc.* [101], i, nos. 609-936. On family links: Holt, 'Patronage and Politics' [474].

The solidarity of counties, on the other hand, was confirmed as royal government imposed ever more duties upon them. The kind of men who were likely to take the lead in county affairs were also quite likely to hold land in more than one county, but almost any county must nevertheless have exerted a stronger pull on its members than could almost any lord, or the community of his tenants, outside the Welsh or Scottish marches. It represented home for many of them, it met regularly, and it carried out regular and important duties of judgement, taxation, and government in general. Panels of knights and freeholders assessed taxes, gave verdicts on behalf of the whole county, and were sometimes summoned to the king's court to report what they had done. Counties could buy privileges from the king and, of course, could be collectively punished by him. They seem to have come to dislike having sheriffs imposed on them from outside and closed ranks when sheriffs bullied them. By the end of the thirteenth century they were regularly electing knights from among their number to represent them in royal parliaments.[24] Pressure from above forced at least some people to take part in county business and forced some sort of working community on them as a result, even when they were divided by political conflict.

This particular pattern of separation between lordship and province was peculiar to England. In France the two became assimilated for a time and when they diverged again with the revival of royal power in the thirteenth century the dividing line was not drawn in quite the same way as it was in England. Most of the Carolingian counties of France (often alternatively known as *pagi*, producing the French *pays*) survived fairly well until the early eleventh century, but many of them then became fragmented. In the Mâconnais the *mallus publicus* met under the count throughout the tenth century and was attended by nobles from the whole *pagus*. It was not until the next century that the count became merely one lord among many, when the nobles based further from Mâcon began to take independent control of their *châtellenies*, and

[24] White, *Self Government* [747]; Holt, *Magna Carta* [475], 52-8; Powicke, *Henry III* [633], 392-3, 404-5, 424-6; Palmer, *County Courts* [619], esp. 76-7, 293-5; below, pp. 308-11.

their humbler neighbours, landowners as well as peasants, were diverted to do suit at their courts instead of the count's.[25] In other areas the position looks similar, with some variation in the chronology and details of fragmentation.[26] The old framework of authority and subordination seems to have been replaced by a loose framework of power and influence, in which more or less anyone able to control his immediate neighbourhood lived in a jurisdictional void. That does not mean that such people—in effect the nobles—lived in a social void: they had family and friends to rally round when they were needed; they allied with each other as prudence, ambition, and affection dictated; and they still met together on occasion to adjudicate disputes. But the pleas which were held on such occasions were amorphous affairs, arbitrations (as we might call them) without any established sanctions between force and public opinion to back them up.[27] It was this situation which provoked the movement to establish rules of conduct under the Peace and Truce of God, which started in southern France and spread fastest where normal secular authority was most weak and fragmented— although, ironically, the great churches which led the movement had, by their quest for privileges, themselves contributed to the fragmentation of comital authority in the first place.[28]

In some parts of France, however, a few counts maintained their authority and extended it, both by accumulating whole counties and by gaining other sorts of right over parts of other people's counties nearby. Flanders, Normandy, and Anjou are the most obvious examples, but we should not assume that even the rulers of these areas always controlled their noble neighbours as effectively as they did later, or through the same means. In Normandy, where the counts of Rouen got control of more counties and by the eleventh century were beginning to call themselves dukes (among other titles), the troubles of William the Conqueror's minority suggest that ducal or comital power was still dependent

[25] Duby, *Société mâconnaise* [381], 95-8, 137-48.
[26] Beech, *Gâtine of Poitou* [243], 42-70; Bur, *Comté de Champagne* [291], 125-6, 147-8, 211-17, 133, 259; Devailly, *Berry* [358], 109-23, 161-75.
[27] Above, p. 27.
[28] Magnou-Nortier, 'Mauvaises coutumes' [565].

largely on personal influence.[29] The Flanders ruled by the tenth- and eleventh-century counts was similarly an area of fluid borders, and not one composed exclusively of complete *pagi*. By the early twelfth century the count of Flanders controlled all the *châtellenies* within his dominions, while all crimes and law-suits, of nobles as well as peasants, were apparently justiciable within the *châtellenie* courts, but comparisons with other parts of France suggest that it would be rash to conclude that that had always been the case.[30] The conflicts which followed the murder of Count Charles the Good in 1127 revealed a body of peers, barons, and *principes* of Flanders which was, according to Galbert of Bruges, prepared to act collectively to find a new count, but their sense of common interest may have been stimulated by the crisis itself and also by quite recent developments in comital government.[31] All through France, therefore, while the followers of a successful man in the eleventh century might form a cohesive group, the choice of allegiance may often have been too open, and the absence of accepted authority too unsettling, for really durable communities to develop.[32]

During the twelfth century things seem to have become more settled. Jurisdiction began to be more systematically exercised and literacy and numeracy came to the help of government at every level. By the 1170s the count of Champagne, although he apparently had little power in his greater subjects' lands, at least had a list of the services they owed him.[33] Nevertheless in many areas the structure of authority was not radically changed before the thirteenth century. Comprehensive civil and criminal jurisdiction still belonged to the lords of small areas, and in Burgundy, for instance, they themselves, as late as the first half of the thirteenth

[29] Werner, 'Quelques observations' [746]; Bates, *Normandy* [239], 156-8, 175-81, *et passim.*

[30] Ganshof, *Flandre* [434], 13-35, 99-100, and *Tribunaux de châtellenies* [436], 57-9, 81-5.

[31] Galbert de Bruges, *Histoire* [31], 8, 76-7, 81, 135-6, 146 (c. 4, 47, 52, 91, 101); Dhondt, 'Solidarités' [361].

[32] Other examples of instability: Guillot, *Anjou* [458], 301-18, 358, 381-2; Feuchère, 'Une Tentative manquée' [415].

[33] Longnon, *Documents de Champagne* [146], i. 1-74; Bur, *Comté de Champagne* [291], 399-404.

century, were still under no effective authority.[34] It seems to
be generally accepted that when change came it took the
form of the establishment of that 'feudal hierarchy' which
had been so lacking in the eleventh century, so that most of
the provinces of the *ancien régime* took shape as 'great fiefs'
under dukes or counts through whom the king began to
extend his control over the kingdom.[35] This may not, however, have been how things looked to most people in the
thirteenth century. A good deal of the country was not
included in any 'great fief' through which the king's relationships with lesser men were mediated, but was not 'royal
domain' in the usual modern acceptation of the expression
either: that is to say, though in some areas (such as Beauvaisis)
a genuine hierarchy of jurisdictions was now established,
there were others in which local lords had primary jurisdiction
but where there was no regular hierarchy of intermediate
jurisdictions between them and the king. Everywhere the
basic units of local government and jurisdiction seem to have
been greater lordships of the sort which Beaumanoir called
baronies and whose lords he regarded as *souverains* within
them. As he implied, however, and as the records of the
king's court show, their jurisdiction was becoming one of
first instance. Appeal from them went, sometimes—as the
model of 'feudal hierarchy' suggests—to the count or duke,
but sometimes—less tidily—direct to the king. Either way,
it was now the king, not God, and not the duke or count,
whose peace was to be preserved in the kingdom, and his
court was the final, if not always the only, court of appeal
in secular matters.[36] Lordships thus became minor divisions
—what one might call provinces or sub-provinces—of the
kingdom in a way that the comparatively jurisdictionless
lordships of England were not.

Above them, however, a new or strengthened layer of
provinces was created or reinforced, partly, by the strengthening of intermediate lordships (the 'feudal hierarchy'), but
also by the needs of royal government itself. Normandy would

[34] Duby, *Société mâconnaise* [381], 402, 420-4, 427-33.
[35] e.g. Lemarignier, *France médiévale* [537], 256-9; Devailly, *Berry* [358], 451.
[36] *Coutumes de Beauvaisis* [61], §§ 295-8, 1043, 1779-80; Devailly, *Berry*
[358], 464; Graboïs, 'De la Trève de Dieu' [448].

have offered a good model of regional government when Philip II took it over in 1204, but even if it had not, he and his successors would have needed units of a comparable size elsewhere—irrespective of the pattern of 'great fiefs'—to mediate the administration of their extensive kingdom. Royal taxation and the increasingly energetic exercise of royal rights required royal officials to summon people before them, and to hold more or less formal assemblies, on this larger regional or provincial scale much more often than did dukes or counts. In Languedoc, where seigniorial assemblies were held in the first half of the century (perhaps in response to a particular need for consultation and collective action in the aftermath of the Albigensian crusade), these were superseded after 1251 by assemblies summoned by royal officials.[37] How most of these larger regions or provinces were delimited is obscure. Normandy and Flanders, of course, were self-evidently defined by over a century of separate but united administration, but that did not apply to, say, Burgundy or Champagne or Berry. The currency of a regional name—even its use as an adjunct to a noble title—would not necessarily have entailed the fixity of boundaries or the existence of a single authority and a corresponding political community within them. The tendency of historians to talk in terms of 'duchies', 'principalities', and 'apanages' may exaggerate the seigniorial aspect which most regions seem to have had at this stage. Contemporaries seem to have often referred to them by their names alone, without any qualifying descriptions like 'the duchy of . . .'. Where there was—or seems to have been—no practical hierarchy of jurisdiction they may not have generally envisaged them in this way. Until royal authority began to press people into new communities of collective government and collective discontent, some regions may have been defined only by customary colloquial usage, with all the variations and inconsistencies which that must imply. In some areas the church provided a missing link of regional or provincial community: diocesan communities met occasionally in parts of the south to try to maintain the peace along the lines of the old Peace of God, and even where laymen were not accustomed to acting in this way, the boundaries

[37] Bisson, *Assemblies in Languedoc* [255], 39-65, 137-43.

of bishoprics were useful simply because, where secular jurisdiction was fragmented and secular boundaries were changeable, they at least were fixed and known.[38]

Royal promises of reform in 1303, together with the
grievances expressed by many local and provincial communities in 1314-15, suggest that by then royal officials
(*baillis, sénéchaux* and so forth) had become pretty active
all over the country and by no means only in the interstices
of seigniorial jurisdiction on what historians call the 'royal
domain'.[39] That being so, we may wonder how far the
boundaries between the districts in which they worked
(which were as yet not permanently fixed[40]) corresponded
to those of lordships great and small. In some areas royal
administration and royal tax-collecting were creating communities of government and grievance which only roughly
and patchily corresponded with the communities of lordships or—so far as they affected lay people—of bishoprics.
Given the readiness of medieval people to act together with
the minimum of legalistic fuss and their insouciance about
overlaps, that would not preclude the formation of strong
provincial solidarities. If and when royal, seigniorial, and
diocesan boundaries did not coincide, then neighbourliness,
kinship, and feelings of shared custom and grievance would
cut across them in much the same way that, at a humbler
level, they cut across the overlaps of village, lordship, and
parish. The reality of such regional solidarities was demonstrated in 1314-15, when royal taxes and oppressions evoked
widespread complaints. It was the Champenois and Burgundians, whose seigniorial links seem to have been relatively
weak, who nevertheless took the lead then in holding provincial protest meetings, electing provincial governors, and
setting up schemes for regular assemblies in future.[41] In so far
as the configuration of the movements and alliances of these
years was determined by administrative boundaries at all, it is
more likely to have been by those of royal than of seigniorial
—or ecclesiastical—government. At this period, however,

[38] Bisson, *Assemblies in Languedoc* [255], 12, 17-19, 102-36.
[39] *Ordonnances* [144], i. 558-9 (5, 8, 11), 562-7 (3, 4, 7, 10, 22); cf. Beaumanoir, *Coutumes de Beauvaisis* [61], § 298.
[40] Henneman, *Royal Taxation* [465], 10 n.
[41] Brown, 'Reform and Resistance' [280]; below, p. 286.

while the provinces and lesser districts of the *ancien régime* were still in the process of formation, regional and local solidarities must have been as various as the patterns of lordship, jurisdiction, custom, and neighbourhood which preceded and shaped them.

This interpretation may underplay too much the loyalty which dukes and counts attracted—quite apart, of course, from that of their immediate servants and retinues, which is not under consideration here. Now that ideas of government and hierarchy were being worked out, the perception of Burgundy as a *patria* may, for instance, have enhanced the standing of its duke, slight though the attendance of the nobles of Burgundy at his court seems to have been. Conflicts of loyalty between service to the duke and service to the king were worth at least theoretical legal discussion—with the explicit example of Burgundy—in the thirteenth century.[42] Nevertheless, despite all the emphasis on feudal or seigniorial government in published work, royal government and sheer neighbourliness look as if they promoted more collective activity at the regional level than did the affairs of dukedoms or counties as such. Everyone, after all, resented summonses to courts, particularly distant courts, that they did not have to attend according to ancient custom. The records of the king's courts and the complaints of 1314-15 show that he and his officials could and did override the restraints of custom, but it would have been harder for most counts and dukes to do so. Many of them—apart from the count of Flanders and (earlier) the duke of Normandy—had no traditional right to suit from anyone outside their immediate domains, no worthwhile jurisdiction to enforce over them, and no established and accepted sanctions by which to enforce it. No one in 1300 could have envisaged that France would come to look so like a collection of 'territorial principalities' as it did—according to many historians—in the later middle ages.[43]

While the assimilation of provinces to lordships may, on

---

[42] Acher, 'Le Droit savant' [213], 161; Post, *Studies* [631], 446; cf. Richard, *Ducs de Bourgogne* [656], 19-28, 80-110, 281-9, 402-516. For a reference to the region of Burgundy as a duchy (against my argument): below, p. 287, n. 92.

[43] Though see Lewis, *Later Medieval France* [550], 2-4, 195-9.

this interpretation, have been partially—and perhaps temporarily—checked in the thirteenth century by the revival
of royal authority, developments in Germany were just then
beginning to go in the opposite direction. There the network
of Carolingian counties (Ger.: *Grafschaften*) survived largely
unchanged until the twelfth century and the *mallus publicus*
seems to have functioned in very much the same way as did
the shire meeting in England.[44] Some counties on the borders
were called marks and others were given to bishops to run
more or less on their own account, but otherwise the chief
difference between the two kingdoms was that the great
duchies (*Herzogtümer*) of Germany were more stable and
important units of government than were the ealdormanries
or earldoms of the smaller kingdom of England. Some of
these duchies had once been independent kingdoms and they
were still regarded as natural units of custom, descent, and
government. How far their solidarity derived from ancient
'tribal' traditions, and how far it threatened the unity of the
kingdom, is discussed in chapter 8, which argues that it
derived primarily from their continued use as units of government and military organization and by no means excluded
either wider or narrower loyalties. A partial list of military
obligations to the king which survives from 981 is arranged
according to the traditional units of duchies or former kingdoms. If the laggard lords who are mentioned in it had sent
their men at the right time these might perhaps have been
formed into contingents county by county as well as duchy
by duchy.[45] There does not seem to be any evidence that
dukes held regular meetings to which suitors came as a matter
of course from the whole duchy as they came to their respective *malli* from the whole of their respective counties, but
dukes sometimes held meetings to do justice—as did the
king on his travels—at which counts and people from a wide
area might be present.[46] Many people must have got into
the habit of acting collectively at the level of both county

---

[44] Schulze, *Grafschaftsverfassung* [683], 15-32, 296-348; Schlesinger, *Entstehung der Landesherrschaft* [679], 237-44.

[45] Werner, 'Heeresorganisation' [743]; hundreds were used for military service on occasion: above, p. 116, n. 39.

[46] *Mon. Boica* [153], no. 116.

and duchy and, if they served in royal armies, of the kingdom too. Except in rebellions the loyalties would not need to conflict.

It is sometimes held that the 'age of territorial princes' in Germany began with the 'feudalization' of land and office in the twelfth century, which both destroyed the last of the old 'tribal duchies' and fatally damaged royal control in general. The concepts involved in this interpretation are, however, rather remote from the twelfth century.[47] The duchies had never been tribal in any meaningful sense. Both they and the counties had long tended to be passed on in families, as were lay offices everywhere. If Frederick I in 1154 and 1158 saw them as a kind of fee (*feudum*), that was probably because his legislation then followed the new Italian usage for what in Germany were generally still called benefices. Anyway, he prohibited their division (except, presumably, by his permission) while allowing the division of other fees, subject to the normal safeguards about services.[48] When counties and duchies were in practice divided (sometimes only for certain of their functions) it was apparently by royal authority.[49] Lords may have had some jurisdiction in disputes between their free and noble tenants, and they may well have developed it *pari passu* with the general growth of legal activity, but counties still served as the main forum of justice, with the king as the ultimate court of appeal over all. The symptoms—by implication pathological—of 'feudalization' might be better diagnosed as the not unhealthy effect of the new definition of jurisdictions and the concomitant ordering of them into something like a hierarchy, and of the better recording of all sorts of delegation.

It was only during the troubles of the mid thirteenth century that the delegation of royal authority turned into its general usurpation by lords. Counties began to be amalgamated or fragmented, with the greater lords carving out lordships for themselves, based on an accumulation of all sorts of property

[47] Below, pp. 289-91.
[48] *M.G.H. Const.* [160], i, no. 177, c. 6—on the assumption that this applied also to Germany (as did c. 5) or at least would have seemed reasonable there.
[49] Ibid. nos. 159, 279; Mascher, *Reichsgut und Komitat* [577], 130-3; Mayer, *Fürsten und Staat* [581], 293, 309-11.

and jurisdiction, and extending their authority over lesser nobles and everyone else within them.[50] Because their titles and the bases of their power were so various, these rulers later came to be given the general description of 'territorial princes': prince was, after all, a general word for ruler in the middle ages and the kings of Germany had often called their great men princes.[51] It is, nevertheless, important to recognize that 'territorial principalities' were not perceived in the middle ages as mere chunks of territory delimited only by their rulers' swords. As Brunner showed, *Land und Herrschaft* were two sides of the same thing: just as government or lordship (*Herrschaft*) had shaped the boundaries and solidarities of the 'tribal duchies' in the past, so now new units of government created new peoples with their own sense of natural boundaries and identity. The peace of which the prince now became protector was the peace of the whole province (*Land*) and its people. The high jurisdiction which territorial princes exercised over their subjects still involved collective judgement and collective obedience, and because many principalities were small they did not need to involve very burdensome or new-seeming duties and loyalties. To contemporaries the new lordships would have differed from earlier duchies and counties because of the absence of effective royal authority over them, not because of any intrinsic difference in the nature of the community which they embodied.[52]

Of all the variations of provincial government in the kingdom of Germany—and indeed in its sub-kingdom of Burgundy—which should ideally be discussed, one cries out for special mention. The origin of self-government in Switzerland is particularly interesting in the context of collective activity in general because, seen like this, it fits so much more easily into the normal pattern than might be supposed. During the twelfth century the dominant lords of the area were the counts of Zähringen, whose lands had been effectively detached from the duchy of Alemannia (or Swabia) in 1098. After their line became extinct in 1218

[50] Mascher, *Reichsgut* [577], 104–10, 134–5.
[51] Below, p. 260.
[52] Brunner, *Land und Herrschaft* [289], 165–239, 357–440.

their estates were divided between shifting lordships, notably those of the various branches of the local family of Habsburg, which already held comital rights in Zürichgau. The Alpine passes, however, were important to Frederick II for his wars in Italy, and this was probably why his son bought out Habsburg rights in the valley of Uri and promised protection to its inhabitants in 1231, and why Frederick himself promised protection to the people of the neighbouring valley of Schwyz in 1231 and 1240.[53] The documents which record these transactions did not bestow any formal liberties or create any new collectivities: on the contrary, they show that the people of Uri and Schwyz already formed communities which were capable of negotiating with kings.[54] No doubt people here and in other Alpine valleys, where local lordship was often divided and there were many free men, ran their own affairs much of the time with little supervision, provided that they paid over the dues to which lords of all sorts were entitled by custom. The position might be compared to that of an English county whose sheriff was a local man who was left without the constant nagging from the central government which had become usual in the much smaller kingdom of England. During the troubles at the end of Frederick's reign the valleys seem to have been free to ally themselves in leagues with local towns so as to protect themselves as best they could. The eventual election of the Count of Habsburg as king in 1273 presumably brought more security, but also, because of his local interests, some reassertion of authority. In 1291, a few months after his death, the men of Uri and Schwyz and of the area later known as Unterwald (*homines vallis Uranie universitasque vallis de Switz ac communitas hominum intramontanorum vallis inferioris*) renewed an alliance they had evidently made earlier and did so in a document which is now considered the foundation charter of the Swiss Confederation.[55] A great deal has naturally been written about it and there has been much discussion of the constitutional position of the three groups, particularly of

[53] Oechsli, *Anfänge der schweiz. Eidgenossenschaft* [165], i. 380-1.
[54] Cf. *Urkundenbuch Zürich* [120], i, no. 203; ii, no. 723, 798; Oechsli, *Anfänge* [165], ii, no. 56.
[55] Oechsli, *Anfänge* [165], i. 381-3; Wartmann, 'Königlichen Freibriefe' [203], 129-31; Bonjour, *Short History of Switzerland* [265], 49-85.

Unterwald, which had not hitherto apparently either received any charter or acted as a single unit. That would not have worried people at the time: collectivities were constantly being formed and reformed, while the difference of wording —the men of Uri, the *universitas* of Schwyz, and the *communitas* of the men of the lower valley between the mountains—looks, when compared with other documents of the kind, as if it was either accidental or designed for elegant variation. There were no legal distinctions for the difference of vocabulary to imply, and the treaty itself is sufficient evidence that all the contracting parties considered themselves capable of acting as independent entities.[56] They did not yet enjoy, or perhaps want, complete independence, nor need their alliance have led to anything so revolutionary. Their emergence as small acephalous provinces, combined in a league which itself constituted another layer of provincial government, all underneath and within the shifting pattern of higher lordships, illustrates very well the haphazard way that layers of collective government evolved, especially where higher authority was distant or ineffective. Chaotic and confused as it seems to us, it did not worry contemporaries, provided, of course, that the customary rights of superior lords were not infringed.

In the kingdom of Lombardy or Italy, as in France, the Carolingian counties (Ital.: *contadi*) seem to have held together in the tenth century but became fragmented thereafter. Within the cities that formed their headquarters many counts found their rights disputed by bishops and citizens, while their control outside was steadily lost to the lords who dominated smaller districts.[57] Duchies or marquisates were superimposed on some areas but except in the south they do not seem to have attained much stability. The most effective units of government and solidarity were apparently the small new *contadi* of cities and the rural lordships which belonged to *castelli*, but their rulers' control of people in the countryside above the level of the peasantry seems to have been weak: one *castello* could too easily be threatened by another,

---

[56] Above, pp. 63, 135-6.
[57] Vaccari, *Territorialità* [722]; Fumagalli, 'L'Amministrazione periferica' [430]; Wickham, *Early Medieval Italy* [750], 175-84.

and some of them were little more than nests of brigands—
'Lombards', as they were sometimes called, or 'nobles'—this
last, perhaps, largely because they lived off others rather than
working for their living.[58] The situation is explicable by the
difficulties and absences of kings, who were in no position to
back up those who maintained law and order on the ground.

In 1037 Conrad II issued an ordinance at Milan which was
destined to become the nucleus of what came to be called feudal law.[59] In view of that later history it is worth noting that
Conrad's law gives no hint of any dual system of 'feudal' and
'public' courts or law. He was not introducing or strengthening a particular sort of law. His primary concern was to adjudicate in a dispute between the archbishop of Milan and
his tenants.[60] In doing so, he extended his judgement so as
to lay down general principles that look as if they would
have seemed right anywhere in western Europe. The terms of
the ordinance suggest that part of his concern in legis-
lating was, apparently, to reconcile lords and men (*seniores*
and *milites*) and to ensure that anyone holding royal or
church land should forfeit it only according to custom and
by the judgement of his peers. This applied both to great men
and their followers (*tam de nostris maioribus vasvasoribus
quam et eorum militibus*). Difficult cases were to be referred,
with due notice and accompanied by a deputation of peers,
to Conrad himself, some of his lords, or a deputy.[61] Presumably *milites* had been liable to oppression because the tribunals
(if any) in which their pleas against their lords had hitherto
been decided were presided over by those same lords, but
there is no indication that these tribunals were separate from
meetings in which other kinds of person and other kinds of
case were judged. Not, of course, that we are at all clear about
such meetings, for some of the pleas recorded from eleventh-
century Italy are difficult to connect with any particular

[58] D'Amico, 'Città e campagna' [219]; Wickham, *Early Medieval Italy* [750],
71-4, 185-8. For the improbability of pure Lombard (or Roman) descent:
Reynolds, 'Medieval *Origines Gentium*' [653].

[59] Lehmann, *Langobardische Lehnrecht* [48], 77; see above, pp. 44-5.

[60] This brief account of Conrad's ordinance has been rewritten in 1996 to
eliminate what now seem the grosser errors of what I wrote in 1983. A fuller
analysis of the circumstances, content, and consequences of the ordinance is
given in Reynolds, *Fiefs and Vassals*, 199-207, 218-19.

[61] *M.G.H. Dipl.* [156], Conrad II, no. 244.

lordship or jurisdiction.[62] What seems clear is that, even when judges claimed to be using Roman law, they presided over meetings which represented—or were intended to represent —some sort of local consensus. It was that consensus which formed the necessary, if not the sufficient, condition for the enforcement of judgements and, in the long run, for the maintenance of conditions in which a real sense of local or provincial community could develop. Where the more powerful and independent inhabitants of the countryside did not throw their weight behind it, local communities were effectively restricted to townsmen and peasants.

In most of northern Italy the establishment of provincial government in the twelfth and thirteenth centuries was the work of towns which brought the surrounding countryside under their rule. To some extent this may have circumscribed the collective government of the lesser towns and the villages of the *contadi*, but in Siena, at least, it seems to have drawn their lords and more important inhabitants into the community of the whole city.[63] Further south, as the thirteenth-century popes established their government more firmly, their officials held provincial parliaments which presumably reflected and developed collective habits.[64] In the kingdom of Sicily there were provincial courts which have been compared to the English county courts. They seem to be less well recorded and presumably had a shorter history behind them, but the vigour of royal government in the twelfth and early thirteenth centuries could well have built up a good deal of collective feeling locally as it did in the kingdom as a whole.[65]

The structure and working of provincial communities

Before records begin to improve in the twelfth century the working of provincial government can only be occasionally and dimly perceived. It seems reasonable to suppose that at

---

[62] Ficker, *Forschungen* [416], iv; Manaresi, *Placiti* [148].

[63] Bowsky, 'Medieval Citizenship' [272]; Caggese, *Classi e comuni rurali* [298], ii.

[64] Waley, *Papal State* [735], 111-19, 304-6.

[65] Marongiu, 'Le "curie generali" ' [570], 9; cf. Jamison, 'Norman Administration' [491]; below, pp. 298-301.

that stage, when the population was relatively small and perhaps rather scattered, and when government was still unprofessional and depended all the more on affective bonds, a fair proportion of any province's inhabitants may have attended its meetings. Quite often provincial headquarters would be in a 'primary town' with a mother church and market which also drew people in the same direction.[66] Especially in troubled times and when higher authority was distant, the collective loyalties which developed among the more independent and warlike of the people when they fought under the lord who presided over their government would be a powerful cement of unity—especially when they won. It was when their solidarity evaporated and separate warbands began to form around separate lords that counties in France and Italy began to break up. Separate warbands did not always mean separate lordships in the sense considered here: sometimes they just meant the dissolution of government. It would, however, be difficult to draw a boundary between the community of a lord and his followers which terrorized a district and the community of a lord and his followers which governed it and formed the core of its own wider community. The solidarity of the warriors might be most readily confirmed and extended to the rest of the population when some of them were settled on their own estates and maintained a fair degree of law and order around them. Whether they obeyed their lord because he presided over provincial affairs as the king's representative, or because they had received their land from him or formally conceded lordship over it to him, or had gone through any ceremony which later writers would consider to be a ceremony of homage to him—whether, in other words, their bond with him was what would come to be called public or feudal— probably mattered less than whether thcy felt that the peaceful enjoyment of life and property depended on his goodwill and on the maintenance of custom and order by all of them under his supervision. Where the lordship was a new one with a new headquarters, its cohesion would be enhanced if the ties of fighting and governing were supplemented by others:

---

[66] Everitt, 'Banburys' [400]; above, pp. 114–20.

if, for instance, old habits of recourse to the old capital were
weakened and replaced by the foundation of a new church
and market.

Throughout the middle ages the kind of people who dominated provincial governments continued to cherish ideals
which had developed out of the old loyalties of the warband:
the mutual loyalty of lord and man and the mutual loyalty
of brothers in arms. In practice, however, this kind of ideal
must have had less and less to do with the working community of any province, seigniorial or royal, except in
moments of special stress. Other equally old and powerful
values were more durable and continued to determine the
forms of collective action even when the new professionalism of government and law began to invade provincial affairs.
People had to act together all the time at this level of government as at every other, whether in obedience to authority or
in opposition to it. Wherever there were common customs
and common interests there was likely to be collective activity
and a sense of community, and whenever common customs
and interests overran the boundaries of lordships or provinces
the boundaries of community would be adapted accordingly.
Within this confusion of communal activity, however, it
remains clear that every established province or lordship was
assumed to constitute a collective group which could be held
legally responsible for its actions. It could be punished or
taxed collectively and could send deputations to represent
itself in legal proceedings or royal assemblies, whether or not
it happened to be called a *universitas* in written documents
which happen to have survived. The binding of local communities to pay taxes agreed upon by their representatives
was no novelty of the thirteenth century, though the rising
demands for money and the rising standards of legal sophistication produced some new and ingenious arguments.[67] The
use of collective words like *populus*, the description of judgements as made *in pleno comitatu* or by the *patria*, and references to the custom of a *pays* or *Land* all illustrate the same
assumptions of collectivity, as do charters which confirm
liberties or customs.[68]

[67] Below, pp. 302-16.
[68] Palmer, *County Courts* [619], 16-19, 76-7, 294-5; Pollock and Maitland,

Relatively few provinces were formally given rights of self-government as were towns or other small local communities, but the documents which confirmed the customs and rights of their inhabitants take for granted that they were groups which could negotiate and enjoy privileges. English counties bought out royal forest rights, paid to have agreeable sheriffs, and paid to limit the sheriff's powers.[69] In 1212 Simon de Montfort the elder, establishing himself and his followers in the newly conquered county of Toulouse, had first of all to make special provision for the treatment of the church and of heretics, but he also took the opportunity to lay down rules of military service; introduce inheritance customs familiar to himself and his men (*ad consuetudinem et usum Francie circa Parisius*); forbid subversive conspiracies; forbid lords to extort anything from their men arbitrarily or tax them unduly; prohibit the imprisonment of those who could give pledges; and generally confirm everyone's customary rights.[70] Charters granted later by French kings to provincial groups naturally concentrated on remedying grievances against royal officials but the emphasis on custom and the assumption of shared interests and the capacity to share rights are just the same—as they are in the charters which German kings gave to the inhabitants of Swiss valleys.[71]

It was normally assumed that those who assembled to give judgements and make governmental decisions in the court of a lordship or province spoke, whether to their lord or to the outside world, on behalf of all. If towns or particular lordships within the province were privileged to run their own affairs they might either be excused from suit or be separately represented. In 1127 the barons or princes of Flanders expected to elect a new count, and were expected by the king to do so, in consultation with him, but the great towns jointly decided to intervene and did so to some effect. Their importance in Flemish society ensured them a voice in the affairs of the province which was not thereafter seriously

English Law [628], ii. 624 n.; Beaumanoir, *Coutumes de Beauvaisis* [61], §§ 3-4, 6-7, etc.; Brunner, *Land und Herrschaft* [289], 180-96, 234-7.

[69] Holt, *Magna Carta* [475], 524.
[70] De Vic and Vaissete, *Languedoc* [201], viii, col. 626-35.
[71] Above, nn. 53-5, and below, pp. 285-9.

contested.[72] The proportion of the whole population which attended provincial courts may have dropped during the twelfth and thirteenth centuries as the business began to be more technical and as obligations to attend began to be recorded and interpreted in more legalistic ways. By the twelfth century lords or their stewards were allowed to do suit to English county courts on behalf of their tenants, and they may have tended to dominate proceedings, but that did not mean that others were excluded. Quite large numbers sometimes turned up when important or controversial business was to be transacted.[73]

Among those who attended courts and councils it was probably taken for granted that the lord or president would lead deliberations, followed by the richer and more important of the rest. Age would secure a particularly respectful hearing on matters of past custom.[74] In some areas the usual habits of deference had been institutionalized since Carolingian times in the presence of a permanent élite of judgement-makers called *scabini*.[75] Rather similar-looking groups called peers appear in the twelfth century in parts of northern France—confusingly in some of the areas that also had *scabini*. How far the two élites overlapped is not clear: the first reference to the peers of Flanders in 1127 gives them a political rather than legal appearance, but the distinction is probably anachronistic.[76] On occasion great men or—perhaps worse—their stewards could arouse resentment: in 1220 an English baron refused to knuckle under to a ruling given by the rest of the assembly in a county court and in 1226 a baron's steward was warned by a prosperous and experienced fellow-member: 'We shall soon be seeing your lord and we shall tell him how you have been behaving in this county [court].'[77] In general, however, advice and leadership from people with exceptional legal and political experience were

[72] Galbert of Bruges, *Histoire* [31], 75-7, 81-4, 140 (c. 47, 52-3, 95); Dhondt, *Estates or Powers* [360], 65-78: the argument of pp. 71-3 seems unconvincing.

[73] Palmer, *County Courts* [619], 56-138; but cf. Maddicott, 'County Community' [562], esp. 29-30.

[74] *Cart. de Saint-Aubin* [99], i, nos. 5, 9; Cam, 'East Anglian Shire-moot' [103].

[75] Above, p. 23.

[76] Feuchère, 'Pairs de principauté' [414] does not mention *scabini*; Galbert of Bruges, *Histoire* [31], 8, 135-6, 146 (c. 4, 91, 101).

[77] *Royal Letters* [187], i. 102-3; *Curia Regis Rolls* [109], xii, no. 2142.

probably welcome, even if they were themselves only the stewards of greater men—provided that they were tactful. Charters and grants of liberties give evidence of discontent against lords and officials but there seems to be little sign of structural conflict among the probably quite wide range of people who attended assemblies. The Swiss treaty of 1291 included a clause pointing out that each man was bound according to his condition to serve his lord and submit to him suitably:[78] those who spoke on behalf of all the people of Schwyz, Unterwalden, and Uri had no intention of abandoning customary rules of good order and subordination. Community did not involve equality and there was no betrayal of principles in preserving seigniorial rights even in a community which was not itself united by submission to a single lord: the courts of provinces without hereditary lords were not intended to be democratic assemblies any more than were seigniorial ones. In 1297 the knights and freeholders of Sussex refused to elect members of parliament in the absence of the archbishop, bishop, earls, barons, and knights who were overseas in the king's service.[79] Their object may have been to avoid paying a parliamentary tax but the idea that great men were a valued part of the community was, after all, entirely conventional. If there was any group that was beginning to arouse resentment by 1300 it may have been the professional or semi-professional lawyers. They were certainly important in some courts and, in England at least, the following century provides ample evidence of their unpopularity.[80]

Provinces and lordships, like other medieval groups, probably hoped to be able to make their decisions unanimously or, failing that, wanted to achieve some sort of consensus in which the wiser and more respected would take the lead. What was needed was a decision which would seem to come from the whole community, present and absent, and the usual indeterminate attendance of unequal people would make a numerical majority rather pointless. In 1277 the king of France and his council ordered, presumably in response to

[78] Oechsli, *Anfänge der schweiz. Eidgenossenschaft* [165], 380-1.
[79] *Parliamentary Writs* [166], i. 60; cf. Illsley, 'Parliamentary Elections' [489].
[80] Maddicott, *Law and Lordship* [563], 59-72, 85-7, *et passim*.

an enquiry from Touraine, that a judgement which seemed good to the *bailli* there should not be deferred merely because one or two knights disagreed with it. If several disagreed then it should be postponed to another session.[81] In thirteenth-century England disagreements in county courts were sometimes expressed by getting up and leaving the court. A judgement given by an assembly depleted in this way could lead to an appeal to the king's court and might be held to be invalid.[82]

Conclusion

Provinces and lordships of the sort considered here form a very amorphous category, but that is not just because it is one created for the convenience of this book. Medieval categories were themselves amorphous. The same principles of justice and authority can be seen, however dimly, at work in lordships and local government areas of very varying sizes and powers. Given the wide variety of collectivities subsumed here, and the different ways in which their political and constitutional surroundings developed, it is impossible to say whether they became stronger or weaker in general during the period. On the whole those lordships and provinces which survived with important civil and criminal jurisdiction into the era when jurisdictions were defined, or which appeared during it, acquired more duties and may therefore have developed more solidarity among their active members. On the other hand, as population rose and the business of courts became more technical, the active members may have become fewer. There is still plenty of evidence of affective solidarity in 1300 but provincial courts were relying more on the submission of the absent than they had once done. More of their solidarity may have come from sheer neighbourliness— sheer provincialism, even—than from the sense of collective responsibility.

That, however, is only speculation. One conclusion which may more justifiably be drawn from the material cited here is

---

[81] *Les Olim* [90], ii, p. 100 (ix); cf. *Bracton's Note Book* [98], no. 1297.
[82] *Curia Regis Rolls* [109], iii. 129; x. 344-6; Walker, 'Local Jurisdiction' [736], 193-6.

a rather surprising one. Although historians are very familiar with the idea of the English community of the shire, of French provincial loyalties, or of German and Italian local separatism, provincial communities of all kinds seem to turn out less impressive than do those of either towns or smaller rural communities on the one hand or kingdoms on the other. They embraced less of their members' lives than did the former and they lacked the supreme authority of the latter. As government around and above them developed, they became merely legal and political communities—communities of people who came to meetings and shared only that public experience with each other. The way that the members of English county courts voted with their feet illustrates how provincial communities were weakened by the possibility that those who disagreed or felt aggrieved could either simply stop participating or could appeal to higher authority. Presumably it was this which explains the relative lack of information about serious or persistent conflicts within communities of this sort. Where higher authority disappeared or was ineffective, of course, things were different. In those circumstances, even though a count or duke would lack the peculiar reverence which was accorded to kings, and his people would form something less than the ideal type of perfect secular community,[83] a county or duchy (or any other lordship, whatever the title of its ruler) became to all intents and purposes as commanding and demanding a community as a kingdom.

[83] Below, pp. 259-61, 321-2.

8

The community of the realm

The preceding chapters have argued that medieval ideas of custom and law facilitated collective action so that communities of all sorts and sizes were being easily and unself-consciously formed, altered, and indeed superseded by each other, all through the period covered by this book. The highest, most honourable, and most perfect of all secular communities was the kingdom. Although at every date there were some kingdoms which looked less united than some smaller units of government, kingdoms as such nevertheless seem to have been normally perceived as the ideal type of political unit, just as kings were perceived as the ideal type of ruler. A kingdom was never thought of merely as the territory which happened to be ruled by a king. It comprised and corresponded to a 'people' (*gens*, *natio*, *populus*),[1] which was assumed to be a natural, inherited community of tradition, custom, law, and descent. So much was this taken for granted that learned writers seldom argued about it directly when they discussed political subjects: they merely made remarks which suggest that it was an unreasoned premise of their political arguments.

One reason why the collective solidarity of medieval kingdoms has been insufficiently appreciated is that historians do not always seem to look very closely at the assumptions about political solidarity from which they themselves start. The first assumption which is seldom examined concerns the nature of representation and the objectives of consultative procedures. Recent generations of medievalists have rightly rejected the nineteenth-century tendency to see medieval councils and parliaments as purposeful strivings towards modern representative government, but in doing so they have sometimes seemed to imply that if medieval demands for consultation did not reflect our principles then they

[1] These words are discussed on pp. 255-6.

reflected none: noble demands for consultation were merely covers for sectional interest or rebellious obstructiveness. That is throwing the baby out with the bathwater. It seems to derive from surely unfounded beliefs that different ranks or classes always perceive their interests to be different, that representation necessarily involves election, and that the only assemblies that can reflect collective solidarity are therefore those which are elected by members of all classes. This is to make nonsense of ideas of representation in a period when it was assumed that the leading men in any community represented the whole of it, whether or not they had been elected.

The second modern assumption which needs to be acknowledged if we are to appreciate the way that medieval people perceived kingdoms as collective entities is that underlying modern nationalism. Most medieval historians would deny that they are nationalists, but that is because, like many historians of the phenomenon of nationalism, they see it as something aggressive, xenophobic, and deplorable, but do not look hard at the ideas which underlie it. Nationalist ideas, however, are more widespread than the unpleasant manifestations of nationalist emotions. The most important is the belief, widely held though seldom recognized and articulated, that 'the world is naturally divided into nations, each of which has its own particular character and destiny'[2] and that nations by their very existence have the right to be self-governing and independent. The nationalist's nation is therefore an essentially corporate body, with essentially political rights. The nation is 'the body which legitimizes the state',[3] whether that state is governed by democratic or authoritarian means, and the nation-state, however governed, is the one sort of state which is by its nature both legitimate and internally cohesive. The fundamental premise of nationalist ideas is that nations are objective realities, existing through history. Some such premise, however unarticulated, seems to be implied in much writings about the history of Europe, including medieval Europe, with its teleological emphasis on

[2] Smith, *Nationalism* [824], 10. Other recent writers have made similar definitions, e.g. Breuilly, *Nationalism* [775], 3-10, though all those concerned with modern nationalism concentrate more on nationalist movements than on what Breuilly calls 'governmental nationalism'.

[3] Emerson, *From Empire to Nation* [781], 96.

the development of modern states—the predestined 'nation-states'. It seems normally to be taken for granted that the nation-states of today are the true nations of history and that only they can ever have inspired loyalties which deserve to be called nationalist. Allowance may be made for units like Scotland or Brittany which are not nation-states but are today claimed to be nations by somebody. None the less, any past unit of government which no one claims to be a nation now is *ipso facto* seen as having been less naturally cohesive in the past. It evidently did not enjoy the manifest destiny to solidarity and survival which is the essential attribute of the true nation.[4]

The trouble about all this for the medieval historian is not that the idea of the permanent and objectively real nation is foreign to the middle ages, as so many historians of nationalism assume,[5] but that it closely resembles the medieval idea of the kingdom as comprising a people with a similarly permanent and objective reality. Not all the kingdoms of the middle ages, however, were destined to become modern states, and if we start from nationalist assumptions we are in danger of prejudging the relative solidarity of those which did and those which did not. A more fundamental distortion arises from the fact that belief in the objective reality of nations inevitably diverts attention from itself: since the nation exists, belief in it is seen not as a political theory but as a mere recognition of fact. The history of nationalism

[4] e.g. Kohn, *Idea of Nationalism* [800]; Hayes, *Evolution of Modern Nationalism* [795]; Trevor-Roper, *Jewish and Other Nationalism* [829]; Hobsbawm, 'Reflections on Nationalism' [796]; Poliakov, *Aryan Myth* [815]; Seton-Watson, *Nations and States* [822]; and, on the middle ages, Werner, 'Les Nations' [745]; discussions of the concepts which I have found particularly useful, apart from those in nn. 2–3, include Brogan, 'Nationalism' [776]; Metzger, 'Generalizations about National Character' [808]; Rustow, 'Nation' [821]; Potter, 'Historian's Use of Nationalism' [816]; Rotberg, 'African Nationalism' [819]; Laslett, 'Idea of the Nation' [801]; Fishman, 'Language and Nationalism' [783]. For distinctions between national consciousness and political nationalism, Smith, *Nationalism* [824], 10–26; Lemberg, *Nationalismus* [802], 40–3; Kamenka, *Nationalism* [799], 14–15.

[5] Including most of those cited in n. 4. The political character of medieval nationalism (or 'regnalism': below, p. 254) is suggested by Bloch, *Feudal Society* [262], 379–83, and more explicitly recognized by Keeney, 'Military Service' [500]; Huizinga, *Men and Ideas* [482], 97–155; Werner, 'Les Nations' [745]; Beumann, 'Bedeutung des Kaisertums' [249]; MacCormick, 'Nation and Nationalism' [559].

becomes less a part of the history of political thought than of historical geography, while the starting-point of political development becomes the nation, with its national character or national characteristics. This pre-existing nation is then seen as moving through the attainment of 'national conscious-ness' to find its own rightful boundaries in the nation-state. Perhaps, however, it might be easier to assess the values and solidarities of the past if we considered whether the process may not sometimes have worked the other way round, with units which are perceived as nations as the product of history rather than its primary building-blocks. National character is that which is attributed to any group thought of as a nation: the nation itself is the product of its members' belief that it exists. In medieval terms, it was the fact of being a kingdom (or some lesser, but effective, unit of government) and of sharing a single law and government which promoted a sense of solidarity among its subjects and made them describe themselves as a people—irrespective of any relationship that we can now trace between the medieval 'people' and its kingdom on the one hand and the modern 'nation' and its state on the other.

A first step towards disentangling the political ideas and loyalties of the past from those of the present may be to avoid the confusions which arise from obviously ambiguous terminology. The word 'national' is nearly always misleading. Talk of 'the rise of the national monarchies', for instance, is liable to be either tautological or teleological, or both. The loyalties of people in 'national kingdoms' under 'national monarchies' presumably developed because of the way they thought of themselves then, rather than because their king-doms developed into nation-states at some later time. It can-not be taken for granted, for instance, that France and England developed directly into nation-states because their monarchies were at all times more 'national' than that of Germany: the point needs to be argued, and it can only be argued by comparing the way people at the time thought of their governments. Calling some monarchies national and others not simply begs the question. The most confusing use of 'national' which still creeps into some medieval histories is that which survives from the nineteenth-century association of nationalism with popular government, and which contrasts 'national' with 'feudal' or 'royal'. 'National armies' were thus armies in which all classes are thought to have served (probably for more patriotic motives than those who served in a 'feudal host') while 'national parliaments' represented everyone in some kind of quasi-democratic way. Language like this casts a blanket of muddled anachronisms over medieval institutions and ideas. Until we can sort out what the medieval idea of a people did and did not have in common with modern nationalism it is better to avoid the words nation and national altogether. The difficulty about avoiding 'national' in medieval contexts is that we lack an adjective derived from 'kingdom'. In this chapter I therefore propose to employ the word 'regnal' whenever I want to describe that which pertains to a kingdom or kingdoms.

Another possible confusion between words and concepts arises from the common translation of the Latin word *gens* as 'race'. This derives from habits formed in the nineteenth century and earlier when 'race' was used widely and loosely —as in 'the English race', 'the German (or Germanic) race (or races)', and even 'a royal race of kings'. In the nineteenth century, as in the middle ages, the groups which medieval writers called *gentes*, *nationes*, or *populi* were actually thought of as units of common biological descent (that is, races in the more exact modern sense of the word) as well as of common culture. The history of races was investigated through philology, and 'national character' was explained in terms of biological transmission. Since people believed that descent and culture were closely connected, it was natural that their terminology should reflect the connection. Now, however, the advance of biology, history, archaeology, and linguistics has shown that human society is more complicated than that. The inhabitants of an area are likely to develop a common culture, particularly if they are governed as a unit, and they will then tend to breed with each other more than with outsiders. But the facts of biological descent in the distant past are probably less important for the transmission of culture than is the creation or maintenance of political solidarity in the present: how far they matter is, of course, highly controversial, since the boundary between genetics and culture, nature and nurture, race and nation, is so hard to trace empirically. Nevertheless it seems clear that the boundary exists, that few of the kinds of social and political change which the medieval historian studies can have been caused by genetic change, and that few of the variations in social patterns can have been genetically programmed.

Medieval *gentes* were not 'races' in any sense in which the word can be used without misunderstanding in the late twentieth century.[6] The traditional idea of the 'races of Europe' is not merely morally repugnant in so far as it has been connected with ideas of a hierarchy of races: it is intellectually defective because it implies that cultural and political communities are in reality and in essence also communities of biological descent. Using the word in the older sense therefore invites confusion between what people in the past believed about their common descent and history and what we believe about them. It thereby tends to prevent us from appreciating the force of their beliefs. Incidentally, it also invites us to assume truly racial reasons for medieval hatreds and distrusts: that is, for instance, to assume that Normans were physically distinct from English or English from British. Yet, although medieval people themselves confused culture and descent, the sources do not suggest that physical differences, even where they existed, were as important to them as they are to modern racists.[7] In the context of this book race is largely irrelevant, and I propose to translate *gens* not as 'race' (nor yet as 'tribe', which as applied to early medieval peoples carries the same misleading connotations of nineteenth-century ideas), but as 'a people'.[8]

'A people' may also serve as a neutral translation of both *natio* and *populus*. There is no foundation at all for the

[6] Cavalli-Sforza and Bodmer, *Genetics* [777], 698, 701, 775. For other views: Baker, *Race* [773]; Ebling, *Racial Variation* [780].

[7] One example of physical differences being noticed is Ambroise, *L'Estoire de la guerre sainte* [6], 206 (1. 7719).

[8] On 'tribes' see Reynolds, 'Medieval *Origines Gentium*' [653], 379-80; Slicher van Bath, 'Dutch Tribal Problems' [691]; Iliffe, *Tanganyika* [798], 8-11, 318-41. The currently fashionable 'ethnic' seems nearly always to combine connotations of both descent and culture: e.g. Smith, *Ethnic Revival* [823], 64-6.

belief, common among students of modern nationalism,[9] that the word *natio* was seldom used in the middle ages except to describe the *nationes* into which university students were divided. It was used much more widely than that, and often as a synonym for *gens*: any individual writer might, of course, distinguish the two, for instance by giving one a more definitely political connotation than the other, or by using them to distinguish types of social and political unit which seemed to him significantly different.[10] There is, however, no reason to believe that words of this kind were used more precisely and consistently through the centuries than they are today: Isidore of Seville's definitions were no more successful in controlling subsequent usage than are those of the Oxford Dictionary. As a matter of fact Isidore himself drew no clear distinction between the two words. For him, as for others, they do not seem to have any exact or exclusive sense.[11] Moreover, while in some contexts *populus* could mean something more like *plebs*, and be contrasted with *nobiles*, in others it was yet another synonym for *gens*.[12] Like a *gens* or *natio*, a *populus* was thought of as a community of custom, descent, and government—a people.

The idea of a kingdom

In 900 the idea of a people as a community of custom, law, and descent was already well entrenched in western society, though peoples were not yet normally envisaged as constituting kingdoms. In recent times the kings of the Franks had ruled over many separate peoples while the English, for instance, had been perceived as in some sense a single people

---

[9] e.g. Smith, *Nationalist Movements* [825], 22; Post, *Studies* [631], 495 (though here nation is equated with state); Albertini, 'L'Idée de nation' [770], 3-4, 9-10.

[10] e.g. William of Alton, quoted by Borst, *Turmbau von Babel* [266], 752-4.

[11] Isidore, *Etymologiarum Libri* [44], 9. ii. 1, iv. 4-6; 15. ii. 1; Müller, 'Zur Geschichte der Wortes und Begriffes "nation" ' [600]; Kahl, '*natio* im mittelalterlichen Latein' [493].

[12] Graus, 'Littérature et mentalité' [454], 61 n.; Ranieri da Forli (quoted by Bertelli, *Il Potere oligarchico* [248], 65), for instance, drew attention to this ambiguity. Anselm of Laon distinguishes *populus* and *natio*: *P.L.* [60], clxii, col. 1521, though his sense seems to be slightly obscured by homoeoteleuton in the printed text.

although they were divided between different kingdoms. About 900 Regino of Prüm wrote that 'Just as different peoples (*diversae nationes populorum*) differ between themselves in descent, manners, language, and laws (*genere moribus lingua legibus*), so the holy and universal church throughout the world, although joined in the unity of faith, nevertheless varies its ecclesiastical customs among them'.[13] Regino lived in Lotharingia, near the boundary between the newly divided kingdoms of the East and West Franks and the older but different boundary between Germanic and Romance languages. How his idea of a people corresponded to the complications of this political and social reality it is difficult to know. By his time there can have been no question of the Franks as a single people in the sense he meant, but whether he thought of the East Frankish kingdom as one people, or of groups like the Saxons and Bavarians—and perhaps his own totally anomalous Lotharingians—as separate, he would have found plenty of overlaps and divisions in the wrong places. For that very reason his remark is a good illustration of the notion that he and his contemporaries had of 'peoples'. The idea of a people, like the modern idea of a nation, was a commonplace that went uncontested just because it was seldom argued, and it is characteristic that Regino should have noted the differences between peoples in passing, as a premise to a more controversial statement about the church. A little over a hundred years later very much the same assumptions seem to be nicely demonstrated from just outside the area with which this book is concerned. King Stephen of Hungary (d. 1038) maintained that a kingdom of one language and one way of life (*unius linguae uniusque moris regnum*) would be weak and fragile. This may seem a paradoxical illustration of the point, but Stephen was arguing that foreigners should be welcomed: their different languages and customs, their example and their arms, would, he argued, enrich the kingdom and deter its enemies.[14] Clearly, therefore, he saw a variety of languages and customs within a kingdom as an exception to be justified—and, moreover, as an exception which derived from immigration. The sort of kingdom he

[13] *Chronicon* [65], p. xx.
[14] *P.L.* [60], cli, col. 1240.

envisaged would normally, without new immigrants, have consisted of something like one of Regino's peoples.

It seems reasonable to suppose that Regino's idea of peoples as units of custom and law would have seemed right to many laymen. Its own law was one of the oldest marks of a people, though the great variety of local custom meant that the unity of a people's law was always more conceptual than practical. Whether as yet many laymen knew much about the myths of the origin and descent of their peoples which learned writers were by now concocting and copying from each other is more doubtful. The earliest of these myths seem to have originated several centuries before in a way which suggests that they owed little to popular tradition, let alone to anything which could be called 'folk memory'. Their details of biblical or classical ancestry and of long migrations would have had little appeal outside learned circles even if they had been known. All the same, the general ideas about peoples as real and permanent entities which they embodied, and the desire for a sense of corporate identity which they fulfilled, were probably shared by laity as well as clergy. From the tenth century, moreover, and even more from the twelfth, such stories proliferated. They were copied in vernacular poems and stories designed for lay audiences and by the thirteenth century political documents were alluding to them. Though the documents were drafted by clerks that must mean that such laymen as were politically active, if no others, were likely to be familiar with the outline of the myths, to find them useful, and—presumably—to accept them.[15]

The essential point about these *origines gentium* from the point of view of political ideas is that, at whatever date they were recounted, they concerned collectivities which formed significant social and political units at that time. By the tenth century that nearly always meant the permanent, settled inhabitants of a reasonably well-defined territory. Because custom, law, and descent were assumed to go together, the stage at which law had become territorialized also seems to have been the stage at which peoples came to be perceived in

---

[15] The content, as well as the earlier history, of these myths is more fully discussed in Reynolds, 'Medieval *Origines Gentium*' [653].

territorial terms too. Mythical stories, telling how a band of migrants under their king had come and conquered the land, normally defined the area of conquest in terms of current political units. They also normally assumed that all the currently settled inhabitants of the area who lived under one law were descended from the conquerors. Medieval descent myths, unlike those of later centuries, did not justify class divisions by postulating different descents for different classes.[16] Inequality was taken for granted: the myths were about political unity, not about social divisions. Land and people were assumed to be one. The constitutional distinction which was drawn in 1830 between a king of France and a king of the French would have been meaningless in the middle ages. With the usual conservatism of official practice an individual chancery might tend to use one or the other formula, but general usage suggests that the difference was immaterial.[17]

Being a political unit with a single law and, probably, a supposed common descent did not necessarily mean being a kingdom. Some political units which claimed both did not achieve such honour. Nevertheless kingship had been a focus of loyalty for centuries and despite the troubles of the post-Carolingian age it still was. Nothing could be more misleading than the textbook idea that a king of the 'feudal age' was merely *primus inter pares*,[18] dependent on 'feudal bonds' for what little authority he had. Only kings were crowned: only kings could draw on the fund of prestige which came from the church and from the kings of the Old Testament. Weak as were the kings of France in the tenth and eleventh centuries, such prestige as they had came from the title of king, not from being at the head of any 'feudal pyramid'. Ideas of feudal hierarchy were only beginning to be worked out in the twelfth century and most of them were not articulated until even later.[19] Even if, untypically, the king of France sometimes

[16] For exceptions, and for the later 'estate myths', see Reynolds, 'Medieval Origines Gentium' [653], 380.

[17] Giry, *Manuel de diplomatique* [443], 320; Chaplais, *English Royal Documents* [315], 13.

[18] I have not found the origin of this expression.

[19] Lemarignier, *Gouvernement royal* [538], 171-6; Brown, 'Tyranny of a Construct' [284].

looked rather like one among the lords or princes of his realm, that did not mean that kingdoms in general were normally seen as loose congeries of lordships or principalities. The very word 'principality' may be misleading: *princeps*, like most words, could be used in various ways but it normally had the fairly general sense of 'ruler'.[20] A king was seen as a sort of prince, not because the ideal type of ruler was a 'territorial prince', any more than it was a 'feudal lord', but because it was a king. Kings sometimes referred to their greater subjects as princes, but that was partly for grandiloquence and partly because kingdoms contained layers of government. Anyone who exercised government at a fairly high level was a sort of prince. Those great lords who, for one reason or another, were most independent were most like princes precisely because they were like kings: the idea of the independent 'territorial prince' as the ideal type of French or German ruler belonged to a later age.[21] The extent to which kingdoms were perceived, even in France, as the political norm of the eleventh and twelfth centuries is exemplified by the occasional references to Flanders and Normandy, two particularly well-governed areas, as kingdoms.[22]

One of the most important political developments of the centuries after 900 was that in many areas the loyalties of kingship came to coincide with the solidarities of supposed common descent and law. Kingdoms and peoples came to seem identical—not invariably, but sufficiently often for the coincidence of the two to seem the norm to contemporaries. It is tempting to think that this happened because the post-Carolingian kingdoms were formed out of units which were already perceived as peoples, but this may be a teleological illusion: peoples—that is, groups which felt themselves to be communities of custom and descent—were perceived everywhere, at every level, interlocking and overlapping. Those which became kingdoms and endured as such were not those which corresponded to pre-ordained peoples but those which

[20] Niermeyer, *Lexicon* [211], 849-50; cf. Werner, 'Quelques observations' [746].

[21] Brunner, *Land und Herrschaft* [289], 165.

[22] Le Patourel, *Norman Empire* [542], 181, 231; Werner, 'Kingdom and Principality' [744], 250, 280; see also Guillot, *Le Comte d'Anjou* [458], 365 n.; Werner, 'Heeresorganisation' [743], 795.

best managed to harness the old solidarities of law and myth to themselves. The change in succession laws which seems to have taken place by the early tenth century was an important factor in this: kingdoms were now seldom shared or divided between sons, so that one king to each kingdom became the norm. That in itself helped both to concentrate authority and to perpetuate regnal solidarity. It is sometimes said that kings lost much of their sacral quality as a result of Gregorian reform, but that may reflect Gregory VII's wishful thinking more than his achievements. Laymen generally supported their kings when they had trouble with the pope and if they did not it was because they saw a chance of pushing their own interests in the conflict. The real effect of church reform on lay society was not to undermine lay loyalties but to spread knowledge of Christianity, increase fervour, and improve education. Kings profited from the growth of literacy and the developments in law and government which ensued from it. Wherever a king maintained or increased his authority over legislation and law-enforcement his subjects would tend to feel themselves to be a people: being under a single law meant being a people.[23]

The effect of all this can be discerned in documentary sources well before academic writers began to say anything notably new about kingship or politics. The ideas about peoples and their laws and customs, and about the sanctity and duties of kingship, which were current in the tenth century, were already old by then, and there was little significant change in the way they were expressed before the thirteenth. Well before then, however, the practice of government had begun to develop, and a new synthesis of traditional ideas and new practices had begun to appear. Each element in it—descent myths, political and legal ideas, the prestige of kingship, and the practice of law and government—was gaining in force from its association with the others. This is obvious almost everywhere from the twelfth century and in some areas it can be seen in the tenth.

---

[23] Above, p. 43. Cf. Graus, 'Entstehung der mittelalterlichen Staaten' [453]; Manteuffel, 'Intégration et désintégration' [569]; Strayer, *Medieval Statecraft* [704], 341–8; Clanchy, *From Memory to Written Record* [327].

Kingdoms as communities

The first great beneficiary of these changes was the kingdom of Germany, but the question of its unity or disunity has become so enmeshed in controversies deriving from later history that it may be easier to start by considering the kingdoms of England, Scotland, and France. The expression 'community of the realm' is particularly associated with England, for it was used there frequently in the thirteenth century. It was also used, though in surviving records rather later and less, in both Scotland and France. It seems to be generally agreed that all three kingdoms were by the thirteenth century beginning to evoke feelings of patriotism and national —or regnal—solidarity.[24] In all three, however, kings might have found it hard to enforce their rule as effectively as they did at the end of this period if their subjects had not already become accustomed to thinking of kingdoms as natural entities. I shall argue that there is quite good evidence that in England and France, at least, they had begun to do so very much earlier.

Until the late ninth century the English had been divided among a number of small kingdoms which were often at war with each other. Nevertheless they seem to have found some solidarity in the sense of being a single *gens* with a shared name and language, and this was fostered by the church.[25] By the tenth century inter-regnal conflicts were practically over: all the kingdoms except Wessex had disappeared and during the following decades the kings of Wessex extended their authority over nearly all the territory hitherto thought of as English, finally conquering the transient Viking kingdom of York in 954. Tenth-century kings used a variety of titles in their charters, often stressing their authority over the whole of Britain, but both charter-titles and the inevitably briefer titles used on coins suggest that the essential basis of royal authority was soon fixed as being that which belonged to them as *rex Anglorum*.[26] Just who was understood to be

[24] Kantorowicz, *King's Two Bodies* [496]; Strayer, *Medieval Origins* [705].

[25] Wormald, 'Bede, *Bretwaldas*, and *Gens Anglorum*' [764].

[26] Kleinschmidt, *Untersuchungen* [505], 64–105, 205–6, 215–19, and list at end; also information kindly supplied by Dr Pauline Stafford from her analysis of Ethelred's charters. On the northern border: Barrow, *Kingdom of the Scots* [235], 139–61.

included among these English needs some consideration. Historians often assume that the descendants of the Danish
invaders were for some time consistently recognized as a distinct group and in some ways excluded from any regnal
community enjoyed by the original English, but this may
need qualification. It is true that, while King Edgar legislated
on some subjects for the whole people (*leodscype*), English,
Danes, and Britons, under his rule (*on ælcum ende mines an-
wealdes*), he left some matters to the Danes to decide for
themselves.[27] His claim to overlordship over the whole of
Britain could account for the appearance of Britons in this
list, but the Danes he mentioned were presumably those who
lived in the north and east of England proper. The distinction
between West Saxon, Mercian, and Danish law survived into
the twelfth century, so that some people who lived under
what they thought of as Danish law may have gone on thinking of themselves as being descended from Danes, whether or
not they really were. All the same, the boundary of the Danelaw may have been less consistently remembered than modern
historians tend to suggest and the division between English
and Danes may have been less generally significant. The
English and Norse languages and customs were not very
different, many of the Danes were quickly converted to
Christianity, and one way and another intermarriage and
social assimilation must quite soon have made them hard to
distinguish. By the end of the century most subjects of the
rex Anglorum probably felt themselves to be as a matter of
course part of the *Anglica natio* which constituted his kingdom. When resistance to the new wave of Danish invaders
collapsed in the later years of Ethelred's reign, the chronicler,
bitter as he was, did not suggest that the divisions of the
kingdom followed what might now be called ethnic lines: the
traitors, like those they betrayed, were English. It was the
invaders who were seen as Danes. That being so, the royal
order to kill all the Danish men in England in 1002 should
be interpreted as applying only to aliens or immigrants, rather
than to subjects of the kingdom who happened to be—or
were thought to be—of Danish descent.[28] It would certainly

[27] Robertson, *Laws* [177], 32, 36 (IV Edgar 2. 1. 2; 12).
[28] *Anglo-Saxon Chron.* [76], 133-5 (C, D, E); *Eng. Hist. Docs.* [119], i,

be more comprehensible on that basis. Later on in the eleventh century Cnut's laws refer once more to Danes as well as English among his subjects, but that was probably because he ruled Denmark too and must thus have brought over followers who did not settle permanently in his English kingdom. Meanwhile, whatever people called themselves, some of them were already capable of a genuine regnal solidarity: the poet who commemorated the battle of Maldon described earl Byrhtnoth telling his troops that he was ready to die guarding 'this country (*eþel þysne*), the land (*eard*) of Ethelred my lord, people and soil (*folc and foldan*)'.[29]

An important factor in the promotion of solidarity was the firm everyday control which the royal government maintained over the kingdom in spite of invasions and civil wars. There has been a good deal of argument about the existence of a royal secretariat and about the administrative means by which royal powers were exercised, but from the point of view of regnal unity the means are less important than the result. Coin finds show that from 973 money was issued in the king's name from mints scattered throughout England south of the Trent, and from at least one (York) further north; that dies and types were regularly and simultaneously changed at all of them; and that, even in the north, there was apparently very little infringement of the royal monopoly and regulations.[30] However royal orders were transmitted they were thus pretty well obeyed all over the kingdom by those who made and handled money. By the eleventh century taxes and military service were assessed by counties and by the hides and carucates into which each county was divided. Historians anxious to explain how England came to be conquered twice in the eleventh century have sometimes dismissed this central control as ineffective in practice: some say that the army was composed of amateur—if patriotic—

no. 127; cf. the reference to Danes in e.g. II Ethelred 5 (Robertson, *Laws* [177], 58). For references to the Danelaw as a territory: Liebermann, *Gesetze* [145], ii. 347-8, but note the alternative geographical terms recorded there. Some of Liebermann's references to Danes are, moreover, clearly to hostile invaders, not to settled inhabitants of Danish origin or descent.

[29] Ashdown, *English Documents* [85], 24.

[30] Dolley and Metcalf, 'Reform of the Coinage' [366]; Campbell, 'English Government' [307].

peasants, or that the power of the earls undermined regnal unity. Nevertheless the government was effective enough to be oppressive and its subjects were united enough to win concessions: in 1014 Ethelred had to promise to rule more justly than he had before and Cnut seems to have started his reign with promises to rule justly and limit his demands for money.[31] Something like the regnal solidarity which we associate with Magna Carta seems to be dimly foreshadowed, if not fully embodied and attested, two hundred years before.

There is, moreover, little evidence to support the notion that English armies of the eleventh century were composed of humbler people than served in contemporary forces elsewhere. The English army was a regnal army not because it included the poor but because the duty to serve in it was owed to the king.[32] As for the earls, they seem to have had no noticeably separatist objectives: none of them, for instance, had his own image and superscription put on the coins of his local mint. Even in the reign of Edward the Confessor, when the king himself had little or no personal following, unity was maintained. Earl Godwin became overmighty primarily because he controlled the king and the government, not because he tried to make his earldom independent. In the confrontations of 1051-2, the other earls first supported the king against Godwin and his sons, and then apparently advised him to pardon them, but on each ocasion the decisive factor in avoiding civil war was that 'it was hateful to almost everyone to fight with their own kinsmen (*agenes cynnes mannum*), for there were few powerful men on either side who were not English; and also they did not want the country to be left open to foreigners while they destroyed each other.' Here we have a classic statement of regnal solidarity, characteristically expressed in terms which imply a sense of common descent.[33] There is, incidentally, little evidence that a consciousness of English or Danish descent determined the policies or factions espoused by the great men of the reign.

[31] *Anglo-Saxon Chron.* [76], 145 (C, D, E); Stafford, 'Laws of Cnut' [693].

[32] Brooks, 'Arms, Status, and Warfare' [278]; Gillingham, 'Introduction of Knight Service' [442]; Harvey, 'Knight and Knight's Fee' [462].

[33] *Anglo-Saxon Chron.* [76], 181 (D). The usual translation 'with men of their own race' expresses this well so long as 'race' is understood in its nineteenth-century sense: above, p. 254.

Even in the Northumbrian revolt of 1065, though both English and Danes are mentioned, the difference between them does not seem to have been politically significant, and it is noteworthy that the Northumbrians neither claimed any sort of independence nor asked for a Danish—or even Northumbrian —earl.[34]

In view of all this it is clear that, even though the boundaries of the kingdom had shifted considerably during the tenth century, the territory within them formed a political unit well before 1066. Many Englishmen must, of course, have felt other loyalties in addition to regnal ones. Locality, lordship, and law all offered opportunities for feelings of community, but they did not always conflict with regnal loyalties. When there was a conflict it was not always the kingdom which lost. The Norman Conquest did not create a new kingdom and the modern use of the tautological expression 'Anglo-Saxon England' is misleading in its implication of a change of categories in 1066. The inhabitants of the kingdom of England did not habitually call themselves Anglo-Saxons (let alone Saxons), but English, and they called their kingdom England. It was not a hyphenated kingdom but one whose inhabitants felt themselves to be a single people.

One reason why 1066 was conclusive was that the English had the habit of obedience to a lawfully crowned king. Once William was crowned king, holding the traditional seat of government, united resistance became difficult, especially since the death of Harold and his brothers had left no one capable of rallying the English forces. In spite of that, English traditions of solidarity ensured that guerilla resistance continued for some years, and even after the English had sunk into discontented submission, a new regnal solidarity took some time to develop. The delay was not so much caused by differences in law and custom between Normans and English, which were few,[35] let alone by differences of 'race', as by the clean sweep of the English aristocracy, the French interests of the king and the new nobility, and the consequent division of languages between ranks.[36] The sense of two separate

---

[34] *Anglo-Saxon Chron.* [76], 190–3 (E, D).
[35] Robertson, *Laws* [177], 232; cf. above, chapter 1.

[See facing page for n. 36]

peoples of separate descents and customs survived well into the twelfth century. As late as 1137 there was a plot to kill all the Normans and hand the government of the kingdom over to the Scots—presumably because the Scottish king's mother had belonged to the old English royal house.[37] In practice, of course, intermarriage lower down the social scale had started long before then. By 1179, though the unfree were assumed to be English and great men, no doubt, were assumed to be Norman, it was admitted to be impossible to know whether free men were English or Norman.[38] One among many reasons for the immediate popularity[39] of Geoffrey of Monmouth's romantic history may have been that its glorification of a British past transcended the uncomfortable divisions between Normans and English.

It has become usual to attribute the recovery of regnal solidarity in late twelfth-century England to the demands which Angevin kings made for men and money in order to fight their wars in France and to the opposition which these aroused. There is obviously a good deal of truth in this, but royal government did not foster unity merely by its oppressions. The extension of royal jurisdiction sent royal justices touring around the country administering increasingly uniform procedures, and took place through procedural changes that do not seem to have been perceived as encroachments.[40] When there were complaints, they were of corruption and oppression in practice, not of the principle of royal control. Angevin government, just because it was strong, demanded a great deal of collective activity. By 1200 an increasing number of towns and some counties were winning collective grants of liberties. Everywhere, even when there was no question of a formal grant, people were having to serve on juries and other panels which negotiated, assessed, and collected taxes, and conducted a mass of other business on behalf of the government and of their local communities. The

---

[36] Clanchy, *England and its Rulers* [325], 52-61; Mayr-Harting, 'Functions of a Recluse' [584], 344.

[37] William of Malmesbury, *Gesta Regum* [83], i. 8-9, 70; ii. 284, 304-6, 313, 355; Orderic Vitalis, *Hist. Eccl.* [57], vi. 494.

[38] Richard fitz Nigel, *Dialogus* [66], 53.

[39] Gransden, *Historical Writing* [452], 201-2.

[40] Clanchy, *England and its Rulers* [325], 143-53.

result of the combination of collective activity with collective
—and individual—oppression was Magna Carta, the classic
statement of regnal solidarity against a king: classic, not
because the ideas it embodies and the society it represents
were unusual in thirteenth-century Europe, but because they
were not.

Magna Carta is noted particularly for its length and detail,
its apparent concern to protect a wide proportion of the
population against royal oppression, and its relative unconcern
with the protection of purely seigniorial rights and jurisdiction. The apparent altruism that this seems to suggest on the
part of the magnates who extorted the charter from King John
has been explained in various ways. One has been, in effect,
to explain it away as the result either of clerical influence or
of a disingenuous effort to win support from the lower ranks
of society. There is, however, little evidence that any of the
clergy helped to formulate the detailed grievances on which
the charter was based, while it seems unnecessarily tortuous
to suppose that it was deliberately drafted to cover up
narrow class interests. No doubt some of the barons, like
other people, were selfish, but they may well not have seen
their own interests as conflicting with those of lesser subjects. That is not to imply that they thought of others as
their equals, and we should not explain the exceptional
qualities of the charter as reflections of a relatively egalitarian
society. There is little evidence that English society was in
general ways particularly equal, or more equal than society
elsewhere: it was not social equality which made the barons
of Magna Carta sympathize with the lower ranks of society
but similarity of oppression. Because royal jurisdiction was so
wide there was relatively little seigniorial jurisdiction to
protect, while a relatively large proportion of the population
was frequently and directly exposed to oppression by royal
officials. Given such a pervasive and potentially oppressive
government, and given the universally accepted ideas of
custom and law, there is nothing surprising in demands—
even demands by the magnates and barons of the realm—that
no free man should be prosecuted except by due process of
law, and that even an unfree man should be punished only in
proportion to his offence. Nor did the provision that all lords

should abide by the same rules in their relations with their own men imply any improbable altruism: many no doubt failed to keep their undertaking, but it would have been unthinkable to deny the obligation.[41] The barons of Magna Carta spoke—and presumably spoke more or less sincerely —on behalf of the community of the realm, not because they thought most of its members were their equals but because they did not. It was the accepted duty of the great men of any kingdom to represent the rest.

Despite its apparent peculiarities, moreover, Magna Carta is very like other charters of liberties, from those of villages upwards, in what it assumes and in the vagueness which continually blurs the edges of its details. It is vague in its assumptions about what is right and it is vague in its assumptions about collectivities. Because England, like other kingdoms, contained many different ranks, and because royal government affected an unusually large number of them, different clauses dealt with different categories of people, sometimes as individuals and sometimes as collectivities.[42] Yet, like other charters, Magna Carta never defines the membership of any category: collective privileges and collective responsibilities, like the existence of different categories with different individual rights, were all taken for granted, and rough edges were left to be settled if and when individual problems arose. The greatest collectivity of all was, of course, the community of the kingdom—the community which was represented at Runnymede, as it was at more normal royal councils, by its greatest men.[43]

Any suggestion that the king did not want to recognize the existence of such a community is misleading because it implies that communities as such had some character that required recognition.[44] Analogies drawn from town communities are erroneous: the towns' peculiarity was that they were republican, but no one seems to have envisaged the community of the realm as autonomous in that sense. Of course no king could recognize the community of his subjects as self-governing without him, but no one seriously wanted

---

[41] Magna Carta, c. 39, 20, 15, 60 (Holt, *Magna Carta* [475], 316-36).
[42] Holt, *Magna Carta* [475], 186-7.   [43] Below, p. 306.
[44] Holt, *Magna Carta* [475], 185-6; above, pp. 59-64.

him to. In 1215 John had to concede—until he could get the charter abrogated—that the commune (*communa*) of the whole land might join in distraining him if he misbehaved,[45] but that was a matter of military and political reality, not of legal or political theory. The community of the kingdom was perceived as a community just as all collectivities were: the argument was not about the nature of the collectivity but about the rights and wrongs of its ruler and his subjects. In moments when external danger threatened the division between king and community could be forgotten. In 1205, when John called upon everyone, *servientes* as well as *milites*, to defend the kingdom against alien invasion, one chronicler represented the measures taken as the formation of a *communa* of the whole kingdom under the orders of the king and all his magnates. His picture of the organization of defence by constables through subordinate communes in counties and towns does not seem to fit the only official record very well; the oaths he says everyone had to take were perhaps only those which all free men had taken since 1181 to bear arms for regnal defence.[46] Nevertheless, however garbled the story, the use of the word 'commune' in such a context, associated with procedures reminiscent of more subversive communes, illustrates the contemporary acceptance of the kingdom as a community—even at a time of division and discontent.

The following reign demonstrates a combination of internal conflict with xenophobia that, in this period, seems peculiarly characteristic of England. No doubt its roots lay in the long history of invasions and conquests from abroad, with their legacy of the royal use of soldiers and advisers from outside, royal interests outside the kingdom, and royal demands on Englishmen to protect those interests.[47] Under Henry III lack of success in war against the French and Welsh, together with the king's inability to inspire trust and respect among his barons, intensified both discord within the realm and

[45] Magna Carta, c. 61.

[46] Gervase of Canterbury, *Opera* [33], ii. 96; *Rot. Litt. Pat.* [178], i. 55; comments: Richardson and Sayles, *Governance* [657], 76-7, 113; Powicke, *Military Obligation* [634], 58-60.

[47] The criticism of Edgar for favouring foreigners was written in the eleventh century and probably after the Danish conquest: *Anglo-Saxon Chron.* [76], 115 (E); cf. *Eng. Hist. Docs.* [119], i, pp. 113, 225.

a compensating need to find scapegoats among those who seemed not to be members of the community which royal government and misgovernment had cemented. Throughout Henry's reign he faced demands that he should rely on his 'natural counsellors'—that is, on his own subjects, not on aliens.[48] In 1258 distrust and dissension erupted in baronial schemes of reform which reflected many of the underlying principles of Magna Carta but whose proponents displayed much more political skill and patience. 'The barons'—as the chroniclers with characteristic vagueness describe the opposition—made the king agree to work with a council of fifteen members. This was elected by what was called in Latin *communitas regni*, in French *le commun* (or *commune* or *communance*) *d'Engleterre* (or *de la terre*), and in English *pæt loandes folk on ure* (i.e. Henry's) *kuneriche*.[49] Presumably the election was made in effect by those who attended the meetings of 1258, with the greatest men taking the lead, but it is notable that though they regarded themselves as representing everyone, they nevertheless took pains both to consult local opinion directly and to publicize their work even to those who only spoke English. Their reforms, moreover, look as if, like those of 1215, they were designed to put right whatever seemed to contemporaries to be unjust, whoever had committed the injustice and whoever suffered from it.[50] Henry had earlier tried to undermine opposition by suggesting that the barons were themselves unjust to their own subjects, and he may well have now tried to exacerbate the rubs between greater and lesser men which for a while impeded reform. In 1259 a group described by a chronicler as the *communitas bachelerie Anglie* received support from his son when they protested that 'the barons' were doing nothing for the public good (*ad utilitatem reipuplice*).[51]

[48] e.g. Roger of Wendover, *Flor. Hist.* [70], iii. 48-51, 66-9, 75; Treharne and Sanders, *Documents* [198], 80 (Pet. Bar. c. 4-6); *Song of Lewes* [71], lines 285-324, 409-10, 496-504, 573-80, 765-94, 954-68; on 'natural counsellors': Clanchy, *England and its Rulers* [325], 242.

[49] Rymer, *Foedera* [179], i (1), 377-8; cf. Treharne and Sanders, *Documents* [198], 116 n.; cf. ibid. 76, 100, 104, 132, 148, 156, 230.

[50] Treharne and Sanders, *Documents* [198], especially nos. 3, 6-13.

[51] Clanchy, 'Return of Writs' [326], 65; Matthew Paris, *Chron. Maj.* [52], v. 744; *Annales Mon.* [7], i. 471 (with spelling corrected from Brit. Library, Cott. MS. Vesp. E III [2], f. 91).

When the unity of the reformers finally broke down it seems to have been less because of directly conflicting interests among them than because most of the magnates felt greater inhibitions against fighting the king than did their followers and subordinates. Again and again protests ended in agreements to submit to arbitration: it was impossible to accept that wise and honest men might not be able to find a just balance between authority and consensus. Again and again arbitrators decided that the last word must rest with the king. Having sowed the wind, however, the great men now had to reap the whirlwind. As a London chronicler said when Louis IX's arbitration came down firmly on the king's side, 'almost the whole commune of the middling people of England' (*fere omnis communa mediocris populi regni Anglie*), who had not agreed to abide by the king of France's decision, entirely rejected it.[52] The fact that when the issue was between submission or outright rebellion it was the 'middling people' rather than the original leaders who felt most obligation to the community and least to the king shows that the community of the realm was no figment of exclusively baronial minds. It was in support of the community of the realm that the villagers of Peatling Magna (Leics.) fought their own little war against a royalist force in 1265.[53]

During the later part of the thirteenth century the sense of regnal community was developed by increasingly regular parliaments to which representatives of the local communities of counties and towns were beginning to be summoned. Conflicts went on, interspersed by moments when Englishmen deflected their frustrations and hostilities outward. In 1290 Edward I sought to awaken patriotic indignation by telling his subjects that the king of France had a detestable plan to wipe the English language from the earth.[54] Despite the common association of language, people, and descent, however, English writers of the thirteenth century do not seem to have expressed any sense of regnal solidarity through a regnal descent myth. Perhaps the claims which their kings made to

[52] Arnold fitz Thedmar, *Liber de Antiquis Legibus* [9], 61.
[53] *Select Cases without Writ* [185], 42-5.
[54] *Parl. Writs* [166], i, p. 30.

overlordship of Wales, Scotland, and Ireland, as well as to inherited fiefs in France, inhibited them from writing in such terms. Such claims, however, found justification in the tradition of history which derived from Geoffrey of Monmouth: by attributing a common ancestry to all the inhabitants of Britain Geoffrey had paradoxically enabled the English to appropriate the myth of Trojan descent which the British had once used against them.[55]

Their neighbours remained none the less defiantly conscious of being distinct peoples. Welsh claims to independence were founded on their separate descent, language, and customs, but the lack of political unity—of a single kingdom of Wales—fatally hampered their resistance to the English.[56] The Scots were better off. Their kings had eliminated all neighbouring and client kings by the mid eleventh century. Intermittent pressure from England probably helped to explain the regnal solidarity which, despite a relatively weak and undeveloped central government, had begun to grow there even before Edward I mounted his great attack at the end of the thirteenth century.[57] In 1291 Edward claimed that, just as the eldest son of the Trojan Brutus was supreme over his brothers, so the English ought to be supreme over all Britain. The Scots argued in return that the threefold division of Britain between Brutus's three sons justified Scottish independence. Later, during their long and increasingly stubborn war of independence, they varied the story. Sometimes they rested their claim to autonomy on the descent of the Scots from a daughter of Moses' Pharoah who had either brought her people to Britain long before the British got there or had conquered Albany from them. Sometimes they simply stressed their continual independence from the time of their travels from Greater Scythia.[58] Presumably many of those who used any of these arguments knew at one level that the inhabitants of their kingdom were variously

[55] Below, n. 58; Geoffrey of Monmouth, *Hist.* [32], 327, 350 (IV. 17; V. 15).
[56] Giraldus Cambrensis, *De Invectionibus* [34], 141-2; *Opera* [35], iii. 320; cf. Bartlett, *Gerald of Wales* [237], 50-1, 164-7.
[57] Duncan, *Scotland* [387], 90-8.
[58] Stones and Simpson, *Edward I* [192], ii. 298-9; Stones, *Anglo-Scottish Relations* [193], 113; Fergusson, *Declaration of Arbroath* [125], 6-11; cf. Borst, *Turmbau* [266], 473, 552.

descended from Britons, Picts, English, and Normans, as well as from the Scots—who, incidentally, inhabited Ireland as well as Scotland. Yet they may not have been entirely dis-ingenuous in claiming a single descent for all of them and then in varying its details. History could no doubt operate at different levels then, as it does now, when politicians who have studied history—or even historians themselves—fall back on popular stereotypes of the past in their rhetoric. Any claim to regnal independence needed to presuppose a people and any people must by definition always have been a people.

By 1320, under the stress of constant attacks from England, the Scottish government produced the most eloquent state-ment of regnal solidarity to come out of the middle ages.[59] The letter to the pope traditionally known as the Declaration of Arbroath was written in the names of eight earls and over thirty barons on behalf of 'the other barons and freeholders and the whole community of the realm'. They appealed to the pope, as the earthly representative of him who makes no distinction between Jew and Greek, Scot and Englishman, for support against the king of England, who should be satisfied with what rightly belongs to him. England had once been enough for seven kings or more, and its king should leave poor little remote Scotland to them, who asked for nothing else. Their argument began with the origin of the Scottish nation (*Scottorum nacio*) in Scythia and went on through their conversion by St. Andrew, and their long history of unconquered freedom in a kingdom ruled by a hundred and thirteen kings of their own royal stock, with no alien inter-vening. Wickedly and cruelly assailed by the English, their liberty had now been restored by Robert I, to whom they were bound by law as well as by his just deserts. Yet even if he gave up the fight they would find another king to carry it on, for they would never submit to English rule (*Anglorum dominium*) so long as a hundred of them remained alive. They fought not for glory, riches, or honour, but for liberty itself, which no good man gives up but with his life.

It is easy to see why this splendid rhetoric has been cherished

---

[59] Fergusson, *Declaration* [125]; cf. Simpson, 'Declaration of Arbroath' [690]; Duncan, *Nation of Scots* [385] and 'Making of Declaration of Arbroath' [384].

by generations of Scots, but it would be wrong to discount it just because of the often anachronistic enthusiasm it has aroused. The fact that the letter was organized and drafted professionally by the royal government as part of its diplomatic manœuvres, that it borrowed its passage about fighting for liberty from Sallust (whom few if any barons would have read), and that many barons were probably less patriotic and virtuous than the letter implies[60]—all this detracts not one whit from its significance as a statement of regnal loyalties. The barons were not proclaiming a merely personal loyalty to the king, for they declared him to be dispensable, while allusions to the English right to England show that they were not merely ethnocentric: they recognized the rights of another people as on the same level as their own. The very quotation from Sallust is nicely amended to make it suit a demand for regnal liberty, made by Christians, rather than the circumstances of a pagan civil rebellion.[61] Even if the rhetoric of the letter were empty and disingenuous it would be fallacious to assume that it would have been used if it had not appealed to values and emotions current at the time. Arguments to the contrary spring from that curious historical cynicism—almost a sort of inverted naïvety—which is determined not to take any statement of feeling or principle at its face value. No doubt the Scottish barons failed, like the English barons of 1215 or 1258 among others, to live up to the principles of their society, but that does not mean that it had none or that they did not share them. Presumably those who sealed the letter knew what it said, at least in outline, so that its contents were intended to appeal to them as much as to the pope. This suggests that, with all its flourish, it is likely to have been based on ideas that were widely shared, at least among the Scots, if not, as they evidently hoped, at the papal curia.

That this was so—that the Declaration was no flash in the pan—is indeed supported by the history of Scotland over the previous thirty-five years at least.[62] It is also noteworthy

[60] Discussion of these points is surveyed by Simpson, 'Declaration' [690].

[61] Barrow, 'Idea of freedom' [234], 28-30; cf. below, n. 105.

[62] Barrow, *Robert Bruce* [236]; cf. Duncan's review [386], 199-200; Keeney, 'Medieval Idea of the State' [499]; Barrow, 'Idea of Freedom' [234].

that the Irish, though not united in a kingdom, had used some of the same arguments about their difference from the English in a similar, though less splendid, letter to the pope a few years before.[63] The Declaration of Arbroath is a peculiarly eloquent statement of sentiments that had long been brewing, in defiance, as happens also with modern nationalist sentiments, of the facts that might be stated against it. Not only did the Scots have no common descent, they did not even have a common language. They were a purely political unit, and not normally a very united one at that, but they believed in their historic regnal unity and their right to independence.

In 900 the division of the Frankish kingdom into two halves, with a disputed territory in between, was still very recent. Both halves were still sometimes called simply the kingdom of the Franks, though as the name of *regnum Teutonicorum* came to replace that of the East Franks, the old undifferentiated title was gradually taken over by the West. It seems likely that in 900 neither half had a great deal of separate regnal solidarity and, despite the survival of the Carolingian line there, and the often valiant efforts of its kings, the western kingdom seems to have been slow to build it up. Even before 900 large areas had begun to fall under the dominance of lords who were beginning to call themselves dukes and princes, while parts of the south and centre formed the sort of political vacuum that suggests a pretty weak solidarity among the upper and middle ranks of society.[64] In some places such persons felt themselves to be members of different peoples—Romans, Franks (*Salici*), and Goths, for instance—living under diverse laws.[65] Though they seem nevertheless to have been able to act together at law, there could be little sense of community where individuals thought of themselves as descended from different origins.

By the time that Hugh Capet made himself king in 987 most of his kingdom paid little attention to him. Recent

---

[63] Bower, *Scotichronicon* [12], ii. 259-67; cf. Otway-Ruthven, *Medieval Ireland* [613], 235-6.

[64] Lemarignier, *Le Gouvernement royal* [538], maps 3, 4, 5; Werner, 'Quelques observations' [746].

[65] *Cart. de Saint-Victor de Marseille* [132], no. 290; Poly and Bournazel, *La Mutation féodale* [630], 60-71, 329-33; James, *Origins of France* [490], 179-96.

judgements have focused on the 1030s as the low point of the French monarchy,[66] but it is difficult to see really consistent signs of recovery thereafter much before the reign of Philip Augustus. Just as the teleology of national historiography has tended to depreciate the unity of medieval Germany and the power of the German kings, however, so it has encouraged historians to keep looking for signs of revival in France, and to attribute it exclusively to the activity and power of the monarchy. The early Capetians must, it seems, have had some special kind of staying-power, some tendency towards ultimate success. Even the extreme restriction of their authority in the eleventh century has been praised as the effect of wise realism, and the chance that produced a long series of direct heirs as evidence of their latent power and fitness to succeed in the long run. Abandoning such imaginative hindsight, one finds little contemporary evidence to suggest that the kings of France between 1030 and 1180 were patiently and gradually enlarging their area of direct control or that they used 'feudal rights' to extend their authority over the great men outside that area. Such territorial gains as were made before 1180 were hardly sufficient to constitute a significant trend, while ideas of feudal hierarchy and legally enforceable feudal rights were the effect, not the cause, of royal power: the vocabulary of fees, homage, and vassals was useful to Philip Augustus and his successors only because royal lawyers were then beginning to give it a new precision. If the words had had any generally agreed legal content before the thirteenth century then they would not have served royal purposes, since kings had not hitherto received regular dues and services from outside those areas of more direct royal control which later came to be called the 'royal domain'.[67]

---

[66] Dhondt, 'Une Crise de pouvoir' [359]; Lemarignier, 'Autour des premiers Capétiens' [535].

[67] Duby, 'Generations of Kings' [379]; Bisson, 'Problem of Feudal Monarchy' [259], 470–5; Stephenson, 'Les "Aides" des villes' [698], 277 n. The terminology in Fulbert of Chartres's letter to William of Aquitaine, for instance, is much less clearly 'feudal' than is sometimes suggested: Letters [29], no. 51, where fidelis is translated as 'vassal' and casamentum as 'fief'. Note the equally vague terminology in ibid. no. 86, especially placitum (translated as 'court': see above, p. 24). For meanings of 'domain', above, pp. 219–20.

Some of the difficulty of understanding how the twelfth-century monarchy pulled itself up by its bootlaces may be alleviated by diverting attention from the king to the kingdom. Any latent power the early Capetians had was not peculiar to France or to their still puny dynasty. Rather the reverse: it was what rubbed off on them from more powerful kings either in the past or in their own time elsewhere, and from the way that everyone tended to think about kingdoms. The absence of an effective king did not at once destroy belief in a kingdom.[68] Though the kings of the East Franks had no compunction about taking over Lotharingia or the kingdom of Burgundy, which had once formed part of the disputed Middle Kingdom, and though they exerted decisive influence on the affairs of the western kingdom on several occasions, even Otto the Great respected its integrity as a separate entity. At the end of the tenth century, when the king had very little authority in most of France, it was still possible to write of the great lords as *primores regni* who should—though they might not—show honour and reverence to him by their aid and counsel.[69] Count William V of Poitou, who called himself duke and was said in his own lifetime to have subjected all of Aquitaine to his government (*imperium*) and, moreover, to be regarded more like a king than a duke, was, after all, only *like* a king.[70] A little later the power of the rulers of Normandy and Flanders would lead people to slip into referring to each of them as a kingdom, but their rulers never went so far as to call themselves kings.[71] It seems to have been accepted that the kingdom had only one king: when his prestige began once more to surpass that of his greater subjects it was partly because being king gave him a unique advantage.

Just as some sense of being a kingdom may have preceded and promoted royal prestige, so royal prestige may thus have preceded and promoted the reality of royal power. There are several indications of the way that this seems to have happened. First, the processes by which government in general

[68] Ehlers, 'Karolingische Tradition' [389].
[69] Abbo of Fleury in *P.L.* [60], cxxxix, col. 478.
[70] Adémar of Chabannes, *Chronique* [5], 163.
[71] Above, n. 22.

was by the twelfth century beginning to become more regular and effective had some impact within the area which the king of France already controlled.[72] That does not on its own explain how royal power came to supplant that of other lords elsewhere, but at the same time the kingdom of the East Franks was coming to be known more regularly as the *regnum Teutonicorum*. That left the identity, myths, and glory of the Franks to seem more like the exclusive property of the western kingdom. To abbot Suger of Saint-Denis, writing the life of Louis VI in the mid twelfth century, nothing showed the glory of *Francia* better than the way that the *Franci* united in 1124 to repel invasion by the *imperator Theutonicus*. The duke of Normandy, to be sure, was allied with the invading Germans, but the other great men of the kingdom (*proceres regni*) who rallied to the king's summons included the counts of Anjou and Brittany and the duke of Aquitaine. Regnal solidarity, it seems, did not exist only in the mind of Suger, though he did much to promote it, not least through the propaganda of his book. Although to a sceptical reader Suger's account shows Louis struggling long and hard to enforce even a modicum of order in the Île de France, and although the *Franci* whom Suger describes as obeying him seem often to have been restricted to that relatively small area, Suger obviously—as his account of the invasion of 1124 shows—thought of the king and his kingdom in much grander terms.[73] He depicts Louis's expeditions to Flanders and the Auvergne, for instance, as forceful exercises of established authority. In fact Louis's interventions in the affairs of lordships outside the Île de France relied largely on force of arms and *ad hoc* negotiations, rather than on any clearly recognized rights, and they were neither unprecedented nor the starting-point of significantly new relationships. Whether either Suger or anyone else at the time thought that any rights which Louis could claim were owed to him as feudal lord rather than as king seems doubtful: Suger's own words lend less support to the idea

[72] Lemarignier, 'Autour des premiers Capétiens' [535].

[73] *Vie de Louis VI* [72], 218-30; cf. 232-4, where *Franci* and Auvergnats are contrasted. Such examples do not suggest to me that Suger thought of the kingdom as consisting only of the Île de France: cf. Poly and Bournazel, *La Mutation féodale* [630], 301-3.

that the twelfth-century kings of France based their authority on specifically 'feudal' rights than do those of his translator and commentators. The speech in which he made the king's spokesman claim that Henry I of England held the duchy of Normandy by Louis's generous liberality *tanquam proprium feodum* was surely not intended to make a point which would be limited by any technicalities of feudal lordship, even if those had been clear at the time. Its point was not that Louis was 'overlord' or 'suzerain' but that he was king— a king for whom it would be particularly wrong to transgress the law since king and law share the same majesty of government (*cum et rex et lex eandem imperandi excipiant majestatem*).[74] To Suger the king was, or ought to be, supreme simply because he was king, not because he possessed any particular or defined powers.

In fact, of course, the relationship between the king and the duke of Normandy was very different from that depicted in Suger's grandiloquent phrases. Rouen, commanding the Seine within eighty miles of Paris, was the centre of a firmly controlled duchy as well, from 1066, as being the seat of another king. Even before the conquest of England a story was told about the descent of the Normans which suggests that they regarded themselves as a separate people.[75] Orderic Vitalis, elaborating it in the twelfth century, makes it clear that to him the *gens Normannorum*, descended as it was from Danes and ultimately from Trojans, comprised all the inhabitants of the duchy.[76] The effectiveness of the political unit was both the cause and the effect of the sense of shared ancestry. Nevertheless, Normans in England were often referred to as *Franci*. Although the government of Normandy and England was for a while quite closely integrated and wars with the king of France were frequent, Normandy continued to be considered in some sense part of the kingdom of France.[77] After 1154, when both Normandy and England, along with much of the rest of western France, came under

[74] *Vie de Louis VI* [72], 106. Among 'feudalizing' translations note e.g. *ost* for *exercitus*, *chevalerie* for *militia*, *la service du vassal* for *servitium*.

[75] Dudo, *De moribus* [24], 130 (I. 3).

[76] *Hist. Eccles.* [57], ii. 274–6, v. 24–6.

[77] Robert of Torigni, *Chronica* [69], 208, 240; Loud, 'Gens Normannorum' [557].

the rule of the count of Anjou, the threat to the king and kingdom looked even greater. Yet, despite Louis VII's often feeble performance against Henry II, his prestige appears paradoxically to have been greater than that of his ancestors who had never had such a powerful enemy on their door-step. Even Henry himself, who was never averse from twist-ing law and events to his own advantage, seems to have felt some slight inhibitions about correct behaviour towards the king of France.[78] So far as he bowed to current ideas of political obligation, they were probably concerned as much with that which was owed specifically to kings and kingdoms as with that which any vassal owed to any lord.

Perhaps it may not be too far-fetched to imagine that one reason why the twelfth-century kings of France came to seem more considerable rulers than their predecessors was the wide and high reputation which the schools of Paris enjoyed. Writing after Philip II had conquered Normandy and Anjou from John of England, Gerald of Wales, who looked back with nostalgia on his student days in France, thought that the French love of learning explained their victories. Whereas the Normans' love of liberty had been enfeebled by tyranny, the kingdom of France, from the time of King Pepin on, had shown how the arts of war and wisdom flourished together, just as they had under the the Greeks and Romans.[79] Former students of Paris included many who were more influential than poor Gerald managed to become. Their respect for Paris, rubbing off on its king, may have been infectious. As well as taking happy memories and admiration of France home with them, English and German students may have left behind them in northern France ideas about the authority of kings, and the respect due to them, which had been rather forgotten there in the last century or so.

However much—or however little—influence Suger and the students of Paris had on lay political ideas, Angevin power did not in the event break the tenuous solidarities which sustained the twelfth-century kingdom. In the long run wars between the kings of France and England promoted the separate solidarities of the two kingdoms rather than that of the Angevin dominions themselves. The Angevin lands never

[78] Warren, *Henry II* [738], 87, 148.   [79] *Opera* [35], viii. 258-9.

developed any internal cohesion, for their government was not systematically integrated and little attempt seems to have been made to bind them together in any other way.[80] Even at tournaments, where knights sometimes formed their teams by provinces, the various contingents from the lands which Henry II ruled did not always fight on the same side.[81] It seems extremely unlikely that anyone thought of their inhabitants as sharing a common ancestry apart from that which belonged to all Franks. Even if Philip II's conquest of Normandy was made easier by a wealth which enabled him to pay for large armies, money was not all-important. A king like Philip, who, unlike his father, was prepared to act his part effectively and use all the advantages of his position, could secure a good deal of service and obedience without having to pay for it in cash.

Whatever the explanation of Philip's initial successes, there is no doubt that the conquest of Normandy and Anjou, quickly followed as it was by the Albigensian crusade, transformed the position of the French monarchy. In the victor of Bouvines France had an effective focus for regnal loyalty, and a sense of community among the upper ranks of society began to develop accordingly. It is no accident that references to the Trojan descent of the Franks—in which the Normans' similar descent could be easily subsumed—began to multiply at around this time.[82] Initially, it was the sense of solidarity of those who lived in northern France which was increased, not only by the elimination of the separate Angevin government there, but by successful wars against southerners, with their rather different language and customs. Once royal authority was established in Languedoc or anywhere else, however, the way was open for regnal solidarity to be strengthened there too. That is not, of course, to say that all separate regional or local loyalties were eliminated: political practicality, the acknowledged validity of local custom, and the very size of the kingdom all combined to prevent the king

[80] Holt, 'End of Anglo-Norman Realm' [473]; cf. *Chroniques des comtes d'Anjou* [18], 223-4.

[81] *Hist. de Guillaume le Maréchal* [42], iii. 20; cf. ibid. 39, 42, 45, 46-7, 51-62, 73.

[82] Bossuat, 'Les Origines troyennes' [269]; Duby, *Dimanche de Bouvines* [376], 194-215.

from enforcing the same royal rights everywhere that he had in his domains around Paris. Nevertheless, wherever contact with the central government was maintained, a layer of regnal feeling tended to be imposed, or strengthened, over the top of the existing layers of local and provincial loyalty. A thin layer of solidarity even slid over the boundary of the kingdom to the east: the clergy in the French-speaking provinces there, having responded to the call to contribute to Louis IX's first crusade, went on paying taxes to his successors throughout the century.[83] Combined with the way that southerners, although undoubtedly part of the kingdom, went on thinking in some contexts of *Francia* and *Franci* as exclusively northern, this illustrates the untidiness which sometimes blurred the coincidence of kingdoms with peoples as they were perceived in the middle ages, just as it blurs the coincidence of states with nations as they are perceived today.

As in England, the improved records of the thirteenth century provide ample evidence of the sense of a community of the realm, though here its development cannot be attributed, as it often is in English history, to persistent conflict between king and nobles. Traditional interpretations of French history may, however, overemphasize both the harmony which prevailed before the reign of Philip IV and the contribution of the monarchy towards the growing sense of regnal solidarity. By suggesting that the French monarchy had an inevitable tendency towards absolutism they obscure the extent to which regnal solidarity in the thirteenth century was the effect of collective government. Traditional emphasis on extensions of the 'royal domain' as the basis of royal power is also misleading. The kings of thirteenth-century France were powerful, not just because they had more of the kingdom under a variety of different kinds of more direct control than their predecessors had done, but because they ruled a whole great kingdom, and their subjects all over it felt enough regnal solidarity to make them, by and large, support and obey royal authority. Contemporaries were beginning to think in terms of a common law that applied to the whole kingdom and of the king as having ultimate

[83] Strayer, 'Crusades of Louis IX' [703], 490. For provincial loyalties, above, pp. 232-5.

jurisdiction over it. Though he did not often find it necessary to do either, the king could on occasion summon large general assemblies and could legislate for the whole kingdom.[84]

Further solidarity came from collective hostility, directed not only against the English and Albigensians, but against the church. In 1205-6 assemblies of barons met in different parts of the kingdom to declare their support for the king in resisting what they saw as encroachments by the ecclesiastical courts on their rights. Though they met in separate local groups some claimed to speak on behalf of the barons of the whole kingdom and of their men and their lands, and the king agreed not to reverse what was agreed with their consent.[85] Collective activity in much the same cause was resumed under St. Louis. In 1246 forty-one lords sealed a document which invited others to join a *compainnie* or *comite* they had formed. Everyone was to pay an annual subscription of the hundredth value of their lands, and the association was to be governed by four great lords. If more than two of the four were to die or be out of the country then ten or twelve of the other rich members of the association could elect four others to replace them. Whether or not these formalities ever worked in practice and the *compainnie* ever amounted to more than an amorphous pressure-group, or series of pressure-groups, the protests and counter-measures of the pope and clergy suggest both that it worried them for several years and that it involved *burgenses* and *rustici* as well as nobles. It is not surprising that the pope was worried, for in 1247, at the council of Lyon, he was confronted not only by a protesting deputation from the barons of France (*nuntii baronum confoederatorum in Francia*) but one from the bishops of France themselves and a formal embassy from the king into the bargain. Louis's ambassador alleged that, in addition to the magnates, the whole kingdom (*omne regnum*) was disturbed by papal taxes, by provisions (especially of foreign clergy), and by other oppressions. The kingdom here is not merely a geographical area, that *douce France* which we

---

[84] Langmuir, 'Concilia' [520] and 'Judei Nostri' [521], 231-5; Wood, *French Apanages* [762], 82-8, 99-102; above, p. 48.

[85] Teulet, *Layettes* [194], i, nos. 762-7, 785; cf. *Actes de Philippe II* [111], nos. 899-900.

know had for long been the object of devotion, but a collective group, the inhabitants of the kingdom, with whose opinion Louis, like Robert I of Scotland in 1320, found it good policy to confront the pope. The fact that, like Robert, he chose on occasion to lead from behind shows that he considered that the collective opinion and action of his subjects was respectable and worthy of attention, and that he assumed that the pope would too.[86]

Meanwhile Louis IX himself, despite later beliefs to the contrary, raised some quite general taxes,[87] and when his successors began to take more their subjects showed themselves fully capable of collective opposition. Philip IV's reform ordinance of 1303 suggests that he was aware of potentially dangerous discontents.[88] On this occasion he forestalled trouble but in 1314, when he failed to cancel a tax which the avoidance of war had robbed of its justification, he was met with simultaneous protests from all over the kingdom.[89]

The movement of 1314-1315 has often been compared with the English movement of a century before. Seen within the context of thirteenth-century ideas of collective rights and action, rather than of the different ways that the constitutions of the two kingdoms developed later, the two movements and the charters which appeased them did indeed have a great deal in common. In both cases the opposition to royal oppression was led by nobles, but in both cases the nobles claimed to speak on behalf of others. In France, as in England, complaints were made against oppression and corruption within the existing system, and demands were for what was just, reasonable, and customary. Apart from an end to what they saw as new and extortionate taxes, the kinds of things the French protesters wanted included open and public trials to be held in the accused's home jurisdiction, restrictions on arbitrary arrest and imprisonment, and the making of collective

---

[86] Teulet, *Layettes* [194], ii, no. 3569; Matthew Paris, *Chron. Maj.* [52], iv. 590-3, 614, vi. 99-112, 131-3; Campbell, 'Protest of St. Louis' [306].

[87] *Rec. Hist. de France* [64], xxii. 152-4 (Geffroi de Paris, ll. 6508-38); cf. Brown, 'Customary Aids' [279], 191-2.

[88] Cazelles, 'Une Exigence de l'opinion' [312].

[89] Brown, 'Reform and Resistance' [280]; Artonne, *Le Mouvement de 1314* [224], 13-26, 44-66.

judgements without interference by *baillis, prévôts,* or castellans.[90] Like all collectivities of the time, moreover, the
various associations and alliances through which opposition
was organized are difficult to fit into the tidier categories of
later history. The documents in which they were recorded
combine precision about mutual obligations with vagueness
and variety of expression about those who were obliged. Lists
of names are followed by general phrases including everyone
else. When medieval people did their sea-lawyering it was not
against the background of the verbal exactitudes characteristic
of modern treaties or the precise rules of membership characteristic of modern associations. Because 'noble leagues' are
a familiar category of later French history, the northern and
central alliances of 1314-15 are often now referred to in
these terms, and distinguished from the southern movement
of local 'communities'. The reason why nobles look particularly prominent in the north may be simply that there they
traditionally paid dues and acted in law and politics apart
from local communities of lesser people whereas in the south
they acted within them. It did not make much difference in
practice in 1314-15. Everywhere, north and south, the word
commun crops up frequently. Sometimes it means particular
local communities which acted as units within larger alliances
(as in *li communs d'Ostun, de Chalon, de Beaune, de Dyjon*);
sometimes it means commoners as distinct from nobles—or
perhaps everyone as well as nobles (as in *li noble et li communs tous de Bourgoingne*); and sometimes it means simply
everyone (as in *le commun du royaulme* or *le gouvernour de
nostre commun*).[91] Communities were everywhere—communities which were thought of, as they were in any town or
province or village which secured liberties, as including everyone in the area and as being able to act together without any
formal definition of membership or boundaries. When the
Burgundians held their first great meeting at Beaune most of
the more important lords of Burgundy (though not the duke)
took part, along with representatives of some abbeys and

[90] e.g. *Ordonnances* [144], i. 555 (Périgord, c. 9), 559 (Burgundy, c. 11),
563, 566 (Amiens and Vermandois, c. 5); cf. the 1303 ordinance: ibid. i. 358,
365, 366 (c. 5, 52, 60).
[91] Duchesne, *La Maison de Vergy* [115], preuves, 232, 234; Brown, 'Reform
and Resistance' [280], 130-2.

chapters and of the *commun* of several towns, and even some women and children. Those present took an oath to resist the current abhorrent taxation and other unreasonable actions of the king, both in their own names and on behalf of all other religious houses and *villes* great and small in the duchy of Burgundy. They also set up a system of governors and meetings for the future.[92] The Champenois may have done the same, and perhaps had already set the pattern. Together Burgundians and Champenois then constructed a network of *alliances* or *convenances*. The word 'league', for what it is worth, does not seem to be used, but the strength of the network depended less on particular words or even on the particular way in which each knot in it was tied than on the assumption that everyone shared common rights, interests, and duties within the *commun du royaulme*—the community of the realm. The whole affair illustrates once again the vague but strong assumptions about collective action and collective rights which are found throughout the period.

Although, however, the values and assumptions of the French opposition of 1314-15 were so similar to those of English opposition movements throughout the previous century, their circumstances were different. The dramatic extension of French royal jurisdiction took place after the boundaries of other jurisdictions had become clearer than they had been in the twelfth century, and after ideas of law and legal authority had been clarified too. It therefore seemed much more like encroachment than the comparable change in England had done: the relative jurisdictional position also explains why resistance to ecclesiastical courts was primarily a matter for the lords in France and for the king in England. In the circumstances it was natural that the French demands of 1314-15 included much more about the protection of seigniorial jurisdiction than had the English demands of 1215. The fact that they did so, together with the usual teleological tendency to project the system of estates backwards in time, explains why the French 'leagues'

---

[92] Duchesne, *La Maison de Vergy* [115], preuves, 232-6: here, and in the royal charter to the Burgundians (*Ordonnances* [144], i. 567), the expression duchy of Burgundy is used, rather than the unqualified name which had been more usual earlier (above, p. 233).

have often been seen as exclusively, or more predominantly, noble. There is, however, no evidence that those customarily subject to seigniorial jurisdiction disagreed with their lords in resenting royal encroachments. Custom was custom, and, to judge from the whole tenor of the complaints, the king's local officials had presented the unacceptable face of royal jurisdiction more visibly than its possible benefits to many Frenchmen.

Furthermore, though justice and government were becoming more centralized, much less tradition of united regnal meetings and regnal activity had developed in France than in the smaller kingdom of England. Some of the local groups of protestors acted together for a while in 1314–15, but others never joined them. Philip the Fair's death and his son's quick and adroit concessions appeased the opposition before it had become either fully united or fundamentally damaging to the crown.[93] With all these reservations, it is none the less clear that many Frenchmen did not see their interests either as exclusively local, or as peculiar to their particular rank or class. Whatever the arguments of local custom or special privilege that were advanced to avoid taxes and oppressions, no one seems to have contested the basic obligation to contribute to the defence of the kingdom or the general principle that the common good and common customs of the realm overrode local privileges.[94] It was to the king that everyone appealed in 1314 to right their wrongs and it was the king who issued charters of liberty and pardon in the following year. To judge from these troubles, from the earlier anti-clerical and anti-papal movements, and from continuing references to the Trojan ancestry of the Franks, John of Paris may have been expressing quite widely held views, though in an exceptionally learned and subtle way, when he wrote his treatise against papal pretensions in 1302–3. He attributed the origin and justification of kingdoms in general to the diversity of climate, languages, conditions of men, and ways of life, while deriving that of the kingdom of the Franks in

---

[93] Brown, 'Reform and Resistance' [280]; Wood, *French Apanages* [762], 118–24.

[94] Strayer, *Studies* [706], 7–23, 47, 56; Brown, 'Customary Aids' [279]; Petot, 'Le Droit commun' [624].

particular from their collective Trojan descent.[95] The myth that had once promoted the glory and solidarity of the seventh-century Franks was now thus applied to all the inhabitants of the kingdom of France. Perhaps in this sort of context even southerners could see themselves as free Franks and descendants of Trojans. The community of the realm of France, though not so clearly expressed or so well developed through collective action as that of England, nevertheless existed in the minds of a fair number of its subjects.

If one compares the evidence of cohesion and conflict in Germany with that for France, England, and Scotland at the same time, some of the controversies about it seem over-strained. They have arisen because the traditional way of looking at medieval Germany starts from the belief that the German nation was doomed to wait in the anteroom of history until the modern nationalist movement summoned it forth in the nineteenth century. In the tenth and eleventh centuries, as the theory goes, the inhabitants of the kingdom of Germany (or, rather, of the East Franks) felt no significant loyalty above the 'tribal' level of the duchies, and the kingdom itself was fatally weakened on the one hand by these separatist duchies and on the other by being subsumed within a supranational empire. Thereafter the monarchy lost all credibility as its powers were undermined first by the 'Investiture Contest' and then by the rise of 'feudalism'. By the thirteenth century the tribal duchies had been replaced by territorial principalities without either internal cohesion or common interests. All this is very unconvincing: the search for the first signs of later fragmentation in Germany is as misleading as the search for the first signs of royal power in France. Nationalist teleology is a poor guide to the values of the past.

In 900 the kingdom of the East Franks, like that of the West, was a recent creation which on the face of it may seem to have been united only through its Carolingian ruler. Some of the component parts of the eastern kingdom may have had particularly strong solidarities of their own. Saxony and Bavaria, for instance, had been conquered by the Frankish kings relatively recently and although they were now governed,

[95] *De potestate regia* [45], 176-8, 180-3, 199, 246-7 (c. 1, 3, 4, 10, 21).

under the king, by dukes rather than by their own kings, they were still sometimes thought of as kingdoms. Historians have often described these duchies or subkingdoms as 'tribal duchies' (*Stammesherzogtümer*)—or, in a curious mid-North Sea formulation, as 'stem-duchies'. The implication of 'tribal' —or, presumably, of 'stem'—seems to be that the inhabitants of the duchies were of ancient common descent and therefore formed naturally cohesive units. That, however, as has already been suggested, is misleading: in so far as the duchies were cohesive it was because they had for some time been governed as units and their inhabitants *felt* that they were units of custom and descent.[96] The Saxons and Bavarians are indeed known to have had their own descent myths, by the tenth and twelfth centuries respectively. They may have had them earlier and so may other groups.[97] Myths, however, is what they were: in reality the boundaries of duchies changed from time to time, so that loyalties and myths changed accordingly.

In any case it is not at all clear that the internal cohesion of the duchies worked against the unity of the whole kingdom. When Louis the Child died in 911 the duchies to the east of Lotharingia did not all go their separate ways and become separate kingdoms. Apparently the dukes and the more important of their subjects felt that the kingdom still needed to exist even if there were no Carolingian left to govern it. The very weakness of Conrad I underlines the consensus: even with an ineffective king, whom not all the dukes may have wanted as king, the kingdom still existed. Conrad himself, according to Widukind of Korvei, wanted Duke Henry of Saxony to succeed him because Henry looked like a winner:[98] kings were supposed to have more authority than Conrad had achieved. Henry was therefore elected by the Franconians and Saxons, and though the duke of Bavaria put in a rival claim it was to the whole kingdom, not to a separate kingdom of Bavaria. Whether or not Henry formally made

---

[96] Werner, 'Heeresorganisation' [743], 792-813; Müller-Mertens, 'Zur Rolle der politischen Formung' [602].

[97] Widukind, *Rer. gest. Sax.* [81], 4-5, 20-1 (I. 2-3, 12); Borst, *Turmbau von Babel* [266], 568, 669, 671.

[98] Widukind, *Rer. gest. Sax.* [81], 33 (I. 25); cf. Beumann, *Historiographie* [250], 461-2, 481.

a rule that the succession should in future be undivided, the precedent for that was already established—as indeed it was in other kingdoms.[99] With stakes as high as Henry's own success made them it is not surprising that there should have been disputes on occasion about the crown. They arose less from any peculiarly fissiparous tendency in the German polity than from the power which Henry had achieved and which had itself increased unity. Those who believe that the German kingdom had no real unity at this stage have sometimes argued that it was not called the *regnum Teutonicorum* until the twelfth century and that so long as the Germans thought of themselves only as East Franks (or East Franks, Saxons, Bavarians, and so on), they could not be united. The argument seems overstrained, not least because it rests on the absence of evidence, which is dangerous at such an ill-recorded period. For what it is worth, recent study suggests that the evidence that the name *regnum Teutonicorum* was *not* used in the tenth century is weak.[100] In any case it is not at all clear that the names of Frank and German (*Teutonicus*) were mutually exclusive. No one yet knew about the labels and hostilities of later history, and the Saxon kings and their subjects may have been as ready to take over the name and glory of the Franks as were people in the western kingdom. Many subjects of the eastern kingdom thought of themselves for much of the time and in many contexts as Bavarians, Saxons, and so forth, and indeed as members of smaller local groups, but Wipo's use of the name *Theutonici* suggests that some of them thought of themselves as Germans too. Even if they did not regularly give themselves that name they surely knew that they were the subjects of a king whose authority and prestige outshone that of any other. They were part of a great kingdom.

Henry I's successes included the annexation of Lotharingia, which had since 911 slipped under West Frankish control, and the creation of a protectorate over the kingdom of Burgundy, which had likewise once been part of the old Middle Kingdom. Thereafter, as the power and prestige

---

[99] Beumann, 'Die Bedeutung des Kaisertums' [249], 345; Schlesinger, *Beiträge* [678], i. 161-4, 261-9; cf. Leyser, *Rule and Conflict* [553], 15.
[100] Beumann, 'Die Bedeutung des Kaisertums' [249], 343-7.

of the kings of Burgundy declined, so their kingdom lost solidarity and independence until it was finally absorbed into the kingdom of Germany under Conrad II.[101] Meanwhile Otto I continued his father's successes to the point where, having taken over the kingdom of Italy—the last important component of the Middle Kingdom—he was crowned emperor in 962. Defeat under his son, a long minority under his grandson, and then two failures of direct heirs did not break the mould. There were plenty of rebellions and conflicts in tenth- and eleventh-century Germany but they do not seem to have been caused by any significantly 'tribal' separatism in the duchies. Personal ambition and grievances against tough and sometimes arbitrary kings accounted for much:[102] the conflicts were those of power, not of weakness. Moreover, just because they were so powerful, the Saxon kings relied all the more on their subjects. The stronger a medieval government was, the more collective action it required. German kings held assemblies at which they judged and legislated by and with the advice of their lords spiritual and temporal— which no doubt explains how at least one eleventh-century German already thought of German law as a single category. Royal armies were regularly raised from all over the kingdom according to local quotas that seem, in the usual medieval way, to have been regarded as fixed and obligatory though in practice they were subject to the drift of custom.[103]

The idea that German solidarity was diluted by Otto's revival of the imperial title seems to derive less from contemporary evidence than from a confusion between the kingdom of Germany and the empire which developed only gradually over the centuries—and perhaps also from an obsession with the contrast between 'Germanic' and Roman inheritances that dates from later still. To tenth-century Germans their king's title of emperor was probably just a mark of his supreme power and prestige and a reminder of the glory and plunder to be won in Italy—or, for the more faint-hearted, of the burden and dangers of military service

[101] Fournier, *Le Royaume d'Arles* [424], pp. i–xxii, 65–7, 523–6.

[102] Leyser, *Rule and Conflict* [553], 9–47.

[103] Above, p. 18; Werner, 'Heeresorganisation' [743]; cf. Gillingham, 'Introduction of Knight Service' [442].

there. German regnal solidarities are prima facie as likely to have been strengthened by wars in Italy as English ones were by wars in France. In the eleventh century Wipo, although he does not refer explicitly to the *regnum Teutonicorum*, appears to distinguish the *terra Teutonicorum* from Italy and, indeed, from the kingdom of Burgundy.[104] Some of what he says about empires, kingdoms, and *res publica* may reflect the ideas of his classical models rather than those of his contemporaries, but not all.[105] In 1027 Conrad II returned from Italy to deal with plots among the Germans and especially with a revolt threatened by the duke of Swabia (*Alemannia*). Working through the traditional methods of collective government he summoned a *colloquium publice* at which the duke submitted because, although he tried to whip up support by appealing to Alemannic traditions of loyalty, his followers refused to join him in rebellion. According to the two counts whom Wipo makes act as spokesmen, it was a mark of their freedom to serve their king and emperor, the supreme defender of their freedom on earth. They would therefore obey the duke only in what was honest and just.[106] Wipo no doubt improved their reasoning and eloquence[107] but he was presumably right in saying that the duke's followers, or most of them, remained faithful to the king. They must have had some reason for doing so: it is less likely to have been a sense of merely personal loyalty than a loyalty which they felt to him as king, the ruler of the kingdom. At many times they could have felt such loyalty without any conflict with more local loyalties, but on this occasion, when there was a conflict, regnal loyalty won.

Several failures of direct succession may have tended to emphasize each new king's dependence on consent, but there is no evidence that as yet the German monarchy was recognized to be more elective than others. Despite changes of family, moreover, each king became king of Italy and emperor, so that these titles were coming to seem traditional

---

[104] *Opera* [84], 38-9, 81.
[105] Beumann, 'Entwicklung transpersonaler Staatsvorstellungen' [251]; below, p. 325.
[106] Wipo, *Opera* [84], 38-41.
[107] Using the same piece of Sallust as the Declaration of Arbroath: above, p. 275.

appendages of the kingdom of Germany. It was Henry IV's conflict with the papacy in the later eleventh century which created the first dangerous precedents of deposition, election-eering conflict, and concession.[108] Nevertheless, as in France, it is a mistake to assume that a king's troubles immediately weakened the sense of regnal cohesion. Even pro-papal polemics show how much contemporaries accepted the king-dom as a fact of political life. Leyser points out that Mane-gold of Lautenbach 'took the existence of a community for granted' when he argued that kings might be deposed if they broke their contract with the people.[109] Not everyone would have agreed with him, but everyone apparently went on agreeing that there must be a king and that he should be powerful. When Henry V died without heirs in 1125 ecclesi-astical influence ruled out the duke of Swabia as too arrogant but everyone seems to have assumed that the king and emperor would have to be one of the three men in the king-dom who were most outstanding in wealth and character (*tam divitiis quam virtute animi*). The narrative of Lothar's election suggests that by now people were unclear whether they were electing a king of the Romans or an emperor but it was still the *regnum Teutonicorum* that they were concerned with.[110] Three years earlier the Concordat of Worms had dis-tinguished clearly between the *regnum Teutonicorum* and the rest of the empire.[111] German claims to the Roman empire did not imply a lack of German regnal feeling: the Germans had conquered Rome and inherited its glories but they saw a dif-ference between Germans and Romans, between the kingdom of Germany and the kingdom of Italy.[112] Confusion about the king's title did not prevent them from envisaging the kingdom as a geographical and political entity.

Throughout the twelfth century, from the royal proclama-tion of peace at Mainz in 1103 to the royal confiscation of the duchies and estates of the kingdom's greatest subject in 1179-80, royal authority and jurisdiction were maintained

---

[108] *Brunos Buch* [15], 85-6.
[109] Leyser, *Medieval Germany* [552], 143-7.
[110] *M.G.H. Scriptores* [54], xii. 509-12; *M.G.H. Const.* [160], i, no. 112.
[111] *M.G.H. Const.* [160], i, no. 108.
[112] *Gesta Friderici* [58], 138; *M.G.H. Const.* [160], i, no. 230; cf. *P.L.* [60], ccxvi, col. 1013, 1028 (Innocent III); Folz, *L'Idée d'empire* [418], 117-28.

and even extended through consultation and collective judge-ment.[113] Ideas that the monarchy had been permanently weakened by the 'Investiture Contest' and that this period saw its further weakening by the growth of 'feudalism' are as implausible as that it was already doomed by being elective.[114] Both derive from the imposition of later categories on twelfth-century documents and from reading German documents without comparing them with others of the time. During the reign of Frederick I the area under direct royal control was built up, while direct royal intervention in some other parts of the kingdom was diminished:[115] it is probably only hind-sight that makes this look like the first stage in a general surrender of royal power. Frederick's legislation and judge-ments, no less than his ability to raise armies for Italy and keep them in the field, suggest that the monarchy was still powerful and still a focus of regnal solidarity. Only the blindest belief in the inevitability of German fragmentation could make the fall of Henry the Lion in 1179-80 and the dismemberment of his lands into a defeat for the king. The emperor decided to grant out the lands rather than keeping them for himself presumably because generosity made good political sense, and he divided them up presumably because Henry had, as it turned out, been dangerously powerful.[116] In so far as Frederick acted with the advice and consent of his great men and of the men of Henry's duchies he was acting according to law but there was nothing new or par-ticularly 'feudal' about that, nor did his decision create any more of a precedent than would any important and famous judgement. Frederick ended his reign as well in control of Germany as any of his predecessors. His attempt to re-establish imperial government in Italy had failed, but if his son's marriage to the heiress of Sicily had not awakened

---

[113] Vita Heinrici IV [79], 438-9 (c. 8); M.G.H. Const. [160], i, nos. 74, 159, 279, 297-8; Appelt, 'Kaiserurkunde' [221].

[114] For relations with the German church: Reuter, 'Imperial Church System' [647].

[115] Génicot, 'Empire et principautés' [437]; Fuhrmann, Deutsche Geschichte [429], 180-2.

[116] Fuhrmann, Deutsche Geschichte [429], 186-9; on possible ways of treat-ing the effect of escheats on undertenants compare e.g. Magna Carta, c. 37, 43: Holt, Magna Carta [475], 210, 218, 326, 328.

papal hostility, historians might now be describing thirteenth-century Germany as another 'national monarchy' which was developing naturally into a nation-state. As it was, all Innocent III's efforts to get the weakest possible king of Germany, who would be unable to assert himself in Italy, barely dented the determination of the great men of the kingdom to hold it together.

Frederick II's reign is commonly seen as marking an important step towards the replacement of royal power by 'territorial principalities', but this interpretation does not seem to be borne out by contemporary documents. None of the clauses of the *Constitutio in favorem principum* sacrifices any significant jurisdiction. Seen in the context of thirteenth-century collective politics in general, the whole document looks much more like a charter of liberties of the usual kind than a foundation charter of separatism. It is granted to 'our faithful men of our realm' as well as to 'our ecclesiastical and secular princes' and though, like the French charters of the early fourteenth century, it certainly lays considerable emphasis on the customary rights of great men, it also, like them, protects the customary rights of others.[117] Within a few years of the *Constitutio*, moreover, another royal assembly dominated by the same great men or princes of the kingdom made a serious effort to develop royal jurisdiction throughout the kingdom.[118] The German princes who in 1237 elected Frederick's son as king of the Romans and his father's heir seem to have thought of the inhabitants of the kingdom as a single people of common descent, for they alluded to their Trojan origins and claimed to be acting as Roman senators in electing a future Roman emperor.[119] In the event, Frederick's death was followed by long years of conflict and a series of contested elections, but these troubles, like the contemporary conflicts of England, demonstrate the general acceptance of the single forum within which disputes were conducted. The college of electors could only have come into existence because its members were felt to represent

[117] *M.G.H. Const.* [160], ii, nos. 171, 304. Cf. especially c. 22 of the two documents and e.g. ibid. nos. 173, 175.

[118] *M.G.H. Const.* [160], ii, no. 196; Leuschner, *Germany* [547], 56-63; above, p. 237.

[119] *M.G.H. Const.* [160], ii, no. 329.

some kind of collectivity—even though one of them, the king of Bohemia, was recognized to be in rather an anomalous position within it. After 1273, moreover, Rudolf I made determined efforts to restore government, notably through the method most characteristic of thirteenth-century kingdoms—that is, legislation at great regnal assemblies.[120]

In all the circumstances it seems probable that many thirteenth-century Germans continued to feel some loyalty to the whole kingdom as well as to their local community. Alexander von Roes, writing about 1280, described the Germans as descended from Trojans who had intermarried with women of the ancient *Theutonici.*[121] A little later another inhabitant of the kingdom described the inhabitants of *Theutonia, Alemania,* or *Germania* as sharing characteristics which distinguished them—favourably—from the men of other barbarian nations. He seems to have envisaged their country pretty well in the terms of the historic kingdom of Germany proper, definitely excluding Italy, and also, apparently, Burgundy and Bohemia.[122] The 'age of the princes' may have been dawning but Germany was still a kingdom whose subjects thought of themselves as in some sense a single people.

The most obvious exception to my argument that kingdoms and peoples were perceived as coextensive is provided by Italy, but it is an exception which illustrates well the general rule that peoples were supposed to coincide with political units. By the tenth century the sense of Roman or Lombard ancestry survived patchily, as did the sense of Frankish, Burgundian, and Roman ancestry in France, and is equally difficult to interpret. Whatever it meant in different contexts it seems to have cut across a good many political divisions, both locally and on a larger scale. Significantly, the kingdom of Lombardy was by now often known alternatively as the kingdom of Italy, and its boundaries were very unclear. When Charlemagne conquered it he had, after all, been called in by the pope. Both he and Otto I exercised authority in Rome

---

[120] Leuschner, *Germany* [547], pp. xvi–xviii.
[121] *M.G.H. Staatsschriften* [55], i. 102, 108–15.
[122] *M.G.H. Scriptores* [54], xvii. 238: differently interpreted by Leuschner, *Germany* [547], pp. xvi–xviii.

and had ambitions further south.[123] Liutprand of Cremona, acting as Otto's ambassador in Constantinople, told the eastern emperor that the people (*gens incola*) and language of that part of southern Italy which the emperor claimed showed it to be part of the kingdom of Italy.[124] Obviously he was making the best case he could for his master, but what he said reflected the real difficulties which contemporaries found in reconciling current political divisions with feelings of a shared culture and history. In practice German kings and emperors could manage little more than intermittent control of parts of Italy. When ideas about the liberty of the church embroiled the papacy in conflict with them even the north began to slip from their grasp, so that, by the time that Frederick I had given up his attempts to bully the towns of Lombardy into submission, regnal solidarity had disappeared apparently beyond recall. The contrast of this quick dissolution of regnal feeling with the contemporary experience of France is hard to explain, especially if one ignores the later history that would otherwise lull one into assuming that France *ought* to be united and Italy divided. Perhaps some explanation could be found in the uncertain boundaries and identity of the Lombard or Italian kingdom, its frequent changes of dynasty, and its nearly always absent kings. All these must have made unity difficult in the face both of a papacy which claimed independent control of Rome and the patrimony, and of towns which could harness local patriotism so effectively. By the thirteenth century it was the city-states, not the kingdom, which seemed to constitute those natural entities which contemporaries thought of as peoples.[125]

The problem of the south had meanwhile been brusquely solved by its Norman invaders. Writing at the end of the eleventh century, William of Apulia said that the first of them taught their manners and language to the local malefactors who joined them, in order to create a single people (*gens efficiatur ut una*).[126] This says more about current ideas of

---

[123] Arnaldi, 'Regnum Langobardorum' [222].
[124] *Opera* [50], 179 (*Legatio*, c. 7).
[125] See pp. 171-2, 213.
[126] *Geste de Robert Guiscard* [41], 108.

normal peoples than about the language and customs that came to prevail in Norman Italy, but it is undeniable that the Normans seem to have created some sort of people, in the terms of the time, out of their conquests. By 1129 Roger II of Sicily had eliminated his mainland rivals, and the disputed papal election of the following year gave him the opportunity to secure a grant of the crown of what Anacletus apparently called the kingdom of Sicily, Calabria, Apulia, and all the lands granted by his predecessors to Robert Guiscard, Roger Borsa, and William of Apulia, with Sicily as the *caput regni*.[127] The title of tenth-century Germany can hardly compete for amorphousness with this lot, yet two chroniclers within the new kingdom pass over the papal share in its creation, making it purely a matter of internal consensus. The kingdom was internally divided in language, legal tradition, and even in religion, and Sicily was perhaps the most divided part of all, but that did not prevent it from being the 'head of the kingdom' and the base of royal power. It was from Sicily that Roger built up the government which bound his kingdom together in much the same way as did the very similar government of England.[128] The similarity of the two kingdoms did not derive from some cultural, let alone 'racial' peculiarity of their Norman rulers, but from the improvements (as they saw them) that ambitious and ruthless kings could bring to traditional methods by making use of the literacy and numeracy which had become available in the twelfth century. Contemporaries described Roger as a tyrant, but that was because he was arbitrary and cruel and threatened the liberties of the church, not—so far as contemporary evidence suggests—because he was some sort of oriental despot who therefore dispensed with the normal consultative methods of legislation and government.[129] However arbitrary he and his successors were and however elaborate the protocol of their court and documents, their leading subjects continued to cherish much the same ideals of government as did their western contemporaries. When William I failed to confide in his nobles they

---

[127] *Italia Pontificia* [140], viii. 37 (no. 137).

[128] Jamison, 'Norman Administration' [491], 244–5, 265–70.

[129] Wieruszowski, 'Roger II, *Rex-Tyrannus*' [751]; Calisse, *Storia del Parlamento in Sicilia* [102], 285–325.

rebelled in alliance with the larger towns. Their spokesmen claimed to represent all the noble men of the kingdom in asking that the customs first introduced by Robert Guiscard and observed by Count Roger I should be restored. Traditional ideas survived into the thirteenth century, when new taxes and oppressions were blamed on the wickedness and foreignness of kings and people looked back to the better days of the twelfth.[130]

Frederick II's death brought war and trouble to Sicily as to Germany. According to one chronicler the people of Palermo who rose against Charles of Anjou in the revolt which became known as the Sicilian Vespers sent messengers throughout the land (*per terram*) to ask everyone to join them for the common welfare and the liberty of Sicily (*per quos petunt universitates intrare per syndicos ad bonum statum communem et Siciliae libertatem*).[131] The ambassador they sent to ask the king of Aragon for help spoke on behalf of the *gens* of Sicily as well as of the *Panormitanus populus*. How far Sicily, on this occasion, meant the island and how far it meant the whole kingdom, is difficult to tell now and may have been unclear then. The original 'head of the kingdom' was the centre of the revolt but in parts of the ambassador's speech the *gens* he represents seems to be that of the whole kingdom.[132] In any case the divisions which inevitably accompanied the collapse of government seem to have been geographical rather than 'ethnic' or religious. The rebels of 1282 resented foreign oppression all the more because they had been made into a community by being governed together—by being a kingdom. The xenophobia of the Sicilian Vespers, like that of thirteenth-century England, was the explosive result of a combination of foreign conquest and oppression with accepted ideas about peoples, their rights, and their natural relationship to their kings. In 1302 Sicily was divided from the mainland by the manipulations of international high politics rather than by any popular separatism, but the success of high politics always depended on voluntary submission: rival

[130] Hugh Falcandus, *Liber* [43], 64–5; Runciman, *Sicilian Vespers* [670], 125–31.

[131] Calisse, *Storia del Parlamento in Sicilia* [102], 312.

[132] *Rerum Ital. Scrip.* [56], N.S. xiii (3), 12; cf. the story of the baronial plot (also on behalf of all): ibid. N.S. xxxiv (1), 8.

kings were never able to ignore pressures from below. Royal government had always been most effective in Sicily and so the sense of being a community was strongest there, in defiance of the sort of 'ethnic' unity which modern nationalism tends to assume.

The conclusion I draw from this survey of kingdoms, incomplete as it is, is that throughout the four centuries under review, the inhabitants of the kingdoms I have discussed, or at least the politically active among them, seem to have taken for granted that their own kingdoms comprised peoples of some sort of naturally collective character. Both oppression —or what was perceived as oppression—and conflict with outsiders stimulated the collective solidarity of kingdoms, but only because people already thought of them in this sort of way. They did not invariably claim that the inhabitants of kingdoms were of common origin and descent: Sicily, so far as I know, understandably enough lacked a myth of the usual sort. So, of course, did the Latin kingdom of Jerusalem. None the less the people of Jerusalem were soon pressed together by their isolation among enemies into thinking of themselves as a people.[133] Laws there were made and regnal custom was evolved in the usual sort of regnal assemblies. Royal elections and the growth of solidarity among the nobility were no obstacle to royal power so long as kings could lead their men to victory against the enemy.[134] The election of a king, in Jerusalem as in the west, was an anxious business to be undertaken only when an obvious heir was not available. In the thirteenth century, when the king was absent and his *bailli* seemed oppressive, the great men, knights, and burgesses (*li riche home et li chevalier et li borgeis*) of the surviving remnant of the kingdom bound themselves by oaths within the framework of an already existing fraternity to protect their rights. Their *communia* or *commun de la terre*, as it was variously known, apparently had officers and councillors, in addition to a bell to sound alarms, but it was probably as amorphous in character and membership as similar associations in the west.[135] Just as

---

[133] Fulcher of Chartres, *Hist.* [30], 748-9 (III. 37).
[134] Prawer, *Latin Kingdom* [636], 94-109.
[135] *Rec. Hist. Croisades: Occ.* [62], ii. 391-3; Prawer, *Crusader Institutions* [635], 57-63.

the kingdom of Jerusalem was the melting-pot of western customs so it was a mirror of western political values and assumptions.

If a sense of common descent was not essential, however, it could nevertheless exist in cases, like that of Scotland, where one would have thought that divided language and still-remembered movements of population would have made it almost as anomalous as it would have been in Sicily or Jerusalem. On the other hand, no one seems to have been worried by the cases where two kingdoms shared a supposed common descent or a language or by the similarities which existed between the laws of all kingdoms. The whole set of ideas about the collective nature of peoples was too un-systematic to create claims to autonomy, or to authority over another people, which would otherwise not have been made. Feelings of community could neither create nor divide king-doms on their own. To do that the ambitions and machina-tions of great men were also necessary. Nevertheless, though politicians could manipulate solidarity and shape the units within which it functioned, its character was determined not by them but by the beliefs about loyalty, law, custom, and government within which they too had been brought up. Within kingdoms, conflict was often caused by personal ambitions and feuds rather than by collective grievances, but assumptions about collective rights and collective activity underlay all of it and could be used by the unscrupulous as well as expressed by the public-spirited. Rebels and dissidents formed collective groups with the same unselfconscious ease as did the law-abiding, unhampered by rules about the constitutions and powers of corporate or non-corporate bodies. Some who called their associations 'communes' may have liked the word because of its revolutionary connotations, but none of them seem to have wanted to follow the urban model of communal government to the extent of being republican. Kingdoms needed kings to rule over them, lead their armies, and preside over their assemblies.

Regnal assemblies and representation

The traditional rules and assumptions about the necessity of consultation for legislation, judgement, and the general conduct of government which can be deduced from the records of what went on in lesser communities naturally applied equally to kingdoms. For kingdoms, moreover, because they were regarded as the most important units of government, we have relatively good evidence throughout the period both of actual consultation in practice and of the belief that it ought to take place. Like the assemblies through which the lesser communities were judged and governed, royal councils seem to have been variable and amorphous bodies, whose character was presumably determined by the usual combination of apparently conflicting values: values which concerned custom and collective judgement and encouraged wide participation, and values which concerned due order and hierarchy and imposed on great men the duty and right to speak on behalf of the rest. When kings decided to take counsel with a wider group than their everyday advisers and assistants one reason prompting them to do so must have been that the business needed the advice and consent of a more fully representative assembly. Those modern historians who have been at pains to deny the representative character of, for instance, 'the Old English *witenagemot*' have been guilty of rather the same sort of anachronism as were their predecessors who saw it as the precursor of the modern parliament. Both were assuming that representation implied election. Before the fourteenth century, however, the representative character of royal councils was not derived from the election of their members any more than it was connected with the association between particular members and any particular part of the kingdom or rank of society.[136] By the early fourteenth century these new ways of thinking about representation may have just been beginning to develop but even then they were articulated in ways which distinguish them clearly from most modern ideas about it.

Abbo of Fleury (d. 1004) was presumably taking it for granted that great men would represent the rest when he said that the election of a king was made by the agreement of the

---

[136] For ideas of counsel and representation similar to those of medieval Europe: Gluckman, *Barotse Jurisprudence* [789], 31-2; Richards and Kuper, *Councils in Action* [818], 1-28; cf. Pitkin, *Concept of Representation* [814].

whole realm.[137] Whether such an election was the mere confirmation of an obvious heir, an agonized decision between
rivals, or an anxious search for a worthy candidate to fill an
heirless throne, the same sort of people would participate as
had formerly advised the last king and would continue to
advise the new one. They would also presumably constitute
the chief witnesses of the coronation and would, on behalf
of their fellow-subjects, hear the new king's promises to rule
justly. Thereafter ceremonial crown-wearings would repeat
and strengthen the link, first symbolically forged at the
coronation, between the majesty and holiness of a king and
his duty to rule justly and with consent.

Some royal councils of the tenth century look almost like
ecclesiastical synods, since they appear in the records as
dominated by the clergy and their concerns.[138] Given that
kings were at this time supposed to look after the church as
part of their normal duties, however, this is not surprising
and should not be taken to imply that they had to consult
more about church matters than about anything else. Consultations about church matters would attract more churchmen and would be more likely to be well recorded. Other
consultations no doubt took place of which we know much
less. In so far as they are recorded at all it is in ways which
make some of them look more like what we, according
to our way of classifying business and meetings, might
call law-courts or even military musters.[139] All these distinctions are anachronistic, as are those sometimes drawn between
'feudal' and other councils. There was nothing particularly
'feudal' about consultation: the presence of clergy, if not of
others, meant that few if any royal councils were composed
solely of feudal tenants in chief, and it is very unlikely that
anyone at the time would have noticed whether they were or
not. What historians refer to as the 'Old English *witenagemot*'
and the Norman 'feudal Great Council' or *curia regis* look
different only because historians use Old English words for the
first and modern English or Latin for the second—throwing
in the word 'feudal' for further obfuscation.

[137] *P.L.* [60], cxxxix, col. 478.
[138] *Councils and Synods* [204], i (1), pp. vi, ix; Krause, 'Königtum und
Rechtsordnung' [512], 34–5. [139] Bisson, 'Military Origins' [258].

In practice kings must often have consulted less widely than contemporary ideas of what was right, vague as they were, may have implied they should. The bigger kingdoms were, and the more actively kings tried to govern them, the more there was to consult about, but the more kings must have slipped into relying primarily on consultation with their well-informed and professional advisers. As a result, magnates who came only to formal councils at great feasts might complain that they were not being properly consulted, since the real decisions seemed to be taken elsewhere. For kings wide consultation increasingly involved at best delay and at worst opposition, above all when it concerned the key issues of military service and taxation. According to traditional ideas, neither ought to be imposed on free men without their consent. By the twelfth century warfare was becoming more organized, armies were larger, and kings were trying to keep them in the field longer, so that demands for men and money were beginning to outrun anything covered by old ideas and customs. The professional or semi-professional soldiers on whom kings increasingly came to rely needed to be paid, and as inflation set in they needed to be paid much more than could be covered by the sort of taxes that people traditionally thought right—that is, aids given freely and willingly by loyal subjects whose lords asked them to help out in an emergency.

Where the need for military service and taxation was most acute, therefore, the rules about consultation were clarified through conflict, and new kinds of assembly began to develop. Both the chronology of their development and the way that contemporaries referred to them suggest that changes were not seen as the result of any new principles of representation and consent. New methods of consultation were the result not of new theories but of the pressure of new conflicts on old ideas. Spain, which is excluded from discussion here, would provide some of the best and earliest evidence to support these arguments,[140] but they can also be illustrated from the kingdoms so far discussed.

The long and well-recorded conflicts between king and barons make the case of England particularly illuminating. It

[140] Procter, *Curia and Cortes* [638].

is worth noticing, for a start, that as controversy about taxation mounted in the thirteenth century, so the usual references to consultation and consent in royal documents which announced levies became fuller. The lists of those consenting to aids were on occasion extended from the usual 'archbishops, bishops, abbots, earls, and barons of the whole realm' to include knights, freemen, and even villeins (*villani*), although the meetings at which the levy was agreed were the normal assemblies of magnates and their followers:[141] when opposition was expected it made sense to emphasize that consent had been given on behalf of all.

The first attempt to set out the proper procedure for summoning an assembly to consent to taxes came in Magna Carta, though clause 14 was probably designed more to ensure that consultation did not involve undue trouble and delay than to define the sort of people who were entitled to attend. The barons had demanded that aids (apart from those for the king's ransom, his eldest daughter's marriage, and his eldest son's knighting) should only be taken by common counsel (*per commune consilium*) of the kingdom.[142] It was therefore in the king's interest to limit the arguments and delays that might be caused once sea-lawyers got to work on the old vague norms of tradition: clause 14, which sets out the procedure of summons, and has no corresponding clause in the baronial demands, may have been inserted from the king's side. What it says is that summonses would be sent direct to archbishops, bishops, abbots, earls, and greater barons, while sheriffs and bailiffs would issue a general summons to all who held of the king in chief. The summons would give due notice of purpose, time, and place, and the business would then go ahead accordingly, ignoring absentees. The combination of the reference to tenants in chief with the description of the three sorts of aid which clause 12 exempted from the procedure gives the whole thing a very 'feudal' look in the sense that English historians use the

---

[141] e.g. *Rot. Litt. Pat.* [178], i. 55; *Close Rolls* [105], *1234-7*, 545-6; Matthew Paris, *Chron. Maj.* [52], iii. 230, and cf. iii. 380-3, iv. 181-2. For the particular thirteenth-century English sense of *villani*: Hyams, *King, Lords and Peasants* [485], 242, 250 n. *et passim*.

[142] Articles of the Barons, c. 32; Magna Carta, c. 12 (Holt, *Magna Carta* [475], 308-10, 320-22); Langmuir, 'Per Commune Consilium' [522].

word. That is probably misleading. In the context of regnal assemblies (as distinct from that of reliefs or wardship, for instance) the distinction between tenants in chief and other great men was probably insignificant to contemporaries. There was a large overlap but that does not mean that tenure was an essential criterion for attendance. The bishop of Rochester, for instance, technically held his lands from the archbishop of Canterbury, not the king, but all bishops were natural advisers to kings. Bishops attended royal councils primarily as shepherds of their flocks, the representatives of their clergy, and the guardians of the spiritual welfare of the laity, not just because they—or most of them—were tenants in chief.[143] The distinction between 'feudal' and 'non-feudal' taxes, indeed between all the different sorts of taxes, was also less clear to contemporaries than to historians. Many people who were not tenants in chief had contributed to the aid for the marriage of Henry II's daughter and even more to Richard I's ransom.[144] It is surely unlikely, in the circumstances, that the barons intended their restrictions to exclude the sort of taxes that John had levied on the movable property of his subjects at large: their immediate successors did not interpret the rules in that way. Given that those who consented did so on behalf of others all these inexactitudes and overlaps did not much matter. Seen against the background of past practice and terminology, clause 14 was a fair attempt to ensure that the king could get taxes agreed within a reasonable time without preventing the great men of the realm, and as many other suitable and public-spirited people as possible, from having a chance to air their views and, if they were determined, reject his demands.

In the years after Magna Carta some individuals and groups succeeded in avoiding taxes by claiming not to have been consulted, but they got away with it more because the government was anxious to avoid trouble than because the general principle of representative consent to taxation and legislation had been superseded.[145] On the contrary, the principle

---

[143] Chew, *Ecclesiastical Tenants in Chief* [318], 175-6.
[144] Reynolds, 'Farm of London' [174], 224-5; Hoyt, *Royal Demesne* [481], 109-15.
[145] Holt, *Magna Carta* [475], 287-8 and 'Prehistory of Parliament' [477], 25-6.

continued to be clearly reflected in the assemblies, sometimes called parliaments, which were fairly regularly held for the discussion of general business, including taxation, during the 1240s and 1250s, unsatisfactory as the barons found them as a means of influencing royal policy.[146] It is also visible in the new constitution imposed on Henry III in 1258. Twelve men were then chosen by the king and twelve by the 'community of the kingdom' to propose reforms. Each group of twelve elected two from the other group, and these four then elected the council of fifteen which was to advise the king on a permanent basis. In addition to the council of fifteen a panel of twelve was elected by the barons—or by the community, which apparently came to the same thing—with the duty of attending the three parliaments which were to be held each year and of consulting with the king and fifteen 'on behalf of the whole community of the land about common business' (*pur tut le commun de la tere de commun busoine*).[147] How they were elected is not explained but they do not seem to be meant to represent any different group or interest from that represented by the fifteen. They simply supplemented and strengthened the representation of the whole community. The scheme reflects much the same objectives as were embodied in the indirect elections and layers of councils currently adopted by some towns: to secure a consensus based on wide participation and on due respect for hierarchy, tradition, and order.

The summoning of elected knights and townsmen to English parliaments in the later thirteenth century has become the subject of such acute and complicated controversy that it is difficult to realise how uncontroversial it seems to have been at the time.[148] That, however, may be a clue to understanding as much of the problem as is most directly relevant to the subject of this book. Despite the partisan character of the parliament of 1265 to which Simon de Montfort summoned representatives of counties and towns, his contemporaries do not seem to have noticed that

[146] Treharne, 'Nature of Parliament' [716]; Langmuir, 'Politics and Parliaments' [523].

[147] *Documents of Baronial Reform* [198], 104, 110.

[148] Fryde and Miller, *Studies* [428] has a recent, though short, bibliography.

their presence marked a constitutional innovation. Representatives had sometimes been summoned from towns and
shire courts before this to discuss particular business with the
king,[149] but 1265 seems to be the first time that they were all
summoned together to what purported to be a full and regular
parliament. Thereafter the precedent was followed, though
sporadically, by Edward I. Chroniclers, however, were not
much interested: they sometimes commented that parliaments
large but, apart from Bartholomew Cotton, do not seem to
have been interested in the presence of elected members, let
alone in the varying list of towns which were represented.[150]
In 1297 the king was accused of getting consent to an un-
popular tax from the people (*plebe*) who happened to be
around in his chamber,[151] but none of the recorded complaints
of that year specified how parliaments ought to be composed.
The magnates wanted large and open meetings, but in an
emergency they still felt that they could speak for all. As late
as 1322 the Statute of York, deliberately and formally reserv-
ing important constitutional issues for decision in parliament,
said that such matters were to be decided 'by our lord the
king and by the assent of prelates, earls, and barons, and
the community (*communalte*) of the realm as has been
accustomed hitherto'.[152] The statute referred variously to
those present at the parliament of York itself as prelates,
earls, and barons, and either *le commun du roialme* or *tote
la commune du roialme. Communalte, commun,* and *commune* all meant the same, but whether they yet in this context meant the elected knights and burgesses whom later ages
would call the House of Commons is unclear. The point at
issue was that parliaments discussing important affairs should
be big, public, and full enough to seem to represent the
whole community of the kingdom. Probably by this time
the accumulation of precedents meant that that implied the
presence of knights of the shires and representatives of a fair
number of towns, but controversy had not yet fastened upon
that point in such a way as to clarify it. Nor indeed had

[149] White, 'Early Instances' [748].

[150] Based on impression (not a search of the sources), but there seem to be
few citations in the abundant secondary literature to suggest otherwise.

[151] *Flores Hist.* [28], iii. 295–6.

[152] *Statutes of the Realm* [190], i. 190.

controversy fastened on the difference, if any, between meetings which were called parliaments and those described as *colloquia, tractatus*, great councils, and so on. Chancery clerks may have had their own definitions for their own purposes[153] but these are in the circumstances unlikely to have been consistent through time or to have affected wider usage.

Against this background it may be possible to bypass some of the controversies which surround the first summons of 'the commons'. It was not at first seen as involving a new kind of representation, only a fuller representation of the old kind. They were not summoned because they represented a lower rank or a wider range of society, for the magnates—and indeed the king himself, in some circumstances—already represented everyone. They were summoned because they were able to speak, with more direct and immediate knowledge than most great men could, on behalf of those who ran local affairs in the shire and borough courts of the kingdom. They were not elected by haphazard slices of countryside but by the members of those courts which were collectively responsible for doing justice, administering counties and towns, and, not least, assessing and raising the taxes which parliaments, however constituted, granted to the king. Hence the vagueness about elections: it was assumed that shire and borough courts would make their elections by the same sort of compromise between the will of the president and that of the members as applied to the rest of their business. If, in the early days, the king or the magnates occasionally nominated people to speak for their shires, the nominees would not necessarily seem to be any the less representative—unless of course conflict had already created distrust and polarized ideas of eligibility.[154] The sort of men who were elected knights of the shire must in any case have been socially indistinguishable from the less important of the still unstable list of those who were summoned individually. At least one in the early fourteenth century moved back and forth between the two categories and as late as 1383 another found himself simultaneously in both. At that date his position was

---

[153] Richardson and Sayles, 'Parliaments and Great Councils' [658].
[154] Holt, 'Prehistory of Parliament' [477], 9-18.

recognized to be anomalous, but one is tempted to guess that there may have been precedents which were not recorded.[155]

To argue whether knights and burgesses were summoned to consent to taxes, witness judgements, or act as channels of communication between court and country, is therefore to split hairs. They were summoned for all these reasons, just as the magnates were. Their consent to taxes was at first no more and no less essential than was that of the barons, so that it is meaningless to ask whether the knights and burgesses alone could or could not refuse it. Under Henry III the magnates often refused outright. Under his son they more often bargained and temporized, but that was probably more a testimony to Edward I's character and toughness than to the nature of his arguments. Meanwhile, so long as great men naturally took the lead, and they and the knights and burgesses saw their interests as the same, there would be no need and no opportunity to decide whether the elected members could act on their own.

Nevertheless, practice by 1300 was evolving in a way that at least foreshadows further distinctions. The early system of using elected representatives to report on local affairs may have become rather overlaid in the general parliaments of the later part of the century, but the controversies that then surrounded taxation ensured that the link between knights and burgesses and their constituencies would be emphasized in a manner that in the end made them seem the only truly representative members of parliament. From the 1280s writs ordering elections used a variety of formulae to stress the binding nature of parliamentary decisions and to insist that taxes granted by representatives would have to be paid.[156] That did not reflect new theories but it helped to create them. The magnates' right to speak on behalf of others was beginning to be undermined, for now the others had their own representatives who attended on the explicit understanding that they—and therefore, it might be inferred, they alone—bound their constituents by their assent. At the same

---

[155] Powell and Wallis, *House of Lords* [632], 314, 391. No example is noted by Edwards, 'Personnel of the Commons': Fryde and Miller, *Studies* [428], 150-67.

[156] Edwards, *'Plena Potestas'* in Fryde and Miller, *Studies* [428], 136-49.

time, the clergy's reluctance to pay taxes for secular purposes, and even to attend lay assemblies, combined with Edward I's efforts to divide his critics (by, for instance, getting consent to customs duties separately from the merchants most directly affected), further emphasized the separate interests of separate groups and their separate representatives. By the 1320s it was possible to maintain that the two knights of a shire carried more weight in granting aids than the greatest earl, and the proctors of the clergy of a diocese than their bishop, and to use the word *communitates* as a synonym for the elected representatives.[157] Such ideas may not, however, have been widely held and it is hard to believe that they were already around in 1300.

In France conflicts about taxation affected regnal assemblies rather differently, but the differences seem to derive more from the way custom happened to develop than from fundamentally different ideas of what was right. Such great assemblies as were held tended to be the traditional, all-purpose affairs, dominated by great men who were assumed to represent the whole kingdom, and they did not turn into the main forum for negotiation of taxes. When people were summoned to negotiate taxes it was more often by regions than all at once. Whether this was because of the size of the kingdom and the diversity of the local precedents, or because kings consciously thought it wiser to divide potential opposition in this way, it is impossible to say. As it was, kings of France seem to have got away for a long time with taxes that were initially granted at everyday councils, without any special effort to make them larger and more representative.[158] Hard bargaining still took place, but it came at a later stage, after the formal grant of the tax. The best evidence of this concerns those towns and other local communities which already had a measure of autonomy in local government and were accustomed to pay their taxes and dues as collective lump sums. Since many of them had charters which exempted them—or which they claimed exempted them—from all dues not mentioned in the charters, separate negotiations

---

[157] *Parliamentary Texts* [59], 77 (*Modus*, c. 23).

[158] Langmuir, 'Concilia' [520] and 'Politics and Parliaments' [523]; Strayer, *Studies* [706], 1-97.

with each were more or less inevitable. That did not mean that towns had to work in isolation from each other. Sometimes they had to send representatives to meetings which royal officials held to negotiate the taxes of a whole region or province at once. Sometimes appeals against taxes went to the king's court in Paris, where a number of local communities could be represented at a single session. When days were set aside for business from a whole province the result could turn, in Bisson's phrase, into something like 'centralized provincial assemblies'.[159] There must have been many opportunities to compare notes and concert strategies. In these circumstances town representatives, though bullied by royal officials and perhaps overawed by the royal court, would not be overruled by the rest of a great assembly as were their opposite numbers in England. Careful definition of their power to bind their constituents was therefore all the more desirable in the interest of the taxpayers, and the evidence shows that French townsmen were no guileless victims of the royal manipulation of phrases drawn from Roman law. Whatever the king and his officials thought and said about the duty of subjects to consent to taxes, the negotiations they conducted with French towns throughout the thirteenth century implied that the towns were within their rights in bargaining and even sometimes in refusing to pay. They were certainly not afraid to try.[160]

As in England there was at first no clear distinction between the types of taxes paid by particular categories of people. It was not until the fourteenth century that a line was drawn between the obligations of the royal domain and those of the rest of the kingdom, and when that happened it was more a convenient way of cutting through a mass of conflicting arguments and precedents than an application of any existing rule.[161] Nevertheless, the practicalities of negotiation with the privileged local communities marked them off from the rest of the kingdom and, in the mean time, as the government manipulated the possibilities of various sorts of taxes,

---

[159] Bisson, 'Consultative Functions' [257], 368 et passim; Stephenson, 'Les Aides' [698].
[160] Brown, 'Representation' [281].
[161] Brown, 'Customary Aids' [279], 191 n. et passim.

another distinct category of taxpayers began to emerge as worth taxing separately, even if it meant separate negotiations. This group comprised all those relatively large landowners, conventionally known as nobles, who, especially in the north, generally stood more or less apart from the local communities which paid their taxes collectively, and therefore invited separate taxation. Although, however, the taxes which Philip IV and his advisers devised to be paid by the rich tended—because most of the rich were the sort of people who were called noble—to be paid by nobles, the concept of nobility was as yet very loose.[162] Nobles did not yet have any particular privileges or obligations as taxpayers. Nor would it have been possible to draw up clear and consistent lists of those who might or should attend the regional or regnal assemblies to which barons, great men (*granz homes*), and other nobles (as they were variously described) were summoned to negotiate taxes. These assemblies were certainly not 'feudal' in the sense that English historians use the word—that is, they were not composed only of those who held their land directly of the king.[163]

The earliest evidence of resistance to taxes in France seems to concern towns and other local communities rather than nobles. This may be an illusion of the sources, but it is possible that in such a large kingdom as France, without frequent regnal assemblies in which great men could give a lead to the rest as they did in England, nobles were at first too widely scattered to be able to co-ordinate their resistance to taxes. They also lacked the local solidarity which long collective responsibility for raising as well as granting taxes had given to the local communities of humbler people. Solidarity, however, became greater as taxes got higher: in 1318, after the great eruptions of the end of Philip IV's reign and the consequent concessions, regional assemblies of nobles were even—exceptionally—allowed to organize the raising of their own taxes and were even told that they could supervise the spending. When Philip V declared to some recalcitrant ecclesiastical taxpayers that the king was not accustomed to bargain about his aids he was whistling in the

---

[162] See also above, p. 223; Rogozinski, 'Ennoblement' [664].
[163] Taylor, 'Composition of Baronial Assemblies' [714].

dark:[164] the twists and turns of fiscal policy in the previous fifty years tell another story. By now, however, the separate taxes and separate negotiations with nobles, towns, and, of course, clergy, had become rooted in custom. Nobles still often spoke in a general way on behalf of everyone, but it was natural that when kings negotiated taxes through either regnal or regional assemblies those assemblies should begin to take the form of what later became known as estates. In 1300, however, that was as much in the future as were the two houses of parliament in England.

Thirteenth-century German kings were seldom in a position to raise the sort of taxes that might have emphasized the difference between different sorts of taxpayer. Nevertheless they held general assemblies and Rudolf I's first great court at Nuremberg was attended by 'princes, an honourable crowd of counts and barons, and a great multitude of nobles and common people (*plebeiorum*)'.[165] The terminology, seen in a thirteenth-century context, does not suggest that either this or the next regnal meeting that he held were in any sense merely 'feudal' or composed only of those who could reasonably be called 'territorial princes'. Citizens of Lübeck were expected to attend the Nuremberg meeting as representatives of their city,[166] and in view of the independence and importance of the German towns by this time, it is quite likely that others were summoned too. There was, however, no reason why the ranks should meet separately and no evidence that they did so. Presumably the great men took the lead and the rest followed.

The kingdom of Sicily provides clearer evidence of the summons of elected representatives, and of their summons in connection with taxes. In 1231 a tax was granted by prelates, counts, lords, and many citizens of the kingdom.[167] The following year, according to a chronicler, letters were sent to summon two of the better men from every town (*de qualibet civitate vel castro*) to an assembly to be held for the welfare of the kingdom and the general profit.[168] In 1267

[164] Brown, 'Royal Necessity' [282], 164 n. *et passim.*
[165] *M.G.H. Const.* [160], iii, no. 72.
[166] Ibid. no. 58.
[167] Marongiu, *Medieval Parliaments* [572], 105-6.
[168] *Rerum Ital. Scrip.* [56], N.S. vii (2), 183, 205.

Clement IV told Charles of Anjou to consult the prelates, barons, and local communities (*locorum communitates*) of the realm before taxing them.[169] General assemblies continued to be held during the rest of the century, presumably including the same wide range of people but not in formally divided estates.[170] The area ruled by the pope, though not strictly a kingdom, shows the same sort of thing. Consultation was provoked by the financial and military needs of the thirteenth-century popes, and took the form of either general or regional assemblies in which nobles and abbots met along with representatives of towns and lower clergy. The town representatives dominated the meetings numerically and perhaps in other ways too. It was not apparently until the fourteenth century that the powers of representatives began to be defined. Then, as in France, it was the towns themselves that took the initiative by limiting their delegates' powers to bind them.[171] Even at the gates of Rome, and in a polity which surely did not lack canon lawyers, representative institutions were being shaped more by the practicalities of negotiations within the traditional framework of collective consent, than by ideas drawn from Roman law by rulers who wanted to browbeat their subjects.

The unimportance of new theories as a stimulus to new kinds of representation is only one of the conclusions which emerges from this survey. Another is that throughout the period contemporaries thought of their assemblies in unitary terms. That is, although elected representatives of various local groups were beginning to be summoned, people did not yet think of their assemblies in terms of any theory of estates. They did, of course, think of society in terms of 'orders', whether they visualized these as embodying different ranks or different functions or both,[172] but they did not yet assume that orders needed to be separately represented. There is no evidence that, even in France, where nobles, clergy, and representatives of local communities commonly negotiated their taxes separately, anyone thought that this threefold

---

[169] Martène, *Thesaurus* [151], ii, col. 445.

[170] Calisse, *Storia del Parlamento* [102], 285-325; cf. 78-83.

[171] Waley, *Papal State* [735], 52-3, 110-20, 164, 304-6.

[172] Among much recent work on orders, see e.g. Aubenas, 'Inconscience de juristes' [226]; Duby, *Trois ordres* [382]; Oexle, 'Funktionale Dreiteilung' [609].

division corresponded significantly to the common images of the division of society. It would have been odd if they had, for the local communities which were represented were more or less urban in character; if there were only three orders, and they were envisaged as those who pray, those who fight, and those who work, then the *bourgeois* formed an odd and inadequate representation of the third order. Orders did not simply evolve naturally into estates: assemblies were divided to deal with taxes, and then people subsequently began to approximate these divisions to orders in order to explain and justify the way that they had become rooted in custom.

In 1300 that conceptualization was still in the future, but hindsight can help us to detect the forces that produced it. The first break in the unitary kingdom had come from the drawing apart of the clergy. In the ninth century Hincmar had thought that royal assemblies should be held in two parts, ecclesiastical and lay,[173] and though this may not generally have happened, it was the consistent policy of church reformers from the late eleventh century on that the clergy should distance themselves as far as possible from secular affairs. In practice, no king could dispense with the advice of his higher clergy, and thirteenth-century popes themselves seem to have assumed that the clergy formed an integral part of the general consultative process both in Sicily and in their own dominions. In so far as clerical ideas influenced lay assemblies it was through this sort of contact, rather than through purely academic ideas. Papal taxation of the clergy needed consent just as any other taxation did, and it started early enough for clerical assemblies, and their evasive arguments, to provide a useful model to laymen on occasion.[174] Nevertheless, clerical taxes were normally negotiated separately, and when the lower clergy began to elect proctors to represent them in making the grants, they met apart from the laity. It was easy to envisage the order of those who pray as a separate political estate.

The separation between nobles and what was to become known as the Third Estate can be traced back to the way that

[173] *P.L.*. [60], cxxv, col. 1006 (*De Ord. Pal.* c. 35).
[174] Powicke, *Henry III* [633], 344; Marongiu, *Medieval Parliaments* [572], 37–41.

taxes began to be negotiated in the thirteenth century. The resulting distinction was not feudal: that is, assemblies were not consistently divided according to their members' place in any feudal hierarchy or according to their type of tenure. Nor did the division result, as divisions between representative bodies did in some towns, from a conscious recognition of conflict between ranks or classes so that their interests had to be separately represented. Once the division had been made, separate interests were more easily articulated and recognized, but that does not seem to have been its original purpose. The only purpose seems to have been to facilitate the raising of taxes. Even that statement barely allows for the resulting anomalies: in England the division that became final did not accord with that between tax rates, but looks as if it came from the way that the requirement of binding decisions about taxes undermined the old idea that the community was represented as a whole and not by individual delegates.

The distinction often drawn between 'true parliaments' and the earlier assemblies which had included no elected members would not have seemed important in the thirteenth century. Election was not essential to representation. There were no rules about who participated in elections and no one seems to have tried to ensure that there should be no overlap between those represented by elected members and those who attended themselves or were represented by their lords. The refusal of the knights and freeholders of Sussex to elect parliamentary representatives in the absence of great men who would themselves have attended parliament independently would have been nonsense in a system of estates, but, even though in this case it was probably just a ploy to avoid agreeing to taxes, it made sense within the framework of thirteenth-century ideas of communities and their representation.[175] *Communitas* and its derivatives could mean either the whole community, including great men (and in some contexts the king himself), or only the 'common people'. The ambiguity had apparently not yet struck those who were involved in regnal politics as one which needed resolution. Nor do they yet seem to have found it necessary

[175] *Parliamentary Writs* [166], i. 60.

to make formal rules about voting within assemblies, at least in any record which has come down to us. The general impression is that regnal assemblies worked through some kind of consensus or rough majority, influenced more or less by respect or fear of the king. Where groups were accustomed to meet apart they presumably voted apart too, but that again does not seem to have been carefully worked out. Only England, in the revolutionary years 1258-65, provides evidence of anything like the electoral refinements which were practised in towns. Even then the purpose was the same: it was unity and consensus, not the kind of division which was enshrined in later estates or houses of parliament. This was not because those who met in regnal assemblies were too unsophisticated politically to understand the use of numerical majorities: numerical majorities were simply not appropriate to the ideals, objectives, and assemblies of regnal politics.[176]

Kingdoms in political theory

In order to substantiate the argument that the representative institutions and political conflicts of kingdoms, together with lay ideas about kingdoms in general, were less influenced by academic lawyers and other learned writers than is often believed, a closer look at the way that academics wrote about kingdoms is necessary. The purpose here is not to attempt a survey of academic political thought as a whole, but to consider some of the ways that learned men referred to kings and kingdoms, and how their views seem to relate to the evidence of lay attitudes which has already been discussed. The first point that needs consideration is the extent to which intellectuals, like laymen, considered kingdoms to be naturally separate entities consisting of naturally separate and collective peoples. Most modern accounts of medieval political thought do not say much about this, except to suggest that in the later middle ages new humanistic ideas began to combine with new forms of government to shape an essentially new

[176] For some limitations and variations in the use of numerical majorities in other societies: Bailey, 'Decisions in Councils and Committees' [772]; Gilmour, *The Body Politic* [787], 220-1, 223-5; Mackenzie, *Power, Violence, Decision* [804], 204-11.

sort of national consciousness.[177] Perhaps that is because intellectual historians are, understandably, most interested in the more intellectual and more controversial part of their authors' treatises, with the result that they may overlook what is unreasoned and assumed. At all events the idea of naturally separate peoples and their inherited right to separate government seems to me to emerge from a number of works. It does so in the form of unreasoned premises, which I suggest rested on traditional assumptions and beliefs, rather than in the form of doctrines to be formulated and discussed.

Before the academic explosion of the twelfth century treatises of all sorts were comparatively rare. Nevertheless, both Regino of Prüm's remarks about the differences between peoples, and the many stories of the origins and descent of peoples and their kings to which I have already referred, suggest that scholars, like laymen, took kingdoms and peoples for granted. More surprisingly perhaps, there is testimony from Gregory VII himself. In a moment of stress Gregory might allege that the authority of kings and dukes came not from God but from the devil, but he also wrote to the king of Hungary that his kingdom, *sicut alia nobilissima regna*, ought to be subject to no one but the church of Rome.[178] In the mean time, however, the polemics of his conflicts, and of later conflicts between popes and emperors, produced a rather misleading body of literature. It is misleading because when it is seen in isolation it suggests that the idea of a universal empire, and its relations with a universal papacy, were the central if not the only problem of medieval political theory. In fact, of course, they were not.[179] Italian and German writers often referred to the secular ruler as the emperor rather than the king, while the imperialists among them found useful ammunition against the high and universal jurisdiction of the pope in the high and universal-sounding jurisdiction of the ancient emperors. Most of this was sheer

[177] e.g. Ullmann, *Medieval Foundations* [719], 118-22 *et passim*; Wilks, *Problem of Sovereignty* [753], 431-4.

[178] *M.G.H. Epist. Sel.* [158], ii. 218; Carlyle, *Mediaeval Political Theory* [309], iii. 96-8.

[179] Carlyle, *Mediaeval Political Theory* [309], v. 149; Lewis, *Medieval Political Ideas* [549], 430.

political solipsism: many of the arguments were seriously concerned only with Italy and Germany and were therefore simpler and more effective if they ignored other kingdoms.[180] Emperors themselves enjoyed glory refracted through splendid titles from the past, and liked to claim pre-eminence over kings, but they did not make serious claims to authority over such kingdoms as France or England.[181] When the king of France or his subjects declared that he had imperial powers or was an emperor in his kingdom they were not worrying about claims to overlordship from the emperor. Rather, they too wished to claim a share of the glory and authority which he seemed to get from Roman law, and were at the same time concerned to counter such papal claims to override royal power as might be based on the alleged delegation of imperial rights to the papacy by the Donation of Constantine.[182] All this polemic, however, only reached its full flower of ingenuity after 1300. It is a poor guide to beliefs before then.

Meanwhile, in the twelfth century, John of Salisbury wrote in terms of the prince (*princeps*), that is any ruler rather than specifically a king, but there can be little doubt that he was thinking primarily of the king of England, and that the *respublica* or body of which the king was the head was a kingdom and its people.[183] In the thirteenth century, with the reception of Aristotle, treatises on various aspects of politics become more numerous and more closely reasoned. When Thomas Aquinas discussed political matters his first preoccupation seems to have been to assimilate Aristotelian ideas to Christian values. In order to do this he had to ignore Aristotle's premise of human fulfilment in this life and break down (without comment) that which Aristotle calls simply political into social and political. Apparently that was a small price to pay for a rationally articulated conception of the state as an ethical and natural entity which fulfilled those who belonged to it just because they were unequal, exactly as a medieval kingdom was traditionally supposed to do. To

---

[180] For an exception: Post, *Studies* [631], 456-9.

[181] Leyser, 'Hand of St. James' [551]; Folz, *L'Idée d'empire* [418], 117-28.

[182] Lewis, *Medieval Political Ideas* [549], 450-5; Kantorowicz, *King's Two Bodies* [496], 288 n., 325-6; Post, *Studies* [631], 459.

[183] *Policraticus* [46], ii. 346 (VIII. 7) *et passim*; Rouse, 'John of Salisbury' [667], 704-8.

make the fit even neater, Aquinas, though following the Latin translations of Aristotle in describing the perfect community as a *civitas*, sometimes qualifies this by referring to a *civitas vel regnum*, a *civitas vel gens*, or a *civitas vel provincia*. He does not, incidentally, refer to any universal empire over the *civitates* or kingdoms.[184] Adapted like this, Aristotle did not so much provide fundamentally new concepts as make the old ones look rational.

Later Aristotelians elaborated Aquinas' formulation. Egidius Colonna extended Aristotle's hierarchy of communities by explicitly superimposing *regna* over *civitates*, instead of assimilating them as Aquinas had done.[185] Early in the fourteenth century Engelbert of Admont elaborated it further so as to distinguish *gentes* from *regna*, but he then seems to treat the two categories as much the same. The kingdoms of the world, he says, are diverse because of the diversity of *patriae*, languages, manners, and laws. Engelbert may theoretically have envisaged a kingdom which did not enjoy uniformity in these phenomena, but he believed that the peace of the kingdoms depended on their doing so. There could not be one law, or one king and emperor, over diverse *gentes* with their diverse laws, *patriae*, and inherited manners and rites (*patrios mores et ritus*). Engelbert accepted all this even though he was writing in favour of universal monarchy.[186] So, of course, was Dante. Yet he too conceded that a universal empire could not look after little local details, and that *nationes*, *regna*, and *civitates* had their own characteristics and needed their own laws.[187] Both of them, it seems, accepted the diversity of peoples and their kingdoms as a fact, and it looks as if, without thinking much about it, they probably also assumed that the diversity was inherited. John of Paris, with his Trojan Franks, made that explicit.[188]

There are some exceptions, of whom the clearest that I have

[184] *Summa* [75], i. 744, ii. 508, 786, iii. 383, v. 208 (Ia, q. 96, art. 4; Ia IIae, q. 72, art. 4, q. 105, art. 1; IIa IIae, q. 50, art. I; IIIae Suppl. q. 40, art. 6); *Sel. Pol. Writings* [74], 8 (*De Reg. Princ.* I. 1).

[185] Woolf, *Bartolus* [763], 274–5.

[186] *De Mutatione* [26], 754–812 (c. 12, 14, 16).

[187] *Opera* [22], 344, 349 (*De Mon.* I. 5, 7, 14).

[188] Above, p. 288. For canonist and Roman-law views on natural kingdoms see citations in Mochi-Onory, *Fonti canonistiche* [591]; Calasso, *I Glossatori* [299].

found is Marsilius of Padua, who argues that states are united not by any naturally occurring (i.e. involuntary) unitary form (*per formam aliquam unicam naturalem*) any more than by walls and boundaries, but by common will—because the men of one *civitas* or kingdom want one government. Even he, however, talks about the apparently larger *regnum* as well as about the *civitas* and alludes to the possible advantage of separate governments for different regions, especially those with different languages, manners, and customs— though he leaves this aside as irrelevant to his subject.[189] Apparently Marsilius, like the other writers I have mentioned, shared the usual presuppositions of his contemporaries about the connection of common custom, common descent, and political unity. These were the sort of ideas which are around in the air which even the most innovatory intellectual, the most cloistered academic, must breathe. Intellectuals, who, like others, accepted the natural diversity of peoples and their customs, could, like them, do so without feeling that mankind was hopelessly divided. God ruled over all and Christian peoples with differing secular laws nevertheless shared one supreme law, God's law. The Christian community included all lesser communities.[190] It was this, not the occasional special pleading of popes and emperors, which constituted the real universalism of the middle ages.

The ignoring of the underlying assumptions of academic treatises is only one reason for undervaluing medieval ideas about kingdoms. Another is the common belief that the thought of this period, or most of it, had no concept of the state or, indeed, of the public welfare or public interest as such. The first difficulty about this is that concepts of the state are more various, and often more confused, than some intellectual historians of the middle ages seem to imply. The second is that some of the discussions of medieval concepts seem to invite a confusion of word, concept, and thing. Attention has, for instance, been focused on the use of the word *status*,[191] apparently in the belief that it will reveal

[189] *Defensor Pacis* [51], 7 (I. 2. 2, 17. 10-11).

[190] Aquinas, *Summa* [75], v. 208 (IIIae Suppl. q. 40, art. 6); cf. Borst, *Turmbau von Babel* [266], 498, 513, 517, 540-1, 595, 720, 733.

[191] Post, *Studies* [631], 241-558; Mager, *Entstehung des modernen Staatsbegriff* [564].

ideas about the state. Even without the confusing tendency to assimilate state to nation-state or nation, that is surely misdirected. So far as words matter then *regnum* would repay study. So far as the thing—that is, the reality of political systems—is concerned, there seem from the eleventh century to have been some kingdoms (and some lesser units of government) within which their respective rulers claimed the control (though not the monopoly) of the legitimate use of physical force with about as much success as those of a good many modern states. By Max Weber's standards they therefore look not unlike states.[192] Whether their rulers and subjects, even the intellectuals among them, visualized them in the way—any of the ways—in which modern people visualize modern states is another matter. In so far as thirteenth-century writers give the impression of approaching modern concepts it is often because the terminology and style of their discourse foreshadows that of later controversies. They were not really concerned with the same issues. They were not preoccupied with the problems of sovereignty—whether external or internal—which worry some modern theorists. Their view of the supremacy of law and of the layers of authority under it created practical problems rather like those which the modern concept of sovereignty creates for federal states, but neither practising nor academic lawyers seem to have addressed themselves to the underlying contradictions. Nor were they concerned to try to fit the state into any doctrine of fictitious persons, since they had no such thing in the first place.[193] Kingdoms had become states without much help from academics, and when academics began to multiply and become more influential they did not have anything very new to say about kingdoms. They just said it in a more subtle way.

The same sort of objections may be raised to the argument that people in the middle ages did not have any concept of the public welfare before they learned it from the academics. This probably derives ultimately from the later conceptualization of feudalism as a system which combined and confused

---

[192] Weber, *Social and Economic Organization* [830], 156; cf. Runciman, *Social Science and Political Theory* [820], 35, 38 and n.

[193] Above, pp. 59-64.

public duties with private property, reinforced by the idea, probably derived from nineteenth-century anthropology, that 'primitive' people are incapable of abstract, rational thought.[194] Medieval sources may appear to support this in so far as the sort of works which most obviously contain abstract, rational thought become abundant only after the twelfth century. If one only reads the treatises and assumes that every piece of reasoning which appears for the first time in one of them represents a conceptual novelty then one could deduce that the period before the twelfth century was almost entirely devoid of rational thought about politics and society. But the hypothesis that any of the ideas and values of the treatises was new can only be tested by looking at the earlier evidence outside the treatises. That suggests that, although in much discourse king and kingdom were undifferentiated (as government and state are today), and although the boundary between public and private interest and property was not always drawn consistently (any more than it is today), nevertheless some people were capable of making the distinction between king and kingdom, private profit and public welfare, and so on, whenever they needed to do so. Governments then—like governments now—often tried to assimilate the public good to governmental interest and governmental interest to the private interest of the rulers, but that is no argument for a lack of conceptual distinctions. Even before the tenth century kings had on occasion distinguished their family inheritance from the royal office, while laws and oaths of fidelity had implied that obligations could be owed to the public as well as to the king.[195] Coronation oaths imply that a divergence of interest between kings and subjects was, sadly, recognized to be possible. In the eleventh century it was not only the intellectual Wipo who thought that royal property was public property which remained such even in the absence of a king, for Conrad II punished the Pavians for ignoring that rule.[196]

[194] Above, pp. 13–14, 36–7.

[195] Halphen, 'L'Idée d'état' [459]; Southern, review of Kantorowicz, *King's Two Bodies* [692]; Nelson, 'Kingship' [606]. On the boundary between public and private: Brunner, *Land und Herrschaft* [289], 120–33.

[196] Wipo, *Opera* [84], 29–30; Beumann, 'Entwicklung transpersonaler Staatsvorstellungen' [251].

What happened in the twelfth century was that formulations of these ideas became numerous and explicit.[197] Words
like *respublica* came into common use and John of Salisbury
produced an elaborate analogy between the *res publica* and
the body.[198] Organic metaphors must have been so familiar
from the New Testament, however, if nowhere else, that it is
surely implausible to represent this as a conceptual advance.
It certainly did not herald anything like modern organic
theories of the state. Metaphors and allegories, however much
elaborated, remained just that.[199] In so far as the impersonal
and public dimension of government became clearer and
more widely appreciated, it was because government itself
was becoming more complex and bureaucratic, legal systems
were beginning to work with less personal direction from
kings, larger populations (even perhaps larger proportions of
populations) were being more effectively mobilized by
written propaganda. Above all, as conflicts between kings and
subjects multiplied, the difference between their interests
could no longer be swept under the carpet. But although
ideas were now being clarified through argument, no amount
of clarification justifies ignoring the evidence, implicit and
indirect as much of it is, that people living before 1100 were
capable of feeling collective loyalties, distinguishing the king
from the community, and thinking generally in impersonal
terms about society.

The central problem of secular politics during this period
was, however, not so much to define, explain, or justify the
political community, as to define the limits of royal power.
That was first and foremost a question of law but it was not
one to which academic lawyers offered a solution. Roman
lawyers helped Frederick Barbarossa prepare his case against
the Lombard towns who had usurped the regalia.[200] They
may have been responsible for the theory that all governmental authority was exercised by delegation from the king.
On the other hand, such a theory could equally well have

---

[197] Numerous examples in Kantorowicz, *King's Two Bodies* [496] and Post, *Studies* [631].

[198] *Policraticus* [46], i. 282–4 (V. 2).

[199] Dohrn-van Rossum in *Geschichtliche Grundbegriffe* [288], iii. 538–48; cf. Struve, *Entwicklung der organologischen Staatsauffassung* [708].

[200] Above, p. 47.

been deduced from traditional law and the ancient practice of granting charters. Its consonance with tradition would explain the way that it seems to have been very generally accepted by the thirteenth century.[201] That it was so accepted indicates the high view that was generally taken of royal authority, the more so since the theory never seems to have been debated in such a way as to define its impact and limitations, let alone to fit it to the historical reality. The only attempt to apply it with any pretence of thoroughness was in the English Quo Warranto proceedings, when some holders of franchises claimed that as a matter of historical fact they held not by royal grant but by conquest. This argument sidestepped both the theory as such and the king's right to make his subjects defend their exercise of authority in court. So did the final compromise by which unchartered franchises were sanctioned.[202]

With regard to representation, legal practice helped to clarify some points which affected representation at regnal assemblies, but the phrases from Roman law which were used in political documents did not embody new ideas. The analogy from legal to political representation, moreover, depended on the assumption, which does not seem to have needed to be argued, that individual representatives, however strictly instructed, could be overruled by the rest of an assembly. Collectivist assumptions, in other words, were not questioned. That may also explain the absence of discussion about the constitution of electing groups or the relationship between representation and election. It is sometimes suggested that the 'doctrine of necessity' in taxation came into regnal politics from canon law,[203] but it is not clear that the canon —or Roman—lawyers did more than refine and record traditional arguments about the tricky boundary between a ruler's right to obtain help in a crisis and the subjects' right to pay only what was customary or what they had freely

[201] *Liber Consuetudinum Mediolani* [89], 113 (21. 11); Sutherland, *Quo Warranto* [709], 182-9; Riley-Smith, *Feudal Nobility* [660], 166-7; its acceptance is implied in many royal dealings with town governments: above, pp. 168-83.

[202] Sutherland, *Quo Warranto* [709], 182-4; cf. Ehrlich, 'Proceedings against the Crown' [390].

[203] e.g. Post, *Studies* [631], 253-309. For other arguments about Romanist influence, ibid. 61-238; Congar, 'Quod omnes tangit' [336].

conceded.[204] The moral teachings of theologians about taxation which worried French kings were little more than
rationalizations of traditional lay ideas.[205]

On the most fundamental issue of all, the relationship of
kings to law, the revolutionary idea that kings might be above
the law, by right as well as in practice, seems to have come
not from commentators on Roman law but from people
involved in real politics and its conflicts. All references to this
new suggestion seem, moreover, to be disapproving.[206] The
orthodox view remained that a king who failed to maintain
and obey law was a tyrant. Whether that meant he could
be deposed or killed was a problem which remained un-
resolved.[207] Gregory VII's deposition of Henry IV was as
little copied as was his statement that royal power came from
the devil. Political authority was made necessary by sin but
it was in itself good and necessary. Kings, on the other hand,
were men and they sinned.[208] On occasion it might be politic
to blame a king's ministers rather than him for some injustice,
but that was a matter of tactics, not yet of political theory.
The problems of maintaining justice in a world where kings
and their subjects sinned were not susceptible of resolution
by legal or political theory.[209]

To say that academics did not solve these problems is not
to belittle the academics. To start with, many of them were
only concerned with discussing political authority when it
impinged on ecclesiastical authority. In that highly contested field clerical ideas and arguments certainly eroded
some old loyalties, though not significantly among the laity.
Even among the clergy, after a hundred years and more of
church reform and papal pressure, the bishops themselves
were not immune from feelings of regnal loyalty. We can
understand their problems over papal provisions, papal taxes
and—at worst—papal excommunications of kings, only if

[204] Prestwich, Documents [170], 27-30.
[205] Brown, 'Taxation and Morality' [283].
[206] Above, pp. 45-51.
[207] Rouse, 'John of Salisbury' [667]; Carlyle, Mediaeval Political Theory
[309], v. 92-111.
[208] Cf. Maitland, Collected Papers [566], iii. 246-7; Brown, 'Taxation and
Morality' [283].
[209] Graus, 'Social Utopias' [455], 6.

we appreciate the universally acknowledged duties of all people, clergy as well as lay, to their kingdoms. The old values were strong. Another illustration of that is the lack of interest among thirteenth-century Aristotelians in the Philosopher's classification of constitutions.[210] The heads of medieval academics, like medieval kingdoms, had king-shaped holes in them. There was no point in worrying over the differences between aristocracy and oligarchy, polity and democracy. The only significant distinction was that between monarchy and tyranny—in other words, from their point of view, between lawful and unlawful government.

The most important contribution which the schools made to secular politics was in educating the men who directed the new bureaucracies and drafted their documents. How much the resulting clarity of political and legal thought helped to resolve or intensify conflicts it is hard to say. Fundamentally the regnal conflicts of the period seem not to have been the sort for which clear thought on its own would have provided a remedy. So long as the ideal was harmony and consensus under the king and the law there were no neat and crisp solutions to be had. A precise location of sovereignty within the kingdom (or state) would have been repugnant, whether it meant making the king absolute or replacing him by some sort of republican system which might have been derived from the autonomous town and village communities. Instead, people went on trying to combine obedience to superior authority with consultation and consent. To modern eyes the result may look like a conflict between 'ascending and descending themes' of government but that suggests that these were alternatives.[211] To people at the time they do not seem to have been separable. The old ideal was still cherished in 1300 and, however deficient in justice or practicability it may seem to us, there does not seem to be much reason to suppose that intellectuals then found it any more deficient than anyone else did or that the deficiencies were the result of intellectual inadequacy or naïvety on their part. It was simply a different ideal.

[210] Above, p. 198.
[211] Ullmann, *Principles of Government and Politics* [720], 1-19 *et passim*.

Conclusion

Like the chapter on urban communities, this one has been long and yet has left out a great deal. Much is recorded about kingdoms, not only because regnal governments, like urban governments, kept good records, but because people thought that the affairs of kings and kingdoms were important. Chroniclers talk about regnal politics more than any other sort of politics. Kingdoms mattered, or, to put it in a more intellectual way, they were the highest form of secular community that there was.[212]

The community of the realm was therefore not, as English historians tend to assume, a peculiarly English concept, and collective activity on a regnal scale was not the product of thirteenth-century conflicts, bureaucracy, and propaganda. It was something much older and more general. Any kingdom which survived did so because it was in some sense felt to be a community. That is not to say that enduring kingdoms were in reality the political manifestation of peoples of common descent and inherited common culture—what people today usually call nations. People thought of them as that, for politics demanded solidarity and the metaphor of kinship was strong and emotive. All the same, kingdoms were created and preserved not by kinship but by government, and government of an essentially public character. The loyalty people felt to their kingdom was on a different level from that to their family, their lord, or their locality. Some modern scholars, perhaps influenced by Rousseau's belief that solidarity with one group rules out any other, have believed that medieval people can have felt no loyalty except to their lord or local community.[213] Anyone who belongs at the same time to a family, a town, a university, and a nation-state—and may even support a football team into the bargain—ought to find this idea implausible.[214] It makes even less sense when it is

---

[212] Aquinas, *Selected Political Writings* [74], 8 (*De Reg. Princ.* I. 1).

[213] e.g. Kohn, *Idea of Nationalism* [800], 84–5; Seton-Watson, *Nations and States* [822], 17–18, 418–19. This idea is combined by Kohn (op. cit. 78–9) and others with a belief that medieval people were dominated by purely religious ideas and loyalties.

[214] Cf. Gluckman, *Custom and Conflict* [788], 10–26; Mackenzie, *Political Identity* [803].

applied to a period in which there was no idea that sovereignty should be single and precisely located: government consisted of layers of authority, and loyalties were attracted to each layer accordingly.

Kingdoms were units of government which were perceived as peoples. The government and the solidarity were both essential. Government without any voluntary submission was impossible, but without any government collective solidarity evaporated. Whether governments harnessed loyalty, or provoked collective solidarity by oppression, they did so because of pre-existing beliefs about what government should be like and about the duty of obedience to it. In practice kings were often arbitrary and kingdoms were inclined to discord, but the arbitrariness did not imply theories of absolutism and the discord did not imply theories of popular sovereignty. There is, in the end, very little hard evidence of any fundamental conflicts of political ideology. The problem was one of means—how to achieve an agreed standard of justice—not of ends—finding a new sort of justice. Besides, not all kings were always unjust, and when they were the sense of solidarity may have made endurance easier. Kings, as Thomas Aquinas said, are sometimes called the fathers of their peoples, and they rule them for their common good.[215]

[215] Aquinas, *Selected Political Writings* [74], 8 (*De Reg. Princ.* I. 1).

9

Lay collective activity, 900–1300:
a general view

Many of the arguments set out in the preceding chapters are vulnerable to criticism from specialists in the various fields into which my subject has led me, so that the accumulation of errors may leave any general conclusions looking distinctly weak. In spite of that danger, I hope that it may be agreed that between 900 and 1300 lay society and government depended in a mass of different ways on the collective activities of a wide range of people; that this activity was undertaken as a matter of course in support of government, as well as in opposition to it; and that in all its aspects it reveals a very homogeneous set of values, which combined acceptance of inequality and subordination with a high degree of voluntary co-operation. These values, moreover, continued to dominate collective activity throughout the period. Although the twelfth and thirteenth centuries brought new forms of collective activity, clearer articulation of the duties owed to and by communities, and somewhat clearer expression of the values they embodied, the evidence of any fundamental change of values is surprisingly small. By 1300 there are hints of novelty, but no more: rash as it may seem to try to disentangle cause and effect on such a topic, it looks, in other words, as if new practice evoked new theory, not the other way round.

Given this stress on continuity, a reader might well ask what significance, if any, I attach to the changes in collective activity during the period, and how I would explain them. In considering the first question some outside standard by which to measure the change might be useful. So far, although I have found insights from social anthropology and sociology extremely stimulating, I have avoided using any of the obvious classifications of forms of association offered by comparative sociology. It seemed better to try to understand the ways medieval people perceived their communities—the meanings they gave to them—by using their own words, and the circumstances in which they used them, as a guide to their concepts, rather than by starting from modern words and concepts. At this stage, however, enough is established to be able to measure the medieval evidence against modern typologies without forcing it into them. Two especially well-known and influential classifications suggest themselves: those of Tönnies and Weber.

Tönnies saw the middle ages as a period dominated by the sort of natural communities of common will, custom, and sociability that he called *Gemeinschaften*. One way of characterizing the changes between 900 and 1300 might be to see if one could put these centuries into the beginning of his intermediate stage in which a trend towards deliberate, *ad hoc* associations (*Gesellschaften*) was beginning, but in which 'the force of *Gemeinschaft* persists, although with diminishing strength . . . and remains the reality of social life'.[1] The difficulty about this (apart from the fact that the nineteenth-century medievalists whom Tönnies used would not have put the change so early) is that the apparent multiplication of more *Gesellschaft*-like collectivities after 1100 probably owes a good deal to the improvement of the records. Poor as the tenth- and eleventh-century evidence is, it suggests that people then acted together very casually as need and opportunity arose. A lot of the village and guild communities that looked to Tönnies like *Gemeinschaften* may have been as much *Gesellschaften* as some of the better recorded associations of the thirteenth century or later. Even allowing for Tönnies's recognition that actual associations would not fit the ideal types, the distinction seems too blurred to be useful. A second difficulty is that Tönnies's description of *Gemeinschaften* is very idealized, while the ideals only partly correspond to those that medieval people would have recognized: for Tönnies too much inequality of wealth and status are incompatible with *Gemeinschaft*.[2] Yet his picture of *Gemeinschaft* seems to be based on a sentimental view of the middle ages themselves, which reduces its use as a measuring rod for medieval phenomena.

[1] *Community and Association* [828], 271-2.
[2] Ibid. 53, 268, and 42-73 *passim*.

In Weber's terms the period between 900 and 1300 displays the beginnings of a change from traditional and patrimonial government to bureaucratic government, with attitudes towards it—reasonably enough—lagging behind.[3] His classification of forms of association seems more subtle than Tönnies's but some of the distinctions he draws once again cut across medieval categories. It is not just the poverty of the evidence that makes it, for example, so difficult to say whether many communities were, in Weber's terms, open or closed: he himself used ancient and medieval city-states and what his translator calls 'guilds' (*Zünfte*)[4] as examples which shifted between the categories. Another distinction which is not always significant in medieval terms is that between groups formed by voluntary agreement and those formed by imposed authority.[5] It would be impertinent to cite these misfits as criticisms of Weber's typology. He himself stressed that the polarity of his ideal types would always be relative in its empirical application.[6] Polarity may still be useful even if, like the similar polarity of Tönnies's classification, it suggests that what was distinctive about medieval communities was that they tended to straddle the equator. In terms of both typologies, they did not move many degrees of latitude between 900 and 1300.

The doubts that are left after applying these classifications do not derive from the use of ideal types as such but from concern about their empirical, historical foundation. It is impossible to classify collective bodies without reference to the rules and norms of the society to which they belong—and that means looking at the records of political and legal business as actually transacted. While one cannot make sense of the law of any society without reference to its economic and social conditions in general, neither can one make sense of social conditions without reference to the law. The detailed study of medieval records that this would involve had, however, hardly started when the foundations of comparative sociology were being laid and Tönnies's and Weber's typologies

---

[3] *Social and Economic Organization* [830], 341-58.
[4] For the difficulties of these words, above, p. 72.
[5] *Social and Economic Organization* [830], 145. Cf. above, chapters 5 and 6, e.g. pp. 148-52.
[6] *Social and Economic Organization* [830], 152.

were being worked out. Both typologies are apparently still influential,[7] but they are both partly based on interpretations of the middle ages which by now need drastic revision. Emphasis on 'the pre-eminence in medieval society . . . of the small social group' and of 'the centrality of personal status, of *membership* in society'[8] is entirely justified, but only if we recognize that many medieval groups were extremely loose and overlapping—much more like the different groups and networks to which modern people feel they belong than the sociological stereotypes admit. Some of the groups to which medieval people belonged (like some, but not all, guilds) had small fixed memberships, but far more, even at village level, did not. Some communities to which people felt that they belonged (like provinces or kingdoms) were much too large to admit of general inter-personal relationships, so that the sense of membership and the feeling of being a small group were maintained only by the acceptance of gross inequality and non-participation by a large number of people.

Moreover, the romantic view of the middle ages which shaped Tönnies's typology (and, though less obviously, Weber's too) was itself derived from the rather crude developmental anthropology of the nineteenth century.[9] No doubt that is why the typologies lent themselves to even cruder periodization. The description of different sorts of collective groups and different sorts of authority as typical of different stages or periods of history seems to turn imperceptibly into labelling some as more 'primitive' and some as more 'advanced', so that one is invited either to yearn nostalgically for a supposed primitive harmony in the early stages or to applaud the greater cleverness or intellectual subtlety of those who

[7] e.g. Nisbet, *Community and Power* [810], 79–97; Szacki, *Hist. of Sociological Thought* [826], 344–5. More recent classifications seem to stay more within the sociologist's own society (e.g. Reeves, *Dynamics of Group Behavior* [817], 77–106). Anthropologists seem to be as little given to typologies as historians, and, illuminating as I have found their descriptions of collective activities, I have found their fondness for the generally undefined adjective 'corporate' rather frustrating. The most helpful and clearly argued ideal type of community that I have found is in Taylor, *Community* [827]: see above, pp. 1–2.

[8] Nisbet, *Community and Power* [810], 80.

[9] e.g. Nisbet, *Sociological Tradition* [811], 51–82. I have found Goody, *Domestication of the Savage Mind* [791] very helpful on the problem of evolutionary or non-evolutionary approaches.

made the grade to later ones. Medieval collective activity has been seen in both lights. Tönnies's pages on *Gemeinschaft*, with their long quotation from Gierke, are a fair example of the nostalgic view in an early form. More recent manifestations are descriptions of the medieval 'society of orders' as essentially excluding class conflicts, and of village communities as primitive democracies.[10] Examples of the other view, which eschews nostalgia and applauds progress, include characterizations of medieval law as moving from ritual to reasoning and learning how to divide corporate from non-corporate bodies, and of the counting of votes as a manifestation of growing rationality. The evidence I have cited casts doubt on both these ways of looking at medieval collective activity. Medieval ideals certainly excluded class conflict, so that the structures and rules of collective activity tended to mask and mitigate it, but conflicts between lords and peasants in the country, or between rich and poor in towns, were inherent in the underlying structure of both rural and urban society. As for the supposed growth of rationality, there was plenty of serious argument in tenth- and eleventh-century litigation, and no rational room or need for a concept of corporations in thirteenth-century jurisprudence. The early medieval reluctance to count votes was due not to reverence for some 'myth of unanimity' cherished by people of 'Germanic stock',[11] but to the same need for consensus that, in certain circumstances, besets modern councils and committees.[12] 'Primitive' and 'advanced' relationships are found side by side in most societies. *Gemeinschaft* and *Gesellschaft* are not suitable for periodization. Relationships of different sorts do not replace each other any more than reasoning replaces ritual. Modern society is full of *Gemeinschaften* just as modern law-courts are full of ritual—while modern law ties itself into knots sorting groups into corporate and non-corporate.

Other examples of the survival of the developmental typologies of the nineteenth century can be found in attempts to

[10] On the 'society of orders': Razi, 'Struggles' [643]; Arriaza, 'Mousnier and Barber' [771]. Nisbet, *Community and Power* [810], 80–5 closely replicates the nineteenth-century version.

[11] Ruffini, *Ragione dei più* [669], 12–17.

[12] Above, pp. 190–1, 319, and index *sub* decision-making.

make a chronological sequence during the middle ages from kinship to lordship, or from personal to territorial government, with the full concept of the state reserved to be a final, modern achievement. If it can be right at all to regard the family or kin as chronologically prior to other communities, then the time at which it existed alone in Europe, unsupplemented by lordship and by other forms of community, was long past by the middle ages. At the top of any society the relationships between a ruler and those close to him (or among a ruling group) will always be in a sense 'personal', but that does not mean that such people do not have any concept of the public outside—even if they choose to ignore its welfare. Nor, in a society like that of the medieval west, which rested on a settled, agricultural base, can power over persons be significantly distinguished from power over the place where they live and the means of their livelihood. Correspondingly, associations in such a society seldom passed in any significant sense from a purely 'personal' stage (represented, for instance, by guilds or merchant societies) to a territorial one (town governments). Some associations at each stage were purely voluntary, with no physical sanctions, while some had coercive powers, but the membership and authority of either might or might not be territorially restricted. By 900 medieval society was too complex for kinship and lordship, personal and territorial associations, private and public obligations to be mutually exclusive, alternative bases of society. It was a complex society which offered plenty of scope for different sorts of co-operation and different sorts of conflict, both between and within collective groups.

Nostalgia for its primitiveness and applause for its advances seem therefore to be equally inappropriate reactions to medieval collective activity. Medieval communities were not cosy havens of harmony nor does cognitive or conceptual progress seem to have been the motor of their development. Nevertheless they did change, and collective activity did develop new forms between 900 and 1300. As population and the economy grew and government became more complicated, so people were presented with more choices about their collective activity—including more chance of opting out. Whether or not we want to talk in terms of the birth of individualism,[13] we must agree that there was more choice of occupations and more chance of personal fulfilment in different ways in 1300 than in 900, even if only a small proportion of the population could take advantage of it. More varied collective activity did not, therefore, make society more collectivist. The growth of population, wealth, and government also stimulated conflict, not so much by creating new and opposing values as by exposing more clearly the contradictions of existing ones. When old custom was written down, its failure to fit new circumstances became more obvious. When government became more efficient and impersonal, lordship and fraternity seemed more obviously opposed. Consensus—let alone real unanimity—became ever harder to achieve. Even if, as I maintain, people had been, by and large, just as intelligent and thoughtful in their management of law and government in the tenth century as they were in the thirteenth, there were far more complicated problems in the thirteenth century for them to argue about. However little the fundamental social and political ideas of laymen seem to have been affected by academic advances, their arguments were sharpened—in both senses of the word—by the growth of literacy and by the stimulus that intelligent people in contact with those who had been trained in the schools must have got from the development of intellectual argument.

As a result, lawyers found new ways of winning cases, rulers found new ways of getting taxes, and councillors found new ways of counting votes. Arbitrary action by governments was restrained, not by discovering for the first time that it was wrong, but by matching its new forms with new means to prevent it. It is impossible to see all of this as either a Good Thing or a Bad Thing, but it is both possible and essential to notice which aspects contemporaries thought good and bad. Recently historians have tended to stress the arbitrary and violent nature of medieval government. Kings were indeed often arbitrary, greedy, and violent, and some of their subjects were too. That was, however, wrong according to tenth-century ideas and still wrong in the thirteenth century. Many of the ways in which collective activities changed can

---

[13] Morris, *Discovery of Individual* [596]; Benton, 'Consciousness of Self' [246]; Bynum, 'Did the Twelfth Century . . .?' [293].

thus be seen as the responses of people with much the same set of fundamental political values, including much the same contradictions, to increasingly complex problems. Though by 1300 it looks to us as if some groups or individuals had adumbrated some significantly new answers—republican government, absolute government, elective parliaments, consultation by estates, indirect elections—few if any people at the time seem to have recognized any of them as solutions.

As the previous paragraphs may suggest, I find myself driven back on demographic and economic growth as the best that I can manage in the way of a primary cause of the changes I have described. It is not a very satisfactory explanation, and certainly does not account adequately for all the manifold and efflorescent achievements of the twelfth century which lay outside the growth of lay communities but which provided the context in which they grew. I do, however, claim that, as well as casting doubt on the extent to which new academic ideas influenced lay politics and society, I have effectively dismissed some of the traditional national explanations of twelfth-century change. The Norman Conquest cannot have been responsible for all the changes in England which are traditionally attributed to it, nor the 'Investiture Contest' for all those in Germany, when so many of them were so similar and embodied such similar values. Despite the emergent glories of Italian painting and civic architecture, Italian towns were less different from other towns and from the rest of society in their political values and institutions than is often suggested, so that neither the recovery of Roman law nor an inborn Italian propensity for conflict can have been quite so important in shaping them as one might otherwise assume. Any reasons for social and political change that we find must take account of the continuing similarities of collective institutions all over western Europe at least as late as 1300. What happened thereafter is another story, but in so far as it starts from the beginning of the fourteenth century it must start from the values and ideas which were then current. In most of western Europe lay people then believed that government depended on consultation and consent, and that its object was to achieve a harmonious consensus in accordance with the custom and law of the whole community.

List of works cited

Abbreviations

Ag.H.R.	*Agricultural History Review*
Am.H.R.	*American Historical Review*
A.E.S.C.	*Annales: Économies, Sociétés, Civilisations*
A.N.	*Annales de Normandie*
B.E.C.	*Bibliothèque de l'École des Chartes*
B.I.H.R.	*Bulletin of the Institute of Historical Research*
B.P.H.	*Bulletin Philologique et Historique*
Ec.H.R.	*Economic History Review*
E.H.R.	*English Historical Review*
H.J.	*Historisches Jahrbuch*
I.R.M.A.	*Ius Romanum Medii Aevi*
J. Eccl. H.	*Journal of Ecclesiastical History*
L.Q.R.	*Law Quarterly Review*
M.A.	*Le Moyen Age*
Med. Arch.	*Medieval Archaeology*
M.G.H.	*Monumenta Germaniae Historica*
M.G.H., S.R.G.	Monumenta Germaniae Historia: Scriptores Rerum Germanicarum
P. & P.	*Past and Present*
Revue Belge	*Revue Belge de Philologie et d'Histoire*
R.H.	*Revue Historique*
R.H.D.	*Revue d'Histoire du Droit*
R.H.D.F.E.	*Revue Historique de Droit Français et Étranger*
R.N.	*Revue du Nord*
R.S.	Rolls Series (Chronicles and Memorials)
R.S.I.	*Rivista Storica Italiana*
S.C.H.	*Studies in Church History*
Settimane	*Settimane di Studio del Centro Italiano di Studi sull'Alto Medioevo*
S.S.	Selden Society
T.R.H.S.	*Transactions of the Royal Historical Society*
V. und F.	*Vorträge und Forschungen*
Z.R.G.	*Zeitschrift der Savigny-Stiftung für Rechtsgeschichte.*

Ia: *Manuscript Sources*

[1] London, British Library, Additional MS. 6040 (cartulary of St Mary's Priory, Southwark).

[2] London, British Library, Cottonian MS. Vesp. E III (Annals of Burton Priory).

[3] Florence, Archivio di Stato, Diplomatico, Santa Maria Novella 29 aprile 1197.

Ib: *Printed Sources: Chronicles and Treatises*

[4] Adam of Bremen, *Gesta Hammaburgensis pontificum* (M.G.H., S.R.G. 1917).

[5] Adémar of Chabannes, *Chronique*, ed. J. Chavanon (Paris, 1897).

[6] Ambroise, *L'Estoire de la guerre sainte*, ed. G. Paris (Paris, 1897).

[7] *Annales Monastici* (R.S. 36, 1864-6).

[8] Anselm, *Opera Omnia*, iii, ed. F. S. Schmitt (Edinburgh, 1946).

[9] Arnold fitz Thedmar, *De Antiquis Legibus Liber: Cronica Maiorum et Vicecomitum Londoniarum* (Camden Soc. ser. 1, xxxiv, 1846).

[10] Asser, *Life of King Alfred*, ed. W. H. Stevenson and D. Whitelock (Oxford, 1959).

[11] Bede, *Historia ecclesiastica*, ed. C. Plummer (Oxford, 1896).

[12] Bower, W., *Scotichronicon*, ed. W. Goodall (Edinburgh, 1759).

[13] Bracton, *De Legibus et Consuetudinibus Anglie*, ed. G. E. Woodbine and S. E. Thorne (Cambridge, Mass. 1968–).

[14] Brunetto Latini, *Li Livres dou tresor*, ed. P. Chabaille (Paris, 1863).

[15] Bruno, *Brunos Buch vom Sachsenkrieg* (M.G.H. Deutsches Mittelalter, ii, 1937).

[16] *Chronicon Abbatiae Rameseiensis* (R.S. 83, 1886).

[17] *Chroniken der deutschen Städte*, i: *Nürnberg*, i (Leipzig, 1862).

[18] *Chroniques des comtes d'Anjou*, ed. L. Halphen and R. Poupardin (Paris, 1913).

[19] *Corpus Iuris Civilis*, ed. P. Krueger and others (Berlin, 1911-12).

[20] Cosmas of Prague, *Die Chronik der Böhmen* (M.G.H., S.R.G., 1923).

[21] *The Court Baron* (S.S. iv, 1891).

[22] Dante, *Opera*, ed. E. Moore and P. Toynbee (Oxford, 1924).

[23] *Deutschenspiegel* (M.G.H., Fontes Iuris Germ., 1933).

[24] Dudo, *De moribus et actis primorum Normanniae ducum*, ed. J. Lair (Caen, 1865).

[25] Eike von Repgow, *Sachsenspiegel* (M.G.H., Fontes Iuris Germ., 1955-67).

[26] Engelbert of Admont, *De mutatione reformatione ruina et fine imperii*, in M. Goldast ed., *Politica imperialia* (Frankfurt, 1614).

[27] *Fleta seu commentarius juris Anglicani sic nuncupatur*, ed. J. Selden (London, 1647).

[28] *Flores Historiarum* (R.S. 95, 1890).

[29] Fulbert of Chartres, *Letters and poems* ed. F. Behrends (Oxford, 1976).

[30] Fulcher of Chartres, *Historia Hierosolymitana*, ed. H. Hagenmeyer (Heidelberg, 1913).

[31] Galbert de Bruges, *Histoire du meurtre de Charles le Bon*, ed. H. Pirenne (Paris, 1891).

[32] Geoffrey of Monmouth, *Historia Regum Britanniae*, ed. A. Griscom (London, 1929).

[33] Gervase of Canterbury, *Opera* (R.S. 73, 1879-80).

[34] Giraldus Cambrensis, *De Invectionibus* (*Y Cymmrodor*, xxx, 1920).

[35] Giraldus Cambrensis, *Opera* (R.S. 21, 1861-91).

[36] Gislebert de Mons, *Chronique*, ed. L. Vanderkindere (Brussels, 1955).

[37] Glanvill, *The Treatise on the laws and customs of . . . England commonly called Glanvill*, ed. G. D. G. Hall (London, 1965).

[38] Gratian, *Decretum*, in *Corpus Iuris Canonici*, ed. A. Friedberg (Graz, 1955), i.

[39] Guibert de Nogent, *Histoire de sa vie*, ed. G. Bourgin (Paris, 1907).

[40] Guillaume de Jumièges, *Gesta Normannorum Ducum*, ed. J. Marx (Rouen/Paris, 1914).

[41] Guillaume de Pouille, *La Geste de Robert Guiscard*, ed. M. Mathieu (Palermo, 1961).

[42] *Histoire de Guillaume le Maréchal*, ed. P. Meyer (Paris, 1891-1907).

[43] Hugh Falcandus, *Liber de Regno Sicilie* (Fonti per la storia d'Italia, 22, 1897).

[44] Isidore of Seville, *Etymologiarum Libri*, ed. W. M. Lindsay (Oxford, 1911).

[45] John of Paris, *De potestate regia et papali*, ed. J. Leclercq in *Jean de Paris et l'ecclésiologie du xiiie siècle* (Paris, 1942).

[46] John of Salisbury, *Policraticus*, ed. C. J. Webb (Oxford, 1909).

[47] Lampert of Hersfeld, *Opera* (M.G.H., S.R.G., 1894).

[48] *Das Langobardische Lehnrecht*, ed. K. Lehmann (Göttingen, 1896).

[49] *Leges Henrici Primi*, ed. L. J. Downer (Oxford, 1972).

[50] Liutprand of Cremona, *Opera* (M.G.H., S.R.G., 1915).

[51] Marsilius of Padua, *Defensor Pacis*, ed. C. W. Previté-Orton (Cambridge, 1928).

[52] Matthew Paris, *Chronica Majora* (R.S. 57, 1872-83).

[53] *Les Miracles de Saint Benoît*, ed. E. de Certain (Paris, 1858).

[54] *M.G.H.: Scriptores*: folio series (1826-1913).

[55] *M.G.H.: Staatsschriften des späteren Mittelalters*, i (1958).

[56] Muratori, L. A. and others ed., *Rerum Italicarum Scriptores*, new series (Bologna, 1900-).

[57] Orderic Vitalis, *Historia Ecclesiastica*, ed. M. Chibnall (Oxford, 1969-80).

[58] Otto of Freising, *Ottonis et Rahewini Gesta Friderici Imperatoris* (M.G.H., S.R.G., 1912).

[59] *Parliamentary Texts of the Later Middle Ages*, ed. N. Pronay and J. Taylor (Oxford, 1980).

[60] *Patrologia Latina*, ed. J. P. Migne and others (Paris, 1844-1903).

[61] Philippe de Remi, Sire de Beaumanoir, *Coutumes de Beauvaisis*, ed. A. Salmon (Paris, 1900).

[62] *Recueil des historiens des croisades: historiens occidentaux* (Paris, 1844–95).

[63] *Recueil des historiens des croisades: lois* (Paris, 1841–3).

[64] *Recueil des historiens des Gaules et de France* (Paris, 1869–1904).

[65] Regino of Prüm, *Chronicon* (M.G.H., S.R.G., 1890).

[66] Richard fitz Nigel, *Dialogus de Scaccario*, ed. C. Johnson (Edinburgh, 1950).

[67] Richard of Devizes, *Chronicle*, ed. J. T. Appleby (London, 1963).

[68] Rimbert, *Vita Anskarii* (M.G.H., S.R.G., 1884).

[69] Robert of Torigni, *Chronica* in *Chronicles of the reigns of Stephen, Henry II and Richard I* (R.S. 82, 1884–9), iv.

[70] Roger of Wendover, *Flores Historiarum* (R.S. 84, 1886–9).

[71] *Song of Lewes*, ed. C. L. Kingsford (Oxford, 1890).

[72] Suger, *Vie de Louis VI le Gros*, ed. H. Waquet (Paris, 1929).

[73] Thietmar of Merseburg, *Chronik* (M.G.H., S.R.G., 1955).

[74] Thomas Aquinas, *Selected Political Writings*, ed. A. P. d'Entrèves (Oxford, 1959).

[75] Thomas Aquinas, *Summa Theologiae* (Rome, 1894).

[76] *Two Saxon Chronicles Parallel*, ed. C. Plummer and J. Earle (Oxford, 1892).

[77] Usāmah ibn Munqidh, *An Arab-Syrian Gentleman and Warrior in the Period of the Crusades: Memoirs of Usāmah ibn Munqidh*, ed. P. K. Hitti (New York, 1929).

[78] Villani, *Croniche di Giovanni, Matteo e Filippo Villani* (Trieste, 1857).

[79] *Vita Heïnrici IV* in F. J. Schmale ed., *Quellen zur Geschichte Heinrichs IV* (Berlin, 1963).

[80] Walter Map, *De nugis curialium*, ed. M. R. James and others (Oxford, 1983).

[81] Widukind, *Rerum gestarum Saxonicarum Libri Tres* (M.G.H., S.R.G., 1935).

[82] William fitz Stephen, *Vita Sanctae Thomae* in *Materials for the History of Thomas Becket*, iii (R.S. 67, 1877).

[83] William of Malmesbury, *Gesta Regum Anglorum* (R.S. 90, 1887–9).

[84] Wipo, *Opera* (M.G.H., S.R.G., 1915).

Ic: *Printed Sources: Documentary*

[85] Ashdown, M. ed. *English and Norse Documents relating to the reign of Ethelred* (Cambridge, 1930).

[86] Astegiano, L. ed. *Codex Diplomaticus Cremonae, 715–1334* (Turin, 1896–9).

[87] Attenborough, F. L. ed., *Laws of the Earliest English Kings* (Cambridge, 1922).

[88] Ballard, A. and others ed., *British Borough Charters* (Cambridge, 1913–43).

[89] Besta, E. and Barni, G. L. ed., *Liber consuetudinum Mediolani* (Milan, 1949).

[90] Beugnot, A. A. ed., *Les Olim, ou registres des arrêts rendus par la Cour du Roi* (Paris, 1839–48).

[91] Beyerle, F. ed., *Leges Langobardorum* (Witzenhausen, 1962).

[92] Bigelow, M. M. ed., *Placita Anglo-Normannica* (London, 1879).

[93] Blair, C. H., 'Knights of Durham who fought at Lewes', *Archaeologia Aeliana*, ser. 4, xxiv (1946), 183–216.

[94] Bohmer, J. F. ed., *Acta imperii selecta* (Innsbruck, 1870).

[95] Bonaini, F. ed., *Statuti inediti della città di Pisa* (Florence, 1854–7).

[96] *Borough Customs* (S.S. xviii, xxi, 1904–6).

[97] Boutaric, E. ed., *Actes du parlement de Paris*, i (1863).

[98] *Bracton's Note Book*, ed. F. W. Maitland (London, 1887).

[99] Broussillon, B. de, ed., *Cartulaire de l'abbaye de Saint-Aubin d'Angers* (Angers, 1896–9).

[100] Bruel, A. ed., *Recueil des chartes de Cluny* (Paris, 1876–1903).

[101] *Calendar of Inquisitions Miscellaneous*, i (London, 1916).

[102] Calisse, C., *Storia del Parlamento in Sicilia* (Turin, 1887).

[103] Cam, H. M., 'An East Anglian Shire-moot of Stephen's Reign, 1148–53', *E.H.R.* xxxix (1924), 568–71.

[104] Chibnall, M. ed., *Charters and Custumals of the Abbey of Holy Trinity, Caen* (London, 1982).

[105] *Close Rolls of the Reign of Henry III* (London, 1902–75).

[106] *Codice Diplomatico della Repubblica di Genova*, i (Fonti per la Storia d'Italia, 77, 1936).

[107] Conrad, H. and others ed., *Die Konstitutionen Friedrichs II von Hohenstaufen für sein Konigreich Sizilien* (Cologne/Vienna, 1973).

[108] Courson, A. de, ed., *Cartulaire de l'abbaye de Redon* (Paris, 1863).

[109] *Curia Regis Rolls* (London, 1922–).

[110] Davis, R. H. C., ed., *Kalendar of Abbot Samson of Bury St Edmunds* (Camden Soc. ser. 3, lxxxix, 1959).

[111] Delaborde, H. F. and others ed., *Recueil des actes de Philippe II Auguste* (Paris, 1916–79).

[112] Delisle, L., 'Lettre de l'abbé Haimon sur la construction de l'église de Saint-Pierre-sur-Dive en 1145', *B.E.C.* xxi (1859), 113–39.

[113] Diericx, C. L., *Mémoires sur la ville de Gand* (Ghent, 1814–15).

[114] *Domesday Book* (Record Commission, 1783–1816).

[115] Duchesne, A., *Histoire généalogique de la maison de Vergy* (Paris, 1625).

[116] Duchesne, L. and others ed., *Le Liber Censuum de l'Église Romaine* (Paris, 1889–1952).

[117] Eckhardt, K. A. ed., *Lex Salica* (Weimar, 1953).

[118] *Elenchus fontium historiae urbanae*, i, ed. C. van de Kieft and J. F. Niermeyer (Leiden, 1967).

[119] *English Historical Documents*, ed. D. C. Douglas, i: *c. 500–1042* (2nd edn. London, 1979).

[120] Escher, J. and Schweizer, P. ed., *Urkundenbuch der Stadt und Landschaft Zürich*, i–ii (Zurich, 1888–90).

[121] Espinas, G., 'Le Privilège de Saint-Omer de 1127', *R.N.* xxix (1947), 43–8.

[122] Espinas, G. and others ed., *Privilèges et chartes de franchises de la Flandre* (Brussels, 1959–61).

[123] *The Eyre of Kent, 1313–14*, i (S.S. xxiv, 1910).

[124] Fasoli, G. ed., *Statuti del comune di Bassano dell'anno 1259 e dell'anno 1295* (Venice, 1940).

[125] Fergusson, J. J. ed., *The Declaration of Arbroath* (Edinburgh, [1970]).

[126] Fossier, R. ed., *Les Chartes de coutume en Picardie (xie–xiie siècles)* (Paris, 1974).

[127] Foster, C. W. ed., *Registrum Antiquissimum of the Cathedral Church of Lincoln*, iii (Lincs. Rec. Soc. xxix, 1935).

[128] Francheschi, C. de, ed., *Chartularium Piranense*, i (Parenzo, 1924).

[129] *Gallia Christiana*, ed. D. Sammarthanus and others, xi (Paris, 1874).

[130] Giry, A. ed., *Documents sur les relations de la royauté avec les villes en France de 1180 à 1314* (Paris, 1885).

[131] Guasti, C. ed., *Santa Maria del Fiore* (Florence, 1887).

[132] Guerard, B. ed., *Cartulaire de l'abbaye de Saint-Victor de Marseille* (Paris, 1857).

[133] Harmer, F. E. ed., *Anglo-Saxon Writs* (Manchester, 1952).

[134] Harmer, F. E. ed., *Select English Historical Documents of the Ninth and Tenth Centuries* (Cambridge, 1914).

[135] Hearne, T. ed., *Hemingi Chartularium ecclesiae Wigorniensis* (Oxford, 1723).

[136] Hefele, C. J., *Histoire des Conciles*, ed. H. Leclercq (Paris, 1907–52).

[137] Hefele, F. ed., *Freiburger Urkundenbuch* (Freiburg im Breisgau, 1938–).

[138] Herbomez, A. D., 'Cartulaire de l'abbaye de Gorze', *Mettensia* (Paris, 1898).

[139] Inama-Sternegg, K. T. von, *Deutsche Wirthschaftsgeschichte des 10. bis 12. Jahrhunderts*, ii (Leipzig, 1891).

[140] Kehr, P. F. ed., *Regesta Pontificum Romanorum: Italia Pontificia*, viii (Berlin, 1935).

[141] Keutgen, F. ed., *Urkunden zur städtischen Verfassungsgeschichte* (Berlin, 1899).

[142] Lami, G. ed., *Sanctae Ecclesiae Florentinae Monumenta*, ii (Florence, 1758).

[143] Lanfranc, *The Letters of Lanfranc Archbishop of Canterbury*, ed. H. Clover and M. Gibson (Oxford, 1979).

[144] Laurière, E. J. de, and others ed., *Les Ordonnances des roys de France de la troisième race* (Paris, 1733-1847).

[145] Liebermann, F. ed., *Die Gesetze der Angelsachsen* (Halle, 1916).

[146] Longnon, A. ed., *Documents relatifs au comte de Champagne et de Brie, 1172-1361*, i (Paris, 1901).

[147] Madox, T., *Firma Burgi* (London, 1726).

[148] Manaresi, C. ed., *I Placiti del 'regnum Italiae'* (Fonti per la Storia d'Italia, 92, 96-7, 1955-60).

[149] Manni, D. M., *Osservazioni istoriche sopra i sigilli antichi de' secoli bassi*, xii (Florence, 1743).

[150] Marchegay, P., 'Duel judiciaire entre des communautés religieuses', *B.E.C.* i (1839-40), 552-64.

[151] Martène, E. and Durand, U. ed., *Thesaurus Novus Anecdotorum* (Paris, 1717).

[152] Meersseman, G. G., *Ordo fraternitatis: confraternite e pietà dei laici nel medioevo* (Rome, 1977).

[153] *Monumenta Boica*, xxviii (Munich, 1829).

[154] *M.G.H.: Capitularia Regum Francorum* (1883, 1890).

[155] *M.G.H.: Diplomata Karolinorum*, i (1906).

[156] *M.G.H.: Diplomata Regum et Imperatorum Germaniae* (1879-).

[157] *M.G.H.: Epistolae*, iv (1895).

[158] *M.G.H.: Epistolae Selectae*, ii (2) (1955).

[159] *M.G.H.: Legum Sectio III: Concilia*, ii (1906-8).

[160] *M.G.H.: Legum Sectio IV: Constitutiones* (1893-).

[161] Mulholland, M. A., *Early Gild Records of Toulouse* (New York, 1941).

[162] Munoz y Romero, T. ed., *Coleccion de fueros municipales y cartas pueblas* (Madrid, 1847).

[163] Muratori, L. A. ed., *Antiquitates Italicae Medii Aevi* (Milan, 1738-42).

[164] Neilson, N. ed., *A Terrier of Fleet* (London, 1920).

[165] Oechsli, W., *Die Anfänge der schweizerischen Eidgenossenschaft* (Zurich, 1891).

[166] *Parliamentary Writs* (Record Commission, 1827-34).

[167] Pasqui, U. ed., *Documenti per la storia della città di Arezzo*, i (Florence, 1899).

[168] *Placita de Quo Warranto* (Record Commission, 1818).

[169] *Placitorum Abbreviatio* (Record Commission, 1811).

[170] Prestwich, M. ed., *Documents illustrating the Crisis of 1297-8 in England* (Camden ser. 4, 24, 1980).

[171] Prou, M., 'Les Coutumes de Lorris et leur propagation aux xiie et xiiie siècles', *R.H.D.F.E.* ser. 3, vii (1884), 139-209, 267-320, 441-57, 523-56.

[172] Prou, M. ed., *Recueil des actes de Philippe I* (Paris, 1908).

[173] Ragut, M. C. ed., *Cartulaire de Saint-Vincent de Mâcon* (Mâcon, 1864).

[174] Reynolds, S., 'The Farm and Taxation of London, 1154-1216', *Guildhall Studies in London History*, i (1975), 211-28.

[175] Riley, H. T. ed., *Munimenta Gildhallae Londoniensis* (R.S. 12, 1859-62).

[176] Robertson, A. J. ed., *Anglo-Saxon Charters* (Cambridge, 1956).

[177] Robertson, A. J. ed., *Laws of the Kings of England from Edmund to Henry I* (Cambridge, 1925).

[178] *Rotuli Litterarum Patentium, 1201-16* (Record Commission, 1835).

[179] Rymer, T. ed., *Foedera* (Record Commission, 2nd edn., 1816-30).

[180] Salter, H. E. ed., *Cartulary of Oseney Abbey*, vi (Oxford Hist. Soc. ci, 1936).

[181] Sayles, G. O., 'The Dissolution of a Gild at York in 1306', *E.H.R.* lv (1940), 83-98.

[182] Schiaparelli, L. ed., *I diplomi di Berengario I* and *I diplomi di Ugo e di Lotario, di Berengario II e di Adalberto* (Fonti per la Storia d'Italia, 35, 1903; 38, 1924).

[183] Schneider, F. ed., *Regestum Volaterranum* (Regesta Chartarum Italiae, i, 1907).

[184] *Select Cases in the Law Merchant* (S.S. xxii, 1908; xlvi, 1930).

[185] *Select Cases of Procedure without Writ* (S.S. lx, 1941).

[186] *Select Pleas in Manorial Courts* (S.S. ii, 1889).

[187] Shirley, W. W. ed., *Royal and Other Historical Letters Illustrative of the Reign of Henry III* (R.S. 27, 1862-8).

[188] Smith, T. ed., *English Gilds: Original Ordinances of the Fourteenth and Fifteenth Centuries* (Early English Text Soc., xl, 1870).

[189] Solmi, A., 'L'Amministrazione finanziaria del regno italico nell'alto medioevo', *Bollettino della società Pavese di Storia Patria*, xxxi (1931), 5-288.

[190] *Statutes of the Realm, 1235-1713* (Record Commission, 1810-28).

[191] Stenton, F. M. ed., *Documents Illustrative of the Social and Economic History of the Danelaw* (London, 1920).

[192] Stones, E. L. G. and Simpson, G. G. ed., *Edward I and the Throne of Scotland* (Oxford, 1978).

[193] Stones, E. L. G. ed., *Anglo-Scottish Relations, 1174-1328* (Edinburgh, 1965).

[194] Teulet, A. ed., *Layettes du trésor des chartes*, i (Paris, 1863).

[195] Thomas, A. H. and others ed., *Calendars of the Plea and Memoranda Rolls of the City of London, 1323-1482* (London, 1926-61).

[196] Thorpe, B. ed., *Diplomatarium Anglicum Aevi Saxonici* (London, 1865).

[197] Torelli, P. ed., *Regesto Mantovano* (Regesta Chartarum Italiae, 12, 1914).

[198] Treharne, R. F. and Sanders, I. J. ed., *Documents of the Baronial Movement of Reform and Rebellion* (Oxford, 1973).

[199] Vercauteren, F. ed., *Actes des comtes de Flandre, 1071-1128* (Brussels, 1938).

[200] Verriest, L., 'La Fameuse Charte-loi de Prisches', *Revue belge*, ii (1923), 329-49.

[201] Vic, C. de, and Vaissete, J., *Histoire générale de Languedoc* (Toulouse, 1872-1904).

[202] Wackernagel, R. ed., *Urkundenbuch der Stadt Basel*, i (Basel, 1890).

[203] Wartmann, H., 'Die königlichen Freibriefe für Uri, Schwyz und Unterwalden von 1213-1316', *Archiv für Schweizerische Geschichte*, xiii (1862), 107-60.

[204] Whitelock, D. and others ed., *Councils and Synods*, i (1) (Oxford, 1981).

[205] Wopfner, H. ed., *Urkunden zur deutschen Agrargeschichte* (Stuttgart, 1928).

[206] Zdekauer, L., 'La *carta libertatis* e gli statuti della Rocca di Tintinnano', *Bulletino senese di storia patria*, iii (1896), 327-76.

IIa: *Dictionaries*

[207] *Dictionary of Medieval Latin from British Sources* (Oxford, 1975-).

[208] Grimm, J. and W. and others, *Deutsches Wörterbuch* (Leipzig, 1854-1958).

[209] Latham, R. E., *Revised Medieval Latin Word-List* (London, 1965).

[210] *Mittellateinisches Wörterbuch* (Munich, 1967-).

[211] Niermeyer, J. F. and Kieft, C. van de, *Mediae Latinitatis Lexicon Minus* (Leiden, 1976).

[212] *Oxford English Dictionary* (Oxford, 1888-1928).

IIb: *Secondary Works on Medieval History*

[213] Acher, J., 'Notes sur le droit savant au moyen âge', *R.H.D.F.E.* xxx (1906), 125-78.

[214] Aclocque, G., *Les Corporations, l'industrie et le commerce à Chartres du xie siècle à la révolution* (Paris, 1917).

[215] Addleshaw, G. W. O., *The Development of the Parochial System from Charlemagne to Urban II* (2nd edn. York, 1970).

[216] *Album H.M. Cam* (Studies Presented to Internat. Cttee. for Hist. of Repres. and Parl. Insts. xxiii-xxiv, 1960-1).

[217] Alexander, J. W., 'The Alleged Palatinates of Norman England', *Speculum*, lvi (1981), 17-27.

[218] Althoffer, B., *Les Scabins* (Nancy, 1938).

[219] Amico, R. d', 'Note su alcuni rapporti tra città e campagna nel contado di Pisa tra xi e xii secolo', *Bollettino Storica Pisano*, xxxix (1970), 15-29.

[220] Ammann, E. and Dumas, A., *L'Église au pouvoir des laïques* (A. Fliche and V. Martin ed., *Histoire de l'église*, vii, Paris, 1942).

[221] Appelt, H., 'Kaiserurkunde und Fürstensentenz unter Friedrich Barbarossa', *Mitteilungen des Inst. für österreichische Geschichtsforschung*, lxxi (1963), 33–47.

[222] Arnaldi, G., 'Regnum Langobardorum—Regnum Italiae', in T. Manteuffel and A. Gieysztor ed., *L'Europe aux ixe–xie siècles* (Warsaw, 1968), 105–32.

[223] Arnold, C. J. and Wardle, P., 'Early Medieval Settlement Patterns in England', *Med. Arch.* xxv (1981), 145–9.

[224] Artonne, A., *Le Mouvement de 1314 et les chartes provinciales de 1315* (Paris, 1912).

[225] Aston, T. H., 'The Origins of the Manor' and 'A Postscript', in Aston and others, *Social Relations and Ideas* (Cambridge, 1983), 1–43.

[226] Aubenas, R., 'Inconscience de juristes ou pédantisme malfaisante?', *R.H.D.F.E.* ser. 4, lvi (1978), 215–52.

[227] Ault, W. O., 'Village Assemblies in Medieval England', in [216], 13–35.

[228] Bader, K. S., *Studien zur Rechtsgeschichte des mittelalterlichen Dorf* (Weimar and Cologne/Graz, 1957–73).

[229] Bak, J. M., 'Serfs and Serfdom: Words and Things', *Review* (Fernand Braudel Center, Beverley Hills), iv (1980), 3–18.

[230] Banti, O., ' "Civitas" e "commune" nelle fonti italiane dei secoli xi e xii', *Critica Storica*, ix (1972), 568–84.

[231] Baratier, E., 'Les Communautés de Haute-Provence au moyen âge', *Provence historique*, xxi (1971), 237–48.

[232] Barley, M. W. ed., *European Towns* (London, 1977).

[233] Barlow, F., *The English Church, 1000–1066* (2nd edn. London, 1979).

[234] Barrow, G. W. S., 'The Idea of Freedom in Late Medieval Scotland', *Innes Review*, xxx (1979), 16–34.

[235] Barrow, G. W. S., *The Kingdom of the Scots* (London, 1973).

[236] Barrow, G. W. S., *Robert Bruce and the Community of the Realm of Scotland* (London, 1965).

[237] Bartlett, R., *Gerald of Wales* (Oxford, 1982).

[238] Bates, D., 'The Origin of the Justiciarship', *Proceedings of the Battle Conference*, iv: *1981*, 1–12.

[239] Bates, D., *Normandy before 1066* (London, 1982).

[240] Baüml, F. H., 'Varieties and Consequences of Medieval Literacy and Illiteracy', *Speculum*, lv (1980), 237–65.

[241] Beckerman, J. S., 'Adding Insult to Iniuria: Affronts to Honor and the Origins of Trespass', in M. S. Arnold and others, *On the Laws and Customs of England* (Chapel Hill, N. Carolina, 1981), 159–81.

[242] Beckerman, J. S., 'Customary Law in English Manorial Courts in

the Thirteenth and Fourteenth Centuries': London Ph.D. thesis, 1972.

[243] Beech, G. T., *A Rural Society in Medieval France: the Gâtine of Poitou in the Eleventh and Twelfth Centuries* (Baltimore, 1964).

[244] Benson, R. L., 'Political *Renovatio*: Two Models from Roman Antiquity', in [245], 339-86.

[245] Benson, R. L. and Constable, G. ed., *Renaissance and Renewal in the Twelfth Century* (Oxford, 1982).

[246] Benton, J. F., 'Consciousness of Self', in [245], 263-95.

[247] Berger, R., *Littérature et société arrageoises au xiiie siècle* (Arras, 1981).

[248] Bertelli, S., *Il Potere oligarchico nello stato-città medievale* (Florence, 1978).

[249] Beumann, H., 'Die Bedeutung des Kaisertums für die Entstehung der deutschen Nation im Spiegel der Bezeichnungen von Reich und Herrscher', *Nationes*, i (1978), 317-66.

[250] Beumann, H., 'Die Historiographie des Mittelalters als Quelle für die Ideengeschichte des Königtums', *Hist. Zeitschrift*, clxxx (1955), 449-88.

[251] Beumann, H., 'Zur Entwicklung transpersonaler Staatsvorstellungen', *V. und F.* iii (1956), 185-224.

[252] Beumann, H. and Schröder, W., 'Vorwort', *Nationes*, i (1978), 7-10.

[253] Biddle, M. ed., *Winchester in the Early Middle Ages* (Oxford, 1976).

[254] Bishko, C. J., 'Liturgical Intercession at Cluny for the King-Emperors of Leon', *Studia Monastica*, iii (1961), 53-76.

[255] Bisson, T. N., *Assemblies and Representation in Languedoc in the Thirteenth Century* (Princeton, 1964).

[256] Bisson, T. N., *Conservation of Coinage: Monetary Exploitation and its Restraint in France, Catalonia, and Aragon* (Oxford, 1979).

[257] Bisson, T. N., 'Consultative Functions in the King's Parlements (1250-1314)', *Speculum*, xliv (1969), 353-73.

[258] Bisson, T. N., 'The Military Origins of Medieval Representation', *Am.H.R.* lxxi (1966), 1199-1218.

[259] Bisson, T. N., 'The Problem of Feudal Monarchy', *Speculum*, liii (1978), 460-78.

[260] Blair, J., 'Religious Gilds as Landowners in the Thirteenth and Fourteenth Centuries: the Example of Chesterfield', in P. Riden ed., *The Medieval Town in Britain* (Cardiff, 1980).

[261] Bloch, M., 'De la cour royale à la cour de Rome: le procès des serfs de Rosny-sous-Bois', in *Studi in onore di E. Besta* (Milan, 1939), ii. 151-64.

[262] Bloch, M., *Feudal Society*, trans. L. A. Manyon (London, 1961).

[263] Bognetti, G. P., 'I Beni comunali e l'organizzazione del villaggio nell'Italia superiore fino al mille', *R.S.I.* lxxvii (1965), 469-99.

[264] Bongert, Y., *Recherches sur les cours laïques du xe au xiiie siècle* (Paris, 1949).
[265] Bonjour, E. and others, *A Short History of Switzerland* (Oxford, 1952).
[266] Borst, A., *Der Turmbau von Babel* (Stuttgart, 1957-63).
[267] Bosl, K., 'Die Entstehung der bürgerlichen Freiheit im süddeutschen Raum', in [314], 81-95.
[268] Bosl, K., *Frühformen der Gesellschaft in mittelalterlichen Europe* (Munich/Vienna, 1964).
[269] Bossuat, A., 'Les Origines troyennes: leur rôle dans la littérature historique au xve siècle', *A.N.* viii (1958), 187-97.
[270] Boüard, A. de, *Manuel de diplomatique française et pontificale* (Paris, 1929-48).
[271] Boüard, M. de, 'De la confrérie pieuse au métier organisé', *A.N.* vii (1957), 165-77.
[272] Bowsky, W. M., 'Medieval Citizenship: the Individual and the State in the Commune of Siena, 1287-1355', *Studies in Med. and Ren. Hist.* iv (1967), 193-243.
[273] Boyd, C. E., *Tithes and Parishes in Medieval Italy* (Ithaca, 1952).
[274] Boyer, M. N., 'The Bridge Building Brotherhoods', *Speculum*, xxxix (1964), 635-50.
[275] Brand, C. M., *Byzantium Confronts the West* (Cambridge, Mass., 1968).
[276] Brentano, R., *Two Churches: England and Italy in the Thirteenth Century* (Princeton, 1968).
[277] Bridbury, A. R., 'The Farming Out of Manors', *Ec.H.R.* ser. 2, xxxi (1978), 503-20.
[278] Brooks, N. P., 'Arms, Status, and Warfare in Late Saxon England', in D. Hill ed., *Ethelred the Unready* (London, 1978).
[279] Brown, E. A. R., 'Customary Aids and Royal Fiscal Policy under Philip VI', *Traditio*, xxx (1974), 191-258.
[280] Brown, E. A. R., 'Reform and Resistance to Royal Authority in Fourteenth-Century France: the Leagues of 1314-15', *Parliaments, Estates and Representation*, i (1981), 103-34.
[281] Brown, E. A. R., 'Representation and Agency Law', *Viator*, iii (1972), 329-64.
[282] Brown, E. A. R., 'Royal Necessity and Noble Service and Subsidy in Early-Fourteenth-Century France', ΠΑΡΑΔΟΣΙΣ: *Studies in Memory of E. A. Quain* (New York, 1976), 135-68.
[283] Brown, E. A. R., 'Taxation and Morality in the Thirteenth and Fourteenth Centuries', *French Historical Studies*, viii (1973), 1-28.
[284] Brown, E. A. R., 'The Tyranny of a Construct: Feudalism and Historians of Medieval Europe', *Am.H.R.* lxxix (1974), 1063-88.

[285] Brown, J. Wood, *The Dominican Church of Santa Maria Novella at Florence* (Edinburgh, 1902).

[286] Brown, P. R. L., 'Society and the Supernatural: a Medieval Change', *Daedalus*, civ (1975), 133-51.

[287] Brunel, C., 'Les Juges de la paix en Gévaudan au milieu du xie siècle', *B.E.C.* cix (1951), 32-41.

[288] Brunner, O. and others ed., *Geschichtliche Grundbegriffe* (Stuttgart, 1972-).

[289] Brunner, O., *Land und Herrschaft* (5th edn. Vienna, 1965).

[290] Buchda, G., 'Die Dorfgemeinde im Sachsenspiegel', *V. und F.* viii (1964), 7-24.

[291] Bur, M., *La Formation du comté de Champagne* (Nancy, 1977).

[292] Byl, R., *Les Juridictions scabinales dans le duché de Brabant des origines à la fin du xve siècle* (Brussels, 1965).

[293] Bynum, C., 'Did the Twelfth Century Discover the Individual?', *J. Eccl. H.* xxxi (1980), 1-17.

[294] Caenegem, R.C. van, 'Le Droit romain en Belgique', *I.R.M.A.* v. 5. b (Milan, 1966).

[295] Caenegem, R. C. van, 'Public Prosecution of Crime in Twelfth-Century England', in *Church and Government in the Middle Ages*, ed. C. N. L. Brooke and others (Cambridge, 1976), 41-76.

[296] Caenegem, R. C. van, *Royal Writs in England from the Conquest to Glanvill* (S.S. lxxvii, 1959).

[297] Caenegem, R. C. van, 'The State, Society and Private Law', *R.H.D.* xxxvii (1969), 235-45.

[298] Caggese, R., *Classi e comuni rurali nel medioevo italiano* (Florence, 1907-9).

[299] Calasso, F., *I Glossatori e la teoria della sovranità* (3rd edn. Milan, 1957).

[300] Calasso, F., *Il Medio evo del diritto*, i: *Le Fonti* (Milan, 1954).

[301] Calasso, F., *Gli Ordinamenti giuridici del rinascimento medievale* (2nd edn. Milan, 1949).

[302] Cam, H. M., *Law-Finders and Law-Makers in Medieval England* (London, 1962).

[303] Cam, H. M., *Liberties and Communities in Medieval England* (London, 1963 edn.).

[304] *Cambridge Economic History of Europe*, ed. M. M. Postan and others, vol. i (2nd edn., 1966), ii (1952), iii (1963).

[305] Campbell, B. M. S., 'The Regional Uniqueness of English Field Systems? Some Evidence from Eastern Norfolk', *Ag.H.R.* xxix (1981), 16-28.

[306] Campbell, G. J., 'The Protest of St. Louis', *Traditio*, xv (1959), 405-18.

[307] Campbell, J., 'Observations on English Government from the Tenth to the Twelfth Century', *T.R.H.S.* ser. 5, xxv (1975), 39-54.

[308] Carlyle, A. J., 'Some Aspects of the Relation of Roman Law to

Political Principles in the Middle Ages', in *Studi in onore di E. Besta* (Milan, 1939), 185–98.

[309] Carlyle, R. W. and A. J., *A History of Mediaeval Political Theory in the West* (London, 1903–36).

[310] Carus-Wilson, E. M., *Medieval Merchant Venturers* (London, 1954).

[311] Castagnetti, A., *La Pieve rurale nell'Italia padana* (Rome, 1976).

[312] Cazelles, R., 'Une Exigence de l'opinion depuis Saint Louis: la réformation du royaume', *Annuaire-Bulletin de la Société de l'histoire de France, 1962–3* (Paris, 1964), 91–9.

[313] Celli, B., *Pour l'histoire des origines du pouvoir populaire: l'expérience des villes-états italiennes* (Louvain, Inst. d'Etudes Médiévales, ser. 2, no. 3, 1980).

[314] Centre Pro Civitate, *Libertés urbaines et rurales du xie au xive siècle: Colloque internationale, Spa, 1966* (Spa, 1968).

[315] Chaplais, P., *English Royal Documents, 1199–1461* (Oxford, 1971).

[316] Checchini, A., 'I "consiliarii" nella storia della procedura', *Atti del Reale Istituto Veneto*, lxviii (1909), 625–713.

[317] Chénon, E., *Histoire générale du droit français public et privé des origines à 1815* (Paris, 1916).

[318] Chew, H. M., *The English Ecclesiastical Tenants in Chief and Knight Service* (Oxford, 1932).

[319] Cheyette, F. L., 'Custom, Case-Law, and Medieval "Constitutionalism": a Re-examination', *Political Science Quarterly*, lxxviii (1963), 362–90.

[320] Cheyette, F. L., ' "Suum cuique tribuere" ', *French Historical Studies*, vi (1970), 287–99.

[321] Chodorow, S., *Christian Political Theory in the Mid Twelfth Century* (Berkeley, 1972).

[322] Chojnacki, S., 'In Search of the Venetian Patriciate', in J. R. Hale ed., *Renaissance Venice* (London, 1973).

[323] Chomel, V., ' "Francs" et "rustiques" dans la seigneurie dauphinoise au temps des affranchisements', *B.P.H. 1965*, 285–308.

[324] Clanchy, M. T., 'Did Henry III have a Policy?', *History*, liii (1968), 203–16.

[325] Clanchy, M. T., *England and its Rulers, 1066–1272* (London, 1983).

[326] Clanchy, M. T., 'The Franchise of Return of Writs', *T.R.H.S.* ser. 5, xvii (1967), 59–82.

[327] Clanchy, M. T., *From Memory to Written Record: England, 1066–1307* (London, 1979).

[328] Clanchy, M. T., 'Remembering the Past and the Good Old Law', *History*, lv (1970), 165–76.

[329] Clark, J., 'Trinovantum: the Evolution of a Legend', *Jnl. of Medieval Hist.* vii (1981), 135–51.

[330] Classen, P., 'Fortleben und Wandel spätrömischen Urkunden-wesens im frühen Mittelalter', *V. und F.* xxiii (1977), 13-54.

[331] Classen, P., 'Kodifikation im 12. Jahrhundert. Der Constituta usus et legis von Pisa', *V. und F.* xxiii (1977), 311-17.

[332] Clément, M., 'Recherches sur les paroisses et les fabriques au commencement du xiiie siècle d'après les registres des papes', *Mélanges d'archéologie et d'histoire de l'école française de Rome*, xv (1895), 387-418.

[333] Coing, H., 'Römisches Recht in Deutschland', *I.R.M.A.* v. 6 (Milan, 1964).

[334] Collin, H., 'L'Administration des villages lorrains et le système fiscale de l'assise au début du xive siècle', *B.P.H. 1965*, 393-411.

[335] Colman, R. V., 'Reason and Unreason in Early Medieval Law', *Jnl. of Interdisciplinary Hist.* iv (1973-4), 571-96.

[336] Congar, Y. M. J., 'Quod omnes tangit, ab omnibus tractari et approbari debet', *R.H.D.F.E.* ser. 4, xxxvi (1958), 210-59.

[337] Coornaert, E., *Les Corporations en France avant 1789* (2nd edn. Paris, 1968).

[338] Coornaert, E., 'Les Ghildes médiévales', *R.H.* cxcix (1948), 22-55, 206-43.

[339] Coornaert, E., 'Notes sur les corporations parisiennes au temps de Saint Louis', *R.H.* clxxvii (1936), 343-52.

[340] Coornaert, E., 'Une Question dépassée: "l'origine" des com-munautés de métiers', *Tijdschrift vor Geschiedenis*, lxv (1952), 1-10.

[341] Coss, P. R., 'Literature and Social Terminology', in T. H. Aston and others, *Social Relations and Ideas* (Cambridge, 1983), 109-50.

[342] Cowdrey, H. E. J., 'The Peace and the Truce of God in the Eleventh Century', *P. &P.* xlvi (1970), 42-67.

[343] Cowdrey, H. E. J., 'Unions and Confraternity with Cluny', *J. Eccl. H.* xvi (1965), 152-62.

[344] Craig, H., *English Religious Drama of the Middle Ages* (Oxford, 1955).

[345] Cunliffe, B., 'Saxon and Medieval Settlement Patterns in the Region of Chalton, Hampshire', *Med. Arch.* xvi (1972), 1-12.

[346] Czok, K., 'Zum Braunschweiger Aufstand, 1374-86', in *Hansische Studien. Heinrich Sproemberg zum 70. Geburtstag* (Berlin, 1961).

[347] David, M., *La Souveraineté et les limites juridiques du pouvoir monarchique du ixe au xve siècle* (Paris, 1954).

[348] Davis, E. Jeffries, 'A Parliamentary Election in 1298', *B.I.H.R.* iii (1925-6), 45-6.

[349] Davis, R. H. C., 'An Oxford Charter of 1191', *Oxoniensia*, xxxiii (1968), 53-65.

[350] Davis, R. H. C., 'What Happened in Stephen's Reign', *History*, xlix (1964), 1-12.

[351] D'Avray, D. L., 'Sermons to the Upper Bourgeoisie by a Thirteenth-Century Franciscan', *S.C.H.* xvi (1979), 187-99.

[352] Dawson, J. P., *Oracles of the Law* (Ann Arbor, 1968).

[353] Deck, S., 'La Formation des communes en Haute-Normandie et communes éphémères', *A.N.* x (1960), 207-27, 317-29.

[354] Deike, L., *Die Entstehung der Grundherrschaft in den Hollerkolonien an der Niederweser* (Bremen, 1959).

[355] Desportes, F., 'Droit économique et police des métiers en France du Nord (milieu du xiiie - début du xve siècle)', *R.N.* lxiii (1981), 321-36.

[356] Despy, G. and Billen, C., 'Les Jurés dans les villes de Basse Lotharingie au xiiie siècle', *R.N.* lx (1978), 7-29.

[357] Despy, G., 'Serfs ou libres', *Revue belge*, xxxix (1961), 1127-43.

[358] Devailly, G., *Le Berry du xe siècle au milieu du xiiie siècle* (Paris, 1973).

[359] Dhondt, J., 'Une Crise de pouvoir capétien, 1032-4', in *Miscellanea mediaevalia in memoriam J. F. Niermeyer* (Groningen, 1967), 137-48.

[360] Dhondt, J., *Estates or Powers (Anciens Pays et assemblées d'états*, lxix, Heule, 1977).

[361] Dhondt, J., 'Les Solidarités médiévales', *A.E.S.C.* xii (1957), 529-60.

[362] Didier, P., 'Le Droit romain dans la région dauphinoise', *I.R.M.A.* v. 4. f (1979).

[363] Diestelkamp, B., 'Reichsweistümer als normative Quellen', *V. und F.* xxiii (1977), 281-310.

[364] Dodgshon, R. A., *The Origins of British Field-Systems: an Interpretation* (London, 1980).

[365] Dohrn-Van Rossum, G., 'Organ', in [288].

[366] Dolley, R. H. M. and Metcalf, D. M., 'The Reform of the Coinage under Edgar', in R. H. M. Dolley ed., *Anglo-Saxon Coins: Studies Presented to F. M. Stenton* (London, 1961).

[367] Dollinger, P., *L'Évolution des classes rurales en Bavière* (Paris, 1949).

[368] Dollinger, P., *La Hanse* (Paris, 1964).

[369] Dollinger, P., 'Patriciat noble et patriciat bourgeois à Strasbourg au xive siècle', *Revue d'Alsace*, xc (1950-1), 52-82.

[370] Dollinger, P. and others, *Bibliographie d'histoire des villes de France* (Paris, 1967).

[371] Donahue, C., 'Proof by Witnesses in the Church Courts of Medieval England: an Imperfect Reception of the Learned Law', in M. S. Arnold and others ed., *On the Laws and Customs of England* (Chapel Hill, N. Carolina, 1981, 127-58).

[372] Dubled, H., 'La communauté de village en Alsace au xiiie siècle', *Revue d'hist. écon. et sociale*, xli (1963), 1-33.

[373] Dubled, H., 'La Notion du ban en Alsace au moyen âge', *R.H.D.F.E.* ser. 4, xxxix (1961), 30-75.

356 LIST OF WORKS CITED

[374] Du Boulay, F. R. H., 'Law Enforcement in Medieval Germany', *History*, lxiii (1978), 345-55.

[375] Duby, G., *The Chivalrous Society*, trans. C. Postan (London, 1977).

[376] Duby, G., *Le Dimanche de Bouvines* (Paris, 1973).

[377] Duby, G., *L'Économie rurale et la vie des campagnes* (Paris, 1962).

[378] Duby, G., *Early Growth of the European Economy*, trans. H. B. Clarke (London, 1974).

[379] Duby, G., 'Generations of Kings', *Times Literary Supplement*, 21 Jan. 1983, 62.

[380] Duby, G., 'Recherches sur l'évolution des institutions judiciaires pendant le xe et le xie siècle dans le sud de la Bourgogne', *M.A.* lii (1946), 149-94; liii (1947), 15-38.

[381] Duby, G., *La Société aux xie et xiie siècles dans la région mâconnaise* (2nd edn. Paris, 1971).

[382] Duby, G., *Les Trois ordres ou l'imaginaire du féodalisme* (Paris, 1978).

[383] Dufour-Antonetti, G. and Antonetti, G., 'A propos du droit de ban exercé dans la forêt de Roquefort', *B.P.H. 1965*, 377-91.

[384] Duncan, A. A. M., 'The Making of the Declaration of Arbroath', in D. A. Bullough and R. L. Storey ed., *The Study of Medieval Records* (Oxford, 1971), 174-88.

[385] Duncan, A. A. M., *The Nation of the Scots and the Declaration of Arbroath* (Hist. Assoc., London, 1970).

[386] Duncan, A. A. M., review of [236], *Scottish Hist. Rev.* xlv (1966), 184-201.

[387] Duncan, A. A. M., *Scotland: the Making of the Kingdom* (Edinburgh, 1975).

[388] Duparc, P., 'Confréries du Saint-Esprit et communautés d'habitants au moyen-âge', *R.H.D.F.E.* ser. 4, xxxvi (1958), 349-67, 555-85.

[389] Ehlers, J., 'Karolingische Tradition und frühes Nationalbewusstsein in Frankreich', *Francia*, iv (1976), 213-35.

[390] Ehrlich, L., 'Proceedings against the Crown (1216-1377)', in *Oxford Studies in Social and Legal History*, vi (1921).

[391] Endemann, T., *Markturkunde und Markt in Frankreich und Burgund vom 9. bis 11. Jahrhundert* (Constance/Stuttgart, 1964).

[392] Ennen, E. and Janssen, W., *Deutsche Agrargeschichte* (Wiesbaden, 1979).

[393] Ennen, E., *Die europäische Stadt des Mittelalters* (2nd edn. Göttingen, 1975).

[394] Ennen, E., *Frühgeschichte der europäischen Stadt* (Bonn, 1953).

[395] Erler, A. and Kauffmann, E. ed., *Handwörterbuch zur deutschen Rechtsgeschichte* (Berlin, 1964-).

[396] Erler, A., *Bürgerrecht und Steuerpflicht im mittelalterlichen Städtewesen* (Frankfurt, 1939).

[397] Espinas, G., *La Vie urbaine de Douai au moyen âge* (Paris, 1913).

[398] Espinas, G., *Les Origines du capitalisme: Sire Jehan Boinebroke* (Lille, 1933).

[399] Estey, F. H., 'The Scabini and the Local Courts', *Speculum*, xxvi (1951), 119-29.

[400] Everitt, A., 'The Banburys of England', *Urban History Yearbook* (1974), 28-38.

[401] Fagniez, G., *Études sur l'industrie et la classe industrielle à Paris au xiiie et au xive siècle* (Paris, 1877).

[402] Faraglia, N. F., *Il Comune nell'Italia meridionale, 1180-1806* (Naples, 1883).

[403] Fasoli, G., 'Le Autonomie cittadine nel medioevo', *Nuove questioni di storia medievale* (Milan, 1964), 145-76.

[404] Fasoli, G., 'Castelli e signorie rurali', *Settimane*, xiii (1966), 531-67.

[405] Fasoli, G., *Dalla civitas al comune* (Bologna, 1969).

[406] Fasoli, G., *Scritti di storia medievale* (Bologna, 1974).

[407] Fasoli, G., 'Signoria feudale ed autonomie locali', in G. Fasoli and others, *Studi ezzeliniani* (Istituto Storico Italiano per il Medio Evo: Studi Storici, 45-7, 1963), 7-33.

[408] Fasoli, G. and Bocchi, F., *La Città medievale italiana* (Florence, 1973).

[409] Faucher, D., 'L'Assolement triennial en France', *Études rurales*, i (1961), 7-17.

[410] Feenstra, R., 'L'Histoire des fondations à propos de quelques études récentes', *R.H.D.* xxiv (1956), 381-448.

[411] Feigl, H., 'Von der mündlichen Rechtsweisung zur Aufzeichnung: Die Entstehung der Weistümer und verwandter Quellen', *V. und F.* xxiii (1977), 425-48.

[412] Feine, H. E., 'Kirche und Gemeindebildung', *V. und F.* vii (1964), 53-77.

[413] Feine, H. E., *Kirchliche Rechtsgeschichte* (4th edn. Cologne/Graz, 1964).

[414] Feuchère, P., 'Pairs de principauté et pairs de château', *Revue belge*, xxxi (1953), 973-1002.

[415] Feuchère, P., 'Une Tentative manquée de concentration territoriale entre Somme et Seine. La principauté d'Amiens-Valois au xie siècle', *M.A.* lx (1954), 1-37.

[416] Ficker, J., *Forschungen zur Reichs- und Rechtsgeschichte Italiens* (Innsbruck, 1868-74).

[417] Fleckenstein, J., *Early Medieval Germany*, trans. B. S. Smith (Amsterdam, 1978).

[418] Folz, R., *L'Idée d'empire en occident du ve au xive siècle* (Paris, 1953).

[419] Font-Réaulx, J. de, 'L'Origine des villages dans le sud-est', *B.P.H. 1965*, 237-43.

[420] Fossier, R., *La Terre et les hommes en Picardie* (Paris, 1968).

[421] Fossier, R., 'Land, Castle, Money and Family in the Formation of the Seigneuries', in P. H. Sawyer ed., *Medieval Settlement* (London, 1974), 159-68.

[422] Fournier, G., 'Chartes de franchises et fortifications villageoises en Basse Auvergne au xiiie siècle', in [314], 223-44.

[423] Fournier, G., *Le Peuplement rural en Basse Auvergne durant le haut moyen âge* (Paris, 1962).

[424] Fournier, P., *Le Royaume d'Arles et de Vienne (1138-1378)* (Paris, 1891).

[425] Franklin, O., *Das Reichshofgericht im Mittelalter* (Weimar, 1867-9).

[426] Frantzen, A. J., *The Literature of Penance in Anglo-Saxon England* (New Brunswick, 1983).

[427] Fried, J., *Die Entstehung des Juristenstandes im 12. Jahrhundert* (Cologne/Vienna, 1974).

[428] Fryde, E. B. and Miller, E. ed., *Historical Studies of the English Parliament*, i (Cambridge, 1970).

[429] Fuhrmann, H., *Deutsche Geschichte im hohen Mittelalter* (Göttingen, 1978).

[430] Fumagalli, V., 'L'Amministrazione periferica dello stato nell' Emilia occidentale in età carolingia', *R.S.I.* lxxxiii (1971), 911-20.

[431] Ganshof, F. L., 'Charlemagne et l'administration de justice dans la monarchie franque', in W. Braunfels ed., *Karl der Grosse* (Dusseldorf, 1965), 394-419.

[432] Ganshof, F. L., 'Deux chartes de Philippe d'Alsace pour la ville d'Arras', *R.N.* xxx (1948), 97-112.

[433] Ganshof, F. L., 'Le Droit urbain en Flandre au début de la première phase de son histoire (1127)', *R.H.D.* xix (1951), 387-416.

[434] Ganshof, F. L., *La Flandre sous les premiers Comtes* (3rd edn. Brussels, 1949).

[435] Ganshof, F. L., *Frankish Institutions*, trans. B. and M. Lyon (Providence, 1968).

[436] Ganshof, F. L., *Recherches sur les tribunaux de châtellenies de Flandre avant le milieu du xiiie siècle* (Antwerp/Paris, 1932).

[437] Génicot, L., 'Empire et principautés en Lotharingie du xe au xiiie siècle', *Annali della fondazione italiana per la storia amministrativa*, ii (1965), 95-172.

[438] Ghiron, I., 'La Credenza di Sant'Ambrogio, o la lotta dei nobili e del popolo in Milano, 1198-1292', *Archivio Storico Lombardo*, iii (1876), 583-609.

[439] Gierke, O. von, *Das deutsche Genossenschaftsrecht* (1868-1913).

[440] Gilissen, J., 'Loi et coutume: quelques aspects de l'interpénétration des sources du droit dans l'ancien droit belge', *R.H.D.* xxiii (1953), 257-96.

[441] Gillet, P., *La personnalité juridique en droit ecclésiastique* (Malines, 1927).

[442] Gillingham, J., 'The Introduction of Knight Service into England', *Proc. Battle Conference*, iv: *1981*, 53–64.

[443] Giry, A., *Manuel de diplomatique* (Paris, 1894).

[444] Goertz, W. W., *Le Origini dei comuni italiani* (Milan, 1964).

[445] Gouron, A., 'La Diffusion des consulats méridionaux et expansion du droit romain aux xiie et xiiie siècles', *B.E.C.* cxxi (1963), 26–76.

[446] Gouron, A., 'La Science juridique française aux xie et xiie siècles', *I.R.M.A.* I. 4. d-e (Milan, 1978).

[447] Gouron, M. and Gouron, A., 'Un Affranchisement de serfs à Laurens (1270)', in *Hommage à A. Dupont* (Montpellier, 1974), 157–66.

[448] Graboïs, A., 'De la Trêve de Dieu à la paix du roi', *Mélanges offerts à René Crozet* (Poitiers, 1966), 585–96.

[449] Gramain, M., report on defence of thesis on 'Villages et communautés villageoises en Bas-Languedoc occidental', in *Annales du Midi*, xcii (1980), 120–6.

[450] Gramain, M., ' "Castrum", structures féodales et peuplement en Biterrois au xie siècle', in [707].

[451] Grand, R., 'La Genèse du mouvement communal en France', *R.H.D.F.E.* ser. 4, xx (1942), 149–74.

[452] Gransden, A., *Historical Writing in England, c. 550–c. 1307* (London, 1974).

[453] Graus, F., 'Die Entstehung der mittelalterlichen Staaten in Mitteleuropa', *Historica*, x (1965), 5–65.

[454] Graus, F., 'Littérature et mentalité médiévales: le roi et le peuple', *Historica*, xvi (1969), 5–79.

[455] Graus, F., 'Social Utopias in the Middle Ages', *P. & P.* 38 (1967), 3–19.

[456] Green, T. A., 'The Trial Jury and the English Law of Homicide, 1200–1600', *Michigan Law Review*, lxxiv (1975–6), 413–99.

[457] Gross, C., *The Gild Merchant* (Oxford, 1890).

[458] Guillot, O., *Le Comte d'Anjou et son entourage au xie siècle* (Paris, 1972).

[459] Halphen, L., 'L'Idée d'état sous les Carolingiens', *R.H.* clxxxv (1939), 59–70.

[460] Hartridge, R. A. R., *A History of Vicarages in the Middle Ages* (Cambridge, 1930).

[461] Harvey, M., 'Planned Field Systems in Eastern Yorkshire', *Ag.H.R.* xxxi (1983), 91–103.

[462] Harvey, S., 'The Knight and Knight's Fee in England', *P. & P.* 49 (1970), 3–43.

[463] Hatcher, J., 'English Serfdom and Villeinage', *P. & P.* 90 (1981), 1–39.

[464] Hauck, A., *Kirchengeschichte Deutschlands* (5th edn. Leipzig, 1935).

[465] Henneman, J. B., *Royal Taxation in Fourteenth Century France* (Princeton, 1971).

[466] Higounet, C., 'Le Groupe aristocratique en Aquitaine et en Gascogne (fin x^e - début xiie siècle)', *Annales du Midi*, lxxx (1968), 563-71.

[467] Higounet, C. ed., *Histoire de Bordeaux* (Bordeaux, 1962-9).

[468] Higounet, C., *Paysages et villages neufs du moyen âge* (Bordeaux, 1975).

[469] Hilton, R. H., 'Peasant Movements in England before 1381', *Ec.H.R.* ser. 2, ii (1949), 117-36.

[470] Hilton, R. H., *A Medieval Society: the West Midlands at the End of the Thirteenth Century* (London, 1966).

[471] Hirsch, H., *Die hohe Gerichtsbarkeit im Deutschen Mittelalter* (Prague, 1922).

[472] Hoffmann, R. C., 'Medieval Origins of the Common Fields', in W. N. Parker and E. L. Jones ed., *European Peasants and Their Markets* (Princeton, 1975), 23-71.

[473] Holt, J. C., 'The End of the Anglo-Norman Realm', *Proc. of British Academy*, lxi (1975), 223-65.

[474] Holt, J. C., 'Feudal Society and the Family, 3: Patronage and Politics', *T.R.H.S.* ser. 5, xxxiv (1983): forthcoming.

[475] Holt, J. C., *Magna Carta* (Cambridge, 1965).

[476] Holt, J. C., *The Northerners* (Oxford, 1961).

[477] Holt, J. C., 'The Prehistory of Parliament', in R. G. Davies and J. H. Denton ed., *The English Parliament in the Middle Ages* (Manchester, 1981), 1-28.

[478] Holt, J. C., 'Rights and Liberties in Magna Carta', in [216], 57-69.

[479] Homans, G. C., *English Villagers of the Thirteenth Century* (Cambridge, Mass., 1942).

[480] Hoskins, W. G., *Provincial England* (London, 1963).

[481] Hoyt, R. S., *The Royal Demesne in English Constitutional History* (New York, 1950).

[482] Huizinga, J., *Men and Ideas* (London, 1960).

[483] Hurnard, N. D., 'The Anglo-Norman Franchises', *E.H.R.* lxiv (1949), 289-327, 433-60.

[484] Hurnard, N. D., 'The Jury of Presentment and the Assize of Clarendon', *E.H.R.* lvi (1941), 374-410.

[485] Hyams, P. R., *King, Lords and Peasants in Medieval England* (Oxford, 1980).

[486] Hyde, J. K., 'Contemporary Views on Faction and Civil Strife in Thirteenth- and Fourteenth-Century Italy', in L. Martinez ed., *Violence and Civil Disorder in Italian Cities, 1200-1500* (Berkeley, 1972), 273-307.

[487] Hyde, J. K., *Padua in the Age of Dante* (Manchester, 1966).

[488] Hyde, J. K., *Society and Politics in Medieval Italy* (London, 1973).

[489] Illsley, J. S., 'Parliamentary Elections in the Reign of Edward I', *B.I.H.R.* xlix (1976), 24-40.

[490] James, E., *The Origins of France: From Clovis to the Capetians, 500-1000* (London, 1982).

[491] Jamison, E. M., 'The Norman Administration of Apulia and Calabria, more especially under Roger II and William I', *Papers of the British School at Rome*, vi (1913), 211-481.

[492] Jorden, W., *Das Cluniazensische Totengedächtniswesen* (Münster, 1930).

[493] Kahl, H. D., '*natio* im mittelalterlichen Latein', *Nationes*, i (1978), 63-108.

[494] Kaiser, R., 'Cologne au xiie siècle', *Revue belge*, lv (1977), 1071-5.

[495] Kantorowicz, E. H., 'Kingship Under the Impact of Scientific Jurisprudence', in M. Clagett and others ed., *Twelfth Century Europe and the Foundations of Modern Society* (Madison, 1961), 89-111.

[496] Kantorowicz, E. H., *The King's Two Bodies* (Princeton, 1957).

[497] Kauss, D., *Die mittelalterliche Pfarrorganisation in der Ortenau* (Buhl/Baden, 1970).

[498] Ke Chin Wang, H., 'The Corporate Entity Concept (or Fiction Theory) in the Year Book Period', *L.Q.R.* lviii (1942), 498-511; lix (1943), 72-86.

[499] Keeney, B. C., 'The Medieval Idea of the State: the Great Cause, 1291-2', *Univ. of Toronto Law Journal*, viii (1949-50), 48-71.

[500] Keeney, B. C., 'Military Service and the Development of Nationalism in England, 1272-1327', *Speculum*, xxii (1947), 534-49.

[501] Kelley, D. R., 'De Origine Feudorum', *Speculum*, xxxix (1964), 207-28.

[502] Kern, F., *Kingship and Law*, trans. S. B. Chrimes (Oxford, 1939).

[503] Kibre, P., *Scholarly Privileges in the Middle Ages* (London, 1961).

[504] Kitzinger, E., 'The Arts as Aspects of a Renaissance: Rome and Italy', in [245], 637-70.

[505] Kleinschmidt, H., *Untersuchungen über des englische Königtum in 10. Jahrhundert* (Göttingen, 1979).

[506] Köbler, G., 'burg und stat - Burg und Stadt?', *H.J.* lxxxvii (1967), 305-25.

[507] Köbler, G., *Das Recht im frühen Mittelalter* (Forschungen zur deutschen Rechtsgeschichte, vii, 1971).

[508] Kosminsky, E. A., *Studies in the Agrarian History of England in the Thirteenth Century* (Oxford, 1956).

[509] Kraus, H., *Gold was the Mortar: the Economies of Cathedral Building* (London, 1979).

[510] Krause, H., 'Dauer und Vergänglichkeit im mittelalterlichen Recht', *Z.R.G.* lxxv (1958), Germ. Abt. 206-51.
[511] Krause, H., 'Gewohnheitsrecht', in [395].
[512] Krause, H., 'Königtum und Rechtsordnung in der Zeit der sächsischer und salier Herrscher', *Z.R.G.* lxxxii (1965), Germ. Abt. 1-98.
[513] Krautheimer, R., *Rome: Profile of a City, 312-1308* (Princeton, 1980).
[514] Kroeschell, K., ' "Rechtsfindung": die mittelalterlichen Grundlagen einer modernen Vorstellung', in *Festschrift für H. Heimpel* (1972), iii, 498-517.
[515] Kroeschell, K., 'Recht und Rechtsbegriff im 12. Jahrhundert', *V. und F.* xii (1968), 309-35.
[516] Kuhn, J., 'Zur Kritik der Weistümer (nach oberrheinischen Quellen)', in *Festgabe G. Seeliger* (Leipzig, 1920), 29-50.
[517] Kurze, D., *Pfarrerwahlen im Mittelalter* (Cologne/Graz, 1966).
[518] Kuttner, S., *Harmony from Dissonance* (Latrobe, Pennsylvania, 1960).
[519] Lane, F. C., *Venice: a Maritime Republic* (Baltimore, 1973).
[520] Langmuir, G. I., 'Concilia and Capetian Assemblies, 1179-1230', in [216], 29-63.
[521] Langmuir, G. I., ' "Judei Nostri" and the Beginning of Capetian Legislation', *Traditio*, xvi (1960), 203-39.
[522] Langmuir, G. I., 'Per Commune Consilium Regni in Magna Carta', *Studia Gratiana*, xv (1972), 465-86.
[523] Langmuir, G. I., 'Politics and Parliaments in the Early Thirteenth Century', *Travaux et Recherches de la Faculté de Droit et des Sciences Économiques de Paris*, viii (1966), 47-62.
[524] *La Preuve* (Receuils de la Société Jean Bodin, xvii, 1965).
[525] Lattes, A., *Il Diritto consuetudinario delle città Lombarde* (Milan, 1899).
[526] Le Bras, G., 'Les Confréries chrétiennes', *R.H.D.F.E.* ser. 4, xix-xxi (1940-2), 310-63.
[527] Le Bras, G. and others, *Histoire du droit et des institutions de l'église en occident* (Paris, 1958-).
[528] Le Bras, G., *Institutions ecclésiastiques de la Chrétienté médiévale* (A. Fliche and V. Martin, ed., *Histoire de l'église*, xii, Paris, 1959).
[529] Lechner, K., 'Entstehung, Entwicklung und Verfassung der ländlichen Gemeinde in Niederösterreich', *V. und F.* vii (1964), 107-62.
[530] Lees, B. A., 'The Statute of Winchester and *villa integra*', *E.H.R.* xli (1926), 98-103.
[531] Le Goff, J. ed., *La Ville médiévale* (Paris, 1980).
[532] Leicht, P. S., 'La "carta di libertà" di Penna San Giovanni', in *Studi in onore di A. Gregorio* (Cremona, 1954), 114-19.
[533] Leicht, P. S., *Scritti vari di storia del diritto italiano* (Milan, 1943-9).

[534] Leicht, P. S., *Storia del diritto italiano: il diritto privato*, i (2nd edn. Milan, 1960).

[535] Lemarignier, J. F., 'Autour des premiers Capétiens', in W. Paravicini and K. F. Werner ed., *Histoire comparée de l'administration* (Munich, 1980), 117-34.

[536] Lemarignier, J. F., 'La Dislocation du "pagus" et le problème des "consuetudines" (xe-xie siècles)', in *Mélanges d'histoire du moyen âge dédiés à la mémoire de L. Halphen* (Paris, 1951), 401-10.

[537] Lemarignier, J. F., *La France médiévale: institutions et société* (Paris, 1970).

[538] Lemarignier, J. F., *Le Gouvernement royal aux premiers temps capétiens* (Paris, 1966).

[539] Lennard, R., 'Early Manorial Juries', *E.H.R.* lxxvii (1962), 511-18.

[540] Lennard, R., review of [479], *Econ. Journal*, liii (1943), 84-8.

[541] Lennard, R., *Rural England, 1086-1135* (Oxford, 1959).

[542] Le Patourel, J., *The Norman Empire* (Oxford, 1976).

[543] Le Roy-Ladurie, E., *Montaillou: village occitan de 1294 à 1324* (Paris, 1975).

[544] Lestocquoy, J., *Les Dynasties bourgeoises d'Arras du xie au xve siècle* (Arras, 1945).

[545] Lestocquoy, J., *Études d'histoire urbaine* (Arras, 1966).

[546] Lestocquoy, J., *Les Villes de Flandre et d'Italie sous le gouvernement des patriciens* (Paris, 1952).

[547] Leuschner, J., *Germany in the late Middle Ages* (trans. S. McCormack (Amsterdam, 1980).

[548] Lewis, E., 'King above Law? "Quod principi placuit" in Bracton', *Speculum*, xxxix (1944), 240-69.

[549] Lewis, E., *Medieval Political Ideas* (London, 1954).

[550] Lewis, P. S., *Later Medieval France: the Polity* (London, 1968).

[551] Leyser, K., 'Frederick Barbarossa, Henry II and the Hand of St. James', *E.H.R.* xc (1975), 481-506.

[552] Leyser, K., *Medieval Germany and its Neighbours, 900-1250* (London, 1982).

[553] Leyser, K., *Rule and Conflict in an Early Medieval Society* (London, 1979).

[554] Little, L. K., *Religious Poverty and the Profit Economy in Medieval Europe* (London, 1978).

[555] Lombard-Jourdan, A., 'Oppidum et banlieue', *A.E.S.C.* xxvii (1972), 373-95.

[556] Lot, F., *Études critiques sur l'abbaye de Saint-Wandrille* (Paris, 1913).

[557] Loud, G. A., 'The Gens Normannorum—Myth or Reality?', *Proc. Battle Conference*, iv: *1981*, 104-17.

[558] Luzzatto, G., *Dai Servi della gleba agli albori del capitalismo* (Bari, 1966).

[559] MacCormick, N., 'Nation and Nationalism', in C. MacLean ed., *The Crown and the Thistle* (Edinburgh, 1979), 99–111.

[560] Macfarlane, A., *The Origins of English Individualism* (Oxford, 1978).

[561] McIlwain, C. H., *The Growth of Political Thought in the West* (New York, 1932).

[562] Maddicott, J. R., 'The County Community and the Making of Public Opinion in the Fourteenth Century', *T.R.H.S.* ser. 5, xxviii (1978), 27–43.

[563] Maddicott, J. R., *Law and Lordship: Royal Justices as Retainers in Thirteenth and Fourteenth Century England* (Oxford, 1978).

[564] Mager, W., *Zur Entstehung des modernen Staatsbegriff* (Mainz, 1968).

[565] Magnou-Nortier, E., 'Les Mauvaises coutumes en Auvergne, Bourgogne méridionale, Languedoc et Provence au xie siècle', in [707].

[566] Maitland, F. W., *Collected Papers* (Cambridge, 1911).

[567] Maitland, F. W., *Domesday Book and Beyond* (Cambridge, 1907).

[568] Maitland, F. W., *Township and Borough* (Cambridge, 1898).

[569] Manteuffel, T., 'Intégration et désintégration des états européens, ixe–xe siècles', in T. Manteuffel and A. Gieysztor ed., *L'Europe aux ixe–xie siècles* (Warsaw, 1968).

[570] Marongiu, A., 'Le "curie generali" del regno di Sicilia sotto gli Svevi (1194–1266)', repr. in his *Byzantine, Norman, Swabian and Later Institutions in South Italy* (London, 1972).

[571] Marongiu, A., 'Legislatori e giudici di fronte all'autorità dei giuristi', in *Studi in onore di E. Besta* (Milan, 1939), iii, 443–64.

[572] Marongiu, A., *Medieval Parliaments*, trans. S. J. Woolf (London, 1968).

[573] Martin, G. H., 'Church Life in Medieval Leicester', in A. E. Brown ed., *The Growth of Leicester* (Leicester, 1970).

[574] Martin, G. H., *The Early Court Rolls of Ipswich* (Leicester, 1954).

[575] Martin, G. H., 'The English Borough in the Thirteenth Century', *T.R.H.S.* ser. 5, xiii (1963), 123–44.

[576] Martin, G. H., 'The Origins of Borough Records', *Jnl. Soc. of Archivists*, ii (1960–4), 147–53.

[577] Mascher, K., *Reichsgut und Komitat am Südharz im Hochmittelalter* (Cologne, 1957).

[578] Maschke, E., 'Continuité sociale et histoire urbaine médiévale', *A.E.S.C.* xv (1960), 936–48.

[579] Maschke, E., 'Verfassung und soziale Kräfte in der deutschen Stadt des später Mittelalters, vornehmlich in Oberdeutschland', *Vierteljahrschrift für Sozial- und Wirtschaftsgeschichte*, xlvi (1959), 289–349, 433–76.

[580] Mauduech, G., 'La "bone ville"': origine et sens de l'expression', *A.E.S.C.*, xxvii (1972), 1441-8.

[581] Mayer, T., *Fürsten und Staat* (Weimar, 1950).

[582] Mayer, T. ed., *Studien zu den Anfängen des europäischen Städtewesens* (*V. und F.* iv, 1958).

[583] Mayer, T., 'Vom Werden und Wesen der Landgemeinde', *V. und F.* viii (1964), 465-95.

[584] Mayr-Harting, H. M. R. E., 'Functions of a Twelfth-Century Recluse', *History*, lx (1975), 337-52.

[585] Ménager, L. R., 'La Législation sud-italienne sous la domination normande', *Settimane*, xvi (1968), 439-96.

[586] Michaud-Quantin, P., *Universitas: expressions du mouvement communautaire dans le moyen âge latin* (Paris, 1970).

[587] Miller, E. and Hatcher, J., *Medieval England: Rural Society and Economic Change, 1086-1348* (London, 1978).

[588] Milsom, S. F. C., 'Law and Fact in Legal Development', *Univ. of Toronto Law Jnl.* xvii (1967), 1-19.

[589] Milsom, S. F. C., *The Legal Framework of English Feudalism* (Cambridge, 1976).

[590] Milsom, S. F. C., 'Reason and the Development of the Common Law', *L.Q.R.* lxxxi (1965), 496-517.

[591] Mochi-Onory, S., *Fonti canonistiche dell'idea moderna dello stato* (Milan, 1951).

[592] Mollat, M. and Wolff, P., *Ongles bleus, Jacques et Ciompi* (Paris, 1970).

[593] Moorman, J. R. H., *Church Life in England in the Thirteenth Century* (Cambridge, 1945).

[594] Mor, C. G., 'Gouvernés et gouvernants en Italie du vie au xiie siècle', *Recueils de la Société Jean Bodin*, xxiii (1968), 395-420.

[595] Morel, F., *Les Juridictions commerciales au moyen-âge* (Paris, 1897).

[596] Morris, C., *The Discovery of the Individual* (London, 1972).

[597] Morris, C., 'Individualism in Twelfth-Century Religion', *J. Eccl. H.* xxxi (1980), 195-206.

[598] Morris, C., 'Judicium Dei: the Social and Political Significance of the Ordeal in the Eleventh Century', *S.C.H.* xii (1975), 95-111.

[599] Morris, W. A., *The Frankpledge System* (New York, 1910).

[600] Müller, F. W., 'Zur Geschichte der Wortes und Begriffes "nation" im französischen Schrifttum des Mittelalters bis zur Mitte des 15. Jahrhunderts', *Romanische Forschungen*, lviii-lix (1947), 247-321.

[601] Müller, W., 'Der Beitrag der Pfarreigeschichte zur Stadtgeschichte', *H.J.* xciv (1974), 69-88.

[602] Müller-Mertens, E., 'Zur Rolle der politische Formung bei ihrer Volkwerdung', in B. Gramsch ed., *Germanen-Slaven-Deutsche* (Berlin, 1968).

[603] Murray, A., *Reason and Society* (Oxford, 1978).

[604] Nanni, L., *La Parrochia studiata nei documenti lucchesi dei secoli viii–xiii* (Rome, 1948).

[605] Nehlsen-von Stryk, K., *Die boni homines des frühen Mittelalters* (Freiburger Rechtsgesch. Abhandlungen, new ser. ii, 1981).

[606] Nelson, J. L., 'Kingship, Law and Liturgy in the Political Thought of Hincmar of Rheims', *E.H.R.* xcii (1977), 241–79.

[607] Nelson, J. L., 'Legislation and Consensus in the Reign of Charles the Bald', in P. Wormald ed., *Ideal and Reality in Frankish and Anglo-Saxon Society* (Oxford, 1983), 99–129.

[608] Nicholas, D., 'Structures du peuplement, fondations urbaines et formation du capital dans la Flandre médiévale', *A.E.S.C.* xxxiii (1978), 501–27.

[609] Oexle, G., 'Die funktionale Dreiteilung der "Gesellschaft" bei Adalbero von Laon', *Frühmittelalterliche Studien*, xii (1978), 1–54.

[610] Olivier-Martin, F., *Histoire du droit français des origines à la Révolution* (Paris, 1948).

[611] Orestano, R., *Il 'problema delle persone giuridiche' in diritto romano*, i (Turin, 1968).

[612] Orme, N., *English Schools in the Middle Ages* (London, 1973).

[613] Otway-Ruthven, A. J., *History of Medieval Ireland* (London, 1968).

[614] Ourliac, P., 'Les Villages de la région toulousaine', *A.E.S.C.* iv (1949), 268–77.

[615] Owen, D. M., *Church and Society in Medieval Lincolnshire* (Lincoln, 1971).

[616] Pacaut, M., *Louis VII et son royaume* (Paris, 1964).

[617] Packard, S. R., review of [623], *Speculum*, xxiv (1949), 609–14.

[618] Page, W., 'Some Remarks on the Churches of the Domesday Survey', *Archaeologia*, lxvi (1915), 61–102.

[619] Palmer, R. C., *County Courts of Medieval England, 1150–1350* (Princeton, 1982).

[620] Partner, P., *The Lands of St. Peter* (London, 1972).

[621] Perrin, C. E., 'Chartes de franchise et rapports de droits en Lorraine', *M.A.* lii (1946), 11–42.

[622] Pertile, A., *Storia del diritto italiano* (Turin, 1892–1903).

[623] Petit-Dutaillis, C., *Les Communes françaises* (Paris, 1947).

[624] Petot, P., 'Le Droit commun en France selon les coutumiers', *R.H.D.F.E.* ser. 4, xxxviii (1960), 412–29.

[625] Picard, R. le, report on a contribution to 'Le Semaine de droit normand' in *R.H.D.F.E.* ser. 4, xvii (1938), 717–18.

[626] Pirenne, H., *Les Villes et les institutions urbaines* (Paris/Brussels, 1939).

[627] Planitz, H., *Die deutsche Stadt im Mittelalter* (Graz/Koln, 1954).

[628] Pollock, F. and Maitland, F. W., *History of English Law before the time of Edward I* (2nd edn. Cambridge, 1911).

[629] Poly, J.-P., *La Provence et la société féodale, 879-1166* (Paris, 1976).
[630] Poly, J.-P. and Bournazel, E., *La Mutation féodale* (Paris, 1980).
[631] Post, G., *Studies in Medieval Legal Thought* (Princeton, 1964).
[632] Powell, J. E. and Wallis, K., *The House of Lords in the Middle Ages* (London, 1968).
[633] Powicke, F. M., *King Henry III and the Lord Edward* (Oxford, 1947).
[634] Powicke, M. R., *Military Obligation in Medieval England* (Oxford, 1962).
[635] Prawer, J., *Crusader Institutions* (Oxford, 1980).
[636] Prawer, J., *The Latin Kingdom of Jerusalem* (London, 1972).
[637] Prestwich, M., *Law, Politics and Finance under Edward I* (London, 1972).
[638] Procter, E. S., *Curia and Cortes in León and Castile, 1072-1295* (Cambridge, 1980).
[639] Rabe, H., *Der Rat der Niederschwäbischen Reichsstädte* (Cologne/Graz, 1966).
[640] Radding, C. M., 'Evolution of Medieval Mentalities: a Cognitive-Structural Approach', *Am.H.R.* lxxxiii (1978), 577-97.
[641] Radding, C. M., 'Superstition to Science: Nature, Fortune and the Passing of the Medieval Ordeal', *Am.H.R.* lxxxiv (1979), 945-69.
[642] Razi, Z., *Life, Marriage and Death in a Medieval Parish* (Cambridge, 1980).
[643] Razi, Z., 'The Struggles between the Abbots of Halesowen and their Tenants in the Thirteenth and Fourteenth Centuries', in T. H. Aston and others, *Social Relations and Ideas* (Cambridge, 1983), 151-67.
[644] Reicke, S., *Das deutsche Spital und sein Recht im Mittelalter* (Stuttgart, 1932).
[645] Reimann, H. L., *Unruhe und Aufruhr im mittelalterlichen Braunschweig* (Brunswick, 1962).
[646] Renouard, Y., *Les Villes d'Italie de la fin du xe siècle au début du xive siècle* (2nd edn. Paris, 1969).
[647] Reuter, T., 'The "Imperial Church System" of the Ottonian and Salian Rulers', *J. Eccl. Hist.* xxxiii (1982), 347-74.
[648] Reuter, T. ed., *The Medieval Nobility* (Amsterdam, 1978).
[649] Reynolds, R. L., 'In Search of a Business Class in Thirteenth-Century Genoa', *Jnl. of Econ. Hist.* suppl. 5 (1945), 1-19.
[650] Reynolds, S., 'Eadric Silvaticus and the English Resistance', *B.I.H.R.* liv (1981), 102-5.
[651] Reynolds, S., 'The Idea of the Corporation in Western Christendom before 1300', in J. Guy ed., *Law and Social Change in British History* (forthcoming).
[652] Reynolds, S., *Introduction to the History of English Medieval Towns* (Oxford, 1977).

[653] Reynolds, S., 'Medieval *Origines Gentium* and the Community of the Realm', *History*, lxviii (1983), 375–90.

[654] Reynolds, S., 'Medieval Urban history and the History of Political Thought', *Urban History Yearbook* (1982), 14–23.

[655] Reynolds, S., 'The Rulers of London in the Twelfth Century', *History*, lvii (1972), 337–57.

[656] Richard, J., *Les Ducs de Bourgogne et la formation du duché du xie au xive siècle* (Paris, 1954).

[657] Richardson, H. G. and Sayles, G. O., *The Governance of Medieval England* (Edinburgh, 1963).

[658] Richardson, H. G. and Sayles, G. O., 'Parliaments and Great Councils in Medieval England', *L.Q.R.* lxxvii (1961), 213–36, 401–26.

[659] Riesenberg, P., 'Citizenship in Late Medieval Italy', *Viator*, v (1974), 333–46.

[660] Riley-Smith, J., *The Feudal Nobility and the Kingdom of Jerusalem, 1174–1277* (London, 1973).

[661] Roberts, B. K., 'Village Plans in County Durham: a Preliminary Statement', *Med. Arch.* xvi (1972), 33–56.

[662] Rodriguez, M. J., 'Innocent IV and the Element of Fiction in Juristic Personalities', *The Jurist*, xxii (1962), 287–318.

[663] Rogozinski, J., 'The Counsellors of the Seneschal of Beaucaire and Nîmes, 1250–1350', *Speculum*, xliv (1969), 421–39.

[664] Rogozinski, J., 'Ennoblement by the Crown and Social Stratification in France, 1285–1322', in W. C. Jordan and others ed., *Order and Innovation in the Middle Ages* (Princeton, 1976), 273–91.

[665] Rörig, F., *Die europäische Stadt und die Kultur des Bürgertums im Mittelalter* (Göttingen, 1958).

[666] Rössler, H., ed., *Deutsches Patriziat, 1480–1740* (Limburg an der Lahn, 1968).

[667] Rouse, R. H. and M. A., 'John of Salisbury and the Doctrine of Tyrannicide', *Speculum*, xlii (1967), 693–709.

[668] Rubinstein, N., 'The Beginnings of Political Thought in Florence', *Journal of the Warburg and Courtauld Institutes*, v (1942), 198–227.

[669] Ruffini, E., *La Ragione dei più* (Milan, 1977).

[670] Runciman, S., *The Sicilian Vespers* (Cambridge, 1958).

[671] Salvemini, G., *Magnati e popolani*, ed. and introd. E. Sestan (Turin, 1960).

[672] Salvioli, G., *Storia della procedura civile e criminale* (P. de Giudice ed., *Storia del diritto italiano*, iii, Milan, 1925).

[673] Santini, G., *'I Comuni di pieve' nel medioevo italiano* (Milan, 1964).

[674] Santini, G., *I Comuni di valle del medioevo* (Milan, 1960).

[675] Sapori, A., 'Le Compagnie mercantili toscane del dugento e dei primi del trecento', in *Studi in onore di E. Besta* (Milan, 1939), ii, 101–48.

[676] Sautel-Boulet, M., 'Le Rôle juridictionnel de la cour des pairs aux xiiie et xive siècles', in *Recueil de travaux offert à M. Clovis Brunel* (Paris, 1955), ii, 507-20.

[677] Sawyer, P. H., *From Roman Britain to Norman England* (London, 1978).

[678] Schlesinger, W., *Beiträge zur deutschen Verfassungsgeschichte des Mittelalters* (Göttingen, 1963).

[679] Schlesinger, W., *Die Entstehung der Landesherrschaft* (2nd edn. Darmstadt, 1964).

[680] Schlesinger, W., *Mitteldeutsche Beiträge zur deutschen Verfassungsgeschichte des Mittelalters* (Göttingen, 1961).

[681] Schlesinger, W., 'Stadt und Burg in Lichte der Wortgeschichte', *Studium Generale*, xvi (1963), 433-44.

[682] Schneider, J., 'Les Origines des chartes de franchises dans le royaume de France', in [314], 29-50.

[683] Schulze, H. R., *Die Grafschaftsverfassung der Karolingerzeit in den Gebieten östlich des Rheins* (Berlin, 1973).

[684] Schumann, R., *Authority and the Commune, 833-1133* (Parma, 1973).

[685] Schütte, L., *Wik: eine Siedlungsbezeichnung in historischen und sprachlichen Bezügen* (Cologne, 1976).

[686] Seelman, W., *Der Rechtszug in älteren deutschen Recht* (Breslau, 1911).

[687] Sestan, E., 'La Città comunale italiana dei secoli xi-xiii', *XIe Congrès des sciences historiques: Stockholm, 1960: rapports*, iii, 75-95.

[688] Settia, A., 'L'Incidenza del popolamento sulla signoria locale nell'Italia del Nord: dal villagio fortificato al castello deposito', in [707], 263-84.

[689] Sicard, E., 'Notes et hypothèses sur les fraternités', *A.N.* iv (1954), 3-30.

[690] Simpson, G., 'The Declaration of Arbroath Revitalized', *Scottish Hist. Rev.* lvi (1977), 11-33.

[691] Slicher van Bath, B. H., 'Dutch Tribal Problems', *Speculum*, xxiv (1949), 319-38.

[692] Southern, R. W., review of [496], *J. Eccl. H.* x (1959), 105-8.

[693] Stafford, P., 'The Laws of Cnut and the History of Anglo-Saxon Royal Promises', *Anglo-Saxon England*, x (1982), 173-90.

[694] Stafford, P., 'The Reign of Aethelred II', in D. Hill ed., *Ethelred the Unready* (Brit. Archaeol. Rep. 59, 1978).

[695] Steinbach, F., *Collectanea* (Bonn, 1967).

[696] Stenton, D. M., *English Justice between the Norman Conquest and the Great Charter* (London, 1965).

[697] Stenton, F. M., *The Latin Charters of the Anglo-Saxon Period* (Oxford, 1955).

[698] Stephenson, C., 'Les "Aides" des villes françaises aux xiie et xiiie siècles', *M.A.* ser. 2, xxiv (1922), 274-328.

[699] Stock, B. C., *The Implications of Literacy* (Princeton, 1983).

[700] Stoob, H., 'Landausbau und Gemeinde an der Nordseeküste', *V. und F.* vii (1964), 365–422.

[701] Strahm, H., 'Stadtluft macht frei', *V. und F.* ii (1953), 103–21.

[702] Strait, P., *Cologne in the Twelfth Century* (Gainesville, Florida, 1974).

[703] Strayer, J. R., 'The Crusades of Louis IX', in K. M. Setton and others ed., *History of the Crusades*, ii (2nd edn. Madison, Wisconsin, 1969), 487–521.

[704] Strayer, J. R., *Medieval Statecraft and the Perspectives of History* (Princeton, 1971).

[705] Strayer, J. R., *On the Medieval Origins of the Modern State* (Princeton, 1970).

[706] Strayer, J. R. and Taylor, C. H., *Studies in Early French Taxation* (Cambridge, Mass., 1939).

[707] *Structures féodales et féodalisme dans l'occident méditerranéen (xe–xiiie siècles)* (Collection de l'École française de Rome, xliv, 1980).

[708] Struve, T., *Die Entwicklung der organologischen Staatsauffassung im Mittelalter* (Stuttgart, 1978).

[709] Sutherland, D. W., *Quo Warranto Proceedings in the Reign of Edward I* (Oxford, 1963).

[710] Tabacco, G., 'La Storia politica e sociale', in R. Romano and C. Vivanti ed., *Storia d'Italia*, ii (Turin, 1974).

[711] Tait, J., *The Medieval English Borough* (Manchester, 1936).

[712] Taylor, C. C., 'Aspects of Village Mobility in Medieval and Later Times', in S. Limbrey and J. G. Evans ed., *The Effect of Man on the Landscape: the Lowland Zone* (Brit. Archaeol. Rep., 21, 1978).

[713] Taylor, C. C., *The Cambridgeshire Landscape* (London, 1973).

[714] Taylor, C. H., 'The Composition of Baronial Assemblies in France, 1315–1320', *Speculum*, xxix (1954), 433–58.

[715] Toubert, P., *Les Structures du Latium médiéval* (Rome, 1973).

[716] Treharne, R. F., 'The Nature of Parliament in the Reign of Henry III', *E.H.R.* lxxiv (1959), 590–610.

[717] Trusen, W., 'Zur Urkundenlehre der mittelalterlichen Jurisprudenz', *V. und F.* xxiii (1977), 197–219.

[718] Turner, R. V., 'The Origin of the Medieval English Jury', *Jnl. of Brit. Studies*, vii (1967–8), 1–10.

[719] Ullmann, W., *Medieval Foundations of Renaissance Humanism* (London, 1977).

[720] Ullmann, W., *Principles of Government and Politics in the Middle Ages* (2nd edn. London, 1966).

[721] Vaccari, P., 'Diritto Longobardo e letteratura longobardistica intorno del diritto romano', *I.R.M.A.* I. 4. b. ee (1966).

[722] Vaccari, P., *La Territorialità con base dell'ordinamento giuridico del contado nell'Italia medioevale* (Milan, 1963).

[723] Vaillant, P., 'Les Origines d'une libre confédération des vallées:

les habitants des communautés briançonnaises au xiiie siècle', *B.E.C.* cxxv (1967), 301–48.

[724] Veale, E. M., *The English Fur Trade in the Later Middle Ages* (Oxford, 1966).

[725] Verbruggen, J. F., 'Note sur le sens des mots Castrum, Castellum, et quelques autres expressions', *Revue belge*, xxviii (1950), 147–55.

[726] Verlinden, C., *L'Esclavage dans l'Europe médiévale*, i (Bruges, 1955).

[727] Vermeesch, A., *Essai sur les origines et la signification de la commune dans le nord de la France* (Heule, 1966).

[728] *Victoria History of the Counties of England: Middlesex*, iii (1962) and *Oxford*, v (1957).

[729] Violante, C., *La Società milanese nell'età precomunale* (Bari, 1953).

[730] Vollrath, H., 'Herrschaft und Genossenschaft in Kontext frühmittelalterlicher Rechtsbeziehungen', *H.J.* cii (1982), 33–71.

[731] Volpe, G., *Studi sulle istituzioni comunali a Pisa*, ed. and introd. C. Violante (Florence, 1970).

[732] Wade-Martins, P., 'The Origins of Rural Settlement in East Anglia', in P. J. Fowler ed., *Recent Work in Rural Archaeology* (Bradford on Avon, 1975), 137–57.

[733] Wake, J., '*Communitas Villae*', *E.H.R.* xvii (1922), 406–13.

[734] Waley, D. P., *The Italian City Republics* (London, 1969).

[735] Waley, D. P., *The Papal State in the Thirteenth Century* (London, 1961).

[736] Walker, L. E. M., 'Some Aspects of Local Jurisdiction in the Twelfth and Thirteenth Centuries': Univ. of London M.A. Thesis, 1958.

[737] Walraet, M., 'Les Chartes-lois de Prisches (1158) et de Beaumont-en-Argonne (1182)', *Revue belge*, xxiii (1944), 127–62.

[738] Warren, W. L., *Henry II* (London, 1973).

[739] Warren, W. L., 'The Myth of Norman Efficiency', *T.R.H.S.* ser. 5, xxxiv (forthcoming).

[740] Watts, D. G., 'Peasant Discontent on the Manors of Titchfield Abbey, 1245–1405', *Proc. of Hants. Field Club and Archaeol. Soc.*, xxxix (1983), 121–35.

[741] Wenskus, R. and others ed., *Wort und Begriff 'Bauer'* (Göttingen, 1975).

[742] Werkmüller, D., *Über Aufkommen und Verbreitung der Weistümer* (Berlin, 1972).

[743] Werner, K. F., 'Heeresorganisation und Kriegführung im deutschen Königreich des 10. und 11. Jahrhunderts', *Settimane*, xv (1967), 791–843.

[744] Werner, K. F., 'Kingdom and Principality in Twelfth-Century France', in [648], 243–90.

[745] Werner, K. F., 'Les Nations et le sentiment national dans l'Europe médiévale', *R.H.* ccxliv (1970), 285–304.

[746] Werner, K. F., 'Quelques observations au sujet des débuts du "duché" de Normandie', in *Droit privé et institutions régionales: études historiques offertes à J. Yver* (Paris, 1976), 691-709.

[747] White, A. B., *Self Government at the King's Command* (Minneapolis, 1933).

[748] White, A. B., 'Some Early Instances of the Concentration of Representatives in England', *Am.H.R.* xix (1914), 735-50.

[749] White, S. D., ' "*Pactum . . . legem vincit et amor judicium*": the Settlement of Disputes by Compromise in Eleventh-Century Western France', *Am. Jnl. of Legal Hist.* xxii (1978), 281-308.

[750] Wickham, C., *Early Medieval Italy* (London, 1981).

[751] Wieruszowski, H., 'Roger II of Sicily, *Rex-Tyrannus* in Twelfth-Century Political Thought', *Speculum*, xxxviii (1963), 46-78.

[752] Wightman, W. E., 'The Palatine Earldom of William fitz Osbern in Gloucestershire and Worcestershire', *E.H.R.* lxxvii (1962), 6-17.

[753] Wilks, M., *The Problem of Sovereignty in the Later Middle Ages* (Cambridge, 1963).

[754] Williams, G. A., *Medieval London: From Commune to Capital* (London, 1963).

[755] Winchester, A. J. L., 'The Medieval Vill in the Western Lake District: Some Problems of Definition', *Trans. Cumberland and Westmorland Antiq. and Archaeol. Soc.* lxxviii (1978), 55-69.

[756] Winterswyl, R., 'Das neue Recht: Untersuchungen zur frühmittelalterlichen Rechtsphilosophie', *H.J.* lxxxi (1962), 58-79·

[757] Wohlgemuth, H., *Das Urkundenwesen des deutschen Reichshofgerichts, 1273-1378* (Cologne/Vienna, 1973).

[758] Wolf, A., 'Die Gesetzgebung der entstehenden Territorialstaaten', in H. Coing ed., *Handbuch der Quellen und Literatur der neueren Europäischen Privatrechtsgeschichte*, i (1973), 517-800.

[759] Wolf, A., 'Forschungsaufgaben einer europäischen Gesetzgebungsgeschichte', *Jus Commune*, v (1975), 178-91.

[760] Wolff, P., *Histoire de Toulouse* (Toulouse, 1958).

[761] Wolff, P., 'Les Luttes sociales dans les villes du midi français', *A.E.S.C.* ii (1947), 443-54.

[762] Wood, C. T., *The French Apanages and the Capetian Monarchy* (Cambridge, Mass., 1966).

[763] Woolf, C. N. S., *Bartolus of Sassoferrato* (Cambridge, 1913).

[764] Wormald, P., 'Bede, the *Bretwaldas*, and the Origin of the *Gens Anglorum*', in P. Wormald ed., *Ideal and Reality in Frankish and Anglo-Saxon Society* (Oxford, 1983), 99-129.

[765] Worsley, P., 'Village Economies', in R. Samuel ed., *People's History and Socialist Theory* (London, 1981), 80-4.

[766] Wunder, H., 'Serfdom in Late Medieval and Early Modern Germany', in T. H. Aston and others, *Social Relations and Ideas* (Cambridge, 1983).

[767] Yelling, J. A., 'Rationality in the Common Fields', *Ec.H.R.* ser. 2, xxxv (1982), 409–15.

[768] Zdekauer, L., 'Il Parlamento cittadino nei comuni delle Marche', *Atti e memorie della R. Deputazione di storia patria per le Marche*, new ser. x (1915), 91–122.

[769] Zollner, E., *Die politische Stellung der Völker in Frankreich* (Vienna, 1950).

IIc: *Other Secondary Works*

[770] Albertini, M., 'L'Idée de nation', *Annales de philosophie politique*, viii (1969), 3–14.

[771] Arriaza, A., 'Mousnier and Barber: the Theoretical Underpinning of the "Society of Orders" in Early Modern Europe', *P. & P.* 89 (1980), 41–57.

[772] Bailey, F. G., 'Decisions by Consensus in Councils and Comittees', in *Political Systems and the Distribution of Power* (Assoc. of Soc. Anthrop., 2, London, 1965).

[773] Baker, J. R., *Race* (Oxford, 1974).

[774] Beidelman, 'Myth, Legend and Oral History: a Kaguna traditional text', *Anthropos*, lxv (1970), 74–97.

[775] Breuilly, J., *Nationalism and the State* (Manchester, 1982).

[776] Brogan, D. W., *French Personalities and Problems* (London, 1946), 41–55 (essay on 'Nationalism').

[777] Cavalli-Sforza, L. L. and Bodmer, W. F., *The Genetics of Human Populations* (San Francisco, 1971).

[778] Deutsch, M., *The Resolution of Conflict* (New York/London, 1973).

[779] Durkheim, E. and Mauss, M., *Primitive Classification*, trans. R. Needham (London, 1963).

[780] Ebling, F. J., ed., *Racial Variation in Man* (London, 1975).

[781] Emerson, R., *From Empire to Nation* (Cambridge, Mass., 1960).

[782] Finley, M. I., *The Ancient Economy* (2nd edn. London, 1975).

[783] Fishman, J. A., *Language and Nationalism* (Rowley, Mass., 1973).

[784] Fried, M. H., *The Evolution of Political Society* (New York, 1967).

[785] Gellner, E., 'Actions before Words': review of [793], *Times Lit. Supp.*, 15 Aug. 1980, 911.

[786] Gellner, E., *Saints of the Atlas* (London, 1969).

[787] Gilmour, I., *The Body Politic* (2nd edn. London, 1971).

[788] Gluckman, M., *Custom and Conflict in Africa* (Oxford, 1955).

[789] Gluckman, M., *The Ideas in Barotse Jurisprudence* (2nd edn. Manchester, 1972).

[790] Gluckman, M., *Politics, Law and Ritual in Tribal Society* (Oxford, 1965).

[791] Goody, J., *The Domestication of the Savage Mind* (Cambridge, 1977).
[792] Hachmann, R., *The Germanic Peoples* (London, 1971).
[793] Hallpike, C. R., *The Foundations of Primitive Thought* (Oxford, 1979).
[794] Hamnett, I. ed., *Social Anthropology and Law* (Assoc. of Soc. Anthrop., 14, 1977).
[795] Hayes, C. J. H., *The Historical Evolution of Modern Nationalism* (New York, 1949).
[796] Hobsbawm, E. R., 'Some Reflections on Nationalism', in T. J. Nossiter and others, *Imagination and Precision in the Social Sciences* (London, 1972).
[797] Homans, G. C., *The Human Group* (New York, 1950).
[798] Iliffe, J., *A Modern History of Tanganyika* (Cambridge, 1979).
[799] Kamenka, B., *Nationalism* (London, 1976).
[800] Kohn, H., *The Idea of Nationalism* (New York, 1945).
[801] Laslett, P., 'The Idea of the Nation', *Annales de philosophie politique*, viii (1969), 15-21.
[802] Lemberg, E., *Nationalismus* (Munich, 1964).
[803] Mackenzie, W. J. M., *Political Identity* (Manchester, 1978).
[804] Mackenzie, W. J. M., *Power, Violence, Decision* (Harmondsworth, 1975).
[805] Maine, H. S., *Ancient Law* (London, 1905 edn.).
[806] Mair, L., *An Introduction to Social Anthropology* (2nd edn. Oxford, 1972).
[807] Mair, L., *Primitive Government* (London, 1962).
[808] Metzger, W. P., 'Generalizations about National Character', in L. R. Gottschalk ed., *Generalization in the Writing of History* (Chicago, 1963), 77-102.
[809] Miller, J. C., *Kings and Kingsmen: Early Mbundu States in Angola* (Oxford, 1976).
[810] Nisbet, R. A., *Community and Power* (New York, 1962).
[811] Nisbet, R. A., *The Sociological Tradition* (London, 1967).
[812] Ordnance Survey, *Book of Reference to the Plan of the Parish of Iffley* (London, 1877).
[813] Paton, G. W., *A Textbook of Jurisprudence* (4th edn. Oxford, 1972).
[814] Pitkin, H. F., *The Concept of Representation* (Berkeley/Los Angeles, 1967).
[815] Poliakov, L., *The Aryan Myth: a History of Racist and Nationalist Ideas in Europe*, trans. E. Howard (London, 1974).
[816] Potter, D. M., 'The Historian's Use of Nationalism and *Vice Versa*', in A. V. Riasanovsky and B. Riznuk ed., *Generalization in Historical Writing* (Philadelphia, 1963), 114-66.
[817] Reeves, E. T., *The Dynamics of Group Behavior* (New York, 1970).
[818] Richards, A. and Kuper, A., *Councils in Action* (Cambridge, 1971).

[819] Rotberg, R. I., 'African Nationalism: Concept or Confusion', *Jnl. of Modern African Studies*, iv (1966), 33–46.

[820] Runciman, W. G., *Social Science and Political Theory* (2nd edn. Cambridge, 1969).

[821] Rustow, D. A., 'Nation', in D. L. Sills ed., *International Encyclopedia of the Social Sciences* (New York, 1968).

[822] Seton-Watson, H., *Nations and States* (London, 1977).

[823] Smith, A. D., *The Ethnic Revival* (London, 1982).

[824] Smith, A. D., *Nationalism* (*Current Sociology*, xxi (3), 1973).

[825] Smith, A. D. ed., *Nationalist Movements* (London, 1976).

[826] Szacki, J., *History of Sociological Thought* (Westport, Conn., 1979).

[827] Taylor, M., *Community, Anarchy, and Liberty* (Cambridge, 1982).

[828] Tönnies, F., *Community and Association*, trans. C. P. Loomis (London, 1955).

[829] Trevor-Roper, H. R., *Jewish and Other Nationalism* (London, 1962).

[830] Weber, M., *The Theory of Social and Economic Organization*, trans. A. M. Henderson and T. Parsons (New York, 1947).

Index